A Violent Evangelism

LUIS N. RIVERA

A VIOLENT EVANGELISM

The Political
and Religious Conquest
of the Americas

Westminster/John Knox Press
Louisville, Kentucky

Translated from the Spanish *Evangelización y Violencia: La Conquista de América* (San Juan, Puerto Rico: Editorial CEMI, 1991). © 1990 Luis N. Rivera Pagán.

Translation © 1992 Westminster/John Knox Press

Scripture quotations marked TEV are from the *Good News Bible—Old Testament:* Copyright © American Bible Society 1976; *New Testament*: Copyright © American Bible Society 1966, 1971, 1976.

Scripture quotations marked NIV are from *The Holy Bible, New International Version.* Copyright © 1973, 1978, 1984 International Bible Society. Used by permission of Zondervan Bible Publishers.

Scripture quotations marked REB are taken from *The Revised English Bible,* © Oxford University Press and Cambridge University Press, 1989. Used by permission.

Book design by The HK Scriptorium, Inc.

First Edition

This book is printed on acid-free paper that meets the American National Standards Institute Z39.48 standard. ∞

Published by Westminster/John Knox Press
Louisville, Kentucky

PRINTED IN THE UNITED STATES OF AMERICA
9 8 7 6 5 4 3 2 1

Library of Congress Cataloging-in-Publication Data

Rivera, Luis N., 1942–
  [Evangelización y violencia. English]
  A violent evangelism : the political and religious conquest of the Americas / Luis N. Rivera.
        p.   cm.
  Includes bibliographical references and index.
  ISBN 0-664-25367-9 (pb. : acid-free)
  1. America—Discovery and exploration—Spanish. 2. Indians—Missions. 3. Indians—First contact with Europeans. 4. Missions, Spanish—America—History—16th century. I. Title.
E123.R5913 1992
970.01'6—dc20   92-24642

To Luis and Ana,
my parents.

———————

They taught me the dignity
of faith and honesty.

Contents

Foreword

Consider:
How God made the heavens

This is a book about history—about a history that began some five hundred years ago. It is also a book about all of us in the modern world—about our civilization, our culture, and even our faith. This is so, because true history does not lie dead in the past but is still alive and present with us, shaping the way we live and relate to one another, even when we do not know it.

This is what makes the subject of this book so crucial. When, in 1992, we speak of the events that began unfolding in 1492, we are not dealing with matters of antiquarian curiosity, or with stories of heroes and villains. We are dealing with the very birth of modern society as we know it today. To this day, there are millions of people, including each one of us, who are directly impacted by those events. This is obviously true of the Guatemalan Qhiché or the Chilean Mapuche, whose very humanity is repeatedly denied by the dominant society in their countries and whose land has been stolen by that society. It is also true of the Cherokee, whose lands were equally stolen by other Europeans who emulated the Spanish and the Portuguese. And it is true of many others throughout the world. As Luis N. Rivera shows in the pages that follow, the events of 1492 and beyond set the stage for grand-scale African slavery, for modern colonialism, for the development of capitalism, and for a host of other phenomena, large and small, that shape our lives in multiple ways—even when we refuse to acknowledge it, by speaking of "Irish" potatoes, "Italian" tomatoes, and "Swiss" chocolate, all of which are in fact native American.

This is also what makes the controversy about 1492 and its sequel so passionate. The Olympics of 1992 will be celebrated in Barcelona, and there will also be a World's Fair in Seville. The date and place for these events were not chosen at random. The intent is to remind the world of Spain's bygone glories and lost empire. Barcelona is the city where Columbus reported to Isabel and Fernando upon his return from his first voyage. Seville is the city that for centuries held the monopoly on travel and trade with the "Indies." Both at the Olympics and at the World's Fair there will be frequent reminders of these facts. With the same intention, a replica of Columbus's three ships will be retracing his route and then visiting various ports in the Western Hemisphere. Not to be left behind, Genoa will float a similar fleet, in order to remind the world that, after all, Columbus was a Genoese. One can understand that, for after all, both Spain and Genoa have seen better days. Meanwhile, across the Atlantic, the Dominican Republic is planning great celebrations, on the basis that it was there that Columbus founded the first European city in the Western Hemisphere, and that the palace of Diego Columbus still stands there.

Obviously, the purpose in this case is to promote tourism and to bring hard currency into a devastated economy. And that too is understandable.

In contrast, on the fence in front of the Cathedral of Mexico hangs a great sign in bold black letters: "October 12, 1492, day of national disaster!" Throughout Latin America various Native American groups, often supported by churches and other institutions in the dominant society, are planning celebrations for 1992. Yet what they will celebrate will not be the "discovery," nor even the "evangelization" of the Americas, but rather, in their words, "five hundred years of resistance." And in the United States various Native American groups, the National Council of Churches, and a number of denominations have rejected any "celebration" of the "discovery."

This book will make clear why so many people feel it is inappropriate to celebrate the "discovery" of the so-called "New" World. Therefore, I shall not attempt to list here the reasons why such celebration is inappropriate—if each person whose life was destroyed as a result of the events of 1492 is a reason not to celebrate, that in itself provides several million reasons. What I do wish to make clear, however, is that this is a subject whose pertinence will not pass as 1992 draws to a close. The "quincentennial" will indeed serve as a catalyst for much discussion, but if that discussion fades into the background in 1993, it will have been an interesting debate and little more. As Rivera shows, what is called for is a process of "critical reflection, joining academic honesty with moral integrity." That process will take much more than a year or two—even more so, since as we become more deeply engaged in it we shall find ourselves questioning a number of presuppositions upon which our very society and our way of life stand.

For these reasons, although this is a very timely book, being published precisely at the time of the "quincentennial" of 1492, it is also a book that should be studied and debated for many years to come, as we seek to build a more just society for the next five hundred years.

Decatur, Georgia Justo L. González
November 14, 1991

Introduction to the English Edition

The quincentenary of the discovery of the Americas has fertilized historical research to a degree not previously foreseen. A cascade of conferences, essays, articles, monographs, and books has dealt with the origin and birth of the Western Hemisphere, with the encounter of the Old World and the New. Some of this literary work has followed the traditional path of hagiographical paean to Christopher Columbus and the Christian Europeans who dared to colonize, civilize, and Christianize the wild lands formerly inhabited by infidel savage Native Americans (the "merciless Indian Savages" alluded to by the Declaration of Independence of the United States).

Some of the latest publications have followed the relatively useful path of the minuscule research, including issues like the perennial search for Guanahaní, the almost mythical Columbus landfall, or the names of the unfortunate sailors left by the Admiral in the fateful "villa de la Navidad" in Hispaniola. Though the value of such investigation is rarely to be questioned, when taken to extremes it is in danger of debasement to the level of what the Mexican scholar Edmundo O'Gorman, never short in his mordacity, has termed "monographical byzantinism" and "microscopical myopia."

Yet the interest in the quincentenary has had two very positive results for our historical understanding of the process known as "discovery and conquest of the Americas." First, it has stimulated the publication of a substantial number of fifteenth- and sixteenth-century works, some in print for the first time and essential for the better study of the rich complexity of the events. New and better editions of the writings of the main protagonists—Columbus, Bartolomé de las Casas, Hernán Cortés, Francisco de Vitoria, Juan Ginés de Sepúlveda, José de Acosta, Gerónimo de Mendieta, the Spanish Council of Indies, among many others—have enriched our perception of fundamental points, such as who did, said, or wrote what, when, where, and why. The raw stuff of historical understanding is in this manner more to our disposition.

The second result is even more important. The abundance of sources has not produced a convergence of viewpoints. Much to the contrary, the sources have unveiled the intense debates that, since the beginning, accompanied the events and at the same time enriched the diversity of our very different, sometimes even antagonistic, appreciation of those events. With the same object of study, scarce theoretical viewpoints or methodological premises are shared by the books by Kirkpatrick Sale (*The Conquest of Paradise: Christopher Columbus and the Columbian Legacy,* 1990), Felipe Fernández-Armesto (*Columbus,* 1991), David Henige (*In Search of Columbus,* 1991), and Paolo Emilio Taviani (*Columbus: The Great Adventure,* 1991), to mention some distinguished examples of recently published works in English on Christopher Columbus.

Analysis of the issues produces a significant and important fact. Despite the attempts by followers of the "black legend" to perpetuate a homogenized caricature of a sixteenth-century Spain of unmitigated cruelty, the truth is that the nation and the epoch are characterized by an amazing diversity of and contradiction in viewpoints and perspectives. The differences between Bartolomé de las Casas, Juan Ginés de Sepúlveda, Francisco de Vitoria, José de Acosta, and Gerónimo de Mendieta, some of the most prominent theoretical gladiators of the debates, are fundamental and substantial. Indeed, sixteenth-century Spain abounds with different and contradictory voices and perspectives. It truly constitutes a polyphony, and one that is not always symphonic. Many participants of the choir are able not only to make their dissident and discordant voices heard but, like Las Casas and some others, to become quite strident soloists. The basic failure of the black legend is its inability to perceive the critical and important participation of the critical and prophetic voice in the discussions about conquest of the Americas.

These different perspectives have brought to the fore the fact that probably there has never been an empire that in the process of its expansion has discussed its justice and legitimacy with such intensity, with such "heat and light," to borrow Professor Lewis Hanke's apt phrase, as Spain did in the sixteenth century. Those debates caused the ethical conscience of Spain to argue forcibly for a century over the justice of the military conquest of the native peoples in the New World, the fairness of the imposition of slavery or forced labor upon them, their rationality or "bestiality," the legitimacy of the abolition of their autochthonous creeds and religious practices, and the causes of the demographic collapse of several ethnic peoples. And let us not forget the early forced introduction of black Africans, massively imported to substitute for the Native Americans, whose existence oscillated between the stated principle of their natural liberty and the concrete forms in which that principle was denied.

The sixteenth-century Spanish debates had a peculiarity that the historian has to understand and respect, if they are not to be distorted. They were engaged principally in theological and religious conceptuality. Perhaps the main defect of many modern studies of the age consists in not recognizing the primacy of the theological discourse in sixteenth-century ideological production. Truly the Spanish conquerors of the Americas were driven by their quest for God, gold, and glory. But it was the language related to God—*theology*—that served to rationalize avarice and ambition, not vice versa. It was religion that attempted to sacralize political dominion and economic exploitation.

This book is an attempt to rethink the discovery and conquest by Spain of the Americas in their own ideological context, within the horizon of the theoretical debates that accompanied the event, without imposing arbitrary and foreign patterns of interpretation. This is the cause for my extensive citation of the sources. The protagonists of the contemporary debates stated with clarity and intelligence their different perceptions of the issues involved in the history-making process of the globalization of the European dominion and the Christian religion. I know no other instance in which a powerful nation established an empire by the force of its arms, and, simultaneously, argued so forcefully in favor of and against its hegemony. Thus, I try to permit the interlocutors themselves to express their viewpoints, in their own language and discourse.

This book has been the result of several years of academic concentration on the subject. It grew out of a research project sponsored by the Academic Deanship of the University of Puerto Rico, Campus of Río Piedras. However, it is not a morally "neutral" deliberation. On the contrary! It is a tribute of honor and respect to the native peoples of the Americas, militarily defeated and culturally oppressed, offered in sacrifice to the worship of a peculiar messianic providentialism, conjoined with the ambitions and cupidity of the epoch. It is also written in the admiration of Europeans who, like the Dominican friar Bartolomé de las Casas, determined that their personal destiny would be forever linked with the struggle for the liberty and existence of the American peoples and nations.

To render that tribute we do not need to impose foreign and anachronic ethical paradigms. What has a Franz Fanon, or any other modern libertarian thinker, to teach Las Casas about the destructive violence of an emerging empire, or about the cry of the oppressed peoples for justice and vindication? Not much, in my view.

The book is divided in three parts, like concentric circles, that follow the logic of the sixteenth-century debates about the discovery and conquest of the Americas. The first part, "Discovery, Conquest, and Evangelization," narrates the events from a critical perspective, which unveils the intimate connections between discovery and military conquest, a process legitimized by concepts, symbols, and images of a religious order. The second part, "Freedom and Servitude in the Conquest of the Americas," deals with the central elements of one of the great theoretical issues of the epoch: the legitimacy of the abrogation of the autonomy of the Native American peoples and nations, and of the imposition of slavery and forced labor. The third part, "A Theological Critique of the Conquest," attempts to articulate the criticism of the conquest of the Americas from the standpoint of the same theological concepts, symbols, and images claimed by the conquerors as justification of their deeds.

The text is accompanied by several prints of the epoch, contemporary to the dramatic and traumatic process of the encounter between the European Christian culture and the native American communities. They illustrate eloquently that drama and trauma and the artistic attempts to understand the history-making event of the conquest of the Americas. The illustrations for chapters 1 and 3 proceed from Christopher Columbus's famous letter of February 15, 1493, in which he narrates to an astonished Europe an account of the fantastic lands and peoples found during his first expedition, and may be found in *Las primeras representaciones gráficas del indio americano, 1493–1523*, 2d ed., by Ricardo E. Alegría (San Juan: Centro de Estudios Avanzados de Puerto Rico y el Caribe, 1986). The artist is not known. Illustrations for the foreword and remaining chapters come from Guamán Puma de Ayala, an Andean Native American who depicted the discovery, conquest, and colonization of Abya Yala (America, in the Andean native language) from the perspective of the discovered, conquered, and colonized, and were first published in *Nueva córonica y buen gobierno*, by Felipe Guamán Puma de Ayala, at the end of the sixteenth and start of the seventeenth centuries. Original works by Ayala are the property of the Royal Danish Library, Copenhagen.

Every intellectual pursuit is possible thanks to the collaboration of many people. Hereby I would like to express my deep gratitude to two colleagues who offered useful support and relevant advice several times in the process of writing this book: Professors Samuel Silva-Gotay and Jalil Sued-Badillo, of the Social Sciences School of the University of Puerto Rico. The students Fernando Silva-Caraballo and William Font were diligent research assistants who contributed to the progress of the investigation. The assistance given by Carmen González and Gladys Porrata, of the interlibrary loan department at the José M. Lázaro Library of the University of Puerto Rico, was truly invaluable.

The book was published in Spanish in 1990 and reprinted in 1991 and 1992. Special mention of gratitude must be given to the Puerto Rican

Commission for the Celebration of the Quincentenary of the Discovery of America and Puerto Rico for the support it lent to the first two editions, despite the evident difference in our perspectives, beginning with the laudatory name and tone of the Commission, conspicuously absent from this book. Another expression of gratitude is given to the Puerto Rican Presbyterian Synod (Boriquén) for its collaboration in the second edition.

The English edition would not exist if it were not for the support given by several persons and institutions, among them Jovelino Ramos, of the Racial Ethnic Ministry Unit of the Presbyterian Church (U.S.A.); Harry Del Valle, Executive Minister of the Puerto Rican Presbyterian Synod (Boriquén); the Evangelical Council of Puerto Rico and its President, Dr. Luis Fidel Mercado; and Alexa Smith, who, as editor of the General and Professional Books at Westminster/John Knox Press, for several months forced me to rethink the problems from the perspective of North American readers, and in that way helped me in fact to better understand the issues.

My family accompanied the painful birth and development of this work in its different phases: as an idea; as a research project; as a string of articles, essays, and lectures; as three editions of the Spanish version; and finally as this English edition. To my six children—Nina, Omar, Iván, Tamara, Omaya, and Guailí—my recognition of their patience and forbearance with the solitude and quietness demanded so many times by their father. My wife, Dr. Anaida Pascual-Morán, reviewed the several drafts and gave worthy comments, both of content and style. She also gave me the spiritually nourishing serenity needed for scholarly enterprise.

The work is dedicated to my parents—Luis y Ana—to whom I am bound by deep love. They, more than anybody else, taught me the value of faith, honesty, and courage.

Part I

Discovery,
Conquest,
and Evangelization

1

Discovery of the Americas: Myth and Reality

In thirty-three days I was in the Indies with the fleet that the most illustrious King and Queen, Our Sovereigns, gave me. There I found very
many islands inhabited by countless people, and I have taken possession of all of them for their Highnesses, by proclamation and with the
royal banner unfurled.

—Christopher Columbus

It is licit to call it a new world. None of those regions were known by
our ancestors, and for all those who learn about it, it would be something
brand new. . . . My last trip has demonstrated it, for I have found a continent in the southern section, with more towns and animals than Europe,
Asia or Africa.

—Amerigo Vespucci

The Mythology of the Discovery

The 1992 celebration of the discovery of the Americas has reignited
the old debate about the true meaning of that epoch-making event.[1] The
first question that needs to be faced relates to its historical nature: Can
we rightly speak of a "discovery"? Is there really something to "celebrate"?

Are we dealing with a discovery? It was a "discovery" only if we adopt
the provincial perspective of a Christianity cloistered in the mentality of
the European continent at the end of the fifteenth century. The appropriateness of this label "discovery" is quite problematic. The territories that
the Spaniards reached had been discovered and inhabited many centuries
earlier by those who were living there (not to mention the mysterious
journeys of the Normans in the eleventh century). The ships that arrived
at Guanahaní on October 12, 1492, did not find a deserted island. To speak
of a discovery, in an absolute and transcendental sense, would imply the
absence of a prior human and cultural history in the newfound lands. This
is absurd and reveals a deep-rooted and anachronistic ethnocentrism.

Further, the entire debate is colored by the grand irony that Christopher
Columbus did not reach what he really sought and that he arrived where
he did not intend to. The Admiral never understood the nature of his
famous "discovery." Until the end of his days, in 1506, he was still obsessed
by the notion, by then obsolete, of the Asiatic nature of his findings.[2]
Columbus "dies believing he has achieved his dream . . . to sail from
Europe to India" (Varela 1982, xxiii).[3]

His intention was thus described by Bartolomé de las Casas:

So he proposed the following: sailing south by west he would discover great lands, islands and terra firma, very happy, rich in gold, silver, pearls and precious jewels, and innumerable peoples; and through that route he believed he would find the land of India, and the grand island of Cipango (Japan) and the kingdoms of the Great Khan. (Las Casas 1986, 1.1.28:174).[4]

It is absurd to celebrate an event that in the mind of its principal protagonist had a substantially different meaning from what actually occurred. This presents the strange situation of celebrating a colossal incoherence between event and conscience, reality and interpretation. This is what the Spanish historian of Columbus, Consuelo Varela (1982, xxxii), has called "a clear maladjustment between [Columbus's] cognitive capacity and the surrounding [American] world."

This disparity between what was found and Columbus's perception of it increased with time. In his later theory Columbus says he was very close to the earthly paradise of the biblical Genesis in the place he called "*Isla de Gracia*" (Varela 1986, 238–247).[5] This was expressed in his letter of July 1503, when, feverish and lost in Jamaica during his fourth and last voyage, he reiterated his conviction of being near Eden and asserted that he was in the proximity of King Solomon's mines, whence came the gold that built God's temple (ibid., 292–293).[6] Finally he insisted obstinately on the peninsular nature, and therefore, the Asiatic nature, of Cuba.[7]

Columbus seems to have immersed himself in the medieval conception of the triadic nature of the globe, the *orbis terrarum*. In reality, that notion is more theological than cosmographic. It belongs to the long list of reflections and images of the divine Trinity that preoccupied so many medieval theologians. Columbus was unable to learn from his mistakes. His cosmography remained obsolete at a time when European intellectuals were recognizing the amplitude and diversity of the globe.

Edmundo O'Gorman has brilliantly developed a sharp criticism of the idea of the "discovery of America."[8] This caustic criticism can be approved without the need to accept O'Gorman's (1984, 159) later thesis, deeply rooted in Western ethnocentrism, that the "invention" of America together with the development of its Northern Hemisphere is "the decisive and irreversible step toward the fulfillment of the ecumenical program of Western culture . . . the only one with the true potential to bring together the peoples of the earth under the sign of liberty."[9]

An indelible monument to the incoherence of the thesis of the "discovery" by Columbus is the fact that the lands he supposedly discovered were not named after their presumed first finder, but after the person who first conceived them to be *mundus novus*, or New World: Amerigo Vespucci.

Vespucci, in his letter *Mundus Novus*, dated 1503 and published in Augsburg in 1504, says:

> It is licit to call it a new world. None of those regions was known by our ancestors, and to all those who learn about it, it would be something brand new. . . . The opinion of the majority of the ancients was that beyond the line of the equinox and even as far as the meridian line there was no land or sea called the Atlantic. But if anyone was to assert that there was some continent there, he would for different reasons argue that it had to be uninhabited. But that opinion is false and opposed to the truth. My last trip has demonstrated this, for I have found a continent in that southern section, with more towns and animals than Europe, Asia, or Africa.[10]

This was the first time that the newfound lands were identified as a new world, a fourth continent distinct from the other three known ones. In 1507, the cartography of Martin Hylacomilus Waldseemüller assigns for the first time, by way of suggestion, the name of America to the new lands. This was included in the scientific text, entitled *Cosmographiae introductio*, which is also reproduced in Vespucci's correspondence. "Et quarta orbis pars, quam, quia Americus invenit, Amerigam quasi americi terram sive Americam nuncupare licet." (And since it was discovered by Amerigo, it would be licit to call the fourth section of the world Ameriga or America) (Esteve Barba 1964, 42).[11] In contrast, Columbus never had a clear or sure idea of what he had found. The lands found by the Admiral, as well as their inhabitants, were confused within his fantasies, myths, utopias, ambitions, and feverish messianic provincialism.

The letter *Mundus Novus* became extremely popular and was edited and translated repeatedly. The observations by the historian Stefan Zweig (1942, 52–54) merit an extensive quotation:

> [It] had a more transcendental historical influence than all the other accounts, including that of Columbus. But the true celebrity and transcendence of the small pamphlet are not owed to its contents. . . . The event of the letter, properly speaking—strangely not the letter itself, but merely its title (two words, four syllables)—produced an unprecedented revolution in the way of perceiving the cosmos. . . . Those words, few but decisive, make of *Mundus Novus* a memorable document of humanity. They constitute the first proclamation of the independence of the Americas, formulated two hundred seventy years before the other one. Columbus, who lived until his deathbed under the illusion of having arrived at the Indies when he set foot on Guanahaní and Cuba, makes the cosmos—when you think of it—appear narrower to his contemporaries due to his illusion. Vespucci, who disproved the hypothesis that

the new continent was India by categorically affirming that it was a new world, is the one who introduced this concept of a new world, which is still valid today.

Spanish jurists and chroniclers were not happy with the sudden popularity of the name *America*, initially adopted by the non-Hispanic countries, but for centuries resisted by the Castilians. Even Bartolomé de las Casas inveighed against the growing habit of calling "the Indies" America. "What belonged to the Admiral Don Christopher Columbus has been taken away from him . . . as it would have been most appropriate to name it (the land) Columba or Columbo, after the man who discovered it . . . than America after Amerigo."[12]

However, Las Casas does not seem to realize that the crucial element was not who arrived first but rather who was the first to conceive of the area as a continent distinct from the triadic medieval *orbis terrarum* of Europe-Africa-Asia.[13]

The Discovery as Expropriation

Further, there was no activity, either on the part of Columbus or of his successors "in discovering new lands," that was not accompanied by a different action of a juridic nature: expropriation. "In thirty-three days I was in the Indies with the fleet which the most illustrious King and Queen, Our Sovereigns, gave me. There, I found very many islands inhabited by countless people, *and I have taken possession of all of them* for Their Highnesses, by proclamation, and with the royal banner unfurled." (Varela 1982, 140; emphasis added).

In his diary, Columbus describes the expropriation of Guanahaní/San Salvador, the first island he encountered. He told the two scribes accompanying him "to be witnesses of how he was taking possession of said island in front of everyone, in the name of the King and Queen, his Lords" (Varela 1986, 62). This was not an isolated action on his part. It expresses the will of the Admiral to expropriate any lands that he would find. "My will was not to go by any island without taking possession of it" (ibid., 67).

"To discover" and "to expropriate" became concurrent acts. Traditional historiography highlights what happened on October 12, 1492, as a "discovery," avoiding what was central to it. The encounter between Europeans and the inhabitants of the newfound lands was in reality an exercise of extreme *power*. It was an event in which the Europeans assumed power over the native inhabitants, over their lands and their persons. The sixteenth-century Dominican theologian Francisco de Vitoria (Urdanoz, 642), at the beginning of his famous treatise *De indis*, expressed it this way: "All this controversy . . . has been caused by those barbarians of the New World, commonly called Indians, who . . . forty years ago came to be under the power of the Spaniards." Expropriation, as a formal and juridical act, was the unquestioned premise of the parties of the intense debate on the nature of the imperial relation between Castilians and Indians. Only the iconoclastic Bartolomé de las Casas questioned it radically and questioned its juridical validity, especially in his late and unpublished work *Los Tesoros del Perú* (Losada 1949, passim).

"I have taken possession of all of them for their Highnesses, by proclamation and with the royal banner unfurled." This act of expropriation by Columbus was full of symbolism, but it was of a strictly juridical nature. It was not understood at first by the inhabitants of the Antilles. That was no problem for the Admiral. In reality he was not addressing them. As a public act officially registered in the presence of a scribe, the expropriation was directed toward other possibly interested parties, the other European Christian sovereigns. It is a question of establishing firmly that the lands have an owner and that no other Western sovereign can lay claim to them. When Columbus adds to the quote given above the expression "and no one contradicted me," he is not referring to the Indian chiefs— they had no idea of what was happening—but to the probable European competitors.

As a symbol of the expropriation, Columbus placed crosses in strategic sites on the islands he visited. "And in all the lands where the ships of Your Highnesses arrive and in all the capes, I have ordered the placing of a tall cross" (Varela 1986, 245). The cross has a double meaning: the territory thus marked belongs from then on to Christianity, and specifically to the Spanish Catholic Monarchs. In Española, for example, "he placed a very tall cross at the harbor's entrance, a very visible mount, as a sign that the land belongs to Your Highnesses and especially as a sign of Jesus Christ and the honor of Christianity"(ibid., 124–125). Columbus explains the reason for the expropriation: "for until now, no other Christian prince has taken possession of the land nor the island"(Varela 1982, 174).

The Spaniard Francisco Morales Padrón, one of the few historians to recognize the central importance of expropriation as a "phenomenon intimately connected to the discovery, an act that followed immediately after the finding," states it somewhat differently:

> Expropriation happened because the Indies were considered *"res nullius"* [belonging to no one] and Columbus wins and incorporates them *"non*

per bellum' [not by military force] but *"per adquisitionem'* [by juridical procedure], taking possession in the name of the Catholic Monarchs so that no other Christian people could settle on them, since *"vacabant dominia universali jurisdictio non possesse in paganis"* [the infidels do not have the right of jurisdictional authority], and therefore whoever expropriated them would be their lord. (Morales Padrón 1979, 133–134; see also 1955, 321–380; cf. Servin, 255–267)

If the natives were disposed to question the expropriation *per adquisitionem,* Columbus and the Castilians were prepared to ratify it *per bellum.* Hidden behind the evangelizing cross, faintly veiled, was the conquering sword.

Decades later the premise that unbelievers were incapable of exercising dominion and jurisdiction would be questioned, above all, by Dominican theologians (Cayetano, Las Casas, and Vitoria). But initially, in the prevailing mentality of the *orbis christianus,* territorial sovereignty was conceived as the exclusive right of Christians, followers of him who paradoxically had affirmed his radical poverty to the point of comparing himself to foxes and doves, humble dwellers of caves and nests. The lands of the infidels, on the contrary, were seen as *res nullius,* no one's property. The hostile medieval dichotomy between Christians and infidels assumed the shape of a crusade in the very heart of the discovery and acquisition of America.

The "taking possession" (of the new lands) was not an arbitrary individual act by Columbus. It was based on the instructions received from the Catholic Monarchs. On April 30, 1492, from Granada, Fernando and Isabel issued a document that widened and clarified the earlier Capitulations of Santa Fe (April 17). In it, every time the verb "to discover" appears (seven times) it is accompanied by another word, "to acquire." "In so far as you, Christopher Columbus, by our decree are going to discover and acquire . . . certain islands and mainland in said Ocean sea . . . after you have discovered and acquired them . . . thus discovered and acquired."

Only on one occasion are the two verbs separated. But "discover" is the one that disappears, and "acquire" is paired with "conquer": "Of those conquered and acquired by you . . ." (Fernández de Navarrete 1945, 2:18–21).[14] Later, reacting to the acts of "discovery"/"expropriation," they confirmed their original intention of expansion and identified "discover" with "bring under our *power.*" "The many, good, and loyal services that you, Don Christopher Columbus, our Admiral, . . . do for us, and we hope you will continue to do, especially that of discovering and bringing under our *power,* and therefore under our lordship these islands and mainland . . ." (ibid., 2:228; emphasis added).[15]

The principal sign of the discovery as expropriation is the next act of

Columbus, which is to name the newfound islands.[16] "The first island I found I named *San Salvador* [Holy Savior] in commemoration of the Divine Majesty. . . . The second one I named *Santa María de Concepción*; the third *Fernandina*; the fourth *Isabel*; the fifth *Juana*, and thus each received a new name" (Varela 1982, 140). To name the islands has a biblical connotation. In Genesis (2:19–20), the authority of the first human being, Adam, over all other beings of creation is expressed in his naming faculties. To name is an attribute of dominion. In the Christian tradition, on the other hand, the sacrament of baptism and the act of renaming are linked. When an adult was baptized, it was customary to change names. The pagan name was abandoned and a new one was assumed – a Christian one. That renaming – a prominent example, from Saul to Paul – symbolized a profound transformation of the human being, a new personality.

In Columbus's case, the islands had pagan names; therefore, they had to be baptized, christened. About Holy Savior he said that the Indians called it Guanahaní. The act of naming it has a hidden meaning, potentially sinister. It implies an expropriation; the denial of the present inhabitants' authority to name the land they inhabit and, as a result, to possess it. The lands have been baptized by the European – an act in which the natives lack any participation.

We are faced here with an extreme act of renaming. The letter of February 15, 1493, cited earlier, became very popular in Europe, going through several editions in Castilian, Latin, and other languages.[17] This letter was responsible for the name *Indians* for the native inhabitants. This ethnic designation concealed rather than revealed who they were. The first aggression against the native Americans was to deny them proper identity by calling them *Indians*. This was a false term expressive of the mistaken belief of the Spaniards who thought they had reached certain islands on the periphery of the eastern coast of Asia.[18]

There is no doubt we are dealing here with an invention, as O'Gorman asserts. What is significant, however, is its legitimate basis, in that these newfound beings were considered possessions, vassals. The exact condition of their vassalage would be the cause of angry disputes and debates, as we shall see. One possibility that the Admiral suggests is slavery: "Their Highnesses can see that I will give them . . . as many slaves as they shall order"(Varela 1982, 145).

While the Crown, in consultation with theologians and academicians, was deciding on that suggestion, Columbus put into practice the expropriation he had decreed and assumed control over some of the natives with a view to showing them later to the Catholic Monarchs. With full confidence in his juridical authority, and in view of the paganism of the natives and their military inferiority, he wrote to the Crown from Española notifying the Monarchs of something the inhabitants were quite unaware of: "All the men and women here, from this island especially but also from the other islands, belong to Your Highnesses" (Varela 1986, 169).

He also took control of the most interesting fauna and flora in the lands he had found and expropriated. He took back to a fascinated and perplexed Europe samples from this New World that he had taken possession of: spices, fruits, exotic flowers, parrots, and Indians. This scandalized the Christian conscience of Bartolomé de las Casas: "The Admiral acted without scruples, as on so many other occasions during his first voyage. He took free men against their will, without thinking that it was unjust and an offense against God and neighbor" (Las Casas 1986, 2.1.134:17).

Las Casas points out it was usual behavior for conquerors and colonizers to rename the natives, especially the prominent ones: "It was the custom of the Spaniards to rename capriciously any Indians with Christian names" (ibid., 2.2.46:356). Juan Ponce de León, from the beginning of the colonization of Boriquén (the natives' name for the island of Puerto Rico), felt he had authority to change the names of the main *cacique* (chief), Agueybana, and of his parents. First the native people considered it an honor; only later did they discover that it was a subtle manifestation of the act of expropriation of which they had been the object. The Boriquén Indians paid dearly with their blood and suffering for their rebelliousness. The assumption of power over them and their renaming brought about their extinction, not their transformation.

Already Immanuel Kant (1914, 444), at the end of the eighteenth century, had set his critical eye on the concept of the "discovery of America." "When America was discovered . . . it was considered to be without owners since its inhabitants were considered as nothing." They were considered to be "as nothing" for *they were not Christian*. The newfound lands were considered *terrae nullius* (lands without owner), and they were thus classified because they did not belong to a Christian prince. The *orbis christianus* did not seem to need additional legitimacy to extend itself at the expense of infidels. Pedro Mártir de Anglería (1964–1965, 1:267), noted humanist and member of the Council of the Indies, at the beginning of the fifteenth century defended European hegemony over every place in the New World that is "empty of Christians." The discussion became theoretically more complex later in the century as seen in Vitoria's *De indis*, but the result was the same: namely, the supremacy of the rights of the Christians over that of the indigenous "infidels."

But the question arose whether these newfound lands "on the Ocean sea" really did not belong already to another Catholic sovereign. Upon his return from his first journey and even before arriving in Spain, Columbus had a disturbing meeting with the king of Portugal. The monarch seemed ready to lay claim to the newfound territories as falling under his jurisdiction, on the basis of the 1479–1480 Treaty of Alcacovas-Toledo,[19] agreed upon by both Iberian nations. His claim was also based on certain papal bulls that in the fifteenth century had conferred on the Lusitanian Crown sovereignty over the waters extending from the western coast of Africa (Morales Padrón 1979, 13–32; Davenport 1917, 1:9–32).

In this potentially ambiguous and conflicting juridical situation, the Catholic Monarchs took the initiative and went to the Holy See to convince the pope to back their titles of ownership. They got even more than they asked for. Alexander VI's *Inter caetera* bulls (May 3/4, 1493) gave authority to the Catholic Monarchs to expropriate those lands found by Spanish navigators and captains "heretofore not subject to the actual temporal domination of any Christian lord . . ."; ". . . those not owned by another king or Christian princes."[20] The bulls revoked any prior Apostolic Letter or earlier treaty that could be interpreted in a different sense.

The European discovery of the "Indies" became, in short, an event of expropriation, legitimated by reasons and symbols of a theological and religious nature. This factor should not be forgotten when analyzing the indigenous insurrections. Generally resistance against abuse has been highlighted—rape of women, forced labor, cruel treatment, expropriation of treasures, and countless aggravations. All those abuses occurred but should not be isolated from another exacerbating element: *imposed subordination.* Suddenly, the inhabitants of these lands, without any mediating negotiations, found themselves under imposed subordination, and were informed in various ways of their new nature as *owned beings.* They rebelled when they realized that being owned was an essential part of the *discovery.*

This was the source of the surprising change that Columbus detected in the attitude of the natives between his first and second voyage. If what stands out in the first is their *hospitality,* then what leaps into view in the second is their *hostility.* This change endangered the Spaniards, who were not accustomed to providing for their own nourishment in American lands. It had its origin in the natives' recognition that their peculiar guests were changing roles and claiming to be hosts, owners, and lords of their lands, farms, and lives. The natives rebelled when they realized that being owned was a central part of the Spanish discovery.

Columbus's first tales about the aborigines abound with an idyllic vision—they are tame, shy, docile. That perception changed after the first rebellions. A peaceful expropriation became a military enterprise for conquest. In 1499, in the midst of the debacle of the initial illusory plans,

Columbus wrote to the Catholic Monarchs: "Illustrious Princes: When I came here I brought many people for the conquest of these lands . . . and I stated clearly that I came to conquer." In another later letter, the meek and tranquil natives of the first stories who "show so much love that they would give their hearts" are now described as "savages and bellicose" for not accepting the expropriation of their persons (Varela 1982, 236–237, 142, 252).[21]

Las Casas recounts that chief Mayonabex, ally and protector of the persecuted native chief Guarionex, in one of the first confrontations that took place in Española, replied to the Spaniards that they are "tyrants, who have come only to usurp lands belonging to others" (Las Casas 1986, 1.1.120:460). The crime is that of usurpation; the *expropriation* of lands and persons without their consent was the cause of the indigenous war. Their witnessing of the Spaniards taking possession of their lands, coupled with all the personal offenses against them, were the main reasons why the Indians of Veragua (in what today is Panama) changed from an attitude of hospitality to one of hostility toward the Admiral and his companions (ibid., 2.2.27:293).[22]

Several historians, by way of explanation, have attempted to distinguish the discovery from the conquest. According to Demetrio Ramos (1984, 17–63), the initial objective of Spain was not to conquer the American territories. The conquest as a juridical theory, as debate about the "legitimate titles" of ownership over the New World, arises, in his opinion, after the conquest as a historical fact. The actions of Hernán Cortés constitute, as is to be expected, the best evidence for making such an evaluation. The municipal council of Veracruz, in a letter to the Crown, indicates this change in attitude by Cortés: "When he reached the land called Yucatán, on learning about its extent and riches, he decided, not what Diego Velázquez [official superior of Cortés] wanted, which was to take gold, but to conquer the land and win it and bring it under the subjection of the Royal Crown of Your Highnesses." Cortés himself expressed in his third report—sent to Carlos V after the conquest of Technochtitlán—his frustration because prior communications "have not so far seen an answer to any of them" (Cortés 1985, 4, 99).

When Ramos insists that the conquest was not part of the original Spanish plans, and that in good measure it was the result of the isolated actions of active men, he seems to want to excuse the Crown, without critically analyzing the fact that, in every instance, including the endeavor by Cortés, the Crown endorsed the fait accompli of these armed territorial acquisitions.[23] But above all, as we have tried to clarify, Ramos neglects the central premise of the conquest: *expropriation was conceived, from the beginning, as essential to the discovery.* When the natives resisted the vassalage imposed on them, the conquest is revealed as a violent act, and it then is presented as a theory of "licit domination." Unilateral expropriation— essential, as we have seen, to the so-called discovery—of peoples politically organized, as were the American aborigines, inevitably leads to war. It is for this reason that in the notes and letters of his first journey Columbus shrewdly and carefully alludes to the military weakness of the natives. "They have neither iron nor steel, nor arms, and are not concerned with that kind of thing" (Varela 1982, 141). It was not ethnological interest that prompted this observation, but the astute perception of a man who foresees the conditions and possibilities of armed domination.

The correlation between discovery and expropriation is not exclusive to Columbus. It is a constant factor, as the historian Francisco Morales Padrón correctly observes, in all the acts of "entrance" and "discovery" accomplished by the Iberians in the New World during the sixteenth century. A different example among the many that this prominent Americanist scholar offers is the entrance of Alvar Núñez Cabeza de Vaca into Paraguayan territory in 1543. The conqueror himself narrates the story of the expropriation ritual.

> He sent for the clergymen and told them where he wanted the church where they would say mass and the divine office. . . . He had a large wooden cross made, which he ordered planted near the river . . . in the presence of the officers of Your Majesty and of many other people whom he found there; and before the scribe . . . he took possession of the land in the name of Your Majesty.

In regard to the natives, he required them to swear to a double loyalty: to the Castilian Crown and the Catholic church. Finally he informed them of their new juridical situation as "vassals of Their Majesty." Initially the natives seemed to accept their condition of imposed vassalage. However, when the first opportunity presented itself to expel the intruders, they attacked, "saying that the land was theirs . . . that we should leave their land, otherwise they would kill us" (Morales Padrón 1988, 152–153, 179).

From Encounter to Domination

Some participants in the debate about the "celebration of the discovery" suggest a change in terminology. They prefer to speak about "commemorating" the "encounter" between "two cultures" or "two worlds"

(Miró Quesada 1987, 31). This astute semantic reconstruction does not solve the problem. When speaking of "two cultures," the rich and complex diversity of the nations and indigenous peoples is devalued. The importance of the accomplishments and differences, the particular traditions, symbols, customs, languages, and institutions are obliterated. The Argentinian Roberto Levillier (1935, 1:178), in reaction to European indifference, has stressed the richness and complexity of the indigenous cultural accomplishments:

> The Tekestas and Tahinos of Cuba were Indians, tame and hospitable; the cannibal Carib was Indian; the primitive Otomi living in caves was Indian; the wild Jibaro was Indian; the Uro, more fish than man, living in the waters of the Titicaca was Indian. Indian were the artisan stone-cutter Mayan; the Chibchan goldsmith; the wise Inka legislator, and the delicate Yungan ceramist. The Coya weaver was Indian. The heroic Aztec, the cannibalistic Chiriguayo, and the untamable Diaguitas and Araucans were Indians. The shy Juri, the Lule nomad, the sedentary Comechigón and the fierce Guarari were Indians. They were different in intelligence, cruelty, and mildness. Their skin colors, languages, rituals, and theogonies were different. The *veri domini*[24] could be confused with the usurping Indians who subjected them to obedience. They were not the same in their juridical standing, their physical aspects, their language, their tastes, their mannerisms, nor in their creative abilities.[25]

The German scholar Richard Konetzke (1972, 4) shows this enormous cultural diversity in the key aspect of the languages when he states that "133 independent linguistic families have been verified as existing in America."

Furthermore, the reference to "two cultures" badly shortchanges the presence in the Americas, from the beginning of the sixteenth century, of black slaves (Klein 1986, 21–43). The Spanish ladinos (Christianized black slaves) and later the bozales (newly enslaved blacks) from Africa, to which soon were added the other black slaves and the *"criollos"* (often used to indicate blacks born in the Americas in contrast to those who were born in Africa; trans. note), were from the outset actors in the Latin American drama. The date of their first entrance is debatable,[26] but we know the first royal instruction about this matter. It dates from September 16, 1501, and it was sent by the Catholic Monarchs to Nicolás de Ovando, governor of Española at the time. It specifies that the black slaves should be ladinos, born in Spain and Christian (Pacheco et al. 1864–1884, 31:23).[27]

Equally they were early actors in uprisings and rebellions. According to Juan Bosch: "It seems that already in 1503 there were blacks fleeing into the hills, probably with Indians, since that year Ovando recommended that the taking of blacks to Española be suspended because they fled from the ships and spread agitation." Further on he adds: "The first black uprising in the New World took place December 26, 1522, on the same island of Española" (Bosch 1986, 138, 143).[28]

The chronicler Gonzalo Fernández de Oviedo y Valdés points out that diverse unruly blacks joined the uprising led by the Indian chief Enriquillo in Española. That, in his opinion, added an aggravating element to the rebellion. "And it was not to be discounted, especially seeing that each day some blacks, of which there are many on this island because of the sugar refineries making this land look like Ethiopia itself, left and joined that Enrique and his Indians" (Oviedo 1851, 1.1.4:141).[29] Also, the Franciscan Toribio de Motolinía, in Mexico, warned that "blacks are so numerous that at times they have agreed to rebel and kill the Spaniards."[30]

This explains several royal decisions about blacks in America. On May 11, 1526, for example, a royal decree was issued restricting the transportation of black ladinos to the Indies. The text is very instructive about the rebellious attitude of many:

> In so far as I have been informed that the taking of black ladinos who are of the worst kind and of the worst behavior from our kingdom to the island of Española, and that they find no use for them there, for they advise and impose their will on the other tame obedient and peaceful blacks who are on that island at the service of their masters, and that they have tried many times to rebel and in fact have done so and fled to the hills and committed other crimes . . . by means of the present decree we declare and order that no person, now or in the future, can bring to the island of Española nor to the other Indies, or islands and mainland of the Ocean sea nor to any part of them, any blacks who have been for a year in our kingdom or in the Kingdom of Portugal . . . unless we grant a license for their owners to take them at the service of their persons and homes.[31]

It is interesting to note the *"Real Provisión para que se casen los negros"* (Royal provision to have blacks marry), made by the emperor Carlos V a year later to mitigate the black rebellion. Besides being an indicator of the growth of the enforced migration of black slaves, he proposed a clever and manipulative remedy: that the black slaves marry, so that such a civil state might stabilize them. The preoccupation about and affection for wife and children, in the thinking of the Council of the Indies and the Crown, would serve as a restraint on their lack of conformity:

> Inasmuch as we have been informed that due to the fact that many blacks have arrived and continue to arrive daily on the island of Española and

because there are few Spanish Christians there, it could cause restlessness
or an uprising among those blacks, as they see themselves strong and
enslaved, or they might take to the hills and flee . . . having discussed
all this in our Council of the Indies, it has seemed to be a good remedy
to order that the blacks who go to that island, from now on, and those
who are already there, be married, so that each one would have a
wife, because that and the love they would have for their women and
children . . . would be the cause of greater tranquillity among them.
(Konetzke 1953, 1:99)

The emperor adds, as an incentive to win black collaboration and avoid
their rebelliousness, the possibility of their earning their freedom by means
of their work in the Antillean mines. He expresses this wish in a letter
to the governor of Cuba on November 9, 1526: "I have been informed that
to ensure that blacks going to those islands settle down and do not rebel
or flee and be inspired to work and serve their masters more willingly,
besides having them marry it would be a good idea that after serving for
a certain period and paying their masters at least 20 golden marcs, they
be set free" (Sued Badillo 1986, 55).

Carlos Esteban Deive suggests that the flight of black ladinos into the
hills and their unmanageable attitude in Española is to be attributed to
the difference in harshness between their servitude on the Antillean island
and what they had been accustomed to on the Iberian peninsula. "From
a condition as a domestic he went to work as a miner, and that change
made him truly feel the harshness of slavery, its essential injustice and
perversity, pushing him to gain freedom in the thickness of the forest, arm
in arm with the island native" (Deive 1980, 21).[32]

The forgetfulness into which many historians sink regarding the early
black presence in the complex process of conquest and colonization of
America cannot be freed from suspicion of ethnocentrism and ethnic
prejudice. What Deive (1980, xiii) writes in this regard about black slavery
in Santo Domingo is, in general terms, applicable also to other places.

With respect to the valuing of one's own culture, there would be nothing
to say provided it is not accompanied by the devaluing of that of others.
Unfortunately, this is not the case of those who proclaim that the
paradigmatic core of norms, values, and ideas forming society's ethos . . .
is substantially nurtured by Iberian wisdom free from infectious germs.
With reference to the black slaves, that model is instituted as a haughty
and sectarian ideal of a monoculture that considers the culture of the
Africans to be bastardly, illegitimate, and damnable, that displays a
pernicious ethnocentric attitude . . . whose intent is to depreciate the
constructive work of the black as a first-class agent in the dynamics that
produced the growth of the nation.[33]

The label "encounter of two cultures, or two worlds" is neither apt nor convenient, therefore. In criticizing such a concept, veteran Mexican historian Silvio Zavala (1988, 17) put it well in saying that in the events referred to as "the discovery and conquest of America" there is "a multiplicity of encounters between peoples and cultures."

How, then, to "commemorate" an "encounter" that culminates with the abrogation of the sovereignty of some nations over their land and the radical diminution of their inhabitants? It would be historically more faithful to acknowledge that the conquest was a "violent clash of cultures" (León Portilla 1987, 8), in which the nation having superior military technology emerged triumphant.[34] What was staged in the New World was a *clash* or *confrontation;* and that *frontal clash* led to a grave effrontery in which not only was there unequal power but also unequal perceptions. For the native there was perplexity, admiration, and finally fear; for the intruder, aspirations of domination and imposition (Dussel 1988, 39) prevailed — an *animus dominandi.*[35] What started as an encounter between different human groups soon turned into a relation of oppressor and oppressed.[36]

Elegy to Hispanicity

For many, the commemoration of the discovery of America turns into a "feast of Hispanicity," an elegy to Hispanic culture. This line of thought threatens to convert historical reflection into an ideology for imperial conquest, or worse, into hagiographic mythography.

The "elegy to Hispanicity" is not new. It manifested itself splendidly in the great Hispanic American poet Rubén Darío, who played a prominent role in the celebration of the fourth centenary of the discovery. Several of the poems in *Cantos de vida y esperanza* (1905) reflect a profound melancholy in respect to past Hispanic grandeur and nostalgia for its utopian return:

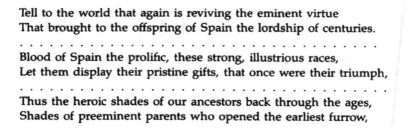

Tell to the world that again is reviving the eminent virtue
That brought to the offspring of Spain the lordship of centuries.
. . . .
Blood of Spain the prolific, these strong, illustrious races,
Let them display their pristine gifts, that once were their triumph,
. . . .
Thus the heroic shades of our ancestors back through the ages,
Shades of preeminent parents who opened the earliest furrow,

May fell in a breath from the fields the signs of the springtime returning,
. . . .
Thus both continents, giving new life to lines old and ancestral,
One in heart, united in spirit and longing and language,
See the moment approaching when the songs they sing shall be new
  songs.

(Darío 1976, 32–33)[37]

This utopian nostalgia stumbles over North American power, manifest in the Hispanic American War. From here comes his poem "To Roosevelt," a favorite of anti-imperialist Latin Americans for decades:

You are the United States,
You are the future invader
Of that ingenuous America of native blood,
That prays to Jesus still and still speaks Spanish!
. . . .
You're rich; to that of Hercules you join the cult of Mammon;
. . . .
Beware, for Spanish America still lives;
The Spanish Lion has a thousand cubs.
'Twere needful, Roosevelt, to be, for God himself,
The terrible rifleman and the hunter strong,
Ever to keep us in your iron grasp.
And you think all's yours: you still lack one thing—
God!

(ibid., 48–50).

Darío realizes that this is not the propitious moment to sing "the heroic shades" of the "blood of Spain the prolific." It is rather the historic occasion of Hispanic decline and sunset and the ascendency of North American power.

There are almost no illusions in our heads,
and we are the beggars of our poor souls.
They preach to us of war with ferocious eagles . . .
but they lack the glories of the ancient sickles,
there are no Rodrigos, nor Jameses, nor Alfonsos, nor Children . . .
Hispanic America as well as all Europe
are fixed in the Orient of their fateful destiny . . .

Will we be turned over to the ferocious barbarians?
Will so many million men speak English?
Are there no noble hidalgos and brave knights? . . .
I feel . . . the death-rattle of a finished lion

(ibid., 68–69).

But, out of the tragic crisis of decayed Hispanic heroism arises, unexpectedly, the illusion of a utopian return to the glories of the past.

> . . . And a black swan said: "The night announces the day."
> And a white one: "The dawn is immortal, the dawn is
> immortal." Oh lands of sun and harmony,
> Pandora's box still holds your Hope!
>
> (ibid.)

In this fashion, the danger that U.S. expansive power represents for many Latin American intellectuals and writers becomes the source of a glorified and distorted view of the Spanish conquest of America. It transforms the conquest into a glorious feat of the Hispanic spirit that could serve as a fertile fountain for Hispanic American utopian thought. In the process, however, the path of critical reflection is paralyzed.

From Celebration to Critical Reflection

The preceding critical observations do not claim to devalue the importance of the so-called "encounter." On the contrary: *The conquest of America is one of the most meaningful events in the history of humanity.* As the Peruvian intellectual Francisco Miró Quesada (1987, 31) asserted: "It cannot be denied . . . that the discovery of America and later, its conquest, are historical happenings of incalculable importance that have contributed in a decisive way to change the course of history. How can we be indifferent in the face of the Fifth Centenary to such momentous happenings?"

Four centuries earlier, Francisco López de Gómara, one of the first chroniclers of the conquest of America, said it in the confessional tone of his day in the prologue of his history dedicated to Carlos V: "The greatest thing after the creation of the world, omitting the incarnation and death of him who created it, is the discovery of the Indies; and so they call them the New World" (López de Gómara 1946, 156). His hero, Hernán Cortés, even though his analogy is different and refers more to the conquest of the Aztec empire—of which he was the central protagonist—than to the discovery, called it "the holiest and highest deed ever started since the conversion of the Apostles" (Cortés 1985, 210). For his part, Christopher Columbus wrote in his *Diary* during his first journey that he believed his maritime adventure, which for the majority of Castilian royal counselors was "a joke," would prove to be the greatest honor for Christianity (Varela 1986, 203).

Pope Leo XIII, in an encyclical celebrating the fourth centenary of "the discovery of an unknown world, close to the Atlantic Ocean, under God's auspices," rates the discovery as "the most grandiose and beautiful deed ever seen by history."[38] He was repeating the thesis of Bartolomé de las Casas, who rated it as "the most illustrious deed ever accomplished by any human"(Las Casas 1986, 2.1.34:176).

It is certainly *the genesis of modern Christianity as a world phenomenon.* Henri Baudet (1965, 3–4) stresses the uniqueness of that era when he points out that for millennia, Europe had been a continent under siege, fighting for its independence and survival against the Persians at Marathon and Salamina, against the Huns of Attila at Rome, and against the Moslem Turks in the Balkans. After the failure of the Crusades, Europe was on the defensive, faced with the threats of the Ottoman Empire that took Constantinople in 1453 and later advanced until it dominated the Balkans, conquered Hungary, and came, in 1529, to the gates of Vienna and to the very heart of Europe (Kennedy 1987, 3–4). Marcel Bataillon (1954, 343–351) highlights the fact that during the first seventy-five years after Columbus's enterprise, Europe acquired more knowledge about other lands than in the preceding millennium, and that it is the "discovery of America" and not the taking of Constantinople that is the decisive event that dramatically marks the beginning of the modern era. For the first time in history a genuine ecumenical and global perspective of human reality can be envisioned (see Scammel 1969, 389–412). It is, however, an imperial ecumenism, civilizing and subjugating at the same time, capable of the greatest religious heights and simultaneously of the most terrible, bellicose cruelty.

With the conquest of the New World not only is there escape from Islamic encirclement, but there is the beginning of European world hegemony, the imperial system that, passing through various phases, has characterized the modern era. European colonialism started October 12, 1492 (Leo XIII says it subtly: "The authority of the European name had an extraordinary increase" [Terradas Soler 1962, 128]);[39] the struggle against it started when the first rebellious native of the Americas took up arms to defend his land and culture. Vitoria's exposition in respect to the "barbarians of the New World" (Urdanoz 1960, 641–726) is not just a critical scrutiny of Spain's legitimate or illegitimate reasons for adjudicating to itself dominion over American lands and their inhabitants; it also masterfully anticipates all the justifications later advanced by the various European imperial systems.

In that European expansion—unthinkable without the technological advances of the compass, the printing press, and gunpowder—*Christian faith played an exceptional role as imperial ideology.* To forget it would be tantamount to falling into vulgar materialism. *In hoc signo vinces* (in this sign thou shalt conquer) was Constantine's motto, but it also faithfully reveals the mentality of the Catholic Monarchs.

This anniversary year is an excellent and unrepeatable occasion to critically reflect on the roots of our historic identity and, at the same time, to deliberate on our future as peoples having common links and challenges. As the Chilean historian Fernando Mires (1986, 13) affirms: "To invert the celebration and to convert it into a date for meditation is, therefore, an ethical duty."

2

Alexander's Papal Bulls

*Spaniards: The holy Catholic faith
and the royal arms and crown*

[A]ll the mainlands and isles found or to be found, discovered or to be discovered . . . by the authority of Almighty God, granted unto us in Saint Peter, and by the office which we bear on earth as Vicar of Christ, . . . we give, grant, and assign . . . to you, your heirs and successors.

—Pope Alexander VI

I beg and require of you . . . to recognize the church as lady and superior of the universe and to acknowledge the Supreme Pontiff, called Pope, in her name, and the king and queen . . . as lords and superiors. . . . If you do not do it . . . then with the help of God I will undertake powerful action against you. I will make war on you everywhere and in every way that I can. I will subject you to the yoke and obedience of the church and of your Highnesses. I will take you personally and your wives and children, and make slaves of you, and as such sell you off . . . and I will take away your property and cause you all the evil and harm I can.

—*Requerimiento*

To affirm, as was done in the preceding chapter, that the discovery-encounter quickly became domination and conquest does not solve the fundamental question of the goals and objectives of its Spanish protagonists. It is not sufficient, either, to point out the obvious *colonization* process that transferred to the New World Spanish settlers who exploited its natural riches to benefit the metropolis. Certainly, material interests were there from the beginning. The ambition for riches was a constant factor from Columbus to Francisco Pizarro, including the smaller actors in this drama. The transferral of very large quantities of gold and silver to Europe during the sixteenth century to subsidize the imperial expansion of Castilla during the reigns of Carlos V and Felipe II is a clear indication of material interests.[1]

But the principal participants in the debate about the conquest pointed to another objective that was of a religious and transcendental nature: the Christianization of the new lands and towns. The Spanish nation, in its dual role as state and church, gave the salvation of the souls of "infidels and gentiles" as the first legal and theological justification for the armed process of domination of the New World. Zavala's (1984, 32) assertion is correct regarding this historic event: "The religious purpose of converting pagans becomes the true title of jurisdictional European expansion."

It is important to note the unanimity among the important theoreticians who participated in the debates about the Spanish domination of the New World in not admitting, and even rejecting explicitly, the territorial expansion or the acquisition of material goods as a just reason for its legitimation. The result was peculiar: one of the largest imperial expansions in history, by an empire that never admitted, even to itself, that such was its intention. The principal objective espoused by all the main actors in the debate was the conversion of the natives, the eternal salvation of their souls. Evangelization was the theoretical banner that the Spanish state waved during the conquest.

From the bulls of Pope Alexander VI (1493), the Will and Testament of Queen Isabel (1504), the Laws of Burgos (1512), the *Requerimiento* (1513), the *Leyes Nuevas* (New Laws) (1542), the debate in Valladolid (1550–1551), "the ordinances for new discoveries and towns" decreed by Felipe II (1573), and finally, the "Compilation of the Laws of the Indies," realized during the reign of Carlos II in 1680, Christianization emerges as the Spanish government's justifying principal objective in the New World. The Christian religion becomes the official ideology for imperial expansion.

In this context, historical primacy belongs to one of the most famous sets of Apostolic Letters ever issued by the bishop of Rome, and perhaps the most important from the perspective of their political consequences for the Christian religion. The decrees of Pope Alexander VI – *Inter caetera* (May 3–4, 1493) and *Dudum siquidem* (Sept. 23, 1493) – "donate," "grant," and "assign" for life, to the Catholic Monarchs and their royal descendants, the newly discovered and yet to be discovered lands, and grant them the exclusive responsibility for converting their native inhabitants to the Christian faith.[2]

It is a sublime irony of history that the great expansion of Christianity toward the New World started under the aegis of a pope notorious for his moral weakness and personal corruption. Alexander VI, Rodrigo Borgia, father of the unfortunate duke Cesar Borgia, is the subject of attention by Machiavelli in *The Prince*: "Alexander VI was always, and he thought only of, deceiving people, and he always found victims for his deceptions. There never was a man capable of such convincing asseverations, or so ready to swear to the truth of something, who would honour his word less."[3] Coming from Machiavelli, this was a compliment. On another occasion he summed up Alexander's tastes thus: "Luxury, simony, and cruelty" (in *Decennale*, ch. 1).

Without the ironies of the prominent philosopher of power, Catholic historians have admitted that the Borgia pope was not a model of chastity or virtue. The Italian humanist at the court of the Catholic Monarchs, Pedro Mártir de Anglería ([1497] 1953, 1:329–330) commented thus on the habits of the worldly pope: "This Alexander of ours, chosen to serve as a bridge to heaven for us, does not concern himself with anything else outside making bridges for his children – whom he shows off without any shame – so that each day they may amass greater piles of riches. . . . These things make me nauseated."

In his extensive study of the origin of the Apostolic Letters, their canonical value, and their different and not always compatible interpretations, Manuel Giménez Fernández (1944), daringly enters—in an untypical way for Catholic Spanish historians—into their not so edifying political genesis. In short, he sees them as a simoniacal exchange in which Alexander VI consents to the petition/demand of Fernando V, against the Lusitanian claims, in return for some very beneficial marriages for his sacrilegious sons, especially the bastard Juan de Borgia, Duke of Gandia.[4] Giménez Fernández (ibid., 26) also highlights the many canonical irregularities committed in the issuing process since "scrupulosity in the fulfillment of legal formulas was not a distinctive mark of the procedures . . . followed by Alexander VI." However, this state of affairs does not discourage or provoke skepticism in this distinguished intellectual, who concludes with a valiant act of trust in divine providence: "The passage of Alexander VI through the see of Saint Peter is the most perfect demonstration of the divine character of the pontifical institution, since it preserved its prestige in spite of the Borgia pope's behavior." For Giménez Fernández, these pontifical decrees, independently of Alexander VI's corruption and Fernando V's avarice, are extraordinary examples of "the decisive importance of the path that God, writing straight on crooked lines, providentially gave to the discovery of the New World by laying the foundation for the political title of its masters in a civilizing and missionary task" (ibid., 45).[5]

This is certainly an impressive expression of faith in the transcendental virtue of the Roman papacy! Non-Catholics, however, can rightfully express their difficulty in accepting the heroic effort made to reconcile the Alexandrian decrees—of little or no canonical validity—and transcendental dogmatic truth.[6]

To understand the papal bulls issued by Alexander, it is useful to place them first in the context of the medieval doctrine of the supreme authority of the pope as *Vicarius Christi* and *dominus orbis,* legate of the absolute and universal will of the Son of God. The study by the Mexican scholar Luis Weckmann (1949) placing the Alexandrian bulls in the medieval tradition of the temporal authority of the pope, especially as proceeding from the apocryphal Donation of Constantine,[7] is instructive. However, Weckmann's exegesis of the bulls—the peculiar nature of papal power over small islands—is not convincing. He neglects a basic hermeneutical principle: the meaning of a concept is to be understood according to its contemporary use, not by its previous usage. The way in which the Alexandrian bulls were understood at the end of the fifteenth century and in the debates of the sixteenth have greater hermeneutical weight than the scrutiny of similar documents from preceding centuries. This is not to deny the relative importance of that latter task.

It is ironic that in the fifteenth and sixteenth centuries, a moment marking the decline of papal power, and more so, of its authority throughout Christendom, there was a growth of extreme papalist concepts among Spanish canonists.[8] It is also paradoxical that, in the case of the Spanish domination of the New World, defenders of regalist and imperialist positions used the papalist theory with the intention of validating the sovereignty of the Spanish crown (see García 1984, 17–63).[9] The development of national monarchies during the Renaissance gives a strong regalist and politically statist hue to documents that seem to highlight pontifical theocracy. What occurs, in the apt phrase of Zavala (Palacios Rubios and Paz 1954, lxx), is "the confluence of ultramontanism and regalism." The pope is proclaimed *Dominus totius orbis* (Lord of the entire world) at a time when the Supreme Pontiff was greatly dependent on the Spanish Crown. It was not very realistic to expect the bishop of Rome, who was also Spanish, born in Valencia, to reject the Castilian "petition" for a *motu propio* (a decree from his own accord). Giménez Fernández (1944, 140) has pointed out that never before had there been such emphasis on the temporal and universal power of the papacy as in these bulls. It was Spanish royalists, interested more in the power of the Spanish Crown than in the authority of the papacy, who stressed to the point of hyperbole what until then was only the opinion of an ultramontane minority.

Papal maximalism, born in medieval times when the Supreme Pontiff had assumed undisputed moral authority among the remaining subjects of the Roman Empire, achieved its greatest expression during the fertile thirteenth century, with the ideas of Cardinal Enrique de Segusa of Ostia. According to him:

> We believe, however, or better, we are certain, that the pope is the universal vicar of Jesus Christ the Savior, and therefore he has power not only over Christians but also over infidels since the faculty received by Christ from the Father was absolute. . . . And it seems to me that after the coming of Christ, all honor and principality and dominion and jurisdiction have been taken away from the infidels and transposed to the faithful, rightfully and for just cause, by him who has supreme power and who is infallible.[10]

The defenders of the Spanish empire resurrected, for the purpose of magnifying the meaning of the bulls of Alexander VI, this kind of papalism just at the time when the nascent nationalism of the European states was beginning to marginalize the Holy See and when the Roman curia was passing through a period of grave crisis and moral corruption. Felipe II's later efforts to reduce to a minimum the jurisdictional functional authority of the Supreme Pontiff would be ironic, considering that the papal bulls gave the Spanish Crown privileges and benefits over ecclesiastical life in the Americas (Shiels 1961, 195–228; Lynch 1987, 335–352).

One should not neglect the way in which that papalist tradition was incorporated into Castilian law, as represented by *Las siete partidas* (Seven divisions of law) of King Alfonso X, "the wise," in the thirteenth century. The ninth law of the first title of the second division, in reference to political and territorial jurisdiction by a monarch, establishes the four "ways to obtain lordship": (1) by inheritance, "when by inheritance, the oldest son inherits the kingdoms"; (2) by election of the subjects, "when he earns them by the will of those in his kingdom"; (3) by marriage, "when someone marries a woman who is heir to the kingdom"; and (4) by papal or imperial donation, "by the concession of the pope or the emperor when they appoint kings in those lands where they have a right to do so." As was to be expected, this last way to obtain legitimate ownership was applied to the bulls of Alexander (Palacios Rubios and Paz 1954, 77–78). Soon there would arise the dispute over the legitimacy of the pope's "right" to "donate" the lands of the New World to Spain. Also there would be motive for intense debate in the question of the manner in which the conclusion from this law was applied or not in the New World: "Monarchs must always safeguard the welfare of their people more than their own" (Alfonso 1807, 2.2.1.9:10).[11]

The bulls of Alexander VI did not set a precedent. They were linked to papal pronouncements that in the fifteenth century had granted the Portuguese monopoly over territories they explored on the western coast of Africa, among them *Dudum cum ad nos* (1436) and *Rex Regum* (1443) of Eugene IV, *Divino amore communiti* (1452) and *Romanus Pontifex* (1455) of Nicholas V, *Inter caetera* (1456) of Callistus III, and *Aeterni Regis* (1481) of Sixtus IV (see Martel de Witte 1953–1958).[12] These papal decrees were the formal and literary precedent for the bulls of Alexander. They were also used by Portugal to claim jurisdiction over the lands found by Columbus and propelled the Spanish Crown to request a "bull of donation" from Alexander (Davenport 1917, 9–55).[13]

The papal bulls gave the Portuguese these concessions in Africa: (1) title of ownership over the newfound and occupied territories; (2) rights of ecclesial patronage; (3) the Crown's collection of tithes; (4) the commission to propagate the faith; and (5) the power to enslave the natives (Morales Padrón 1979, 16). With the important exception of the power to enslave the natives, a difference that generated an intense controversy, the bulls conferring rights over the territories in the Americas to the Spanish monarchy follow the pattern established by those issued earlier for the Lusitanian Crown.[14]

Let us cite some passages from the most famous of the Alexandrian bulls, the second *Inter caetera* of May 4, 1493.

> Alexander, Bishop, servant of the servants of God: to our beloved son in Christ, King Fernando, and to our beloved daughter in Christ, Isabel, Queen of Castilla, León, Aragón, Sicilia, and Granada, greetings and apostolic blessings.
>
> Among other works acceptable to the Divine Majesty and according to our own hearts' desire, this certainly is the most important, that the Catholic faith and Christian religion, especially in this our time, may in all places be exalted, amplified, and enlarged whereby the health of souls may be procured, and the barbarous nations subdued and brought to the faith. . . . [A]nd understanding you to be true Catholic Sovereigns and Princes, as we have always known you, and as your noble and worthy deeds have declared you . . . as your expeditions restoring the kingdom of Granada from the tyranny of the Saracens do plainly declare your actions to be for the greater glory of the Divine Name. . . . We are informed that lately you were determined to seek and find certain isles and mainlands remote and unknown (and not heretofore found by any other) with the intention of bringing their inhabitants to honor our Redeemer and to profess the Catholic faith. . . .
>
> We greatly commend your godly and laudable purpose in our Lord and, desirous to have the same brought to a worthy end and the name of our Savior to be known in those parts, we exhort you in our Lord and by the reception of your holy baptism, which binds you to Apostolic obedience and earnestly requires you, by the innermost mercy of our Lord Jesus Christ, that what you intend for the zeal of the Catholic faith to carry out such endeavor . . . to bring the people of said mainlands and isles to the Christian religion. . . .
>
> Furthermore we command you . . . to send to said lands and islands honest, virtuous, and learned men who fear God and are able to instruct the inhabitants in the Catholic faith.[15]

This missionary charge carries with it the *donation in perpetuity* to the Spanish Crown of the discovered and to be discovered lands. The evangelization of the natives, therefore, has an important political consequence. The missionary task implies political hegemony. All of this is a transaction between the pope and the Catholic Monarchs, outside the will, consent, and knowledge of the native peoples of the "said mainlands and isles." Thus the ideological bases for the Spanish Christian empire were established.

And that being authorized by the privilege of the apostolic grace, you may more freely and boldly take upon yourselves such an important enterprise, we *motu propio* [of our own will],[16] . . . of our own generosity and certain science, and by the fullness of Apostolic power, do give, grant, and assign to you, your heirs and successors, all the mainlands and isles found or to be found, discovered or to be discovered [here is added the famous line of demarcation between the Spanish and Portuguese overseas possessions] . . . that were not already possessed by another Christian sovereign or prince . . . by the authority of Almighty God granted unto us in Saint Peter, and by the office which we bear on earth as Vicar of Christ, . . . we give, grant, assign [*donamus, concedimus, et assignamus*] . . . all those lands and islands, with their dominions, territories, cities, castles, other places, and villages with all the rights and jurisdictions and all their belongings to you, your heirs and successors to be lords with full and free power, authority, and jurisdiction. (Fernández de Navarrete 1945, 2:45; Zavala 1971, 214–215).

The effective Christianization of the discovered or to be discovered lands "that were not already possessed by another Christian sovereign or prince" (the sovereign's religion determines the validity of his titles to sovereignty) becomes the juridical-theological foundation for the donation, in perpetuity, of political authority. During the next century, the Spanish Crown would allude to these papal bulls to legitimate its dominion over the New World, both before the indigenous owners, and in the face of the pretensions of other European princes. The ironic phrase of Francis I, French king in 1540, is well known: "I would be pleased to see the clause in Adam's testament that excludes me from a share in the globe" (in Leturia 1959, 1:280).[17] For her part, Queen Elizabeth I of England disdained a territorial "grant" ceded by an ecclesiastical hierarchy to which her Crown did not pay homage. She insisted that she "could not be convinced that [the Indies] were legitimately owned by Spain by decree of the pope of Rome, in whom I do not recognize any prerogatives in such matters, much less that he can oblige Princes who do not owe him obedience" (Zorraquín Becú 1975, 587).

The German Catholic historian Joseph Höffner (1957, 264–291), based on Staedler's research (1937), argues against the commonly held theses that the edicts of Alexander VI are "bulls of donation." Alluding to medieval usage and customs, he insists that they follow the writing style and formula for enfeoffments. His line of argument is not convincing. The crucial hermeneutical key cannot be a medieval tradition (such an approach would convert the analysis into a labyrinthine philological disquisition), but rather the key is the way in which the bulls were utilized and understood in the debates over the legitimacy of Spain's dominion of the New World at the beginning of the sixteenth century. Höffner is forced to recognize that the formula "*donamus, concedimus, et assignamus,*" was interpreted in the manner of a grant, whose initial theoretical foundation was the universalist theocracy in vogue among the proponents of a militant and militaristic evangelization. The departure from that understanding had nothing to do with esoteric enfeoffment formulas, but with the reinterpretation of the decrees of Alexander VI as primarily a missionary charge. But as the reflections of Las Casas and Vitoria show, the evangelical-missionary dimension was never totally disconnected from the problem of the legitimacy of political domination.

The intense debate in Spain about the legitimacy of its domination of the New World during the sixteenth century centered in general on the decrees of Alexander VI. His "*donamus, concedimus, et assignamus*" had historical and political resonance unlike any other pronouncement from ecclesiastical authority. All the actors in the intense disputes over the legitimacy of Spanish hegemony in the Americas, over the wars to sustain it, and over the freedom and servitude of its pre-Colombian inhabitants have raised as their war banners their particular interpretation of these papal decrees. Giménez Fernández (1944, 142) is not exaggerating when he categorically asserts that

> during the whole unfolding of the political domination of the Indies by Spain, there is not one single ideological movement intended to reform Spain's established legitimacy, nor the direction of the governance of the Indies by the State, that in various ways does not allege the historical fact of Alexander's letters in respect to the Indies to support its thesis, interpreting them in the light of its own conceptions.

The prevalence of these references to the authorized nature of the Alexandrian bulls was maintained steadfastly among Spanish theologians, as is shown in a memorandum by the Franciscan Alfonso de Castro, in 1553, in which he asserts: "The right of the monarchs of Castilla to lordship of the Indies is by decree of the Apostolic See, which the pope granted in favor of the Catholic faith" (Pereña Vicente 1982, 593).

It would be legitimate to assert that the Valladolid debate between Juan Gines de Sepúlveda and Las Casas centered on the correct interpretation that should be given to the Alexandrian bulls. Against Las Casas, Sepúlveda holds on to the literal interpretation of the formula "*donamus, concedimus, et assignamus.*" According to this reading, Castilian sovereignty of the New World does not at all depend on the free consent of the natives. Sepúlveda, at about this time, wrote another treatise, entitled "Against those who devalue and contradict the bull and decree of Pope Alexander VI granting the Catholic Monarchs and their successors authority to conquer the Indies and subjugate those barbarians, and by this means convert them to the Christian religion and subject them to their power and jurisdiction" (Hanke 1985, 94). Yet in his exegesis of the bull Las Casas sees it as the entrusting of a missionary responsibility with an implied political sovereignty that has to be balanced by the right of the Indians to self-determination.[18]

In the juridical area, the Alexandrian bulls maintained their authorized character, as shown by the first sentence in the first law of the first chapter of the third book of "the Compilation of the *Leyes de Indias*" (1680), which recognizes them as the first foundation for the possession in perpetuity of the Americas by the Crown of Castilla.

> By donation from the Apostolic Holy See . . . we are Lord of the Western Indies, isles and mainlands of the Ocean Sea, discovered and to be discovered and incorporated in our Royal Crown of Castilla . . . [so that] they may always remain united for their greater perpetuity and firmness, we forbid their being taken away. And we order that at no time may they be separated from our Royal Crown of Castilla. . . . And we give our faith and royal word, and the Kings our successors, so that they can never be taken away or separated, in all or in part, for any reason or cause whatsoever. (*Recopilación* 1841, 3.1.1, 2: 1)

This law is based on consecutive royal declarations by Carlos V and Felipe II, who during the sixteenth century propounded the doctrine of Castilian dominion in perpetuity over the Ibero-American peoples. All those declarations allude to the Alexandrian bulls as the crucial point of reference.[19]

Although we cannot dwell on this point, it is appropriate to point out that at the beginning of the nineteenth century the papal grant in perpetuity was used as justification for discrediting the Latin American independence movement (see Leturia 1925, 31–47; 1947, 423–517).

The Requerimiento — *Conversion or War*

The Spanish theological and juridical debates during 1512 and 1513 over the legitimacy of armed interventions against the indigenous people were provoked by the first protests against the abuse of the natives made by Dominican friars of Española and by some dangerous uprisings in the Antilles, above all in San Juan Bautista (Puerto Rico).[20] These debates culminated in a document of decisive importance for understanding the religious ideology of the conquest of America— *"el requerimiento."*[21] This was an attempt to give theological legitimation to the papal grant of the New World to the Castilian sovereigns for the purpose of evangelizing it.[22] It is an exceptional attempt to give a Christian veneer to a process of conquest by war, and to highlight the civilizing and religious mission in the expropriation of the new lands. It has been labeled the "first awakening of human consciousness in the colonization efforts beyond the sea" (Konetzke 1972, 156).

The *Requerimiento,* as a formal official document, was prepared in 1513 for Pedrarías Dávila's expedition to begin the colonization of the mainland. This document was to be read to all native communities in their initial encounter with the Spanish colonizers. From the very beginning of the conquest, however, there was the custom of requiring the natives to pledge obedience to the Catholic Monarchs and convert to Christianity. If they refused, they were victimized and enslaved. We can see this approach in the royal decree issued by Queen Isabel, in October of 1503, to justify the forced subjugation of the Carib Indians:

> We sent with them [the military captains] some religious men to preach to them and to indoctrinate them in matters concerning our holy Catholic faith and to "require" them to place themselves under our service . . . they have been required many times to become Christians and convert and to be incorporated into the communion of the faithful and under our obedience.

When the Caribs rejected that requirement, the queen authorized war against them and said "that they could capture them . . . and sell them and make use of them" (Konetzke 1953, 1:14–15).[23] In the same way, in July of 1511 the Crown gave an order to Juan Cerón, then principal royal official on the island of San Juan Bautista, regarding the rebellious natives of Boriquén:

> Make your requirements formally, two or three times: and if after having done so they do not wish to submit and serve as do the Indians of Española, publicly declare war against them; and gather our people, and . . . it is good to make war by fire and blood, and those captured alive should become captives and treated as such . . . you should try to take control of these miscreants so that they become our slaves or be subjected to hard labor in our mines. (Coll y Toste 1914, 2:74–75)

The "requirements" of this passage seem to refer to the reading of a memorandum, prepared in the court especially for the rebellious natives of San Juan Bautista. This memorandum was probably the precursor to the famous document that we analyze in this section.

The *Requerimiento* of 1513 begins with a brief exposition of the divine creation of the world and the unity of the human species under one God, passing immediately to treat of the supreme authority of the bishop of Rome: "God placed all this people under the care of one called Saint Peter, so that he would become prince, lord, and master of all peoples of the world." It immediately tells how a past pontiff granted these "islands and terra firma of the Ocean sea" to the monarchs of Spain. The central point is a call to render double obedience, to the Catholic church and to the Castilian Crown.

> I beg and require of you . . . to recognize the church as lady and superior of the universe and to acknowledge the Supreme Pontiff, called pope, in her name, and the king and queen . . . as lords and superiors . . . by virtue of said donation; and consent to have these religious fathers declare and preach these things to you. If you do so, you will be acting well, and those who are over you and to whom you owe obedience, and Their Highnesses and I [whosoever leads the Spanish expedition in question] in their name would welcome you with love and charity.

To the misfortune of the American natives, the rejection of Christian preaching converted them, ipso facto, into rebels against the faith, into provokers of a grave offense against God and the cause of the just war against them, the confiscation of their property, and their possible enslavement.

> If you do not do it . . . then with the help of God I will undertake power-ful action against you. I will make war on you everywhere and in every way that I can. I will subject you to the yoke and obedience of the church and of Their Highnesses. I will take you personally and your wives and children, and make slaves of you, and as such sell you off . . . and I will take away your property and cause you all the evil and harm I can. (Oviedo 1851, 3.2.29.7:28–29)[24]

The *Requerimiento* tries to mark the boundary between obedience to the church and the Spanish Crown and conversion to the Christian faith. It demands the first, not the second. "And they will not compel you to become Christian, unless you, after being informed of the truth, want to convert to our Catholic faith." This was by way of conforming to the idea, held by the majority of theologians, of the voluntary nature of the faith (Saint Thomas Aquinas: "The act of faith is an action proper to the will" [2–2.10.8]). This distinction, however, ends up as something arbitrary. How could one demand that peoples and nations "recognize the church as lady and superior of the universe and to acknowledge the Supreme Pontiff, called pope, in her name," and also accept the validity of the grant that this so-called Supreme Pontiff had made, to sovereigns unknown to them, of political jurisdiction over them, without the recognition required of them implying some kind of prior conversion to the Christian faith?

It was to the credit of some Spanish theologians that they recognized this inconsistency. Vitoria and Las Casas, contemporaries of the edict, called it absurd. According to Vitoria: "Nothing, therefore, is more absurd than what is being taught, that if the barbarians can reject with impunity the reign of Christ, they are, however, obliged to subject themselves to the dominion of his vicar under penalty of being forced into war, deprived of their goods, and condemned to punishment" (Urdanoz 1960, 682–683). According to Las Casas, "It is absurd to make them acknowledge the dominion of the Church under penalty of losing their power to rule, since they cannot even guess at this without the teaching of the faith" (Casas 1974, 119).[25]

There is an intrinsic connection between the Alexandrian bulls and the *Requerimiento*. Their starting point is the fundamental attitude that medieval Christianity adopted toward the pagan nations, gentiles or "infidels."[26] The missionary monotheism of the primitive church, when it took hold of the reins of the state, converted the sword into an instrument for the expansion of the evangelical faith. The existence of non-Christian nations was perceived as a religious, political, and military challenge to the *orbis christianus*. As Joseph Höffner (1957, 6, 33, 44) states:

> The *orbis christianus* was not only a tenaciously defended patrimony but also a religious and political motto for the conquest of the world. Therefore the propagation of the reign of Christ was entrusted to the emperors and kings in liturgical solemnity and as a sacred duty. . . .
>
> These ideas were and continued to be a spiritual power until the sixteenth and seventeenth centuries. . . .
>
> Their importance is not insignificant for the understanding of the Spanish colonial ethics of the sixteenth century. Because, taken to its ultimate conclusions, universal domination could not stop within the limits of the *orbis christianus*. Beyond those limits were the infidels. Just as the unity of the faith, from which universalism was born, was preserved in an intolerant way within the Christian world, so also was the attempt to raise up the cross in the lands of the infidels. It was an attempt to convert the gentiles, or annihilate them if they were enemies of the cross of Christ.

The greatest effort in the history of Christianity to expand the *orbis christianus*—the conquest of the New World and the evangelization of its inhabitants—takes place, ironically, just at the sunset of the Holy Roman Empire. It is an event concurrent with the birth of nation states that had little loyalty to the vague ideas of "Christendom," and with the irreversible fragmentation of the church. Perhaps only in Spain, with its peculiar intimate confusion between nationalism and Catholicism, could the vision of *orbis christianus* last as the ruling ideal and ideology of an exceptional imperial expansion. Tommasso Campanella (see Góngora 1974) affirmed that in the Spanish empire the sun never set ("neque unquam in eius imperio noctecescit" [ibid., 109]). It would have been more correct to say that there was never an instant in which, somewhere in the territories incorporated in the empire, a mass was not being celebrated.

Oviedo (1851, 3.2.29.7:31) relates how he read the *Requerimiento in Spanish* to an *empty* native village (a procedure he characterized as laughable). He reports how he said to the Spanish captain: "'Sir, it seems to me that these Indians do not want to listen to the theology of this *Requerimiento,* and you do not have someone to get them to understand. Let your grace keep it until we have one of these Indians in a cage so that he can learn it slowly and the lord bishop get him to understand.' And I gave him the *Requerimiento,* which he on his part took with much laughter and so did the others who heard me." Martin Fernández de Enciso, in his *Suma de geografía,* written in 1519, tells the reaction of the Indians of Cenú, when he read them the *Requerimiento:*

> They answered me that regarding what it said about there being only one God who governed heaven and earth and who was lord of all, that seemed fine to them, but in so far as what it said about the pope being lord of the universe in God's place, and that he donated the land to the king of Castilla, they said the pope must have been drunk when he did that because he gave what was not his to give, and that the king who asked for and took the grant must have been crazy because he asked for what belonged to others, and that he should go there to take it so they could hang his head from a stick as they had hung other heads . . . belonging to their enemies . . . and they said that they were lords of their land and did not need another lord. (In Casas 1986, 3.3.63:45)[27]

However, such an arrogant response did not take into account European superiority in military technology. The Spaniards took by force what the proud aborigines refused to surrender willingly.

Another person who provided a critical account of how the *Requerimiento* was read was the scholar Alonso de Zuazo in an instructive memorandum sent, on January 22, 1518, to Guillermo de Croy, or Monsieur de Xèvres, as the Flemish tutor of the young monarch Carlos was known in Spain. He tells of the entrance of Juan de Ayora in 1514 into Central American territory:

Ayora . . . showed them from afar the *Requerimiento* he was carrying so that they would come under obedience to the Catholic king. And Ayora asked a scribe in whose presence the *Requerimiento* was read to testify that they had been *"requeridos"* (requested to submit). And then the captain would declare them slaves and at a loss of all their possessions since they seemed not to want to obey the *Requerimiento,* which was read to them in Spanish, which neither the chief nor the Indians could understand; and it was also proclaimed from so far away that even if they knew the language, they could not have heard it. . . . And in this fashion, they used to come to the villages at night and there steal from them, send dogs to attack them, burn them, and carry them off as slaves. (Pacheco et al. 1864–1884, 1:316–317)

The fatal consequence—war and enslavement—of not accepting the call to the required double loyalty gives rise to the obvious question, Did the Spanish commanders prefer a positive or a negative answer? Vasco de Quiroga, first official of the court in New Spain and later bishop of Michoacán, is one of the many who espoused the skeptical view of the sincerity of the colonizers (although never of the Crown or church).

The words and "Requerimientos" that they say to them, . . . they [the colonizers] do not understand them, or they do not know what they say, or they cannot get the Indians to understand them as they should, both because of lack of knowledge of the languages or because of the absence of goodwill on the part of our people in this matter since they are not without a strong interest in having slaves for their mines . . . for which they take greater care than in helping the Indians understand the preaching and the "Requerimientos." (Herrejón 1985, 60)

Las Casas rated the *Requerimiento* as "unjust, profane, scandalous, irrational, and absurd," the product of the ignorant, very grave, and harmful shortcomings of the King's Counsel concerning this same affair: "[It] makes mockery of truth and justice and [is] a great insult to our Christian faith and to the piety and charity of Jesus Christ . . . having no legality" (Casas 1986, 3.3.57–58:25–31; 167:409–410).[28] His repudiation was so intense that he dedicated the last lines of his monumental *Historia de las Indias* to condemn it.

The criticism to which the Dominican friar Vitoria subjected the *Requerimiento,* without mentioning it by name, was meticulous and rigorous. For the scholastic from Salamanca, (1) the pope has no temporal power over the native peoples that would allow him to "donate" them to a different national authority; (2) It is not reasonable to expect that with merely exposing them to the need to believe in the Christian faith they will convert without a period of preaching and explanation of its theological contents (which, if necessary, should be accompanied by "miracles and other proofs"); (3) If "those barbarians of the New World," as he calls them, do not wish to embrace the Christian faith, "it is not sufficient cause for the Spaniards to declare war on them, nor to act against them with the right of war."

Besides, Vitoria is not persuaded that the requirement that the natives convert has been confirmed by "religious examples of living" on the part of the Spaniards. He suspects, rather, that "interests . . . far from that" have prevailed, which have caused the stream of "news of many scandals, cruel crimes, and profanities" (Urdanoz 1960, 676–701).

As has been pointed out by Demetrio Ramos (1984, 44), who has attempted to temper the traditional criticism of the documents: "The *Requerimiento* allowed no other response but submission. . . . It was not a matter of an offer, based on conveniences granted, that you could reject; it was a notification of something already resolved with the [papal] grant and of which they were being informed."

The *Requerimiento* had been preceded by the opinions of jurists and theologians such as Juan López de Palacios Rubios and Fray Matías de Paz, O.P., who in the meeting in Burgos (1512) presented memoranda about the legality of the Spanish domination of the recently discovered lands and the kind of servitude to be imposed on their inhabitants. This unleashed the preparation of the first treatises and academic manuscripts about the problem.

Palacios Rubios, the apparent author of the *Requerimiento* (as suggested by Las Casas and Oviedo), a jurist in the confidence of the court, in a treatise provoked by the debates of 1512 entitled "Of the isles of the Ocean sea," considers in the theocratic pontifical tradition enunciated by Segusa from Ostia that the Supreme Pontiff, as successor of Saint Peter, is universal and general vicar of Christ in both his spiritual and temporal powers. Therefore, the maximum authority over all the kingdoms, of both the faithful and the infidels, belongs to the pope. That authority he exercises for soteriological ends. The grant given by Alexander VI to the monarchs of Castilla and León is the practical application of that maximum jurisdiction. The infidels of the New World, however, do not yet know about the supreme papal power, nor of his grant. Therefore, it is indispensable to admonish them to accept the authority of the church and, by extension, that of the Castilian Crown. It is necessary to make the requirement (*Requerimiento*) so as to allow the natives to accept Spanish authority and the Catholic faith. If after that admonition they resist giving their consent, the Spanish monarch can subject them by force; always, naturally, keeping in mind the salvation of their souls.

> All power and jurisdiction . . . were canceled by the coming of Christ, who passed on all jurisdiction and power, according to the opinion of Hostiense [sic]. . . .
> He had, not only spiritual power over spiritual matters, but also temporal power over temporal matters, and he received both scepters from his Father. . . .
> Christ, therefore, entrusted to Saint Peter . . . both powers and jurisdictions he possessed . . . namely the temporal and the spiritual. . . .
> The Roman Pontiff is the successor of Saint Peter in that perfection of power and in the dignity of vicar. . . .
> Supreme dominion, power, and jurisdiction over these islands belong to the church whom the entire world and all men, including infidels, have to recognize as owner and superior, and if required to do so, they refuse, the church could in that case, either by itself or with the help of Christian Princes, bring them into subjection and expel them from their own lands. (Lopez de Palacios Rubios and Paz 1954, 79, 81, 84, 89, 128)

Matías de Paz, Dominican theologian,[29] in another writing of the same period titled "*Del dominio de los Reyes de España sobre los indios*" (see Lopez de Palacios Rubios 1954, 211–259), argued that it was licit for the pope, with a view to increasing the Christian faith and for the benefit of the eternal salvation of the souls of the natives, to cede the dominion of their lands to the Catholic Monarchs. That could not be done, however, for the enrichment of Spain, but for the fulfillment of the evangelical mission command. "It is not licit for Christian princes to make war on the infidels for a whim of domination or for the desire to gain riches, but only inspired by the zeal of faith . . . so that the name of our Redeemer be exalted and praised throughout the entire world" (ibid., 222).

The pope could make such concession as universal and general vicar of Christ, who "as man, was true monarch of the whole world from the beginning of his nativity." Papal authority, inherited from Christ, is complete and absolute. "Christ was given the entire earthly orb . . . and as a result his vicar has the right, founded on Saint Peter's faith, to dominate the entire earth." The fact that he does not always exercise it may be due to impeding circumstances or expediency. In the case of the recently discovered peoples in the Ocean sea, the Supreme Pontiff has considered it convenient with a view to their prompt and expeditious entry into the Catholic Church, since "after the advent of the Redeemer no one can be saved outside his Catholic Church" (ibid., 240; 243).

By the authority of the Supreme Pontiff and in no other way, our Catholic
and unconquered monarch will be permitted to govern the said Indians
with royal power. . . .

Being . . . the pope, monarch of the entire orb, in the name of
Christ . . . he could, if convenient for the Catholic faith, impose on them
a Catholic king who would govern with royal power and under
whom . . . the faith in Christ would be maintained. And this, if considered carefully, would benefit the governed rather than the governor.
(ibid., 233, 252)

This royal power, Paz reiterates on several occasions, is legitimate
"whenever it is exercised out of zeal for the faith and not for the desire
to dominate and be enriched" (ibid., 247). Besides, what should prevail
is the preaching, not warlike actions, and the natives who agree to convert shall not be enslaved nor ill-treated. Paz, in fact, becomes the mouth-
piece of the angry protests by the Dominican friars in the Antilles who
have denounced the unmerciful exploitation suffered by the natives for
the personal enrichment of the Castilian colonizers. In the disputes of
Burgos in 1512, in which Dominican friars confronted Castilian colonizers,
Paz takes side with his brothers wearing the habit.

To them I think should be given greater credence than to those very
people who oppress the Indians with insufferable slavery. Neither Christ
nor the pope wished such evils, nor did our Catholic Monarch or right
reason. The religious we allude to have given an account of the countless
Indians who have perished because of that servitude, people who if left
free or not subjected to slavery, would now adore Christ. (ibid., 255)

Lopez de Palacios Rubios and Paz have as their starting point the medieval theocratic theory according to which spiritual goals are superior to
temporal and civil ones and the latter are politically and legislatively subordinate to the former. The corollaries of that theory, with respect to the
peoples of the New World, are: first, the Christianization of the natives
is the only valid end for legitimate Spanish sovereignty; second, the
Supreme Pontiff, successor of Saint Peter in the bishopric of Rome, is Vicar
of Christ in the supreme and universal power, spiritual and temporal, of
the latter, and has full authority to give Spain exclusive rights to bring the
Catholic faith to the inhabitants of "the isles and mainlands of the Ocean
sea"; third, the natives should be admonished to accept the supremacy
of the Catholic faith and the sovereignty of the Castilian Crown; fourth,
if the natives reject such admonitions, the Spanish monarchs can,
legitimately, declare war on them and subject them to their authority by

force; fifth, the entire enterprise of conquest is carried out primarily for spiritual and religious purposes.

The *Requerimiento* persisted, in spite of the criticism, during a decisive time for the Spanish conquest of the New World. Hernán Cortés tells of different instances in which he required the Mexican natives to pledge double obedience — to Christianity and the Crown. And he threatens them with war and servitude if they do not accept his *Requerimiento*.

> Through me, in your royal name, I had required them . . . to have and adore only one God . . . and abandon all the idols and rituals they had until now. . . . And that at the same time they would come to know how on the earth it is your majesty [Carlos V] that the universe obeys and serves by divine providence; and that they too had to submit and be under the imperial yoke. . . . And if they did not do so, action would be taken against them. (Cortés 1985, 228)

Two decades after its original composition, March 8, 1533, Carlos V sent a version to Francisco Pizarro so that he would read it to the natives of Peru.[30] Fray Martín de Jesús read a substantially more extensive version of the *Requerimiento* to the rebellious natives of Nueva Galicia in 1541 (Pacheco et al. 1864–1884, 3:369, 377).[31] Even after the approval of the so-called New Laws in 1542–1543, the spirit of the *Requerimiento* endured in many royal instructions intended to guide continued discoveries and occupations.

Instructions given by the Crown on May 13, 1556, to the Marqués de Cañete, Don Andrés Hurtado de Mendoza, at the beginning of his functions as viceroy of Peru, preserve that spirit. As was customary, the instructions insisted that an attempt be made to convince the natives peacefully to convert to Catholicism and accept the Spanish lordship. Behind the silk glove, however, the sword is hiding.

> Furthermore, if said natives and their lords do not wish to welcome the religious preachers after these have told them the intent they bring with them . . . and *after being "required" many times* . . . said religious and Spaniards may enter their land and province by the force of arms and oppress those who may resist and force them into obedience. (Konetzke 1953, 1:338; emphasis added)

This peculiar call to Christian faith and political obedience had a long and controversial life.

3

National Providentialism and Messianism

*King Fernando on his throne regards
three Spanish caravels at sea.
A group of native Americans waits
on the opposite shore.*

As Catholics and Christians, our principal intention must be directed toward the service and honor of God, our Lord, and the reason the Holy Father granted the Emperor, my Lord, dominion over these peoples . . . is that these peoples be converted to our Holy Catholic faith.

Hernán Cortés

The monarchs of Spain, to the benefit of the faith, received from the Apostolic See the charge and the responsibility for proclaiming and spreading, throughout that vast world of the Indies, the Catholic faith and the Christian religion, which of necessity has to be done for the conversion of these people to Christ.

Bartolomé de las Casas

The Spanish Crown and Evangelization

Fernando and Isabel, Catholic Monarchs of Spain, gave Christopher Columbus the following instruction at the beginning of his second journey.

Because it pleased God our Lord in his great mercy to grant the discovery of those islands and mainlands to the King and Queen . . . by means of the hard work of Don Christopher Columbus, as admiral, their viceroy and governor . . . who learned that there are in them people very suited for conversion to our holy Catholic faith, because they do not have any laws or sect. . . . Because of that, your highnesses, wishing that our holy Catholic faith be increased and augmented, order and charge said admiral . . . that by every means and ways possible he should try to persuade the inhabitants of said islands and mainlands to be converted to our holy Catholic faith. (Konetzke 1953, 1:1)

To that end, the monarchs sent a group of religious men with the Admiral to begin the evangelization of the natives, who, according to Columbus, did "not have any laws or sect" and were "people very suited for conversion to our holy Catholic faith." Of course the monarchs did not consider the question of the validity of such restrictive affirmations made by Columbus, a person whose superficial contacts with the Antillean inhabitants were filtered through linguistic incompatibility as well as his own fantasies and ambitions.

In the codicil of her will and testament, November 23, 1504, the dying queen Isabel included the following clause:

Whereas, from the time when the Holy Apostolic See granted us the isles and mainlands of the Ocean sea, which have been or will be

discovered, our principal intention at the time when we asked Pope Alexander VI of happy memory to grant us the said concession was to try
to lead and bring the peoples of the said areas and convert them to our
Holy Catholic faith, and to send to the said islands and mainlands of
the Ocean sea prelates and religious and clerics and other learned and
God-fearing persons to instruct the natives and inhabitants of those lands
in the Catholic faith, and to teach them doctrine and good behavior . . .
therefore, I beg the King, my lord, with much affection, and I charge
and command the Princess, my daughter, and the said Prince, her
husband, to carry out and fulfill this charge, and that this be their principal aim, and may they apply much diligence in carrying this out . . . for
this is what is enjoined on us and commanded us by the Apostolic Letters
of the aforementioned grant. (*Testamento*, 66–67)[1]

King Fernando commanded Diego Columbus, the Admiral's son, on
June 6, 1511, to have the Indians instructed in the "matters of our holy
Catholic faith, since this is the principal basis for the conquest of those
parts" (Hanke 1967, 54). The Laws of Burgos, which constituted the first
legal corpus approved by the Spanish Crown to regulate the relationships
between Spaniards and American natives, reaffirm the education of the
natives in the Catholic faith as a first preoccupation of the royal court. These
laws were approved at the end of 1512 after the first theological and juridical
debates about the treatment of the natives of the New World. The debates
were provoked by the rapid depopulation of Española, the revolts on the
island of San Juan (Puerto Rico), and the first criticisms on the part of the
Dominican friars. The text begins this way: "Don Fernando, etc. In so far
as I and the most serene Queen, Doña Isabel, my dear and beloved wife,
may she enjoy heavenly glory, always had strongly willed that the chiefs
and Indians . . . would come to learn about our holy Catholic faith, and
for that purpose we ordered that ordinances be drawn up and so they
were . . ." This intention is reaffirmed in the new legislation for the Indies.
"Because my first desire and of said most serene Queen, and very dear
and beloved daughter [Juana], is that in those places and in each one of
them our holy Catholic faith be planted and take deep roots, so that the
souls of said Indians be saved" (Konetzke 1953, 1:38, 45).

In 1526, with the "Ordinances about the good treatment of the Indians"
(ibid., 89–96), Carlos V tried to have the violence of the conquistadors
mitigated by the spiritual authority of religious missionaries. Every expedition should "be accompanied by at least two religious men or ordained
clerics, who should be presented to our Council of the Indies, with information about their life, doctrine, and example, to be approved as people

beneficial to God's service. . . . We also ordain and command that said religious or clerics be very careful and try diligently to see that the Indians be treated like neighbors who are looked after and favored"(ibid., 92).

The *Leyes Nuevas* of 1542, approved by Carlos V, were intended to eliminate the servitude of the American Natives and to bring order to the chaotic, violent situation prevailing in the New World. They reaffirm the same transcendental objective for Spanish domination: "Our principal intent and will has always been and is the preservation and increase of the Indians and that they be instructed and taught in the things of our holy Catholic faith" (ibid., 217).

The same aim is stressed by Felipe II's "Ordinances regarding new discoveries and towns," approved in 1573, which were yet another attempt to channel the impetuous stream of conquests, conflicts, and ambitions. The ordinances decreed that every expedition to new Indian territories should be accompanied by "two clerics and religious whose concern would be [the natives'] conversion"; ". . . for that is the principal end for which we order new discoveries and settlements to be made"; ". . . the zeal and wish that we have is that all that is yet to be discovered be discovered, so that the holy gospel be made public and the natives come to the knowledge of our holy Catholic faith" (Pacheco et al. 1864–1884, 8:489, 498–499, 494–495).[2]

The monarch even grants religious orders priority in the rights of discovery and settlement, and commands that missions be protected from the interference of conquistadors and entrepreneurial colonizers.

> If there are friars and religious from orders that wish to go to the Indies with the desire to serve our Lord, who may wish to discover land and make the holy gospel public in them, they should be charged before others with the discovery . . . and they should be favored and provided with all that is necessary for this holy and good work, at our expense. . . .
> In those parts where the preachers of the gospel are sufficient to pacify the Indians and convert them and bring them to peace, do not allow other persons to enter who may disturb the conversion and pacification. (ibid., 495, 536)

This last expression, "pacification," plays a key role in the Ordinances. It is substituted for the traditional term "conquest," which is excluded from the official vocabulary of Spanish legislation for the Indies. Even armed actions are referred to as pacifying actions. Religious critics of the conquests achieved, at least, a decisive lexicographic victory.

Finally, in 1680, in the reign of Carlos II, the so-called *"Recopilación de Leyes de Indias"* [Compendium of the Laws of the Indies] was accomplished.

The "first law" serves as a declaration of the primary objective of Spanish dominion over the "Western Indies." It points out that the great Spanish empire is a gift from "God our Lord" who "by his infinite mercy and goodness" thus distinguished the Spanish Crown. That divine grace imposed an exceptional missionary obligation on the Castilian court, namely "to work so as to make God known and adored in the whole world, for the one true God that he is and creator of all that is visible and invisible." This duty, it says, has been abundantly accomplished. During almost two centuries the royal Spanish house has tried, "and being desirous of the glory of our God and Lord, we have happily succeeded in bringing to the body of the holy Roman Catholic faith the innumerable peoples and nations who inhabit the Western Indies."

The descendants of the Catholic Monarchs reiterate their missionary and salvific objective: "So that all may universally enjoy the admirable benefit of redemption, through the blood of Christ our Lord, we pray and charge the natives of our Indies . . . since our aim in preparing and sending our preachers is to procure their conversion and salvation . . . firmly to believe and simply to confess . . . everything that the holy mother, the Roman Catholic Church, holds, teaches, and preaches." But of course, the threats in case the natives would not obey those "commands" or should fall into rebelliousness, apostasy, or heresy against the Catholic church could not be absent. "If they were to persist stubbornly in their error and become obdurate in not accepting what the holy mother church holds and believes, they shall be punished with the penalties imposed by law" (*Recopilación*, 1.1.1.1:1).

During the first century of its colonization of the Americas, the Spanish state created and subsidized six ecclesiastical provinces, thirty-two dioceses, sixty thousand churches, and four hundred monasteries (Höffner 1957, 423). I say that "the Spanish state created" them because it was the state, thanks to the rights of the *Patronato Real*, that was charged with the institutional promotion of the church in the Americas. This leading role was accepted and made official by Pope Julius II in his bull *Universalis ecclesiae*, of 1508 (in Hernáez 1879, 1:24–25).[3] Already Alexander VI in another of his bulls in favor of the Spanish empire in the New World, *Eximiae devotionis* of November 16, 1501, had granted power to the Catholic Monarchs over tithes collected on American soil (in Hernáez 1879, 1:20–21).[4]

The supremacy of royal authority over the church in the Americas was expressed in open caesaro-papalism in the *Capitulaciones de Burgos*, May 8, 1512, in which the three newly appointed bishops for the recently discovered lands—Fray García Padilla, prelate of Santo Domingo; Don

Pedro Suárez de Deza, hierarch for Concepción, also in the island of Española; and Alonso Manso, with the same functions on the island of San Juan Bautista—recognized the Spanish Crown as having those temporal and spiritual faculties in almost every way over their ecclesiastical jurisdictions (in Hernáez 1879, 1:21–24). As it expanded in the sixteenth century, the *Patronato Real* involved the concession, on the part of Rome, of the right to found churches, the geographic demarcation of dioceses, the presentation of miters and ecclesiastical benefits, the collection of tithes, and the selection and sending of missionaries.

That faculty for ecclesiastical patronage was pursued vigorously by the Spanish monarchy, always making clear its authority over all matters in the New World—spiritual as well as temporal—in such a way that one could speak of a *royal vicariate for the Indies*.[5] Those accustomed to the constitutional principle of the separation of church and state, a fundamental axiom of modern social pluralism, would be surprised by the decision-making functions the Castilian Crown assumed in strictly religious and ecclesiastical matters in the Americas. Ecclesiastical disputes of every kind were sent to the Crown to be clarified, not to Rome. It is not strange, for example, that in the dispute between the ordinary clerics and the mendicant friars (Dominicans, Augustinians, and Franciscans), a monk, on expressing his point of view to the monarch, called Felipe II "the lieutenant on earth of the Prince of heaven" and trusted the son of Carlos V to find a solution "whose remedy depends . . . on the royal protection, zeal, and patronage of Your Majesty" (Cuevas 1975, 398, 403).[6]

In summary, in spite of the many changes in the political strategies of the Spanish Crown, the conversion of the natives to Catholicism was continually made explicit as their transcendental objective. According to Paulino Castañeda Delgado: "From the first moment of the conquest, the interest of the Crown for the evangelization of the Indians was manifest and efficacious. That was a constant that was never retracted" (Castañeda Delgado 1974, 178).

This assertion, however, is seriously deficient in not distinguishing between making an objective "manifest" and making it "efficacious." The extinction of the Antillean natives and the death of millions of other natives from other parts of the Americas place in doubt the "efficacy" of that "manifest" evangelization. The contradiction between the theoretical objective of evangelization and the historical reality of the oppression of the Indian communities would give rise to the explosive debate over the legitimacy of Spain's action and presence in the New World.

Conquest and Christianization

Even the ambitious Cortés, in his reports and chronicles, insists on Christianization as the principal purpose of the conquest of Mexico ("to warn them and attract them so that they would come to the knowledge of our holy Catholic faith" [Cortés 1985, 11]). In his military ordinances at Tlaxcala, proclaimed before initiating the siege of the Aztec capital, he declares that the principal motive for the war is the spiritual and religious benefit of the natives:

> Inasmuch as . . . the natives of these parts have a culture and venera-
> tion of their idols, which is a great disservice to God our Lord, and the
> devil blinds and deceives them so they venerate him highly, by separating
> them from so much error and idolatry, and bringing them to the knowl-
> edge of our Holy Catholic faith, our Lord will be very well served. Now
> let us go . . . to separate and uproot the natives of these parts from those
> idolatries, and bring them to, or at least have a desire for, their salvation
> so that they will come to the knowledge of God and of his Holy Catholic
> faith, because if war is carried out with any other intention it would be
> improper, and in logic constitute an obstacle requiring restitution. . . .
> And therefore, in the name of his Catholic Majesty, my principal motive
> in undertaking this war and any other one I should undertake, is to bring
> the natives to the knowledge of our Holy Catholic faith. (Pacheco et al.
> 1864–1884, 26:21–22)[7]

After his victory over the Aztec empire, in establishing the normative policies of the rebaptized Nueva España, Hernán Cortés reiterates the same evangelizing objective. "As Catholics and Christians, our principal inten-tion must be directed toward the service and honor of God, our Lord, and the reason the Holy Father granted the Emperor, my Lord, dominion over these peoples . . . is that these peoples be converted to our Holy Catholic faith."[8] It is not a mere coincidence that Hernán Cortés had a cross in his banner accompanied by the following Latin inscription, *Amici, sequamur crucem; si nos fidem habuerimus, in hoc signo vincemus* (Friends, let us follow the cross, and if we have faith, in this sign we shall win the victory).[9]

His critic, Bartolomé de las Casas, also legitimates domination by the Spanish Crown, keeping in mind "the principal end . . . the salvation of those Indians that will be made possible through Christian doctrine" (Las Casas 1972, 86). In spite of his continuous and severe criticism of the behavior of his compatriots, Las Casas would maintain unchanged his belief in the legitimacy of the papal donation to the Catholic Monarchs of the discovered lands, so that they could facilitate the preaching of Christianity. In a treatise written almost four decades after the one just cited above he asserts: "The monarchs of Spain, to the benefit of the faith, received from the Apostolic See the charge and the responsibility to proclaim and spread, throughout that vast world of the Indies, the Catholic faith and Christian religion, which has to be done for the conversion of these people to Christ."[10]

The colonization of the Americas takes place at the end of the reconquest of Spain, a long period of holy war against Islam and of the expulsion of Iberian Jews. This link was recognized by the protagonists in the "discovery." In his first entry in the log of the first journey, Christopher Columbus links the phrases "in this year of 1492," "Your Highnesses concluded the war with the Moors," and "after having banished all the Jews from all your kingdoms and realms" with the fact of the beginning of his journey to convert the Great Khan (Varela 1986, 43–44; Las Casas 1986, 1.1.12:65).[11] On another occasion, he sketches the idea of a worldwide Christian empire, free from infidels and heretics, as the great contribution of the Catholic Monarchs to the church and to history.

> By knowing the language of the Indians, devout and religious persons could see to it that all [the Indians] would become Christians, and I hope in our Lord that Your Highnesses would be determined to act in this matter with great diligence, so as to turn to the church such great peoples and convert them, just as you have destroyed those who did not want to confess Father, Son, and Holy Ghost [Moors and Jews], and at the end of your days (for we are all mortal), you shall depart your kingdoms in a very peaceful state and clean of heresy and wickedness . . . to increase the holy Christian religion." (Las Casas 1986, 1.1.46:232)

The Admiral insists that it is therefore necessary to supervise carefully the orthodoxy of those going to the newfound lands. "Your Highnesses should not permit any foreigners to come here, except Catholic Christians, for that is the beginning and the end of the enterprise that it be for the increase and glory of the Christian religion, and that no one who is not a good Christian be allowed even to come to these parts" (Varela 1986, 111).

It is a time when Hispanicity and Catholic orthodoxy seem synonymous, in which one can observe a profound "identification between confession and nationality, country and religion," according to which: "The central dominating force of the will of Spain was a transcendental idea, an ideal, a religious conception of life, incarnated in the Catholic church. . . . Fernando and Isabel conceived the idea of making Spain into a homogeneous nation unified by faith" (Ríos 1957, 37, 144).

That "identification between confession and nationality, country and religion" is expressed in various ways in the missionary-political words and actions of Castilians in the Americas. There was probably a widespread consensus with the Franciscan evangelizer in Nueva España, Fray Francisco de Vitoria (not to be confused with the Dominican theologian of the same name), when he writes to Carlos V: "The patrimony of our teacher and redeemer Jesus Christ and that of the Royal Crown of Spain are so united in these parts . . ." (in Gómez Canedo 1977, 224).

The Spanish domination of the New World takes place also at the beginning of the schism of Western Christianity. Its character is profoundly marked by a Hispanic Catholic Christianity furiously antagonistic to "infidels," "apostates," and "heretics" and restrictive in regard to alternative possibilities for interpreting the religious experience.[12] Domingo Bañez, renowned Castilian theologian of Spain's Golden Age, echoes that symbiosis between state and church in defending the execution of the heretics. "The king punishes heretics as enemies, as extremely wicked rebels, who endanger the peace of the kingdom, which cannot be maintained without the unity of the faith. That is why they are burnt in Spain" (in Höffner 1957, 116).

Fernando de los Ríos (1957, 42) makes an accurate diagnosis of the unity between church and religion in the Spain of the era in question, and its consequent intolerance: "In a state conceived as an instrument for a religious goal and with a precise dogmatic content, in a state that . . . does not allow outside itself anything that represents disagreement from dogma, which is its reason for being, in such a state there is no place for minorities, heterodoxy, or discrepant positions because it is a state-church. Such is the Spanish state of the sixteenth century."[13]

That unity between church and state, so characteristic of Spanish history, was forged for centuries. It is so characteristic that the "first partida" of Alfonso X is fully dedicated to religious legislation: "Of the ecclesial state and Christian religion, that makes man to know God through belief" (Alfonso 1807, vol. 1.1.1:1). The official confessional character of the Castilian state was sustained and developed by the centuries-old fight against Moorish Islam.

This means that one must be very cautious, in the context of the conquest of the Americas, when speaking of "Spanish racism," such as prevailed later in the Anglo-Saxon empires. When a Spaniard from the fifteenth or sixteenth century bragged of having "uncontaminated blood" or about "the purity" of his blood, he was not referring merely to racial characteristics, but to having a totally Christian ancestry, without Jewish or Moorish/Islamic mixtures. The certificates of "blood purity" were not analogous to the Anglo-Saxon or Nordic ideal of racial uniformity. That was not possible in the Spain of that time. It implied, rather, an image of indissoluble unity between nation and Catholic orthodoxy. For that reason descendants of Jews and Moors, up to the fourth generation, were excluded from religious orders. That was also the reason for the ferocity with which the Spanish Inquisition persecuted dissidents in doctrinal matters.[14]

What is evident in the texts from the sixteenth century is a deeply rooted sense of national religious superiority. Spain conceived itself as the providential guardian of Catholic devotion. That feeling which is initially directed against Moors and Saracens overflows later in the Counter-Reformation and the expansion of Catholicism in the emerging empire overseas. Symptomatic expressions of this feeling are found in Juan Ginés de Sepúlveda (1951, 33–34) when he praises "the prudence and ingenuity of the Spaniards . . . [their] fortitude, humanity and justice. . . . Regarding the Christian religion, I have seen many clear proofs of how deeply rooted it is in the heart of Spaniards."[15] His work, *Demócrates segundo o de las justas causas de la guerra contra los indios* (The Second Democrates or of the just causes for war against the Indians), is a very good example of the messianic and providential character of the imperial conceptions. The extraordinary talents of the Spaniards – "prudence, ingenuity, magnanimity, temperance, humanity and religion" (ibid., 113) – are signs that make evident the providential operation of divine grace. Those qualities make the Spanish nation the only one deserving of a great transoceanic empire. The natives also can share in the same providential benefits, in the way in which servants share in the happiness and grandeur of their masters, if they obey Castilian sovereignty. If they rebel, they are criminals guilty of subversion against the Spanish Crown and divine will.

A century later, when referring to the providential conquest of the New World by the Spaniards, Solórzano y Pereyra (1930, 1.1.11:113) would credit it to "being firmer, purer, and cleaner in the Catholic faith, and obedient to the Holy Roman Catholic Church, and being free from heresy, which has marred so many other nations . . . so that such a spiritual and sacred conquest could not be entrusted surely or prudently to them."

What were the consequences for those – the Erasmians, reformed heterodox, atheists – who proposed alternative visions of the relation between humanity and divinity? "An inquisitional attitude in respect to consciences, and terrorizing of dissenting persons" (Ríos 1957, 46).[16] The spirit of the crusade endures, and the Spanish nation is identified with the Christian empire's ideal. The Catholic passion nurtured by centuries of struggle against the Moors does not stop in 1492 with the taking of Granada and the vanishing of the Jews.[17] It rushes on, a warlike and missionary, dogmatic and persecuting heterodoxy in the New World. As the Jesuit historian Pedro de Leturia (1959, 1:10) asserts, "the crusade of Granada continues in the Indies." Or, as it has been affirmed many times, under the patronage of "the Apostle James . . . from killer of Moors to killer of Indians" (Flores Galindo 1987, 40).[18]

It is instructive to point out that las Casas, the great critic of Spanish behavior in the colonization of the New World, asked for the Inquisition to be transferred there.

> I beg you . . . that you order the sending here of the Holy Inquisition, for which I think there is great need in these isles and Indies, for where the faith is to be newly planted as in these lands, there may be someone sowing some very bad heretical weed, since two heretics have already been seized and burned, and there is a risk that more than fourteen still remain; and because those Indians, who are simple and believe easily, could be in a situation wherein some evil and diabolical person might trick them into his damaging doctrine and heretic stance. (Las Casas 1972, 76.)

This request, dating to 1516, favorably impressed Cardinal Francisco Jiménez de Cisneros, then general inquisitor and regent of the Spanish government, who approved it on July 21, 1517, but his death a few months later would delay the transferal of the Holy Office to the New World (Pérez Villanueva and Escandell 1984, 662–665). Although the preoccupation of Las Casas and Cisneros, at that time, was the Judaizing and Islamizing tendencies of the so-called "new Christians" (Jewish and Moorish converts), soon the Inquisition turned into an army of combat against all "other signs of Lutheranism" (Las Casas 1965, 1:147).[19]

Fernando Mires (1987, 218) allows his enthusiasm for Las Casas to cloud his historical judgment when he asserts that the great defender of the natives was also "a precursor of the idea of the freedom of religion," a remarkable title for a clergyman from the fanatic Spanish church of the Counter-Reformation.[20] What happened was that Las Casas valued the religiosity of the natives as a type of *praeparatio evangelica*, a preparation for devotion to a supreme being. That is very different from being a promoter of the modern notion of "freedom of religion," which begins with the core concept of a secular state, with its contingent privatization of religion and its relegation to the realm of subjective intimacy.

Las Casas always took care to highlight his Catholic theological and doctrinal orthodoxy. That care is responsible for his never having had truly serious problems with the Inquisition. Others of his noted compatriots — Ignacio de Loyola, Fray Luis de León, Teresa de Jesús, and Juan de la

Cruz—were not so lucky, and at different times suffered from the dreaded rigors of the Spanish Holy Office.[21]

In general, all the principal Hispanic actors in the theological and juridical debates about human liberty in relation to the conquest of the Americas accept without question the Catholic tradition of state and ecclesiastical use of force against the so-called heresies. That tradition started modestly with the declaring of someone to be anathema (cursed)(cf. 1 Cor. 16:22; Gal. 1:8–9) who did not accept the doctrines supported by the majority of the bishops gathered in an ecclesiastical council. After the positive theological exposition of the doctrinal question, it concluded with the condemnation of the heretics. For example: The doctrinal formula approved by the Council of Nicaea (A.D. 325) concludes in the following severe fashion: "To those who affirm that: there was a time in which [the Son] did not exist, and that before he was engendered he did not exist, and that he was made from nothing, or to those who say that he is from another hypostasis or from another substance, or that the Son of God is changeable or mutable, the Catholic church declares these people anathema" (Denzinger 1963, 24).

During the fourth century, in the process of converting Christianity into the official religion of the Roman Empire, the first step was taken. The state initiated the practice, urged by the church, of juridically punishing the so-called heretics: expropriation of goods, imprisonment, and banishment. Its classic defense was provided by the extensive epistle of Saint Augustine (1958, 8:615) of A.D. 408 to Vincent "a rogatist," in which he defends the laws approved by the empire against the Donatists, affirming that the "terror produced by these laws" has been beneficial, "and with their promulgation, the kings serve God through the fear they induce."

In Augustine, state discipline against the heretics seems to affect the liberty and the belongings of the heretics, not necessarily their lives. It did not take long, however, to reach the final stage: *capital punishment as the penalty for heresy.* The classical basis for this repressive measure is found in the *Summa theologica.* Saint Thomas asserts that the faith is voluntary. No adult can be obliged to convert and be baptized. But after having done so, he can be obliged to maintain Catholic doctrine. "Acceptance of the faith is a matter of the will. Whereas keeping the faith, when one has received it, is a matter of obligation. Wherefore, heretics should be compelled to keep the faith" (2-2.10:8). What happens if some "heretic" refuses to subordinate his conscience to the doctrinal dictates of the church? The consequences are two: ecclesiastical excommunication . . . and state execution. "If . . . he remains contumacious, the church no longer waits for his conversion, but looks to the salvation of others by excommunicating and separating him from the church; and, furthermore, delivers him to the secular tribunal to be exterminated thereby from the world by death" (2-2.11:3).

That was the principle that prevailed in Spain and—it should not be forgotten—in all of Europe, during the sixteenth and seventeenth centuries, including non-Catholic areas (it was Calvinist Geneva that executed Miguel Serveto for heresy). Bartolomé de las Casas also upholds it. As a result, when he insists on the strictly voluntary character of the acceptance of Catholic church doctrines and customs by the unbelieving natives, he cannot resist the temptation to point to the Thomistic distinction between infidel and heretic. "It is great blindness . . . to require that the infidels, . . . quite a different case from the heretics, who having once voluntarily accepted the Catholic faith accept it with all its requirements, claims, and threats, . . . be placed in the same category so that they may lose their farms, their bodies, and their souls" (Las Casas 1986, 2.1.173:160).

It was impossible for the Castilian state to conceive of the conquest and colonization of the Americas in terms other than missionary evangelization. It could not articulate the legitimacy of the imperial empire from an exclusively political and economic perspective. The logic itself of the Spanish state carries inevitably the confusion between conquest and Christianization. What for other nations who exercise hegemony had been possible—namely, to claim control of the instruments of power while allowing their subjects to find a spiritual refuge for their troubled subjectivity by living out their native religiosity—was by the very nature of its confessional self-definition, a closed road for Spain. Its messianic conscience was inevitably "of an essentially combative nature" (Höffner 1957, 173).

The attitude of the Franciscan historian Gerónimo de Mendieta is typical when in his *Historia eclesiástica indiana* (1596) he praises the Spanish Crown, first that of the Catholic Monarchs and then of their successors, for being the Christian European principality that had confronted "Judaic perfidy," "Muslim falseness," "idolatrous blindness," and the "household malice of heretics." Because of that eagerness and evangelic zeal, God, "who glorifies and exalts those who seek his divine honor and glory," has rewarded the Spanish monarchy with "the conquest and conversion of numberless idolatrous people, and from such remote and unknown regions" ([1596] 1980, 1.2:17–18).

Solórzano ([1648] 1930, 4.24.3:359) identifies the principle governing the legislation that indissolubly links the state and Catholicism and excludes tolerance for religious and theological diversity. "Heresy . . . is such that if it is not stopped and uprooted altogether when it is first germinating, it would not merely be harmful to religion, but could totally pervert and subvert the political state. Thus in no republic that is Catholic and well governed should diversity of religions be allowed."

Providentialism and Messianism

This principle of religious uniformity brought with it the notion of the formation of a strong messianic conscience, characterized by Enrique Dussel (1972, 54) as "temporal Messianism" — by which the process of discovery-conquest-conversion acquires the providentialist attributes of divine action. The Spanish historian Beatriz Pastor (1984, 42–46) has analyzed the messianism and belief in divine providence of Christopher Columbus, and his keen consciousness of being chosen by God to find the fabulous lands he pursued. This providentialist conscience appears in the *Diary* of the Admiral and in a good portion of his correspondence. "It was our Lord who clearly opened my understanding regarding the need to travel from here to the Indies, and he opened my will so that I would carry it out. And with the fire of this experience I approached Your Highnesses. . . . Who shall doubt that this light was from the Holy Spirit . . . ? . . . Our Lord wished to perform a very evident miracle in this matter of the voyage to the Indies" (Varela 1982, 253).

This messianic consciousness is particularly sharp at the time of doubt and despair, from which no one who considers himself chosen by the divinity can escape. Columbus goes through many such dark moments, for example in the midst of the terrible storm at the end of the first journey when he fears that all his efforts are for naught, due perhaps "to his little faith and faltering confidence in divine providence." At another time of doubt and despair, he alleged having received a divine revelation, a voice that tells him: "Oh foolish one and slow to believe and serve your God, God of all! Could he have done any more for Moses or for David his servant? From your birth, he always took great care of you. . . . The Indies, such rich parts of the world, he gives to you" (Varela 1986, 188, 287).[22]

This providentialism and messianism are intensified in Hernán Cortés. Unlike Columbus, Mexico's conqueror is convinced of the military invincibility of the divinely chosen. Statements such as this one are common in his accounts: "As we carried the banner of the cross, and were fighting for the faith . . . , God gave us so great a victory that we killed many of them without our people suffering any harm" (Cortés 1985, 38). At a moment of grave danger, he encourages his frightened troops and reminds them that the battle is a holy war led by God.

> He inspired them by telling them they should see that . . . as Christians we were obliged to fight against the enemies of our faith, and that we would as a result earn glory in the next life, and in this one such great honor and fame as no other generation has merited until now. And that they should observe that we have God on our side, and that nothing is impossible to him, and they should be convinced of it through the victories we had had in which so many enemies have died, but not one of us. (ibid., 39–40)

The providentialist formulas he continually uses – "it pleased God," "it seemed that God was fighting for us," "how God our Lord gave us victory each day," "after having attended mass" – come out of the Iberian Reconquest and the crusades. They are graphic representations of the hermeneutical perspective of Christians-against-infidels that is artificially superimposed on the war against the Indians. They are not mere rhetorical expressions without ideological content. If they were, Cortés would not have begun each day with mass. They reveal profound convictions forged during long centuries of anti-Islamic contests. When Cortés refers to the temples of the American natives he calls them "mosques," echoing the recently ended war of reconquest against the Muslims, and the struggle against the Ottoman Empire.[23] The battle against the Mexican natives is converted into an ideological holy war, with its double dimension of battle for the faith and contest led by God.

Bernal Díaz del Castillo (1986, 527–528), the first historian of the Spanish confrontations in Mexico, in his vivid description of the complex personality of the conqueror of the Aztec empire, asserts: "I prayed for some hours in the morning and attended mass with devotion. I was very devoted to the Virgin Mary, Our Lady." On one occasion when Cortés was unsure as to which action to take, he decided to consult the divine will: "I had arranged for mass, processions, and other sacrifices, begging God to show me the way" (Cortés 1985, 268). With that fervor coexisted intense desire for personal glory, unlimited ambition, and an insatiable lust.

Because of this combative crusading spirit, the pope was petitioned from time to time to issue a bull granting plenary indulgences for those who might perish in the campaigns. The tenth favor granted Diego Veláz-quez (who, before it even dawned on Cortés to do so, dreamed of being the first one to acquire possession of the riches of the Mexican territory) read: "That the Crown would beg the pope to issue a bull so that the Spaniards killed in that battle would be absolved of guilt and punishment" (in Las Casas 1986, 3.3.124:258). It was a procedure that had been designed for the crusades and was applied, in the same confrontational spirit, against the infidels in the conquest of the Americas. On his own initiative and following the established procedure, Pope Clement VII granted Cortés and his troops bulls of indulgence, after accepting gifts, part of the booty gained in the victory against the Aztec empire, which the conquistador remitted to him (Díaz del Castillo 1986, 527–528). The bull issued April 16, 1529, affirms: "Not sparing yourself hard work of any kind for many years, exposing your life to every danger, and finally fighting valiantly, you triumphed and won Western India, presently named Nueva España, for the yoke of Christ and obedience to the Holy Roman Church" (in Zavala 1971, 349).

Beatriz Pastor (1984, 224) observes about this bellicose providentialism:

> Within this providencialist framework, the will expressed in each of the actions of the person . . . is transformed into one of obedience. The person does not choose but is chosen by God for the endeavor, and limits himself to execute, not his own projects, but divine will. Knowledge consistently appears as divine inspiration; an action resulting from that inspiration is implicitly defined as a holy war and the project is transformed into a mission.

This providentialist messianism was sustained by Fray Toribio de Motolinía, one of the twelve Franciscans (known as "the twelve apostles") who arrived in Mexico in 1524 to evangelize the natives. In his opinion, before Cortés arrived in Mexico, "God our Lord was much offended . . . and the devil, our adversary, was greatly served through idolatry and the cruellest homicides ever seen." The work of Cortés consisted of:

> Impeding and eradicating these and other abominations and sins and offenses against God and neighbor, and planting our Holy Catholic Faith, and raising up everywhere the cross of Christ and the confession of his holy name. . . . Through this captain, God opened the door for us to preach the Holy Gospel, and for the Indians to reverence the holy sacraments and obey the ministers of the church. (in Gómez Canedo 1977, 205–206, 221)[24]

Note that an important aspect of the spiritual or religious dimension of the politico-military conquest of Cortés was his intention to plant a "new church" in the New World. Shortly after defeating the Aztecs, he petitioned the Crown to send missionaries—friars with conviction and education, and of exemplary life—for the conversion of the natives. Two things stand out. First, his emphasis on the friars being from the mendicant orders, Franciscans and Dominicans. They would dedicate themselves exclusively to

the spiritual well-being of the Spaniards and natives. The rejection of the
secular clergy is abrupt and reveals his opinion of the secularization of
the Renaissance church. "Having bishops and other prelates they would
still follow the custom which they have acquired, due to our sins, of dis-
posing of the goods of the Church by wasting them on luxuries and on
other vices or by leaving the right of succession to them to their children
or relatives" (Cortés 1985, 203). Second, that thanks to those missionaries
a "new Church" could be established, superior in religious zeal and conviction to European Christianity, "wherein, more than in all the churches
in the world, God our Lord would be honored and served" (ibid., 280).[25]

This providentialist interpretation of the conquest is not left unquestioned. Bartolomé de las Casas inverts the hermeneutical perspective and
interprets what had been done as inspired by satanic avarice, and he censures at the same time the religious ideology of the conquest.

> And these sad, blind people, allowed by God to come to a reprobate
> understanding and not seeing the very just cause nor the many rights
> in total justice that the Indians have by natural, divine, and human law,
> make bits of the Indians if they have the forces and arms to do so. They
> cast them off their lands. They have a totally unjust and iniquitous
> attitude, condemned by laws of every kind, toward them, and this is
> over and above the many insults and forms of tyranny and enormous
> and unforgivable crimes they have committed against them. Again and
> again they go to war against them. They think and say and write that
> the victories they have over the innocent Indians whom they are assault-
> ing are given them by God because their evil wars are just, as if they
> are rejoicing and giving praise and thanks to God for their tyrannies.
> (Las Casas 1989, 101)

Through his active, constant, and tireless campaign for five decades
(1514–1566), the fiery Las Casas made the concept of "conquest" cease to
be synonymous with "valor" and transformed it into a term of doubtful
reputation. Speaking about some old and impoverished colonizers whose
sense of worth rested exclusively on their "illustrious armed deeds," he
was quick to discredit, as he always did, the prestigious word: "There are
many neighbors, old conquistadors, the most infamous of titles, even
though they take it as being a great honor."[26]

This rigorous criticism of the violence of the conquest, however, cannot hide the fact that Las Casas has a missionary and providential sense
similar to that of his rivals. Also, for the great Dominican friar, the discovery
of the Indies by the Spaniards is the result of divine providence, of the
history of human redemption planned and arranged by God. At the beginning of his monumental *Historia de las Indias*, he defines the discovery as

"the time for God's marvelous mercies," the moment in which the church's commandment to evangelize would be fulfilled for the New World. The discovery is, in the ultimate and fundamental sense, the product of the "universal providence" that "in the abyss of its just judgments," determines when "the hidden nations are discovered and learned about," the occasion for isolated peoples, descendants of Adam, to arrive at their "time for divine mercy . . . to hear and receive Christian grace."

Divine providence selected Christopher Columbus for the purpose of initiating the predestined conversion of the natives of the New World.

> The divine and supreme Master chose from among the children of Adam present on the earth at this time that illustrious and great Columbus . . . as his first minister and apostle in these Indies . . . chosen man. . . . Christopher, a name one should know signifies *Christum ferens*, which means carrier or bringer of Christ, . . . brought our Savior Jesus Christ and his blessed name to these very remote lands and kingdoms until then unknown . . . [and] zealous and desirous of the conversion of these peoples, . . . he brought about the sowing and spread of the faith in Jesus Christ all throughout those parts. (Las Casas 1986, 1.1.1–2:23–30)[27]

This providentialist perspective confers an apocalyptic and eschatological character to the Columbus journeys. The question about the end of history, promised in the biblical *Apocalypses* and indefinitely postponed, had been addressed regularly by theologians in reference to the church's universal missionary command: Christ's *parousia* and the culmination of all times would take place after the gospel had been preached to all the nations. Hence the eschatological importance of the discovery, as sign of the imminent approach of the *eschaton*, the end of history.[28] Las Casas assumes that Alexander VI, the Supreme Pontiff, should "give God . . . much praise and glory because he had seen in his days the opening of the road for the beginning of the last preaching of the gospel and the final call . . . which is, according to Christ's parable, the eleventh hour" (Las Casas 1986, 1.1.79:336–337).

The relationship between missionary preaching in the New World and eschatology provides a theological explanation, or better, a demonic one, for the tenacious resistance that the proposals of Columbus would receive: "The army of hell pits greater forces against these undertakings that are most acceptable to God and most profitable for his holy church, in the knowledge that it has little time left as it is written in the *Apocalypse*" (ibid., 1.1.29:160).[29]

History, therefore, finds itself in "the eleventh hour of the world" (Las Casas 1965, 2:673).[30] This apocalyptic context confers genuine universal significance on the discovery of the Americas. The apocalyptic providentialism of Las Casas is accompanied by an emphatic messianism. Certainly, for Las Casas, in the extraordinary cosmic drama of the discovery and the conquest of the Americas, there are two providential and messianic figures: Christopher Columbus, who opened the path for the evangelization of the inhabitants of the Indies, and Bartolomé de las Casas himself, chosen by God to denounce the injustices and cruelties of the Europeans and to save the bodies and souls of the natives.[31]

The "discovery" of the New World is not a mere historical fluke; it is understood by Las Casas as well as by his theoretical rivals, in the context of the universal history of salvation, as one of its most important episodes. It is very well recognized that one Las Casas work, *Del único modo de atraer a todos los pueblos a la verdadera religión*" (On the only way to attract all peoples to the true religion),[32] is nothing other than an extensive theological deliberation on the conditions for the fulfillment of the mission command of Jesus, his last instruction prior to what the New Testament calls his ascension: "I have been given all authority in heaven and on earth. Go, then, to all peoples everywhere and make them my disciples: baptize them in the name of the Father, the Son, and the Holy Spirit" (Matt. 28:18–19). It is much less known that Francisco de Vitoria's theological treatise *De indis* (Urdanoz 1960, 642) begins with the exposition of the same biblical text, the evangelical command to universal preaching and its implications for missionary activity in respect to "those barbarians from the New World, commonly called Indians." Las Casas and Vitoria proceed from a similar premise: the conversion of the New World infidels, by fulfilling Christ's mission command, announces the approaching end of history.

Fray Gerónimo de Mendieta, Spanish Franciscan missionary in Nueva España, shares the Las Casas vision of Columbus's providentialism. He asserts, at the beginning of his opus, *Historia eclesiástica indiana* ([1596] 1980), that: "God chose Columbus as means and instrument to begin to discover and open the road to this New World, where he wished to manifest himself and communicate with so many souls who did not know him."

Contrary to Las Casas, however, he also considers Cortés a providential figure, as was the norm among Franciscan missionaries in Nueva España. For that reason the sentence above continues: "As he also chose Fernando Cortés as instrument and means of the most important conversion in the Indies that has been accomplished."[33] Mendieta carries to the limits his providentialist conception of Cortés, to the point of including details that have meaning only from that perspective. The day Cortés was born, in 1485, two crucial events for understanding the evangelization of Nueva España took place. On the one hand, Martin Luther was also born that year, the devil's instrument to damage the authentic faith. Cortés was without knowing it an anti-Luther, in such a way that what was lost in the Old World could be recovered in the New.

> Without any doubt, God chose . . . as instrument this courageous captain Don Fernando Cortés so that through him he could open the door and open the way for the preachers of his gospel in this New World, where the Catholic church could be restored and recompensed through the conversion of many souls for the loss and great harm that the accursed Luther had caused at the same time in the old Christendom.

On the other hand, as a second sign of the providential nature of Cortés, that same day some 80,400 people were sacrificed during the idolatrous Aztec festival of the consecration of the Main Temple of Tenochtitlián. That "cry of so many souls and so much spilled blood in offense against the Creator" served as the somber background to the event of the birth of one who would introduce the knowledge of the true and only God among native infidels and barbarians. Therefore, Mendieta considers Cortés as a new Moses, but this time a Moses who would introduce the people of God to the Canaanite land of the Indies (ibid., 3.1:173–177; cf. Phelan 1956).

Cortés, epitome of conquest violence, was constantly praised by the Franciscan missionaries in Nueva España. On this point, as on many others, Mendieta closely follows Fray Toribio de Motolinía, for whom Cortés was a divinely chosen one whose deeds "place him in the tapestry of history and put his person as a model on an equal footing with anyone of the captains, kings, and emperors of antiquity" (Benavente 1984, 3.8:152).

Praise of Cortés is also found scattered throughout the work of another Franciscan, Fray Bernardino de Sahagún ([1582] 1985, Prologue, 12:719–721), who compared him to El Cid, and for whom there is no doubt that "our Lord God ruled over this great man and Christian." All the work of the conquest of Mexico was a succession of divine miracles, carried out under the direction of "this noble captain, Don Hernando Cortés"; "in whose presence and through whom God our Lord worked many miracles in the conquest of this land."

Acknowledgment of the messianic providentialism of Cortés was not limited to the Franciscans. The Jesuit José de Acosta concluded his important work, published in 1590, *Historia natural y moral de las Indias*, with an elegy to Cortés. He admits to the dark side of the conqueror, his avarice and ambition, and that his work was not always "sincere and in accord with Christian means as it should have been." But it is the crooked way for God to write straight. The warrior violence of the conquistador reveals the unfathomable divine mystery since "God is wise and marvelous and with his own weapons defeats the adversary . . . and with his sword beheads him." How could you tell that God was moving and protecting Cortés? Here the Jesuit Acosta outnumbers the Franciscan Sahagún in the enumeration of the war miracles that God, through James the Apostle and the Virgin Mary (cf. Valle 1946),[34] accomplished to grant victory to the Iberians and defeat the Mexican natives ("God favored the business of the Spaniards with many miracles"). He criticized "the learned and religious" who "with commendable zeal, but too much of it" had censured the violence of the armed conquest. They forget, he said, that even through war God also accomplishes his redemptive purposes.

> Our Lord has been careful in favoring the Christian faith and religion, defending those who hold it, even though they did not on their own deserve such heavenly gifts and favors. . . . For even though they were mostly greedy and rough . . . the Lord of all, although the faithful were sinners, favored their cause and side for the good of the unbelieving ones who would afterward convert because of that to the same gospel; for the ways of God are high and his plans are marvelous.

It is true, Acosta admits, that as a result of the cruel war many natives perished. "But the sins of those cruel murderers and slaves of Satan begged to be punished by heaven"(Acosta 1985, 7.26–28:370–377).[35]

I disagree, in consequence, with the Jesuit Uruguayan Juan Villegas, who attributes to Las Casas alone the conception of the history of the Indies as inserted in the divine dispensation for the salvation of all humanity. According to Villegas (1976, 21), the foes and critics of Las Casas "lacked *a providentialist vision* of the events." The fact is that their providentialism is triumphalistic and bellicose while that of Las Casas is evangelical and peaceful.

4

The Christian Empire: Reflections on Las Casas and Vitoria

Consider: God died for the world
and for poor sinners, the children of Adam and Eve.
He was crucified for their sins.

The influence of Padre Las Casas and the scruples he gave the emperor and also the theologians were so great because they followed that priest's false information to the point that His Majesty wished to leave those kingdoms to the tyrannical Incas, until Fray Francisco de Vitoria told him not to do so, otherwise Christendom would be lost.

Anónimo de Yucay (1571)

If a good portion of the barbarians has been converted to faith in Christ, willingly or unwillingly—that is, by threats or terrors or in any other unjust manner so long as they become true Christians—whether they ask for one or not, the pope with reasonable cause could give them a Christian prince and remove the other infidel lords.

Francisco de Vitoria

The Christian Empire
and Indian Self-determination

I do not think the interpretation of Las Casas as anti-colonialist presented by the Colombian Juan Friede (1976) is on target.[1] The terminology used by Friede reflects a certain peculiar semantic confusion between "Indigenist" and "anti-colonialist." Las Casas never proposed the withdrawal of the Castilian Crown from the New World. He defended, rather, a vision of tutelage by the Spanish empire, transformed by intense utopian idealism, that would redound in "temporal and spiritual benefits" for the natives of the New World.

His great polemic for half a century was against violent conquest and the *encomiendas* (a system of servitude to which the natives were subjected; trans. note). But in his *"Octavo remedio"* (Eighth remedy), written in 1542 and published in 1552 (1965, 2:643–849), the recommendation he extensively reiterates is for the Crown to assume direct jurisdiction of the natives, to recognize them as "free vassals"; that is to say, the Crown would exercise its sovereignty over them without colonizers and *encomenderos* as intermediaries. In his own words: "Your Majesty is obliged, by right and divine precept, to rescue them from under the power of the Spaniards and not to subject them to the *encomienda* system and even less as vassals, but to incorporate them in perpetuity as proper subjects of the royal Crown of Castilla" (ibid., 681).

His imperial paradigm is paternal and beneficial; it does not deny the freedom of the natives, but rather, is founded on their condition as free beings, individually and collectively, as autonomous peoples. The relationship of these free peoples with the Crown should be similar to that of the free cities of Europe and Spain, which recognize the emperor as their ultimate sovereign, without such an authority canceling their autonomy and powers for self-determination. "All those nations and peoples are free . . . [they owe] Your Majesty service and obedience, not unrestrictedly, but like that owed by the free peoples and cities to their universal king . . . [the relationship] rests on the *free consent* of the subjects" (ibid., 743, 747; emphasis added). Imperial control should have the temporal and spiritual well-being of its native vassals as its goal, not their economic exploitation.

> The lordship and jurisdiction that Your Majesty has over those people, and did not have before, has been given by God and the church mainly for the spiritual and temporal profit of all those peoples, and this is a privilege granted them, not Your Majesty, so they can achieve their salvation. (ibid., 681)

Here there is not essential contradiction between the indigenous lordship and the Castilian empire. There is in Las Casas an intense effort, continually frustrated but refusing to admit defeat, to combine both levels of political authority.

> One is the service and obedience and tribute that they owe their natural lords, and this is very privileged, because it is primary and natural. The other is the obedience and service that they owe Your Majesty as superior and lord of the universe, and this is also secondarily privileged. And it is not only natural, given their assent, but also by divine right, because it is founded on the preaching of the holy faith, and they add up to two and should be seen as one. (ibid., 733)[2]

Thus the "primary and intrinsic" sovereignty combines with the secondary one in a Thomist fashion: the sovereignty of the natives is "intrinsic," coming from natural law; Castilian sovereignty comes from divine grace. Grace does not destroy, but perfects and completes nature. Where can the natural right and the grace from gospel preaching be combined? In the free self-determination of the native peoples and nations. The image is that of a humanitarian and evangelizing empire, mediated by the consent of the vassals. The schema excludes the authority of colonizers and *encomenderos*, which does not correspond to natural right nor to the needs of evangelization.

> The other and third lordship, the one that the Spaniards demand and enforce, is so unbearable and hard that it surpasses all the tyrannies of

the world and is like that of the devils. This is violent and unnatural, tyrannical and against all reason and nature. (ibid.)

From this perspective, the act of taking possession of the indigenous peoples, of expropriating their lands, goods, and persons, violating their autonomy and self-determination, goes against all law and justice. Las Casas resents the use of the expression "for their very own" referring to the Indies, "because it was already owned," as they had their own legitimate lords who cannot be displaced arbitrarily and should be respected by all the Castilian monarchs and by the pope. "Neither the monarchs nor the pope who gave them power to enter there, could dispossess them of their public and particular sovereignty, their civil estates and liberty (Las Casas 1986, 1.1.124:474). His criticisms were accompanied by a demand for restitution. The Crown should facilitate the devolution of all the goods taken unjustly, "namely, their lands and domains, their dignity and honor . . . their own liberty and that of their people" (Las Casas 1942, 542–543). The dispossession of goods and the servitude of work was attained against the free consent of the peoples of the Americas. On this principle he remained unmoved: "No submission, no servitude, no burden can be imposed on the people without the people . . . giving their free consent to such imposition" (Las Casas 1969, 33).

Since some of his adversaries interpreted his very harsh denunciation as an absolute rejection of the Spanish empire over the New World, Las Casas wrote and sent to the Consejo de Indias in 1552 a treatise entitled *"Treinta proposiciones muy jurídicas"* (Thirty Very Juridical Propositions) (in Las Casas 1965, 1:460–499), in which he tried to reconcile Iberian sovereignty over the indigenous nations while respecting the sovereignty and rights of the latter. His explicit purpose was to set out

> the true and very strong foundation on which rests and is balanced the title and supreme and universal sovereignty that the monarchs of Castilla and León have over the realm that we call the Western Indies. It is by means of this they are constituted universal lords and emperors in these lands above many kings. (ibid., 461)

This way of making the content of this treatise explicit manifests his vision of the relation between the Castilian Crown and the native authorities. The dominion of the first does not eradicate the second. On the contrary, it is a matter of being "emperor over many kings" (Las Casas 1965, 2:1129). The authority of the Catholic Monarchs derives from the concessions made to them by Alexander VI, which ensue from the vicariate that gives the successor of Peter in the episcopate of Rome universal spiritual power over all nations.[3] This power is exercised for the well-being of these nations and pertains to their eternal salvation. Under the premise that the society with natural ends should be subordinate to that of supernatural ones, the pope can grant imperial power to the Spanish monarchs over the infidels of the Indies. The monarchs' responsibility is to promote the evangelical conversion of the natives and their spiritual improvement. The Alexandrian bulls, far from being a gift to the Spanish monarchs, "impose upon them an awesome and frightening formal precept" (Las Casas 1986, 1.1.79:339): to procure the common good of the inhabitants of both the discovered and to-be-discovered isles and mainlands.

Las Casas tries, with unequaled fervor, to reconcile the spiritual authority of the Supreme Pontiff, the temporal dominion of the Spanish monarchs, and the preservation of the native lords. To achieve that, various things are necessary. In the first place, it necessitates reinterpreting the Alexandrian bulls as a beneficial, evangelizing, and educational command. Second, it requires a drastic restriction of the greed and avarice of the Europeans. For that, as a third condition, it is required that the ecclesiastical and governmental authorities approve strict and severe legislation for the protection of the natives and punishment for their exploiters.

Last, as a key factor so that the Spanish lordship can be legitimate, there must be present the mediation of the free will of the native peoples. The goodness of the Christian faith and the virtues of Spanish sovereignty should be preached to them in a manner persuasive to their understanding and attractive to their will, without military force. The objective is to constitute a Christian empire, governed first by the converted chiefs and second by the Castilian monarchy, and spiritually linked by their adherence to the Catholic faith.

Proposition XVII

The monarchs of Castilla and León are true princes and universal lords and emperors over many kings, to whom rightfully belong all that great empire, and universal jurisdiction over all the Indies, by the authority, concession, and donation of the Holy Apostolic See, and therefore, by divine authority.

Proposition XIX

All the kings and natural lords, cities, communities, and towns from those Indies are obliged to recognize the monarchs of Castilla as universal and sovereign lords and emperor in the manner expressed, after having received by their own free will our holy faith and baptism. (Las Casas 1965, 1:481–483)

In the last one of the "thirty propositions," Las Casas intends to reconcile the two opposing poles of his concept of the Spanish-native relations.

Without harming "the title and universal lordship that belongs to the monarchs of Castilla over the realm of the Indies," he declared that all the conquests and dividing up of the natives realized thus far "have no value or force of law" (ibid., 499).

In another of the 1552 treatises he faced the legitimacy of the ownership rights and political sovereignty of the native peoples. In *"Algunos principios que deben servir de punto de partida en la controversia destinada a poner de manifiesto y defender la justicia de los indios"* (Some principles that should serve as the starting point in the controversy destined to expose and defend the just cause of the Indians) he insists that both rights come from the natural law and the laws of nations; they do not depend, therefore, on religious faith or the absence of it (ibid., 2:1234–1273). The native peoples, by the mere fact of being gentiles, cannot be dispossessed of their political or territorial sovereignty. Alexander VI's bulls are reinterpreted as a *pact* between the Holy See and Castilian Crown, which carries with it for the latter a promise to promote the spiritual and temporal well-being of the nations in the Americas. If they did the opposite, the Spaniards would become tyrants and, even worse, would be violating a formal commitment that "they had made with God, his church, and the peoples themselves . . . to reign over and govern them by a kind and good regime . . . guaranteeing the preservation of their life, liberty and sovereignty, civil estate, jurisdiction, etc., both of their goods and of their persons" (ibid., 1271–1273).

In his chronicles, Las Casas tries innumerable times to reconcile the main opposing interests. On the one hand, there is the legitimacy of the supreme Castilian sovereignty on the legitimizing basis of the pontifical bull. "We confess that the king of Castilla and León, due to the concession by the Apostolic See, in order to convert those people, is a sovereign prince of that entire realm." As one can see, the hermeneutical emphasis of the Alexandrian bulls is mission and evangelization, not politics and economics. On the other hand, the validity and permanency of the native sovereigns is reiterated. "It does not follow that those peoples' natural kings and lords should be deprived of their estates and sovereignty, for that would be . . . against natural and divine law." That primary natural sovereignty includes the ownership of mineral resources, the object of European greed. "Because as a result of the apostolic concession the kings did not lose their mines, nor any other thing which they justly possessed within their kingdoms and provinces" (Las Casas 1986, 2.3.11:467–468).

Las Casas brought this idea of a benevolent empire to its climax in his *"Duodécima réplica"* (Twelfth response) during his Valladolid debate with Ginés de Sepúlveda, in April of 1551 (Las Casas 1965, 415–459). He stresses a factor that conditions imperial hegemony: *the free consent of the native nations* ("And in this sense I understand and declare and limit the nineteenth proposition of my thirty propositions . . ."). Although he insisted that after their conversion and baptism, which for him are the priority, they should recognize the temporal sovereignty of the Spanish Crown, this should be achieved without compulsion or violence. In not wishing to recognize Spanish sovereignty, the natives would sin ("if they do not receive them they would sin"), but if the Spaniards resort to war to subject the natives, their sin would be greater ("without a very grave mortal sin they cannot be subjected to war"). Peaceful persuasion is the only legitimate way for the evangelization of the natives of the New World and to achieve their acceptance of the dominion of the Iberian Crown. The optimism of Las Casas is extraordinary; he has full confidence in the efficacy of loving and peaceful persuasion.

> Therefore, the Christian and reasonable way to introduce, plant, and perpetuate the princely rule and sovereign lordship over those kingdoms, which our illustrious kings ought and are obliged to have and undertake as a task, is the way that is peaceful, kind, loving, and Christian, winning by love and good and efficient deeds the disposition and goodwill of those people, lords, and subjects. They, without delay or doubt, would open their arms, with dancing and rejoicing to become your subjects and serve you quickly and generously. (ibid., 433–435; Las Casas 1986, 2.1.136:29)

Las Casas highlights again, almost at the end of his life, the decisive significance of native self-determination.

> So that our kings may acquire, legitimately and rightfully, the supreme princedom of the Indies, that is without reproach and in the right circumstances, it is necessary that the consent of the kings and of the peoples take place, and also that they consent to the donation made by the pope to our kings. (Pérez de Tudela 1958, 495)

The free consent of the native nations, which does not abrogate their political autonomy, but confirms it and frames it in the context of the Spanish empire, becomes for Las Casas the cornerstone of the truly just regime for the New World. The empire, therefore, should not take away but add freedoms for the inhabitants of the incorporated territories. "Without diminishing the liberty of the people; because the gospel and the presentation of the faith does not deprive kings of their kingdoms, nor the individuals of their freedoms, lands, and estates, rather it affirms them (Las Casas 1986, 3.3.55:19).[4]

In the same way in his late treatise *Los tesoros del Perú*, he amended his "*Tratado comprobatorio*," in the sense of stressing, to satiety, the primacy of the free consent and the people's acceptance (*liber consensus et acceptatio populi*) for the legitimation of Iberian authority. The free consent, without any sign of coercion and fear, is the "natural foundation" of the second pact, between the native nations and the Castilian Crown (Las Casas [1563] 1958, 265).

> Our kings have in their favor the papal selection and institution and with it, title and right to those kingdoms which do not belong to another Christian, but they need to obtain another more important and crucial right: the consent of those peoples and their kingdoms to the juridical validity of the papal institution and [their acceptance of our kings] as universal lords and supreme princes . . . so that our kings may acquire the right over this thing . . . and if said peoples and inhabitants, with their kings, do not freely consent, etc., our kings . . . do not have any power to exercise their jurisdiction or to act as supreme princes.

Until such act of free native self-determination happens, the Apostolic Letters only grant the right to authority (*ius regna*), not the royal authority over the native peoples (*ius regnis*) (ibid., 281).[5]

It is a utopian and idyllic vision, based on the profound Christian conscience of the dedicated Dominican friar and which is in painful clash with the ruling colonial violence.[6]

Vidal Abril-Castelló (in Ramos 1984, 229–288, passim), a twentieth-century interpreter of Las Casas, goes too far when speaking of the "revolution of the twelfth response [to Sepúlveda]" and seeing an important change in the position of Las Casas, which caused him to distance himself from his prior sacro-imperialistic attitude, opting for the freedom of the natives over the power of the Crown.[7] Las Casas never posed the problem in such a radical, absolute way: namely, the withdrawal of the Spanish State from the lands of the New World. He even defended, in his "*Tratado comprobatorio*" (Jan. 8, 1553), published after the "twelfth response" (Sept. 10, 1552), the validity of the perpetual nature of the papal donation of the Indies to the Castilian Crown. The imperial dominion granted by the Supreme Pontiff is equivalent to a "perpetual monarchy over all those Indies" (Las Casas 1965, 1103–1109).

Also, the ideas expressed in the "twelfth response" are not so original in the writings of Las Casas as Abril-Castelló pretends. In a memorial to Carlos V, in 1543, signed in conjunction with Fray Rodrigo de Andrada but showing every indication of coming from Las Casas's pen, Las Casas establishes a distinction — using scholastic terminology — between the sovereignty of the Castilian Crown in possibility (*in potentia*) and in fact (*in actu*). Sovereignty *in potentia* comes from the Apostolic Letters of 1493. It becomes effective (*in actu*) when it is recognized by the natives. "And after they [the natives] recognize Your Majesty, the sovereignty would be *in actu*, and now is only *in potentia* as far as their knowing about it" (Pérez de Tudela 1957, 5:192). For that to happen a pact has to be in place, an exercise of free association or free submission, not forced by fear or ignorance. Las Casas even goes into the difficult matter of proposing diplomacy through which it could take place. He suggests that a commission of friars and royal officials

> negotiate, assent, and make a contract between Your Majesty and said lords and chiefs and nations, calling all to assent of their own will and in freedom . . . and give their own consent to subject themselves to Your Majesty on the question of temporal reign and government, since they are free nations and free vassals, giving them first the opportunity to come to a good understanding . . . according to law and reason and justice. (ibid., 183)[8]

It was an idea Las Casas held until his death. He stressed it in relation to Peru in *Los tesoros del Perú* and in the *"Tratado de las doce dudas"* (Treatise on the twelve doubts). The cruel and unjust death of the Inka Atahualpa and the conquest of his empire brings with it the imperative of restoring his sovereignty to his heirs. However, the restoration would not imply a return to the year 1530 (before the Spaniards' arrival), but the remaking of the relation with the Castilian Crown by means of a pact that should be authorized by the natives. This obligation is rooted in an ethical-political principle that Las Casas generalizes for all "the Indies." Las Casas proposes

> that a pact and agreement be carried out between Their Highnesses, or their officials in their name, and the kings and nations of the Indies, with the promise by the kings of Castilla to govern them justly and protect their estates, dignity, laws, customs, and freedoms that are not or would not be against our faith. And on the part of the kings and nations of Indians, they should offer freely, without any force or fear, obedience and fidelity to Their Highnesses and some tribute as a sign of their universal sovereignty. (Pérez de Tudela 1958, 110:497–498)

What is posed in the "twelfth response" with perhaps the greatest insistence is the imperative to respect free native self-determination, even if this is contrary to the Castilian domination, an idea reaching its climax in *Los tesoros del Perú*. The free consent of the native nations conditions—here is the razor's edge of the argument—the juridical actualization of the papal decree. The pope also should respect natural law. In Las Casas, however, optimism rules: the native nations will favorably accept the benevolent and paternal Christian-Spanish sovereignty, as long as they are approached in peace and cordiality.

If after they are Christians they do not wish to receive and obey such
supreme lord [the Castilian monarch] (which is unlikely since the Indians,
especially the nations, are very meek, humble, and obedient), it does
not follow that in that case you can declare war against them (as Doctor
Sepúlveda says). (Las Casas 1965, 433)

His attitude toward the rebellion of the Indian chief Enriquillo in
Española shows again the internal tension of the dialectical conception of
Las Casas about the Castilian and Christian empire. On the one hand,
the uprising is absolutely just, not only because of the ill treatment and
abuse to which the natives had been subjected but because of the criminal
violation of their right to sovereignty over their lands and towns. Spanish
sovereignty never passed the crucible of the test: its free acceptance by
the native peoples.

Because the natural kings and lords of these lands never recognized the
king of Castilla as their superior, but rather, from the time they were
discovered until today, in fact and not by law they have been tyran-
nized . . . always with the utmost cruelty. . . . This is the motto of the
jurists and what natural reason dictates and teaches.

This illegitimate usurpation of the intrinsic native sovereignty, to which
was added cruel treatment, makes Enriquillo's war just and right. However,
Las Casas does not bring out the apparently obvious conclusion, the legal
necessity for a Castilian withdrawal. Against all historical evidence he
remains firm in his utopian idea of a Christian benevolent empire, protected by the spiritual legality of the papal decrees.

What has been said does not abrogate the supreme and universal principality of the monarchs of Castilla over all this realm, granted by the
Apostolic See, if they would come into it and use it as they should, for
everything has to be ordered and guided . . . by reason. (Las Casas 1986,
3.3.125:262–263)

When in a letter to Bartolomé Carranza de Miranda (August 1555) Las
Casas asserts that it is necessary to "free the Indians from the power of
the devil and place them in their pristine liberty, and restore their estates
to their kings and lords" (Fabié [1879] 1966, 71:393), he is referring to the
eradication of the *encomienda* system, which should be replaced by a direct
relation between the emperor and the native system of chieftains. That
letter develops his thesis on the relation between the Castilian empire and
the native kingdoms in two ways. In the first place, he posits the relation
as a mutual contract, which, on the one hand, expresses and preserves
the free consent of the vassals as autonomous communities, subjects with

self-determination; on the other hand, Las Casas stresses the contract's benevolent nature for the inhabitants of the Americas.

> I say, Father, that the king of Castilla has to be recognized in the discovered Indies as supreme prince and emperor over many kings, after the natural kings and lords of those kingdoms and their subjects the Indians have been converted to the faith and made Christians[9] and after having subjected to the yoke of Christ their kingdoms by their own will and not by violence or force, and having been preceded by a treaty, agreement, and pact between them and the king of Castilla, with the king of Castilla promising by oath their good and useful superiority, and to keep and preserve their liberty, their lordship, and dignity, and rights, and reasonable prior laws. They (the kings and nations), promising and vowing to the kings of Castilla to recognize that superiority of supreme lordship and princely status, and [to give] obedience to their just laws and commandments. (ibid., 410–411)

In the second place, if "their lordship, and dignity, and rights, and reasonable prior laws are preserved" there is no need for so many Spaniards to be in the Indies. The conquerors and *encomenderos* would definitely be excluded, since their activities would be forbidden. The number of royal representatives would be reduced, since "the Indians do not have need for a Spanish police." Their principal function would be not to govern the natives but to protect them from the Castilians who try to violate the laws and abuse them.

Las Casas presents, therefore, a dialectic between the presence and absence of the Spaniards in the Indies. His emphasis is on the need of "not being" there since the "harmful root of tyranny and captivity that is destroying them . . . is the continuous conversation of the Christians" (Pérez de Tudela 1957, 5:186). "Being" present there seems to be reduced to a minimum number of royal representatives "to maintain and preserve the superiority and sovereign lordship of the kings of Castilla" and missionaries, religious men of known and verified moral integrity and theological competence.[10]

From his theoretical foundation Las Casas draws a corollary of extreme importance: natural and mineral resources in the Indies belong to the natives and cannot be the object of private exploitation without their authorization and consent. If they have been the object of expropriation or royal grants they should be returned, especially lands with "salt mines, metallic mounds, ports, and other similar things" (Pérez de Tudela 1957, 5:184).[11]

The vision he develops is of a new type of empire, very different from the traditional ones, the legendary biblical empire of Nimrod, Alexander's

Macedonian empire, and the Roman Empire of the Caesars, as he affirms in the *"Tratado comprobatorio."* It would be a Christian empire, directed to the temporal well-being—above all the spiritual—of the vassals, that in no way should "rest on only weapons and power" (Las Casas 1965, 921).

In this context one must clarify the relation of his criticism to the mid-thirteenth-century doctrine of Enrique de Segusa, cardinal of Ostia, commonly called "the Ostiense." What Las Casas rejects in the Ostiense's theory is the idea, which he calls a "blind and detestable and sacrilegious error . . . a formal heresy," namely, that after Christ's resurrection infidel kings and lords, because of their unbelieving character, lose all their political sovereignty (ibid., 1087). The pontifical theocracy of the Ostiense denies the validity of political sovereignty for authorities of non-Christian nations and in general implies the rejection of true autonomy for the political realm.[12]

This criticism does not bring Las Casas to deny papal authority, which he considers to be supreme on temporal matters related to meriting eternal bliss. Through that authority, the bishop of Rome could constitute the Catholic Monarchs as supreme lords of the Indies. What the pope could definitely not do, without having first incurred some previous harm from the native nations, is to take away the authority of the native princes, nor impose on them, without their willing consent, Castilian supreme jurisdiction. The solution to the dilemma, at least at the juridical level, is to reconcile both levels of authority: the primary and natural authority of the native princes and the evangelizing and ultimate authority of the Castilian monarchs.

The hypothesis, affirmed by diverse and prestigious authors,[13] suggesting that the fiery Dominican friar originated a supposedly severe crisis of conscience in Carlos V about the legitimacy of the conquest and domination of Peru is doubtful. Such speculation seems to originate in the document commonly called *"Anónimo de Yucay,"* written on March 16, 1571 (Salvá [1848] 1964, 13:425–469).[14] According to this anti–Las Casas treatise, the friar would have convinced the emperor to abandon Peru and restore its government to the Incas, had it not been for the intervention of the theologian Francisco de Vitoria, who clarified the emperor's Christian and political responsibility for his "legitimately acquired" territories.

> The influence of Padre Las Casas and the scruples he gave the emperor and also the theologians were so great because they followed that priest's false information to the point that His Majesty wished to leave those kingdoms to the tyrannical Incas until Fray Francisco de Vitoria told him not to do so, otherwise Christendom would be lost. (ibid., 433)[15]

According to the author of this enigmatic document, Las Casas had extraordinary persuasive powers, and his passionate preaching against the alleged injustices of the Spaniards in the Americas "frightened and terrified the emperor, the Council and *encomenderos*, friars and bishops and confessors, and every theologian in Spain." This alleged manipulation by Las Casas of Carlos V's conscience was seen as diabolical in origin, "a very subtle work of the devil to persuade the world so suddenly of such deceit" (ibid., 431, 426).[16]

A similar opinion about the alleged "doubt of Carlos V" about Peru is included the following year (March 4, 1572) by Pedro Sarmiento de Gamboa (1942, 29) in his prologue to the *Historia de los incas*. The "devil," seeing that his worship was declining and was devalued by the advances of the Christian faith among the natives, astutely made use of his own enemies, the friars, above all Las Casas, to question the law and justice of Spanish dominion over Peru and the Indies in general.

> Therefore, Emperor Don Carlos, of glorious memory, was at the point of leaving them, which was what the enemy of Christ's faith [i.e., Satan] sought so as to return to his possession the souls that he had kept in blindness for so many years. And all of that happened . . . due to certain information from the bishop of Chiapa, who, moved by passion against some conquistadors of his diocese, . . . said things about dominion over this land . . . that are far different from what have been otherwise seen and clarified.

The reference seems to be to the debate that preceded the reconfiguration of the *Consejo de Indias* and the approval of the *New Laws* in 1542. It makes of Las Casas a defender of Spain's retreat from its territories in the Americas, or at least, from Peru. As has been well pointed out by critics such as Juan Pérez de Tudela, Marcel Bataillon, and Manuel Lucena, this testimony is very late (the French Hispanist calls it a "late myth"); it arises three decades after Carlos V's supposed "crisis of conscience" and is not confirmed by the documents of 1540 to 1546 (the latter the date of Vitoria's death).[17] It is part of a systematic anti-Las Casas campaign aimed primarily at demonstrating that Spain has greater right than the Incas to govern the Quechuas, based on Vitoria's argument of the legitimacy of armed intervention to rescue the innocent ones from a cruel tyranny. The campaign's second objective was to support the primacy over the Indian hierarchies of the colonizers, more and more of whom were *criollos* (children of Spaniards born in the Americas; trans. note). This primacy was questioned by the writings of Las Casas. The myth distorts the posture of Las Casas, but it is based on a correctly understood point. The idea about the obligatory restitution of everything that had been stolen from the natives— political dominion, goods, and individual liberty—as Las Casas applied it to Peru in such works as "*Tratado de las doce dudas*" and *Los tesoros del Perú*, gave a rude blow to the self-interest of the European colonists and *encomenderos*. They took the offensive against Las Casas with the same passion and intensity with which he had assaulted the strength of their socioeconomic interests.

As the Dominican theologian Teófilo Urdanoz (1960, 495) suggests, the objective for Las Casas was to design a "just colonial government," ruled by benevolent norms of "colonial ethics." This regime would include guidelines for political, economic, and religious administration that would reconcile the interests of the Spanish state, the Catholic church, and the indigenous communities. Las Casas, therefore, tries something that in the sixteenth century was like squaring a circle: to reconcile the authority of the Spanish Crown—in his opinion required for the Christianization of the aborigines and their protection from the greedy robbery of the *encomenderos*—and the liberty of the natural inhabitants of the New World. He understood this liberty as having inseparable dual meanings: *free will and political autonomy*. José Antonio Maravall (1974, 377) is undoubtedly right when he says: "The tutelage . . . to which the 'imperial' jurisdiction of the Castilian kings was reduced, would acquire a utopian character."

This free will and political autonomy reach a greater depth in some of the texts in which Las Casas protests the exclusion of the voice of the Indians from the decision-making processes on matters crucial for the destiny of the Indies. In a memorandum he sent to Felipe II in 1556, he warns the king not to accept the offer by the Peruvian *encomenderos* colonists to sell him in perpetuity the allotments of native lands, and he demands that the voice of the Indians be heard, for they are the most affected. "According to natural and divine law they should be called, and given citations, and counseled, and heard, and let them report on what is best for their rights" (Las Casas 1969, 217). Those who have been violently deprived of their voice, in good measure because of their lack of literacy, should be heard and their feelings and opinions taken as decisive.

Marcel Bataillon (1976, 45–136) points to another factor that Las Casas takes into account: the Castilian material and economic interests. According to his sharp, and not at all hagiographic, reading, Las Casas is trying to reconcile "good greed" with the temporal preservation of the natives and their spiritual benefits. This effort to couple missionary spiritual aspirations with economic temporal ones appears in abundant detail in the famous plan by Las Casas to colonize the northern coast of what today is South America (Las Casas 1986, 3.3.132:281–286).[18]

Even after what Bataillon (1954) calls the "second conversion of Las Casas,"[19] in his examination of conscience while cloistered in the Dominican

Friary in Española, Las Casas would not forget this factor. In a letter to the Council of the Indies dated January 20, 1531, Las Casas insists on the good treatment and the preservation of the natives as the only sure path "to inestimable gifts and temporal goods, easily had . . . , which would bring great temporal riches to the King's State." If a colonizing policy beneficial to the natives had been put in place at the outset, "the King would have today more gold and silver and precious stones than Solomon in all his grandeur" (in Fabié [1879] 1966, 70:465, 479, 481). His strategy is to bring the natives out of their servitude under the *encomenderos* and convert them into taxpayers to the Crown, which in turn would have obvious economic interest in aiding their preservation and multiplication. In his *"Treinta proposiciones"* he understands that the Spanish Crown, in exchange for its missionary labors in the Indies, commanded by the pope, can receive from the Supreme Pontiff "remunerative donations from said kingdoms" (Las Casas 1965, 1:473). In *Historia de las Indias* he accuses the conquerors, colonizers, and royal functionaries of a simultaneous double fault: tyrannical homicide against the natives and, with the drastic reduction of taxpaying vassals of the Crown, the elimination of the social base for possible abundant income for the Crown.

> [A]nd they are guilty, before God and the king, of all evil and spiritual and temporal harm and perdition of so many souls and so many treasures that the king would receive if they had the truth . . . of the known law.
>
> With the killing of millions of them [natives] (even if they only paid a single *maravedí* [a third of a silver real; trans. note] as tribute, deprived them [sovereigns] of the greatest and most sure riches that any king or princes in the world have ever owned). (Las Casas 1986, 3.3.118:234–235)

The economic incentive, however, is clearly and firmly subordinated to the spiritual well-being of the natives and the fulfillment of the providential mission God had entrusted to Spain.

Las Casas, a person of undeniable courage and bravery, avoided at all costs falling in Antigone's dilemma—the irrevocable contradiction between the religious principles of conscience and the royal decrees. He tried always to maintain open channels of communication with the Castilian Crown in hope of obtaining beneficial legislation for the natives. If Antigone's dilemma had occurred, what would have been his position? All indicate that he would have followed the principle that he states on a certain occasion: "One should weigh in the balance more the fulfillment of the law of Jesus Christ than the displeasure of the kings" (Las Casas 1986, 1.1.106:420).

Las Casas held that the necessary initiative to establish balance between the Spanish empire and native autonomy should come from the Crown. From this initiative Las Casas expected the juridical project and political action to forge an alliance between the state and the church in defense of the natives against conquerors and *encomenderos*. This explains his constant litany exonerating the monarchs, whose innocence rested on their supposed ignorance of the abuses suffered by their Indian subjects. When Hierónimo de Peñafiel, the Dominican friar, told him about the reaction of Cardinal Tomás de Vio Cayetano, Master General of the Order of Preachers, who, when learning through him of the maltreatment inflicted on the natives, said: *"Et tu dubitas regem tuum esse in inferno?"* (Do you have any doubt that your king is in hell?), Las Casas insisted it would not be the king, but the members of his Royal Council, who would go to hell for tolerating such injustices, hiding them from the monarch, and fraudulently participating in the illicit profits derived from the New World (Las Casas 1986, 2.3.38:563–564).[20]

Even in a late writing, as in his *"Tratado de las doce dudas,"* he asserts, regarding the Indian *encomiendas*, that "they were always against the will of the Castilian monarchs," which he intends to prove true of the Catholic Monarchs to those of the present (1564) (Pérez de Tudela 1958, 110:513–515). Since that categorical affirmation is difficult to sustain, Las Casas admits that the Crown was forced to accept the system of enforced labor imposed on the natives to avoid the worse damage of a rebellion by the Spanish colonizers. It is a notable although illusive effort to establish an alliance between the Crown, and the ethical claims of the Christian conscience and the native peoples of the Americas.

The idea of a Spanish empire that would benefit the Indians was not exclusive to Las Casas. His great theoretical adversary, Ginés de Sepúlveda, also defends it when he affirms that the end of Iberian domination is "to cause some good to all the conquered . . . some usefulness to the winner, but even greater benefit to the defeated barbarians . . . [the] public well-being of those people"; namely, conversion to the true faith, cultural advancement, and civilizing development (Ginés de Sepúlveda 1951, 27, 29).

The enormous difference between Las Casas and Sepúlveda, however, proceeds, first, on the existential experience the former had of the colonialist cruelty, in its bellicose phase and its later phase of servitude;[21] second, on their different understanding of the natural ability of the natives to govern themselves freely and autonomously. While on some occasions the Dominican friar highlights the good regime that prevails in the Indian communities, the learned Aristotelian humanist devalues the natives and considers that they should be subjected, if necessary by force, to a master administration that would instill in them the habits and manners inherent in a civilized and cultured life. The first conceives the Spanish government as an empire that would not deny political freedom to the Indian peoples. For the second, such vision sins from false utopianism.

International Law and Christian Empire

The rootedness of the concept of a Hispanic Christian empire, of an imperial theology that legitimizes the conquest through justifications of a religious nature, is found in Francisco de Vitoria's position. His refusal to recognize the alleged universal authority of the pope that allowed the donation of sovereignty over the inhabitants of the New World has been reiterated to the point of satiety by Vitoria's interpreters. His repudiation of sacro-imperial papalism is complete. "The pope is not the civil nor the temporal lord of the entire orb" (Urdanoz 1960, 678).

The powers of the pope give him jurisdiction only over Christian individuals and nations and refer only to spiritual affairs, in Vitoria's view. His authority over temporal and political matters arises only when these have a clear and necessary link with spiritual and religious matters of faith and morals. Certainly, the Spaniards have the right to preach the faith, and the natives have the duty of not interfering with that exercise. But conversion cannot be forced, nor can its rejection be considered *casus belli* (legitimate cause for war). Even less so can it be affirmed that not heeding the call to obey the church and the pope could be a licit motive for armed conflict.

> Even in the case where the barbarians did not want to acknowledge the pope's dominion, war could not be declared against them nor their possessions taken from them. In the event that the barbarians should not wish to recognize Christ as lord, that would not be a reason for declaring war against them nor for causing them the least discomfort. . . .
>
> Even after the faith has been announced to the barbarians in a practical and sufficient way, and they have not accepted it, it is not licit, for this reason, to make war against them nor to dispossess them of their goods. (ibid., 682, 695)

What happens, however, if a good number of natives convert to Catholicism? Vitoria's answer manifests the depth with which a crusading spirit had penetrated in the Spain of that day, even in moderate and serene spirits such as his:

> If a good portion of the barbarians have been converted to faith in Christ,
> *willingly or unwillingly, that is, by threats or terrors, or by other unjust man-*
> *ner,* as long as they become true Christians, the pope could, *if they ask*
> *for one or not,* with reasonable cause, give them a Christian prince and
> take away the other infidel lords. (ibid., 719; emphasis added)

I have stressed some parts of this fourth "legitimate title" — to assume
sovereignty over the "barbarians of the New World" and declare war against
them — because they are highly indicative of the intimate union between
imperial reason and Christian faith in the Spanish conquest of the
Americas.

To our modern mentality, placed in the context of the birth of the secular
states in which faith has become a matter for the intimate jurisdiction of
individual subjectivity, the process of preaching the faith and becoming
an adherent appear as an exclusively personal and spiritual matter. Vitoria,
on the contrary, remains within the ideological realm of Christendom, of
orbis christianus, even though his modern interpreters have written so much
contradicting this fact. The conversion, therefore, of "a good portion of
the barbarians" (how many is "a good portion"?), independently of the
legitimacy of the means used to obtain it ("willingly or unwillingly, that
is, by threats or terrors, or by other unjust manner"),[22] becomes a serious
political act: "The pope could . . . give them a Christian prince." Generally,
the followers of Vitoria stress the conditional clause, "with reasonable
cause," indicating that pontifical action cannot be arbitrary nor despotic,
but they forget the second, "if they ask for one or not," which cannot be
glossed over to make it compatible with respecting the free consent of the
peoples that the scholastic insists on calling "barbarians."

The Mexican Antonio Gómez Robledo is one of the few Vitorians who
criticize the Salamancan theologian in regard to the "fourth legitimate title."
He finds that Vitoria falls into "inconsistency with himself." It is not, however, a matter of "inconsistency" but rather the uneasy convergence in
Vitoria of the attempt to postulate a universally valid law and at the same
time preserve the predominance of Christianity, something that in another
passage the same Gómez Robledo recognizes. "Within ecumenical society,
in fact, there continues to exist, with its own and specific characteristics,
the *respublica christiana,* to which belong some immanent powers or faculties
that Vitoria does not dare to attribute to the universal community" (Vitoria
1985, lxxiv, xlvii).[23]

There is revealed in Vitoria, as Fernando de los Ríos points out, an
uneasy junction between medieval and modern factors. The first point to
the prevalence of the *orbis christianus* idea; the second to the modern "law
of nations" or international law, before which all states are juridically similar,

irrespective of religious differences. I differ, therefore, with the Spanish Dominican historian Teófilo Urdanoz, for whom Vitoria embodies "new conceptions," "new points of view," and "new theoretical paths" to "new problems." In the same way, it seems to me that the interpretation made by the North American jurist James Brown Scott is excessively modern; according to Scott, the Spanish scholastic, by allegedly overcoming religious differences between states, becomes the founding father of modern international law. On the contrary, it seems to me that for Vitoria, the missionary mandate peculiar to Christian princes and states plays a prominent role in the determination of rights, including sovereignty. Otherwise some of the "legitimate titles" of the Castilian empire over the New World would be incomprehensible (Ríos 1957, 109–130; Urdanoz 1960, 509–510; Scott 1934, 283). Joseph Höffner (1957, 408) is on target when he affirms:

> In Vitoria's conception of the world, the church continued to occupy a very important place. Not only in the sense that Vitoria, naturally, wished and expected the conversion of the whole world, but also, in so far as he in some way extended the juridical realm of the church to the entire world, including that of the gentiles.[24]

Höffner finds in Vitoria, and in the remaining Spanish scholastics of the Golden Age, the junction of two sources: natural law and revealed Christian theology (ibid., 510). This junction, not highlighted by a good many of the exegetes, is what confers on the thought of the theologian from Salamanca his peculiar ambiguity and duality. Contrary to Brown Scott, I think that, in the last instance, it is the ideal of a Hispanic Christianity that prevails.

This is especially evident in Vitoria's discourse *De iure belli*, given a few months after *De indis* and frequently known as *De indis, relectio posterior*, which, on the one hand, presented some universal rules to regulate military conflicts, and on the other hand, distinguished between a war ethic specific to the conflicts between Christian princes and another one for those in which these princes face Turkish infidels and Saracens, "perpetual enemies" of Christianity. Against the second, a harsher behavior is allowed, such as enslaving women and children (Urdanoz 1960, 811–858).[25]

Most Catholic Spanish scholars seldom criticize Vitoria's discussion of Spain's relation to the "barbarians of the New World" (ibid.; Manzano 1948, 79–80; Hernández 1984, 345–381). On occasion, the work of Höffner suffers a similar defect, although it is very insightful in many other respects. He highlights and accents the second part of *De indis*, neglecting the theoretical priority of the third part, which refers to the "legitimate titles" of the Spanish empire. His thesis is equally mistaken that "the leading

thought of Vitoria was *tota christianitas*, not Spanish nationalism," break-
ing the balance between the two that he initially detected in Vitoria (1957,
427). One of Vitoria's central objectives is the theoretical and theological
justification for Spanish hegemony over the New World. This is manifested
in the unresolved contradiction between the principle of liberty in international commerce, which inspires the first legitimate title, and the
exclusivity and monopoly of economic exploitation that acknowledges
Spain, allegedly to allow Spain to be a more efficacious missionary. Richard
Konetzke (1972, 32) does not go far from the truth when he asserts that,
finally, in Vitoria "the national interest voids anew the universal validity
of *ius gentium* [the law of nations]."[26]

I also differ from Juan Manzano's opinion (1948, 62–82), according to
which Vitoria would have set aside the pontifical supremacy expressed
in the bulls of Alexander VI. Manzano interprets them as an authorized
and exclusive missionary command that carries with it the monopoly of
commercial contacts and political domination. Paulino Castañeda (1971)
examines how Francisco de Vitoria and the school of Salamanca, beginning in the fourth decade of the sixteenth century, abandoned the initial
interpretation, by then obsolete, of the Alexandrian bulls as a "donation"
of lands. The pope, no longer the *dominus temporalis totius orbis* (lord of
the whole world on temporal matters), could hardly give away what did
not belong to him. However, Vitoria and his disciples, from a different starting point, arrive at an objective similar to that of the followers of the
medieval theory of a universal papalist theocracy; namely, to justify, in
the first instance, Spain's exclusive dominion over the lands of the New
World (including the commercial monopoly) and—a crucial matter for the
ethical discussion—the validation of the wars against the Indian nations.

You find in Vitoria a *reinterpretation*, not a refusal, of the Alexandrian
bulls. From that perspective, they do not refer to the concession or donation of sovereignty, but to an evangelizing command. This command is
given exclusively. According to this exegesis it is the Spanish Crown that
has the missionary monopoly, the sole concession to *ius predicandi*, the
right to preach in the New World. Vitoria adds that, for the benefit of the
propagation of the faith, this monopoly of the *ius predicandi* carries with
it exclusive rights to commerce and colonization. Although the starting
point is different, the result is the same: thanks to the command of the
Supreme Pontiff, Spain has the exclusive and unique right of being present
and to legitimately assume sovereignty over the "recently discovered"
lands. If some prince from another Christian state dared to intervene,
excommunication would fall on him and, in view of the pope's indirect
power over temporal matters, possibly deposition (Urdanos 1960, 715-720).

If, on the contrary, the native lords do not accept some of the essential clauses of the pontifical decree, then Spain may make war against them.

Therefore, if the pope is considered temporal lord of the whole world, according to the theocratic theory, or sovereign in giving the missionary command, as for Vitoria, the result is identical: Spanish sovereignty is legitimized and the wars against the rebellious natives are declared just. In that sense, the distinction between nationalism and Catholicism in Vitoria made by Castañeda with his affirmation that Catholicism, not nationalism, was the motivation for his considerations regarding "the recently discovered Indians," seems to me superficial. It is certain that for Vitoria Spain was the undisputed vanguard of Christendom. In his thought there is an obvious consonance between the Spanish state's reason for being and its Catholic missionary sense.

In this regard, if it were true that Vitoria opens some type of new "law of nations," that law would be one in agreement with the theoretical needs of European expansionism in the sixteenth century, the decisive historic moment in which European and Christian civilization aspire for world hegemony. It cannot escape our attention, either, that in the last section of his famous lecture Vitoria presents for the first time a plethora of possible justifying arguments for Spanish domination, which would serve as the theoretical arsenal for later European empires in southern lands.[27]

The irreversible character of Castilian domination over the native lands strongly colors Vitoria's analysis. As a result *De indis* concludes: "After the conversion of many barbarians there, it would not be convenient nor licit for the prince to abandon completely the administration of those provinces" (Urdanoz 1960, 726), above all because it would indicate the abandonment to their own devices of the converted natives, something unthinkable for a monarch whose honorary title is that of principal defender of Catholicism. And *De iure belli*, in turn, begins stressing the legitimacy of Spanish dominion as well as the wars against the natives: "The possession and occupation of the provinces of those barbarians . . . can at last be defended above all by the right to war" (ibid., 814). The dichotomy between *tota christianitas* and Spanish domination, referring to the "barbarians of the New World," is artificial.

It should be recognized that, according to Vitoria, in order to justify Castilian domination over the New World, that domination must be "just." The problem is that in his analysis the determination of justice should not have remained, as it in fact does, at the theoretical level, without clarifying the events. The *quaestio iuris* cannot be separated from the *quaestio facti*. The juridical question is based on the supposition, clearly sketched in the first part of the lecture, of the irreversible reality of the Spanish empire.

Contrary to the anti-imperialist interpretation of Vitoria made by Teófilo Urdanoz, I consider more correct the observations made by Luciano Pereña:

> Francisco de Vitoria never . . . questioned the legitimacy of the conquest. It was a proposition that he took for granted. . . . This axiom was his starting point. Vitoria delivers his lectures on the Indies at Salamanca not to attack the emperor nor open a discussion of his right but rather to justify him against the attacks being made by Frances I of France . . . to defend the Spanish monopoly against the protests of the French king.

Pereña then generalizes with respect to the school at Salamanca and the disciples of Vitoria:

> From 1534 to 1573, the teachers at the School . . . unanimously condemned the abuses of the conquerors. . . . The abuses were condemned without reserve from Vitoria to Acosta. But . . . the personal or individual behaviors did not invalidate the fundamental right of the Crown to Spanish domination. They did not even doubt the legitimacy of the Spanish presence in the Indies. . . . They never questioned the conquest by considering it from a global perspective. They supposed that it was legitimate. (Pereña 1984, 299; 340–341)[28]

It is difficult, however, to share the enthusiasm of this eminent Spanish historian, when, in a previous work, for the purpose of exalting "the mission of Spain in America," he makes the scholastic theological school (initiated by Vitoria and continued by Domingo de Soto, Bartolomé Carranza, Melchor Cano, Diego de Covarrubias, and Juan de la Peña) into the theoretical designer of the classic Christian and humanitarian empire, based on "these two concepts—equality and sovereignty of all the nations, and right to intervene . . . to defend and guarantee the rights of the person. . . . Always for the benefit of the barbarians themselves" (Pereña 1956, 310–311). And all in the face of the extraordinary human and social cost that the latter had to pay.

An objection could be raised against this critical interpretation by referring to the letter of Carlos V, dated November 10, 1539, to the prior of the Dominican faculty at Salamanca, forbidding the discussion of the legitimacy of Spanish dominion over the New World and ordering him to gather all dissertation copies treating this theme, a clear reference to Vitoria's theological lectures about the Indians.

> The King: Venerable father, prior of the Monastery of Saint Stephen of the city of Salamanca, I have been informed that some religious teachers from that house have been talking and in their sermons dealing with the rights we have to the Indies . . . and because to treat of similar matters without our knowledge and without first notifying us, besides being

harmful and scandalous, could entail great inconveniences . . . and harm to our royal crown over those kingdoms . . . we have agreed . . . that neither now nor at any other time, without our express permission, should you deal with nor preach, nor argue about this, nor print any writings pertaining to this, otherwise I would feel ill served. (Vitoria 1967, 152–153)[29]

The emperor reacts, however, not to the content of Vitoria's lecture (it is possible he was not even aware of it) but to the fact that there was independent discussion ("without our express permission") of the legitimacy or lack of it of the right of the Castilian empire over the New World. The later consultations by Carlos V himself with Vitoria about core issues and his desire to make him be a part of the Spanish delegation to the Council of Trent show that there was not animosity against specific positions of the scholastic from Salamanca.[30] The monarch's purpose was to centralize and monopolize the entire discussion about the Indies.

This was the same motive that led Carlos V, two years earlier, to protest before Pope Paul III about some papal decrees and edicts concerning indigenous liberty and to force him to an agreement, by means of a papal decree issued June 19, 1538, that he would not make any declaration on the subject without it being first seen and approved by Castilian authorities (Hanke 1937). It was not so much the content of the papal declarations that worried the emperor, but his need to deter the Supreme Pontiff from becoming an autonomous active protagonist in the politics of the Indies. In 1539, the Crown ordered the bishops in the Americas that all communication with the Supreme Pontiff should be channeled through the court, which would pass judgment on its worth. The famous "royal approval" (*Regium exequatur*), imposed by the emperor on the papacy, implied that the last word about the ecclesiastical determinations were in fact in the competence of the state (cf. Shiels 1961, 169–181).

The guide to the royal actions was the control of the entire process related to the Indies and the avoidance of any autonomous space for debate and questioning. It was especially important to avoid letting the ecclesiastical institutions, with their potential symbolic power to challenge, break the close link that subjected them to the Crown and that shaped what Miguel de Unamuno, in irony, called the "Spanish Catholic and Apostolic Church."

Isacio Pérez Fernández (1988) has published an excellent contribution to the comparative study of Las Casas and Vitoria.[31] He avoids the common temptation to equate the ideas of both Dominican thinkers and subtly perceives the double posture of Las Casas vis-à-vis the scholastic theologian. Las Casas, he says, refers to Vitoria's ideas when he considers them useful, and keeps a respectful silence when he understands that Vitoria's abstract investigations are not applicable to the concrete case of the New World.

> Regarding the theme of the juridical titles of the Spanish domination of the Indies . . . Padre Las Casas only coincides with Vitoria in rejecting those that the latter rejects. . . . But Padre Las Casas rejects also all the titles that Vitoria proposes as 'legitimate.' . . . What he does not admit is that those titles *apply to the concrete case of the Indies.* (ibid., 262–263; emphasis added)[32]

The reference is to the brief and cautious critical observation of Las Casas in his debate with Sepúlveda about Vitoria's "legitimate titles":

> Anyone who reads the two parts of the *Prima Relectio* of that scholar [Vitoria] will easily see that, in the first part, he proposes and in a Catholic way refutes the seven headings by which war against the Indians would seem to be just. In the second part, however, he introduces eight titles by which, or by some of which, the Indians would come under the jurisdiction of the Spaniards. . . . He is a little more careless, however, regarding some of those titles, since he wished to moderate what seemed to the emperor's party to have been rather harshly put, although for lovers of the truth, nothing he discussed . . . has not merely been true in the past but is Catholic and certainly very true. He indicates this well enough by speaking conditionally, fearing that he might suppose or make false statements instead of true ones. Now since the circumstance that this learned father supposes is false, he says some things hesitantly . . . (Las Casas, 1974, 340–341)[33]

Part II

*Freedom
and Servitude
in the Conquest
of the Americas*

5

Freedom and Servitude: The Enslavement of the Natives

Conquest: Don Francisco Pizarro puts fire
to Capa Apo (powerful lord) Guamann Chava,
demanding gold: "Give me gold and silver, Indians!"
He burns the major Indian lords in Cuzco.

Their Highnesses can see that I will give them as much gold as they
should need . . . and as many slaves as they should order.

Christopher Columbus

We order and command that from now on not for reason of war or for
any other reason, not even for rebellion, should the Indians be made
slaves.

Leyes Nuevas (1542)

Servitude of Infidels

The conquest as an act of taking possession of the lands discovered
by the Iberian armies provoked the complex dilemma of the relationship
between the inhabitants and the invaders. The difficult historical conjunction of cruel, violent events on the one hand, and the sense of human
dignity inherent in the Christian faith on the other, gave rise to one of the
most extraordinary and intense debates in human history: the dispute concerning the free status (freedom) or servant status (servitude) of the natives
of the Americas.

Pedro Mártir de Anglería (1953, 12:387–388), in 1525, wrote in one of
his letters:

Several opinions regarding the freedom of the Indians have been widely
discussed, and until now nothing has been found to be valid. Natural
law and the pontificate say that all of humanity should be free; imperial
law makes distinctions and its use causes adverse feelings.

On this point we are touching on something extremely important, as
the second *partida* of Alfonso the Wise in the legal code so dear to Castilians
affirms: " . . . freedom . . . is the highest good that a man can have in this
world" (Alfonso 2.2.29: 326). It would be Bartolomé de las Casas, not surprisingly, who would insist for decades on this principle of juridical ethics:
"Nothing is certainly more precious in human affairs, nothing more
esteemed than freedom" (Las Casas 1965, 1:615; 2:1317).

If the problem hardly seems debatable from a moral point of view, it
is because our societies abolished legal slavery a little more than a century
ago. At the end of the fifteenth century this issue caused no scandal to
juridical or religious consciences. The two principal foundations or roots
of Western culture–the Greco-Roman and Judeo-Christian–allowed enforced servitude. Plato in *The Republic* makes explicit his repudiation of
the slavery of Greeks by Greeks, but in *The Laws* he clearly accepts the

same state of subjugation for non-Greeks or barbarians. Aristotle in his *Politics* stresses even more the legitimacy of the enslavement of barbarians by the Greeks (see Schlaifer 1936; Davis 1961, 62–90).

In the same way, the Hebrew Pentateuch tolerates and allows the enslavement of strangers. Leviticus 25:44–46, dealing with freedom legislation during the jubilee year in which Hebrew servants must be freed, establishes the first important exception:

> Your male and female slaves are to come from the nations around you; from them you may buy slaves. You may also buy some of the temporary residents living among you and members of their clans born in your country, and they will become your property. You can will them to your children as inherited property and can make them slaves for life, but you must not rule over your fellow Israelites ruthlessly (NIV).

Paul in some of his epistles seems to tolerate the legality of slavery. He even urges evangelized servants to obey their masters with greater diligence and fidelity (1 Cor. 7:20–24; Eph. 6:5–9; Col. 3:22–25; 1 Tim. 6:1–2; Titus 2:9–10).

In both cultural traditions there were dissident minority voices that proclaimed the kinship of humanity. In Greece and Rome, stoicism, starting with the universality of reason, set down the bases for an implicit cosmopolitanism. Among the Hebrews, from the perspective of the universality of God, the prophetic tradition envisioned the unity of humankind. For centuries, however, those alternate visions were not able to impede the juridical and theoretical legitimacy of slavery.

Slavery was given legitimacy by two arguments that granted it social and religious functions. Medieval thinkers reiterated on innumerable occasions the classical idea that the only alternative for the defeated enemy was *death or servitude*. From that perspective, to enslave a subjugated adversary seems to be a relatively compassionate act. That idea is still operative in the sixteenth century, as can be seen in this judgment by Domingo de Soto ([1556] 1967, 1.1.5.4:44–45; 2.4.2.2:289): "The law of slavery was deduced from the same principle, for it was the only way to free the war enemy from death." Servitude "is not only licit, but also the fruit of mercy."[1]

The second idea comes from Saint Augustine. The bishop of Hippo formulates the principle that although slavery is not part of the Creator's purposes nor of the redemptive objectives, it comes from sin. Slavery is *the punishment for and the remedy of sin*. It will subsist as a social institution so long as there is moral evil. That vision of sinfulness as the transcendent root of servitude still persists in the sixteenth century, as shown by Soto (ibid., 290):

Punishment followed from sin . . . and one type of punishment is legal servitude. From original sin followed, in effect, the need for servitude and the countless wars that reduce men to slavery.

Saint Augustine (*City of God*, 19.15) combines both traditions in a passage that deserves extensive mention because of the great importance it had for canon law and theology during the almost millennium and a half since it was penned.

The origin of the Latin word for slave is supposed to be found in the circumstance that those who by the law of war were liable to be killed were sometimes preserved by their victors, and were hence called servants. And these circumstances could never have arisen save through sin. . . . The prime cause, then, of slavery is sin which brings man under the dominion of his fellowman. . . . But by nature, as God first created us, no one is the slave either of man or of sin. This servitude, is however, penal and is appointed by the law . . . until all unrighteousness pass away, and every principality and human power be brought to nothing, and God be all in all.

During the European Middle Ages the practice of enslaving Christians was discontinued for two reasons: first, the brotherhood of the faith was considered contradictory to the master-servant relationship;[2] and second, the social importance of slavery diminished after the crisis of the Roman Empire until the sixteenth century. However, the servitude of pagans or gentiles was considered legitimate. Joseph Höffner (1957, 87, 92–93) points out:

Continual wars caused many individuals from independent pagan nations to fall into the hands of Christians. Only those prisoners would become the lowest human category within the *orbis christianus:* that of slaves. . . . No scholastic ever doubted that it was licit to make slaves of pagan prisoners captured in a just war. Even in the sixteenth century all theologians held that opinion. In the Code of Canon Law slavery figured also among the institutions of *ius gentium.*[3]

The following distinction made by the jurist from Salamanca, Diego de Covarrubias (1512–1577), is instructive: "Between a captive and a slave there is a great difference; a captive is an enemy, independently of his condition in life, who is captured in a good war; *slave* is the same but an infidel; a prisoner is he who is *catholic* and can be ransomed" (in Bataillon 1976, 136, n. 222).

This distinction also has its base in the Alfonsian code, already cited. The first law of the twenty-ninth title of the second *partida* distinguished between prisoner and captive or servant. The first, defeated in war, pre- serves his life and freedom, thanks to the community of religion with the conqueror. The second could lose them by reason of his being an infidel, for having a different faith than the adversary. "By law, captives are those who are imprisoned by men of another faith; because these men can kill them after they imprison them if they reject their law . . . or they can use them as servants . . . or sell them whenever they wish" (Alfonso 1807, 2:327).

The intense hostility, toward the end of the Middle Ages, between Christians and Muslims created a reciprocal slave market. Christian forces felt entirely free to force Moors, Turks, and Arabs into servitude. At the same time, the Muslims did not feel moral or theological inhibitions in enslaving those who did not worship Allah. If the Christians had an estate, the Muslims offered to emancipate them in exchange for a substantial ransom.

In this context of antagonism between Christianity and Islam, the European discovery of many diverse infidel nations at the end of the fifteenth century and the beginning of the sixteenth offered the possibility of their enslavement (cf. Verlinden 1951). A central element in their intrinsic difference was that of being *non-Christian*. This gave rise to an ironical paradox of history. While during the medieval period Christians are an obstacle to the possible expansion of slavery, they become in the fifteenth and sixteenth centuries its promoters. As long as the contact between Christians and infidels was relatively limited, their enslavement had little social and economic significance. With the journeys to Africa and America and the increased contacts with densely populated nations with inferior military technology, the principle of allowing the enslavement of non-Christians became the basis for the extraordinary expansion of enforced servitude.[4]

It also generated an intense debate, which has merited this judgment from the distinguished Spanish historian Rafael Altamira: "The most interesting and fundamental aspect of our colonization [of America] was the tragic debate between those who were for slavery and those who were against it" (in Zavala 1984, 8).

Columbus and the Enslavement of the Indians

Christopher Columbus was the first to suggest the enslavement of the natives. In his famous letter of February 15, 1493, when narrating the happenings of his first journey, he writes about the attractive aspects of the lands he has found: "Their Highnesses can see that I will give them as much gold as they may need if Their Highnesses would give me a little help . . . and spices and cotton . . . *and as many slaves as they shall order."* Columbus reiterates the ease with which the aborigines can be taken, for their military technology is very primitive: "They have no iron nor steel nor weapons, nor are they fit to use them . . . they are wonderfully timid" (Varela 1982, 141–145; emphasis added).

In the Columbian correspondence from the first journey there is a serious contradiction that arises from two opposing visions about the natives. On the one hand, they are meek and peaceful; supposedly lacking an organized religion, they would be easy to Christianize and make into faithful subjects of the Spanish monarchs. On the other hand, they are infidels who can be enslaved and used for Spanish economic gain. From the first encounter between Europeans and natives, two discordant objectives emerge: evangelization and avarice.

In that same text Columbus mentions the existence of other Indians, the Caribs, allegedly cannibals, who would serve, as we shall see, as the opening for the legal enslavement of some natives.[5] In another letter, written later on March 14, he highlights the value of the lands he has found as a source of slaves: "And so many slaves for service . . . as many as Their Majesties demand" (in Fernández de Navarrete 1945, 1:321). He insists again on the defenselessness of the natives: "They lack arms, go naked, and are very cowardly." In his *Diary,* Columbus insists on the natives' potential as slaves, their defenselessness, and their fitness for servile manual labor. "They are good for receiving orders and working and sowing and doing everything else that is needed and for building towns" (Varela 1986, 132).

Las Casas (1986, 2.1.150:71–72; Varela 1982, 224) transcribes another letter from Columbus, written during the second journey, in which he praises the financial opportunities of the Indian slave market. "From here, it is possible, in the name of the Holy Trinity, to send all the slaves that could be sold." The mention of the triune nature of the Christian God in a recommendation to enslave the Indians is symptomatic of the confessional mentality of Spain at that time. It is probably a reference to baptism; that is to say, that they would be baptized native slaves (however, according to canon law their baptism did not emancipate them). The Admiral adds his favorable estimation of the possibility for enrichment:

> Because in Castilla and Portugal and Aragon and Italy and Sicily and the islands of Portugal and Aragon and the Canary islands many slaves are required, and I think not many come from Guinea any longer; and as you could see with your own eyes one slave from here is worth three from there; and I have recently been at the Cape Verde Isles where people do a great market of slaves and continually send ships to pick them up

and they are all present at the gate, I saw them ask 8000 *maravedís* for
a very weak one.

In his desire to convince the Crown to allow the legal enslavement of
the inhabitants of the New World, Columbus makes two assertions that
would soon become controversial: (a) that the black African market is
almost exhausted; (b) that the Indians are better than the Africans for servile
work. That is part of the "process of fictionalization" to which Beatriz Pastor
alludes. Regardless of the capacity for work of America's natives, Las Casas
(1986, 2.1.150:71) recognizes the enslavement intention of the Admiral and
his fiscal objectives. "For the Admiral, this [Indian slavery] was the main
profit from which he thought and hoped to cover the costs incurred by
the monarchs."

Columbus did not limit himself to the proposal. According to Las Casas
he proceeded to capture more than five hundred Española natives and
send them to Spain (Las Casas 1986, 1.1.102:405). This action of the
Admiral's seemed to rest on solid historic grounds. The Portuguese, with
papal blessings, had been doing that for a few decades in African raids.[6]
In line with the theory that the black Africans were pagans and Saracens,
several papal bulls prescribed the legitimacy of their enforced servitude,
transforming Lusitanian incursions into anti-Islamic crusades. Eugene IV,
in his bull *Dudum cum ad nos* (1436), called them "enemies of God, entrenched persecutors of the Christian religion . . . , Saracens and in other
ways infidels"(Rumeu de Armas 1975, 1:43–46). Similar terms are used by
Nicholas V in his bull *Romanus pontifex* (1455), in which he grants the
Portuguese Crown "full and free faculty to invade, conquer, combat, defeat,
and subjugate . . . any Saracens and pagans and enemies of Christ, and
reduce their persons to perpetual servitude (*in perpetuam servitutem*) . . ."
(in Morales Padrón 1979, 23; Davenport 1917, 16, 23). The black slave market
began, therefore, with the full blessing of the *Vicarius Christi*.

The Spaniards, in their invasions of the Canary Islands, also subdued
and sold as slaves a good many of the natives.[7]

The Genoese Michéle Cuneo accompanied the ships with the aborigines sent by Columbus to Spain and relates their sad condition: "Upon
entering Spanish waters about two hundred of them died, which we threw
into the sea, and I think the reason was the cold to which they were not
accustomed. . . . We landed in Cadiz with the slaves, half of them sick.
They are not suited for hard work; they suffer a lot from the cold and do
not have a long life" (in Sauer 1984, 138). Columbus learned about the
failure of his slave market plans but did not back down. He trusted that,
in time, the natives would overcome the difficulties of the transatlantic

voyage and acclimatize themselves to the Iberian cold. "Even though they die now, that will not always be the case; that was the way it was for the blacks and the Canarians at first"(Las Casas 1986, 2.1.150:72).

Later, Bartolomé de las Casas would bitterly recall Columbus's action. He censured it severely as a lamentable fact, a type of "original sin" of the European presence in the New World. In his opinion, the involuntary detention of the natives "was nothing more than the tacit or interpreted violation of natural law," which is "common to all nations, Christians and gentiles, and of any sect, law, state, color, and condition, without any difference whatever." With profound sadness he condemned the action of the Admiral, whom Las Casas generally held to be "a good and Christian man" (ibid., 1.1.41:107–108):

> Not being astute enough or prepared for the evils that could happen as they happened . . . ignoring also what he should not have ignored regarding divine and natural law and right reasonable judgment, he introduced and started to establish such principles and planted such seeds, from which terribly deadly and pestilential weeds grew and spread and were so deeply rooted as to be enough to destroy and desolate all these Indies.

Columbus's attitude is "very culpable ignorance, which does not excuse anyone from observing natural or divine law" (ibid., 1.1.114:444). Las Casas gave the same explanation when recounting the first violent encounter between the Admiral's men and a group of natives.

> That was the first injustice . . . that was committed against the Indians and the beginning of the great bloodshed which was to flow abundantly on this island. . . . I know the Admiral's intention was good, but . . . it was great ignorance of the law. (ibid., 193:380–382)

He attributes to Columbus two types of ignorance. The first has to do with the newfound lands, and it is expressed in three errors in his thought: (a) that they were on the Oriental edge of Asia; (b) that the extraordinary riches of Solomon's mines were found there; (c) that Cuba was a mainland [in Asia]. The second type of ignorance, of greater significance, is the devaluing of natural and divine law in the abusive treatment of the Indians. This provokes divine punishment: the anguish of the Admiral at his arrest and dispossession of all the distinctions he boasted (ibid., 2.2.38:329–332). In reality, Columbus and Las Casas had opposing ideas regarding the *law* governing that unprecedented new situation: the encounter between European Christians and infidel peoples of lesser technological development.[8]

The initial reaction of the Catholic Monarchs was ambivalence. First they authorized the sale of slaves. In a royal decree, April 12, 1495, addressed to Bishop Fonseca (who was supposed to monitor the slave trade and its fiscal aspects), they asserted: "Regarding what you wrote to us about the Indians coming in the ships, it seems to us that they can be best sold in Andalucia rather than in any other place; you should sell them as you best see fit" (Konetzke 1953, 1:2). But four days later, they expressed reservations about the sale, without stopping it, until "scholars, theologians, and canon lawyers" could analyze the reasons for their enslavement.

> The King and Queen. Reverend Father Bishop in Christ of our council. In another letter we wrote that you could sell the Indians sent by the Admiral Don Christopher Columbus in the caravels that arrived recently, and because we wanted *to be informed by scholars, theologians, and canon lawyers if they, in good conscience, can be sold or not as slaves,* and this cannot be done until we know *the reason why they have been sent to us here as captives,* . . . therefore, as to the sale of Indians you make, hold the money on credit for a brief period, for in that time we shall know if we can sell them or not. (ibid., 2–3; emphasis added)[9]

The determination took more or less five years, during which time the practice started of paying for the services of those who ventured in the expeditions to the Indies with captured Indians. Las Casas tells how his father, who had been one of those adventurers, returned home, in 1500, with one of those natives. That is how the young man who would later become the vehement protector of the American natives saw one of them (Las Casas 1986, 2.1.176:173). The expansion of the custom of capturing Indians and of giving them as payment for services rendered, and the beginning of their introduction into the European slave market, forced the conscience of the Crown and brought it to a crucial decision: the natives of the New World are free vassals of Spain and cannot, without a just cause, be subjected to slavery.[10]

Apparently the royal decision was taken because the Indians of the New World had not, at least initially, committed any crime against the Spaniards, nor could they be treated as Saracens or Muslims, the well-known "enemies of Christianity." The Alexandrian bulls, in contrast to those issued by prior pontiffs in favor of the Portuguese incursions into Africa, did not include the enslavement of the aborigines. On the contrary, they exhorted the Catholic Monarchs to provide for their well-being.[11]

On June 20, 1500, in Sevilla, this royal decree was issued:

> The King and Queen. Pedro de Torres, steward of our house. You have sequestered in your power, by our order, some Indians from among those who were brought from the Indies and sold in this city and its Archdiocese and other parts of Andalucia by order of our Admiral in those

Indies, and now we order you to set them free and we have ordered the religious superior Fray Francisco de Bobadilla to take them back to the Indies with him . . . with not one missing. (Konetzke 1953, 1:4)[12]

The Indians were gathered—with the exception of those desiring to remain in Spain—and returned as free persons to the Antilles. Las Casas tells of the anger of the queen on learning of Columbus's intention to maintain the practice of paying for services by means of Indians: "What power does the Admiral have from me to give anyone my vassals?" (Las Casas 1986, 2.1.176:173). When the monarchs learned that Cristóbal Guerra, commissioned to undertake some expeditions in the New World, had brought natives to Spain and sold them as slaves, they ordered the prosecutor in Jeréz de la Frontera to investigate, and

> as many as Cristóbal Guerra brought, and as many as he sold, and to whom and at what price . . . and thus knowing the truth, and if it happened as has been said, to take from Cristóbal Guerra and from his possessions all the *maravedís* and the price for which those male and female Indians were sold and to retrieve them from the power of the persons who have them . . . and thus retrieved and gathered under your care . . . they can be brought to the island from which they were taken and set free. . . . And in the meantime . . . take Cristóbal Guerra prisoner and set a high bond for him. (Konetzke 1953, 1:7-8)[13]

To this general principle that the natives of the New World are free vassals who cannot be captured and enslaved, however, would be added some exceptions and reservations. These exceptions allowed the metamorphosis of the "perfect legalism" of Castilian colonial policy into the cruel exploitation of enforced manual labor.[14]

Caribs and Cannibalism

The first exception is in regard to the Caribs, alleged cannibals. From Columbus's first trip, the monarchs had been informed of the presence of these supposedly ferocious savages who continually raided the peaceful natives of the other Antillean islands.[15]

On January 30, 1494, Columbus sent a memorandum to the monarchs through Antonio Torres, suggesting the enslavement of Caribs and that they be sent to Spain. The objectives are diverse, reflecting the complex perspective of Columbus: (a) to educate them and to serve as language interpreters with other natives ("here we do not have a language for teaching these people our holy faith"); (b) to take away their deadly custom of cannibalism ("they need to be rid of their inhuman custom of eating men"); (c) to facilitate their Christianization ("and there in Castilla understanding the language they will receive baptism more quickly and benefit their souls"); (d) to improve the standing of Spaniards among the natives who fear the ferocious cannibals[16] ("Seeing that we take and capture those who inflict harm and whom they fear so much that even their name frightens them"); (e) to exchange them for other necessary goods for which they have ventured into the Indies ("to obtain from them cattle and other things to fill the fields and utilize the land . . . and those things could be paid for with slaves from among those cannibals") (Varela 1986, 212–214).

On October 30, 1503, Queen Isabel authorized their enslavement.

> In case those cannibals resist and do not wish to be indoctrinated in the things of our holy Catholic faith and be in my service and render obedience, they can be captured and taken to the lands and islands where needed so that they can be brought here to my kingdoms and realms and other parts and places where you wish and which you find good, paying us whatever part belongs to us, so that they can be sold and utilized without incurring any punishment as a result. (Konetzke 1953, 1:15)

The religious character of the Spanish state was present also in this reservation. Queen Isabel, while indicating the punitive nature of the enslavement of the Caribs, stresses its evangelizing function: "Bringing them from those lands and being utilized by Christians, they [Caribs] could be more quickly converted and attracted to our holy Catholic faith" (ibid.). From this exception came, naturally, the geometric multiplication of the number of alleged cannibals in the accounts of conquerors and adventurers. The traditional policy of captivity allowed by right of war was applied to them.[17] As Carl Sauer (1984, 244, 193) affirms:

> The provision was a carte blanche for future expeditions: any captain could affirm that the natives were cannibals and resisted Christianity and thus proceed as he pleased. . . . It was only necessary to declare the inhabitants of an island to be Caribs in order to legitimate the hunt for slaves.

The animosity toward the indomitable Caribs (whose fierceness assumed legendary attributes) is shown in the following royal proviso issued by Queen Juana, daughter of Isabel and Fernando, in which the Crown, as an incentive to fight and enslave them, dispenses from the payment of required tribute (one fifth of their earnings) those who carry out such actions.

I grant license and power to arm all those who wish to make war against the Caribs, and those who are taken can be made slaves or used as such without any of them having any obligation to give the fifth. (*Colección* 1885–1931, 5:260–261)

Hostility toward the Caribs increased after the natives' rebellion in the Island of San Juan (Puerto Rico), in 1511. This was attributed to an alliance—unusual from the Spaniards' perspective—between the brave Caribs and the natives of San Juan, which was the first serious threat to the stability of Spanish hegemony in the New World.[18] By the same token, King Fernando, after asserting his respect for the freedom of the natives, authorized toward the end of that year the war against the Caribs and their enslavement, while reiterating the incentive of exemption from tributes.

The Caribs . . . cleverly and in a diabolical way committed treason and treachery by killing Don Cristóbal de Sotomayor, deputy of our Captain on that island, and Don Diego de Sotomayor, his nephew, and many other Christians who were on that island . . . and after they rose and rebelled against us they have caused all the remaining Indians in the island to rebel . . . [and] they incited and urged those Indians and brought many Caribs for that purpose to that island of San Juan. . . . They have tried and are trying to protect themselves from being indoctrinated or taught the things of our holy Catholic faith and continually war against our subjects and natives, and many Christians have been killed, and . . . they are hardened in their ways, dismembering and eating other Indians. . . . Therefore, through this decree, I grant license and power to any and all persons . . . to make war against the Caribs . . . to be able to capture them and to do so . . . in order that they can be sold and taken advantage of without incurring any punishment whatsoever or paying any tribute. (Konetzke 1953, 1:32–33)

The instructions of Cardinal Cisneros, regent of the Crown, to the Jeronomite Fathers whom he sent to the New World in 1516 to study the grave demographic problem posed by the drastic diminution of the natives, maintain in effect the enslavement of the Caribs. This measure is one of the remedies offered the Spaniards in compensation for the projected emancipation of the natives who had been illegally subjugated. "In the same way they would profit a great deal if Your Highness grants them ships properly supplied with food and other necessities to capture the Caribs who eat other men." The reason given for the hunt is a religious one: "And those are slaves because they have not received our preachers and are very bothersome to the Christians and those who have converted to our holy faith, killing and eating them" (in Las Casas 1986, 3.3.88:130).

The Puerto Rican historian Jalil Sued Badillo (1978, 75–90) shows that the test confirming that the natives of any region of the Antilles, island or mainland, are cannibalistic Caribs, was based not on any objective study of their customs but on circumstantial economic necessities.[19] If, due to its mineral resources, a region was attractive for exploitation through Castilian colonization, the inhabitants were classified as non-Caribs and were apportioned by means of the *encomienda* system, in which, in theory at least, they were free vassals, though compelled to render certain services or pay certain tributes. If, on the contrary, the island was considered "useless" from a mining perspective, the inhabitants were labeled Caribs and looted and captured as slaves for other places in the process of economic exploitation.

A good number of religious men who defended the natives shared, however, this hostility against the Caribs. The Franciscans in Española, while defending the natural and social freedom of the Arawaks, considered as legitimate the enslavement of the Caribs, *"quia delinquunt in lege naturae"* (because they transgress the natural law) (in Gómez Canedo 1977, 91–92). Even the Dominican friar Pedro de Córdoba, mostly responsible for the first protests against the abuse endured by the natives and promoter of the first battles of Las Casas on their behalf in the royal court, in a letter to Fray Antonio de Montesinos—of the same religious order and companion in the struggle—recounts a homily he had preached against the enslavement and illegal market of Indians and states an exception to his censure: "As to the Caribs, I clearly said in the sermon that they could be given as slaves because of their sin" (in Pérez de Tudela 1988, 164).[20] It can certainly be affirmed that the "Carib Indian did not enjoy any measure of protection" (Otte 1975, 190).

In several decrees and ordinances, Carlos V maintained the enslavement of Caribs, exempting those who defeated them from paying the royal fifth, which was the 20 percent due the Crown as tax on certain types of trading income. An example is the commission granted on March 18, 1525, to Gonzalo Fernández de Oviedo, who would pay a fifth on everything captured, "except the Carib Indians taken in just war, for this is our will and desire that at this time nothing be paid" (in Castañeda 1970, 120).[21] Even at such a late date as 1612, Bernardo de Vargas Machuca defended the enslavement of Caribs: "They are Caribs and of bad tendencies and eat human flesh . . . they well deserve the juridical punishment given them, and not merely punishment, but to be given away as slaves" (in Fabié [1879] 1966, 71:251).

The Caribs became the symbol of a savage, bestial people deserving strong and unmerciful treatment. In spite of the attempts made by the court of Carlos V to reduce to a minimum the formal enslavement of the natives, colonists reiterated their demands that the Caribs be reduced to servitude and forced to work. On May 4, 1547, the Crown authorized the residents of Puerto Rico to attack the fierce Carib natives and to capture males older than fourteen years of age. In 1558, a similar decree was issued by way of concession to the colonists in Española (in Milhou 1975–1976, 39–41). It was reissued by Felipe II in 1569 as a general license for all Spaniards in the Antilles. This last decree was still considered in effect at the time of the issuance of the document known as *Recopilación de las Leyes de los Reinos de las Indias* (1680) (*Recopilación* 1841, 2.6.2.13:226).

In 1588, the Jesuit José de Acosta, in his taxonomy describing the third type of "barbarian," namely, those "savages similar to beasts, who barely have human sentiment; without law, king, or pacts," mentions first "the Caribs, always thirsty for blood, cruel with strangers, who devour human flesh, go around naked, and barely cover their shame. This type of barbarian was mentioned by Aristotle when he said that they could be hunted like beasts and tamed by force." Finally he stated that the Caribs "are the most bloodthirsty ones" (1952, 2.5:159).

In the eighteenth century there are still royal instructions that seem to presuppose continuity with the enslavement policy against the Caribs. On February 7, 1756, there is an order to free three enslaved Indians brought to Santo Domingo by a French brigantine since "in any instance, at no time or place can the Indians who are not Caribs be enslaved, in accordance with the law" (in Konetzke 1953, 3:276–281).

Anthropophagy became the favorite topic of anti-Indian propaganda.[22] It was one of the "legitimate titles" that, according to Francisco de Vitoria (Urdanoz 1960, 720–721), justified the war against the "barbarians of the New World" and allowed the "rights of war" to be exercised against them, one of which was enforced captivity. "Another title can be . . . the killing of innocent humans to eat their flesh." The defense of the "innocent" is right and the responsibility of the Castilian princes, even "without the need for pontifical authority" and independently of the will of such innocent ones. "It is not an obstacle that the barbarians consent or not . . . or that they do not wish the Spanish to rid them of such customs. For they do not have self-determination on this point." This same thesis, developed in greater detail, is set out by Vitoria in his lecture *De temperantia* (1537) (ibid., 1024–1054). He concludes: "The Christian princes can make war against barbarians because they feed on human flesh" (ibid., 1050).

Vitoria's interpreters have discussed the inconsistency between his negation—in the second part of *De indis*—of the violation of natural law as a just cause for war against the "barbarians of the New World" and his affirmation of the "defense of the innocent"—in the third part—as a legitimate rationale for war. Höffner summarizes the common posture among Catholic scholars who reject the hypothesis of such inconsistency, indicating that "Vitoria admits the legality of military measures, not because cannibalism and human sacrifices are contrary to natural law, but only for the defense of innocent men" (Höffner 1957, 439). He limits himself to a quote from *De temperantia:* "The reason by virtue of which barbarians can be fought in war is not that eating human flesh or sacrificing men is against natural law, but that they inflict injuries on other men" (Urdanoz 1960, 1051).

The distinction made by Vitoria and repeated by Höffner seems spurious. Human sacrifices and anthropophagy can be rated as violations of natural law, exactly because they are mortally harmful for the innocent. The conceptual contradiction exists, and an attempt is made to resolve it through rhetoric.[23] Besides, the apparent fact that in several native nations human sacrifice and cannibalism were acts linked to their beliefs and religious ceremonies is kept hidden (Friederici 1986, 1:217–218). Those natives belonged to a culture that held a worldview the Spanish empire wished to eradicate. That objective probably had greater strategic weight than the humanistic considerations about "the rights of the innocent." The natives, deprived of their cultural and religious values, were ideologically unprotected from the invader, who imposed the rules of the game and proceeded to enslave anyone who did not follow them.

Vitoria's view of this "legitimate title" became very popular. It managed to convert a bellicose invasion into a redemptive action. Thus, it began the long history of European interventions, with the excuse of juridical legitimacy to help the "innocent" in countries of lesser social and economic development.

Slavery Due to Rebelliousness

The second exception refers to rebellious Indians. Apparently it was first imposed by Christopher Columbus in Española in 1495 during the conflict between Spanish and Indians. The Spanish were victorious in the battle because of their superior military technology. They applied to the survivors the "right of captivity," proper to a "just war" against infidels. "All those they captured alive, and they were many, were condemned to slavery" (Las Casas 1986, 1.1.104:414). War against and enslavement of the rebels rested on the premise of the alleged right of the Catholic Monarchs through their authorized representatives to take possession of the "discovered" lands. No Spaniard then ever asked the pertinent question later formulated by Las Casas in his narration of the battle: "Those who are not subjects, how can they be rebels?" (ibid., 415).

Beginning in 1504, several royal decrees authorize the enforced servitude of the natives who persist in their obstinate rebelliousness (Rumeu de Armas 1975, 59).[24] The famous *Requerimiento* includes a clause that threatens slavery against those who battle the Spanish, who refuse to accept Castilian sovereignty and the Christian faith:

> If you do not do it . . . with the help of God I will use all my power against you and will battle you everywhere and in every possible way, and you will be subject to the yoke and obedience of the Church and their Highnesses, and I will take your people and your women and children, *and make them slaves;* and as such I will sell them, and I will inflict on you all the harm and damage possible. (in Oviedo 1851, 3.2.29.7:28–29)

The document establishes an intimate link between the papal donation—"a previous pontiff, successor of Peter . . . donated these islands and mainland of the Ocean sea to the aforementioned King and Queen"—and the requirement of obedience and the Spanish right (in case of "malicious" rejection) to war and enslavement of those captured.

Something similar is included in Carlos V's instructions sent to Hernán Cortés upon his appointment as governor and captain general of Nueva España. After insisting that the natives be well treated and their goods and freedoms respected, he indicates the critical importance of requiring that they submit to the Catholic religion and be obedient to the Castilian Crown. This call to faith and obedience to the Spanish state must be done respectfully and by peaceful means, showing goodwill and the desire to benefit the natives. What happens, however, if the natives reject the requirement and use arms to resist their subjugation? The answer comes immediately:

> There will be some Christians who can speak their language; through them you will first make them understand all the good that will come to them if they place themselves under our obedience, and the evil and damage and death that will come to them from war, and especially for those taken alive *who will become slaves;* and so that they be informed and cannot pretend ignorance, notify them of this, *so they can be taken as slaves* and Christians can have them with a clear conscience. (*Colección* 1885–1931, 9:175; emphasis added)

Cortés informs the emperor of his determination to enslave the Zapotecs and Mixes because of their obstinate rebelliousness.

These, for being so rebellious, having been given the *requerimiento* so many times . . . and having caused so much damage, I ordered them to be enslaved; and I ordered that they be branded with the mark of your Majesty, and having taken the portion which belongs to your majesty, they be divided among those who conquered them. (Cortés 1985, 195)

In the same way, he launched an expedition to subject the Chichimecas, who would become famous for their strong resistance to the attempts to subject them to Spanish domination. The troops carried with them instructions to present the *requerimiento* with its double dimension of obedience to Carlos V and adherence to Christianity. But if they did not submit to the *requerimiento*, they would be enslaved. "If they do not . . . wish to be obedient, make war against them and take them as slaves." Cortés adds the various justifications for such a severe measure: (a) the benefit to the Crown ("taking these barbarians as slaves, who are savages, Your Majesty will be served"); (b) the benefit to the colonists ("and the Spaniards would benefit for they shall mine the gold"); (c) and finally, the benefit to the Chichimecas ("in relating to us some of them may be saved") (ibid., 282).

In this category of slaves by reason of rebellion, the warring Chilean Araucans gained special notoriety for their exceptional ability for armed resistance. It was said about them that "never has a king subjected such fierce people proud of freedom," in the famous epic poem *La araucana*, by Alonso de Ercilla ([1945] 1984, 1, 41 [37]). Decades later the jurist Juan de Solórzano y Pereyra ([1648] 1930, 1.2.1:131–140) called them "among the greatest warriors, the most proud, and haughty of all those discovered so far." According to Felipe III, in 1608:

The Indians who are upset and at war in the provinces of Chile . . . have arisen and rebelled without legitimate reason . . . and have refused obedience to the church and rebelled and taken up arms against the Spaniards . . . therefore they deserve any punishment and rigor used against them, *even being given as slaves.* . . . By these means I declare and order that all Indians, either men or women, of the rebellious provinces of the kingdom of Chile . . . *be held and kept as slaves.* (Konetzke 1953, 140–142; emphasis added)[25]

During the second half of the sixteenth century and the first half of the seventeenth, decrees and ordinances were repeated, authorizing the enslavement of the Araucans.

The war of the provinces of Chile has been so long and troublesome. . . . Thus it demands that we think of every means to end it, and it has been necessary to take as slaves those rebellious Indians who were taken

during the war. . . . Most of the theologians and scholars who discussed
this issue and problem resolved that *it is legal to enslave those Indians.* (ibid.,
136; emphasis added)

Since it is peculiar to the confessional Spanish state, where Catholicism
was the theoretical raison d'etre of public policy, the enslavement of the
Araucans is justified principally for religious reasons:

> The very same rebellious Indians given as slaves would enjoy great
> spiritual well-being because they would be instructed and taught the
> things of our faith. . . . Their enslavement can be best founded on their
> refusal to obey the church . . . and while their stubborn refusal to obey
> the church lasts, we order them to be given as slaves. (ibid., 137–138)

Alonso de Ercilla explains the religious intentionality of the war against
the Araucans in this way:

> We explained that our intention
> And our expedition's motive
> Was religious. For the rebels
> Erst baptized we brought redemption.
> They contemned the Holy Wafer,
> Flouting law received, and breaking
> Firm-sworn faith with treacherous mischief,
> and illicit arms resorting.

The Araucans, however, were not convinced of the purity of the
Castilian religious conscience. Arcilla places on the lips of the valiant native
Galvarino, both of whose hands the Spaniards had severed as exemplary
punishment, this skeptical pronouncement:

> . . . "for the occasion that has brought them
> Here through seas and alien countries
> Is seductive gold deep-buried
> in the fecund veins of Chile."
> 'Tis a false decoy and specious,
> To pretend their prime intention
> is to extend the Christian tenets;
> Pure self-interest is their mainspring,
> and from greed flows their pretension.
> All the rest is fraud and feigning.
>   (Ercilla, 16:301 [162]; 23: 401 [210])

The case of the Araucans presents a double dimension of rebelliousness—political uprising and religious apostasy. The brave Indians were
accused of both things. The close link between Hispanicity and Christianity

brings a double rupture, both political and religious. The rebels cease to be considered infidels and come to be regarded as apostates, a crime that according to the traditional laws of Christianity was punished very severely. This religious dimension constituted the escape hatch for the consciences of many friars and ecclesiastics who persevered in supporting both the war without quarter against the Chilean natives and the enslavement of the survivors.[26] In this way, as Master Melchor Calderón stresses in an opinion issued in 1599 in Santiago, Chile, war can be made against the Araucans and they can be subdued "not only as rebels, but as enemies of God and of us and also enemies of Christianity" (in Jara 1971, 200).

In the end, the key principle of the natural freedom of the inhabitants of the New World, codified in many ways in the Indian legislation, was imposed also in the case of the rebellious Chileans. In 1662, King Felipe IV forbade the sale and exportation of Araucan slaves, since it was apparent that the practice had caused the indefinite prolongation of the conflict.

> It is my will that imprisoned Indian men, women, and children cannot be sold as slaves nor taken out of the kingdom, because, due to the selling and taking away of those who had thus far become prisoners, it has become clear that peace and tranquility have become impossible in those provinces. (in Konetzke 1953, 2:492–493; *Recopilación* 1841, 2:227)

He gave orders also to convoke a session in which the bishops of Santiago and Conception and the superiors for the Franciscans, Dominicans, and Jesuits should meet to discuss the enslavement of the rebellious Araucans. The session recommended that the practice of enslaving those older than ten be continued.

> This resolution or opinion in this matter is motivated by the cruelty with which the Indians treat the Spaniards, . . . taking their lives in cruel and barbaric ways, and if those Indians are not enslaved when taken, it would encourage their fierceness, and the continuation of a greater war. (in Konetzke 1953, 2:607)[27]

In spite of this recommendation, subscribed to by the main Catholic authorities in Chile, after a long and intense history of pressures and debates, the principle of natural freedom for all natives including the Araucan was imposed. In 1679 King Carlos II ended the dispute about the possible emancipation of the Araucans, who were decimated and impoverished by the unmerciful war:

> Having resolved, that the Indians of Chile can enjoy full liberty. . . . We ordered the governor of those provinces that all Indian slaves be given their natural freedom . . . and that no imprisoned Indian men, women,

and children could be sold into slavery . . . as they are vassals and cannot be oppressed. . . . And we have charged the governor there to treat them well, convert them, and put them into a *reducción* (reservation) in the most gentle and benign ways possible, and mainly through the preaching of the holy gospel, and the propagation of our holy Catholic faith. . . . In the future, not for any pretext whatever, even a just war, can they be enslaved. (*Recopilación* 2:227)

Servitude by Purchase

From 1506 on, it was legitimate to buy as slaves those bought as such from the natives themselves. On occasion the chiefs were allowed to substitute the tribute that they should pay with slaves, which led to the practice of enslaving free Indians to send them as servants for the Spaniards.

Carlos V, for example, on March 8, 1533, through a royal decree, granted the conquerors of Peru authorization "to buy, rescue, and own the slaves that the chiefs of those lands have justly made into slaves, without placing any obstacles nor any opposition." The reason, it is alleged, is that "the chiefs of that land have for themselves Indian slaves, whom they give you to serve as your slaves" (Konetzke 1953, 1:142). The Crown adds the obligation to investigate whether those slaves were legitimate ones.

This practice was criticized by Las Casas, who alleged often that the great majority of the Indians enslaved by other Indians had been unjustly subjected to servitude; therefore, when the Spaniards acquired them they were perpetuating a perverse iniquity. A central tenet of the Las Casas position is the incompatibility between the Christian gospel and the enslavement of Indians. In the "eighth remedy" he insists that the authentic propagation of the Christian faith requires a necessary link between the people and their freedom to be evangelized or not. Preaching demands respect for the freedom of the native communities, because the "evangelical law of Jesus Christ . . . is a law of supreme freedom" (Las Casas 1965, 2:665).

In his essay "*Tratado sobre la materia de los indios que se han hecho esclavos*" (Treatise on the subject of enslaved Indians), Las Casas confronts a difficult objection to his denunciations of Indian slavery—namely, that it existed before the arrival of the Spaniards. His response does not deny this nor that some were legitimate slaves (i.e., obtained in a just war). But he made a double assertion of doubtful coherence: (a) slavery among the natives was "easy and gentle"; the servants are a little less than the children of the family (Las Casas 1965, 1:589) and (b) the great majority of the natives enslaved by their own people had been enslaved unjustly and therefore could not be acquired legitimately as such by the Spaniards. His idyllic vision of Indian servitude is related to his perspective of the "noble savage" from which he perceived the natives;[28] but this vision is not compatible with the many ways in which, according to him, the Indians managed through malice and fraud to enslave one another.

The criticism of the corruption in the slave market was not limited to the fiery Dominican. The first bishop of Mexico, Fray Juan de Zumárraga, in an extensive letter sent in 1533 to Carlos V, makes the following denunciations:

> Free Indians were branded by the thousands as slaves, and when I examine them according to the laws, among a thousand that they had captured [purchased] for branding, there was not one [legal] slave. . . . They sold as slaves those who were free and sent them to their mines in as many ships as they could find on the shores, without any examination, against the ordinances and royal provisions of Your Majesty, to be sold to the islands. . . . From this it seems and it can be proved that from the province of Pánuco and Nueva España at least fifteen thousand free Indians were taken out to be sold to the islands, and as to the others only God knows and it will be known on the day of judgment whether there were more who threw themselves into the sea in despair. (in Cuevas 1975, 29–30)

In the context of the long and harsh struggle against slavery waged by innumerable friars and religious men, there stands out the opposition of the Franciscan monks of Nueva España in a collective letter to the Crown, July 31, 1533:

> The unbelievable day has come when a soul is valued at two pesos, and it is thus that the slaves are sold. The granting of branding is against divine law, which does not permit that free men be made slaves, even when royal authority is involved in such servitude. We say that here only free men are being branded, and the reason is that the Spaniards are too greedy and they importune the chiefs to capture slaves for them in exchange for the tribute they have to pay them; and the poor ones to be free of them give them their free vassals as slaves, and these out of fear do not dare claim their freedom. Such a grant is against your imperial office, which is to protect the church and free those captured unjustly and . . . against the condition under which Your Majesty received from the Roman pontiff these lands, to convert these people, not to sell them. . . . It is against good government that wishes to preserve and increase these lands and kingdoms, not to destroy them. (ibid., 14–15)[29]

The Crown finally acceded to the pressures from religious men. In 1538 the emperor forbade the purchase of Indian slaves. This decision was an important step in the theoretical affirmation of the natural freedom of the original inhabitants of the New World.

> Insofar as we are informed that the chiefs and leaders of Nueva España had the custom to enslave and take as slaves their native subjects, for very flimsy reasons and with great facility, and sell them thus to the Spaniards. . . . We have provided that by no means whatsoever may a Spaniard from now on, buy or take as a way of ransoming them, any of those Indians. . . . We order and maintain that now, and from now on, none of those chiefs nor leaders, nor any other Indian, can enslave any Indian, nor sell, nor ransom any one, and if anyone does, we declare them free. (Konetzke 1953, 1:188–189)

Personal Freedom as Juridical Principle

In light of the opinion of many important theoreticians of the day, it is remarkable that Spanish legislation refused to accept their reasoning as cause for enforced servitude. Juan Maior, for example, in 1510 pointed out the natural inferiority of the natives as shown by the barbarism of their collective life: "they live bestially . . . savage men . . . hence the first to occupy those lands can rightly govern the people who inhabit them for they are by nature servile" (*populus ille bestialiter vivit . . . et sub polis vivunt homines ferini quia natura sunt servi*).[30] Juan Ginés de Sepúlveda[31] applied to the natives of the New World the Aristotelian theory of the legitimacy of enslaving "barbarians," inferior by nature.[32]

In general, the Aristotelian theory that barbarians are by nature slaves due to their being congenitally inferior, was considered a violation of the theological doctrine of the substantial equality of human beings, as children of Adam and creatures of the one God (Pagden 1982, passim). According to Celestino del Arenal's (1975–1976) well-documented position, the majority of influential Spanish theologians adopted as their axiom the principle, foreign to Aristotelian Hellenocentrism, that every human being is by nature free and that, therefore, no nation by natural law deserves to be enslaved. Melchor Cano (Pereña 1956, 102–103) expressed it this way: "nullus homo est natura servus" (no man is a slave by nature); Diego de Covarrubias (ibid., 184–185): "omnes homines natura liberos esse, non servos" (all men are by nature free, not slaves); and Domingo de Soto ([1556]

1967, 288): "iure naturali omnes homines nascuntur liberi" (by natural law all men are born free).[33] Slavery proceeds not from natural law but from human law.

At most, as in the last legitimate title given by Vitoria for making war against the Indians (but which he does not confirm completely), the perception of the Indians' cultural inferiority took hold to validate a tutelary government rather than one of masters as recommended by Sepúlveda (Urdanoz 1960, 723–725). One has to recognize, however, that if a native nation did not accept a tutelary regime, to which they were enjoined for their Christianization and civilization, the practical difference between this form and slavery was not much. Besides, even though logically and juridically the thesis of bestiality was not accepted as the official reason for slavery, such a pejorative vision was kept alive and reappeared continuously, even among royal functionaries, as shown in this quote from Juan de Matienzo, of the Peruvian Audiencia: "All the Indians of all nations discovered so far [1567] are . . . pusillanimous. . . . They were naturally born and raised to serve, and it is more profitable for them to serve than to give orders" (in Hanke 1985, 168).

In the dispute over the freedom or servitude of the natives, no voice claimed with greater vigor than that of Las Casas, respect for the natural autonomy of the aborigines as human beings protected by law. In his opinion, reiterated innumerable times: "Those Indians are free men and must be treated as men and as free" (Las Casas 1972, 66); "all Indians who have been enslaved in the Indies of the Ocean sea, from their discovery until today, have been unjustly enslaved" (Las Casas 1965, 1:595). To violate the freedom of the natives constitutes a grave transgression against natural law, since every rational creature is by nature free; against human law because the natives have not committed any injury against Spain that can justify their enslavement; and against divine law because it is God who gives them their autonomy.

The majority of exceptions mentioned before were abolished by the *New Laws* of 1542. Before that, the introduction of American natives to the European slave market was avoided by means of a royal decree made on July 21, 1511, which was intended to impede "the bringing or sending by any means whatsoever any Indian slaves from that island [Española] for Castilla" (Konetzke 1953, 1:29).[34] The *New Laws*, considered by some as "the Magna Carta of the Indians" and "the greatest monument to the freedom and dignity of the human person" (Pereña 1956, 3),[35] affirmed the juridical principles of the personal freedom of the natives and forbade their enslavement:

We order and command that from now on because of war or any other cause, even by reason of rebellion or for ransom or any other way, no Indian can be made slave, and we wish them to be treated as vassals of the Crown of Castilla, for so they are. . . . From now on by no means whatsoever are Indians to be made slaves. (in Konetzke 1953, 1:217)

6

Freedom and Servitude: The Encomienda

Priests: Dominican friar, very bad-tempered
and haughty, who oppresses the native women
and forces them to weave.

The perpetuity of the faith and Christian religion of the natives of this land depends on the perpetuity of the Spaniards there. . . . And because in this land there cannot be perpetuity without rich men, nor rich men . . . without the service of the Indians . . . it follows clearly, that it is necessary for the service of God and the perpetuity of the land, and the stability of the faith of the natives, that the Spanish have assigned [*encomendados*] towns.

—Dominican friars from Nueva España

This enforced apportioning places a considerable obstacle to what principally and above all should be the purpose for governing these Indies, that is, the exaltation and increase of our holy Catholic faith and of the holy gospel. . . . And what is worse is that in the name of faith . . . they wish to cover up and paint over their tyrannies, thefts, and avarice.

—Fray Gaspar de Recarte

Origins of the Encomienda

Slavery was not the only system of forced labor imposed on the natives. The institution known as *encomienda* lasted longer. The name comes from the Latin *commendo(are)* and has a positive connotation: to entrust a person with the care of someone or something.

The first official order regarding this peculiar labor institution was given in March 1503 by the Catholic Monarchs, instructing the authorities of Española that "to bring about the salvation of the Indians' souls by means of the people there who hire them, it is necessary that the Indians be apportioned in towns for community living." The supposed purpose of this *repartimiento* (apportioning), a word often used as a synonym for *encomienda*, of natives was to evangelize them, to teach them good and proper customs ("so they will not do the things they used to do, nor bathe, nor purge themselves as often as they do now"), and to give them the discipline of work (Konetzke 1953, 1:9–13).[1]

Differences in daily hygiene as practiced by inhabitants of the tropics and of colder climates were not the only reasons prompting the Spanish to restrain the Indians' daily bathing. Of greater import was the moral problem: the Indians bathed in the rivers without any of the European Christian scruples for showing their naked bodies often and publicly. *Nakedness* was one of the peculiar and strange characteristics of Antillean Indians stressed by Columbus, Vespucci, and Pedro Mártir. Spanish thinkers had a dual response to it. For some it expressed frugality and Edenic harmony with nature – the mythic and idyllic vision of the "noble savage." For others, it was part of their immorality and lack of culture – the mythical and anti-idyllic image of the "fierce savage" (cf. Elliot 1984, 38–40). Todorov (1987, 57) sees behind this dual mythologizing the European incapacity to allow the natives to be themselves, free from imposed interpretations, or to respect their otherness. "These two contradictory myths . . . have a common base . . . lack of knowledge of the Indians."

The most passionate expression of an idyllic vision of the natives is found perhaps in "Información en derecho del licenciado Vasco de Quiroga," which contrasts their simplicity – reflecting in their communal life the lost "golden age" of humanity – with the superficiality of the Europeans, who in that respect show themselves to be in the "iron age" (Herrejón 1985).[2] It was to be expected, however, that after the initial seduction (à la Renaissance), the majority of ecclesiastical and state authorities would espouse the second perspective, and that, in the words of the Dominican Fray Bernardo of Española, they would consider "that Christian honesty cannot tolerate men and women going naked" (in Las Casas 1986, 3.1.94:150).[3]

Yet it is interesting to note that from the mythical perspective of the Antillean Indians, European attire assumed a macabre dimension. When they tried to explain the European invasion that deprived them of collective sovereignty, individual freedom, and finally their existence, the Arawaks referred to a strange apocalyptic prophecy, described by the Jeronomite friar Ramón Pané, the first Spaniard who attempted to decipher their religious beliefs.

> And they say that this chief confirmed that he had talked to Yucahuguamá [supreme Arawak deity; trans. note], who told him that those who remained alive after his death would only enjoy their dominion for a short time because *dressed people* would come and subjugate and kill them, and they would die of hunger. . . . They believe it is a reference to Columbus and the people who came with him. (Pané 1987, 48; emphasis added)

The Spanish attire becomes an ominous apocalyptic sign for the natives, the unavoidable sign of their collective tragedy.

The material profit of the Spaniards can certainly not be forgotten – "in what way could we better utilize the Indians . . . so that our income would increase and the residents of the Indies benefit more?" (Konetzke 1953, 1:13). In a secret instruction to Governor Nicolás de Ovando that accompanied that decree, the monarchs indicate that the Indian settlements should be located "near the gold mines so that more can be obtained" (Pacheco et al. 1864-1884, 31:176).[4]

Months later, when the Crown was informed that many natives had not reacted favorably to that instruction, the official order was made compulsory through a decree from the Castilian queen.

> Doña Isabel. . . . Having learned that because of all the freedom the Indians enjoy, they run away and separate themselves from relating to and communicating with Christians . . . and they become vagabonds . . . in the future [I] *compel and urge* those Indians to relate and converse with the Christians of that island [Española] and work in their buildings, in gathering and mining gold and other metals and tilling the soil and producing food for the Christian residents.

The queen insists that this command is for the well-being of the natives: both spiritual ("to indoctrinate them so that they be converted to our holy Catholic faith") and temporal ("so that they acquire good work habits"); and, above all, that official enforcement should not violate the general principle of their personal freedom ("so that they act and comply as the free persons that they are, and not as servants, and see to it that the said Indians be treated well")(Konetzke 1953, 1:16-17; emphasis added).[5] In spite of these reservations, the meaning is unmistakable: the forced labor of the natives is legalized, and the *encomienda* is codified as a qualified servitude.[6]

The term *encomienda* is apparently used for the first time in an authorization given to Diego Columbus, then admiral and governor of the Indies, by King Fernando on August 14, 1509, to regulate the distribution of the natives. The king states:

> Know that since the Indian islands and mainland of the Ocean sea were discovered through the grace of our Lord, the Indians have been *entrusted* to the settlers who have gone to reside in the island of Española . . . it seems that those settlers who received the *encomienda* used the Indians in that certain form and manner. (Konetzke 1953, 1:20-21; emphasis added)

That same day another royal decree was issued clarifying that the distribution was not for life. "The apportioning of the Indians . . . is not for life, but only for two or three years." The monarch's aim seems to be, among others, to distinguish this new institution of forced labor from slavery: "They shall be marked as servants and not as slaves" (ibid., 22).[7]

Juridically, the authorization of the *encomienda* belonged to the Crown, but most *encomienda* certificates were actually issued by colonial functionaries representing the Crown. Silvio Zavala (1935, 295) includes several decrees or certificates of *encomienda*. These reveal the dual nature of the institution, which underlies all its legal variations: Christianization and the spiritual well-being of the natives on the one hand; material and economic benefit for the Spaniards, on the other. This example, from 1514, was issued for someone in Española:

> Through this decree, [John Doe], resident of the village of . . . , is entrusted with the leader and dwellers of . . . , to make use of them and so that they help you in your plantations and their cultivation and . . . with the charge to teach them about our holy Catholic faith, giving them all the possible and necessary vigilance and care. (Savala 1935, 295)

One can detect in those documents a certain tension between those two objectives. In theory, the evangelizing objective is primary. It links, for example, instructions from 1536, the *encomienda*, and the missionary task prescribed in the Alexandrian bulls.

> The principal reason for the Holy Apostolic See to grant dominion of the kingdoms of the Indies to the Catholic Monarchs . . . was the preaching there of our holy Catholic faith and the conversion and salvation of those people so as to attract and subject them to the universal membership of the church, and for His Majesty to fulfill his Catholic responsibility he ordered the Indians to be apportioned to the Spaniards. (*Colección* 1885–1931, 10:360–361)

It is difficult, however, to avoid concluding that *in practice,* material interest prevailed and culminated in the serious exploitation of Indian labor.[8]

The legitimacy of forced labor was defended by the Dominican theologian Fray Matías de Paz (Lopez de Palacios Rubios and Paz 1954, 219, 223) in his treatise from the second decade of the sixteenth century. It is born from the premise that Spanish hegemony is beneficial for the spiritual life of the natives.

> Otherwise and as a result of the great distance that separates them from the Christians, they would soon lose their Catholic faith if there were no one to help them remain in it, which would be the greatest evil. So it is very appropriate for the salvation of the Indians to maintain them under the monarch's dominion, who with help from the Highest, attracted them to the knowledge of the Catholic faith.

This benefit carries very high costs, which are morally reasonable, and they are to be paid above all by the labors of the natives.

> It will be licit, therefore, even after their conversion, to exact from the Indians certain services, greater perhaps than those expected from the Christian residents of those lands, so long as those services be in conformity with the faith and right reason, taking into account the expenses

and work necessary for getting there and so that our Catholic and very prudent king maintain . . . under the very gentle yoke of Christ, such distant lands.⁹

Seven decades later, however, the Franciscan Gaspar de Recarte, in his "Tratado del servicio personal y repartimiento de los indios de Nueva España (1584)" (Treatise on the personal service and apportioning of the Indians of Nueva España) (in Cuevas 1975, 357, 364), would judge very harshly the evangelizing result of the Indian *encomiendas*.

> This enforced apportioning places a considerable obstacle to what principally and above all should be the purpose for governing these Indies, that is, the exaltation and increase of our holy Catholic faith and of the holy gospel. . . . And what is worse is that in the name of faith . . . they wish to cover up and paint over their tyrannies, thefts, and avarice.

Freedom and Existence of the Indian in the Encomienda System

The centuries-old controversy over the *encomienda*, or apportioning, of the Indians took on a double aspect. The first point in question is whether, in spite of resting on the theoretical, juridical, and theological premise of the *freedom* of the Indians, that right is violated in practice. The dispute is fully understood only if the *encomienda* is accepted as an attempt to combine enforced labor with the formal and juridical acknowledgment of the freedom of the natives and the missionary and civilizing task. The theoretical and juridical difference between *encomienda* and slavery is stressed by Pedro Mártir de Anglería (1964–1965, 2.7.4:606), member of the Council of the Indies, when describing the new labor system: "That those apportioned by royal pleasure as subjects to whomsoever shall be held as tributaries and subjects, *not as slaves.*" The practical reality of *encomienda*, its daily operations, make a scrupulous historian such as Carlos Esteban Deive (1980, 15) state categorically: "The *encomienda*—we will not tire of saying it . . . was in reality, concealed slavery."

It is not a new judgment. Even after the many efforts by the Crown to humanize the *encomienda* and to ban abuses, Bartolomé de las Casas always considered it to be in violation of the natural freedom of the Indian nations. When the bishop of Charcas, Fray Matías de San Martín (in Fabié [1879] 1966, 71:441–451), writes to him distinguishing between the conquerors, whom he censured for trespassing against the instructions of the Crown, and the *encomenderos*, who acted within the limits of the law, Las Casas (ibid., 453–454) responds:

> The *encomenderos*, who have only been *encomenderos*, and not conquistadors, do not be deceived, Your Excellency . . . they are tyrants . . . because those people are free by right and natural law and did not and do not owe the Spaniards anything. . . . *Encomiendas* in themselves are bad, wicked, and intrinsically depraved, not in harmony with any law or reason, because to give or apportion free men against their will, commanding them for the good and usefulness [of the Spaniards] . . . and behind their backs to deprive kings of their kingdoms and princes and natural lords of their domains – is there greater infernal depravity, wickedness and iniquity, impiety and tyranny? . . . It is the *encomenderos* . . . who are obliged to make restitution to the Indians. I am not talking about excessive tributes without rates nor the subtle ways of stealing and oppressing the Indians . . . but of the tributes that have been appraised and imposed as reasonable.

The other side of the issue, a second questionable matter, has to do with the *existence* of the natives. What was the relation between the apportioning of the Indians and its concomitant enforced labor with the demographic disaster that they suffered and that caused the extinction of nearly all the pre-Colombian Antillean communities?

The complexity of the evaluation of the *encomienda* is shown in a paradoxical judgment made in 1517 by the Franciscan Fray Pedro Mexía, for whom "it is bad to take away the Indians from the Spaniards and it is bad to leave them." It is bad to take them away because, it is alleged, the economic aspirations of the colonists would be shattered and the grants from the Crown would be violated. Also, without Spanish vigilance the Christian faith would not be rooted in the natives for "without someone to compel them, in ten days they would have forgotten the Hail Mary they now say." On the other hand, it is bad to leave them in *encomiendas* "because by leaving them, all the Indians of these lands will perish" (in Gómez Canedo 1977, 218).

The convergence between the dual challenge presented by the *encomienda* and the freedom and existence of the Caribbean natives is shown strongly in the fate of the residents of the islands north of Cuba and Española, the first islands found by Columbus in his first trip, today called the Bahamas, then called Lucayas. The drastic reduction in the number of pre-Colombian inhabitants of Española led to the decision to import native laborers from those islands lacking gold mines, called by the Castilians "useless nearby islands" (in Fernández de Navarrete 1945, 2:412).

There is double justification: the spiritual and religious well-being of the Lucayans and the economic profit of the Castilians. King Fernando authorizes the practice through various decrees, for example this one in 1511:

> After having discussed and considered with some members of our Council about bringing some Indians from the islands without gold to those with gold, so that the Christians there may make use of them and teach them the things of our holy Catholic faith, so that they will not be idle and practicing idolatry in those other islands, we grant license to bring those Indians from those islands, paying us a fifth from all those that are brought . . . for I have been told that by bringing those Indians, our Lord is well served and the island of Española benefits greatly. (Konetzke 1953, 1:26–27)

It was not the first decree in this regard. On August 14, 1509, the king had instructed the treasurer general, Miguel de Pasamonte, "to bring Indians from other places" to Española (Pacheco et al. 1864–1884, 31:441–442). That same decree authorizes the slavery of the Lucayans, who resisted their transferal as servants to the gold-rich islands. The choice for these unfortunate natives, as a result, was simple: If they accepted being taken from their homes and lands to work on foreign soil, they would become *naborias* [personal servants]; if, on the contrary, they fought that destiny, they would become slaves.

The dual end—Christianization and procuring cheap manual labor—for the capture and enforced migration of the Lucayans has gold mining as its axis. This becomes a critical problem for the freedom and existence of the Antillean natives. On the islands with gold, the natives are forced to work in the mines, which speeds up their mortality. In those without gold, the population becomes easy prey for the hunters of laborers, and, though in theory free, in practice is forced to work. For them the way to the grave is hastened by enforced labor aggravated by the transfer to a strange environment. The abrupt rupture with their natural milieu, in which they had developed a simple subsistence economy, was a traumatic experience, as detailed by Las Casas (1986, 2.1.43–45:346–355). Their tragedy was made official in the twenty-seventh law of Burgos; it could not be substantially stopped after that law was eased by the instructions issued in 1516 to the Jeronomite fathers (cf. Konetzke 1953, 1:53; Las Casas 1986, 3.3.89:133). Their existence was made vulnerable by the baroque dialectics of Christianization ("to . . . indoctrinate them in the things of our holy faith") and avarice ("and increase of my royal subsidies") (in Fernández de Navarrete 1945, 2:412). Gold became the source of misfortune even for those who were born far from it.

It cannot be forgotten that the *encomienda* had as its principal theoretical justification the Christian conversion of the natives. According to scholar Max Puig from the Dominican Republic, however, during the first decades of the colonization of Española, there was no structured and systematic effort to evangelize the natives.[10] This opinion is a repetition of one expressed in the second decade of the sixteenth century by the Dominican friars residing on that island. In their opinion, the burdensome and excessive work imposed on the Indians by the *encomenderos* did not allow any time or energy for religious instruction. According to their biblical analogy, one cannot be at the same time wolf and shepherd to a herd of sheep.[11] During that same period the native Antillean population diminished very quickly.

That negative judgment is not necessarily denied by the information that Lino Gómez Canedo (1977, 1–22, 148–150) gives about the Franciscan missionary work in the Antilles during the first two decades of colonization. Although its objective is more to inform than to evaluate, his data show the precarious nature of the evangelization efforts. Gómez Canedo does not have courage to admit that it was not only the "indecisions of the Antilles" (150) but the complete failure of the evangelization of its pre-Hispanic population. How does one evaluate a missionary enterprise that ends with the extinction of the subjects to be converted? The categorical judgment passed by Las Casas is closer to the truth: "No ecclesiastical or secular person had at that time the least care to teach doctrine or the knowledge of God to those people, but they all only wanted to make use of them" (Las Casas 1967, 1.3.120:634). He was not alone in that severe appraisal; it was reiterated by the Franciscan Gerónimo de Mendieta (1980, 1.6:36; cf. 3.47:301): "All of them were more after gold than after their neighbors; there was no one to have pity on them, nor zeal to save their lives . . . in the end all those [Antillean] Indians were exterminated."

The correct integration between the desire for quick material gain and the evangelization and preservation of the native nations fatally eluded the Crown; the result was the tragic extinction of most Antillean natives and the drastic reduction of the pre-Colombian inhabitants of the mainland. Judge Rodrigo de Figueroa presented the dilemma to the court clearly on July 6, 1520: "If the present system is maintained in the *encomiendas*, everyone here says that it is impossible for [the Indians] not to be exterminated and quickly, no matter how well we try to preserve them"; if, on the contrary, the *encomienda* is eliminated, the Spaniards would leave: "to take them [the natives] from the Christians would depopulate the island for sure" (Pacheco et al. 1864–1884, 1:419).[12] He was wrong. In reality, what happened was the massive importation of African slaves to do the hard work that produced so much profit.

In Peru, Fernando de Armas Medina (1953, 125), who in general shares the nationalistic and Catholic perspective of the Hispanics in the Americas of his generation, admits, however, that at least during the first years the *encomenderos* fulfilled their legal duty of contracting "curas de Indios" (teachers of doctrine for the Indians; trans. note) more out of self-interest than for the purpose of evangelization. "The *encomenderos* hired for the work of indoctrination those curates who helped them get the greatest earnings."

In the opinion of Las Casas—the harshest criticism in the sixteenth century—the *encomienda*, although it was born from Queen Isabel's correct intention to entrust the spiritual and temporal well-being of the natives to certain Spaniards, in the end turned out to be an "illusion and diabolical artistry . . . a true death that has killed, destroyed, and depopulated . . . so many and such vast kingdoms . . ."; "thick and greedy blindness . . . destructive plague of such large portion of the human race" (Las Casas 1965, 1:799; 1986, 1.1.119:417). It fails in its founding purpose, causes the death of the natives, and violates their natural condition as free beings, not only because it is masked servitude, a badly disguised extraction of riches by means of the sweat and fatigue of the natives, but also because it "lacked the consent of all those people." Therefore, whoever defends and promotes it "does not have anything of the Christian name . . . and truly is God's enemy and cruel exterminator of his neighbor" (1965, 1:803, 837). Las Casas sustained a long campaign, for almost half a century, fighting both juridically and theologically against all attempts to legitimate Indian servitude. In his opinion, expressed in an August 1555 letter to Bartolomé Carranza de Miranda (in Fabié [1879] 1966, 71:409), the *encomienda* practiced as a system of unjust enrichment based on servile labor shows the falseness of the theory as an evangelizing institution:

> The deceit comes from saying or thinking that said *encomiendas* or apportioning originated so that the Spaniards would teach the Indians Christian doctrine. This is false; but on the contrary . . . whoever [invented] it . . . did not pretend to give the Indians any doctrine . . . but riches to the Spaniards.

The Franciscan Mendieta is no less severe or critical than his Dominican colleague. Not only does he call the *encomienda* "harsh slavery" and "perpetual captivity," but he also considers it "the main and most harmful offense [and contrary] to Christianity." It is an institution imposed "against their will and by force"; it is born out of violence and coercion, and therefore it is opposed in practice to that which the Spaniards say is their theoretical objective: to teach the Indians the biblical "law of charity." It is a perversely inverted analogy to what the Christians of Apostolic times suffered. Now "the Christians [inflict] on those who convert to our faith . . . the penal works that the gentiles in the days of the primitive church imposed on the martyrs who refused to deny their faith in Jesus Christ. . . . What greater wickedness and inhumanity can there be?" The natives are the new martyrs tormented by the inhuman work imposed by the self-appointed Christians turned into "wolves." In keeping with the typical demonology of the times, Satan has the ultimate responsibility—the *encomienda* is "what the devil promotes for perdition" (Mendieta 1980, 4.37–38:519–529).

Dispute in New Spain

It is instructive to note the different opinions of Carlos V and Hernán Cortés regarding the *encomienda*. The conquistador, on March 20, 1524, informed the emperor of his decision to establish the Indians' apportioning system in Nueva España (in Pacheco et al. 1864–1884, 26:135–148 and 163–170).[13]

The response of the king was not what Cortés expected.

> Because of the long experience that we have had as a result of the apportioning of Indians on the island of Española and on the other islands that have been settled thus far where the Spanish Christians were entrusted with them, they have decreased greatly because of the ill-treatment and excessive work given them plus the very grave damage and loss in the death and decrease in the number of those Indians and the great disservice done to our Lord which has caused and impeded the Indians from coming to the knowledge of our holy Catholic faith so they could be saved; therefore having seen those damages brought about by the apportioning of those Indians and the need to satisfy that which the holy Apostolic See entrusted us by the concession and granting bull, . . . I order you that in that land do not allow any apportioning in *encomienda* nor keeping the Indians there, but allow them to live freely as our vassals live in our kingdom of Castilla.

The unfavorable judgment in respect to the *encomienda* is extensive and surprisingly firm. It reveals the hand of the "religious theologians and learned persons of good and holy life who are in our Court," who, when consulted by the Crown and being free of interests in Nueva España, suggested that the distribution, at least as practiced thus far, was not licit.

"Thus it seems to us in good conscience because God our Lord created those Indians to be free and not to be subjected and we cannot order them to be in *encomienda* or distributed to the Christians" (*Colección* 1885–1931, 9:170–171).

Cortés was not a person to be intimidated by political or theological authorities. His answer to the emperor is characterized by strength and tact. He begins daringly, saying that he has maintained the royal instructions in secret and without implementation. He argues that the theologians and religious who had been consulted do not know the prevalent situation in Nueva España. The conquerors are greatly in debt, for they have financed the war against the great Aztec empire with their own funds and credit.[14] The only way that they can remain in the land conquered by their arms and colonize it is by being allowed some earnings from the Indians' work and service.

> The Spaniards do not have any other type of projects, nor way of living or earning their sustenance, unless they receive help from the natives, and without that help they could not survive, and would be forced to leave the land.

The last point, abandoning the land recently conquered, he is quick to point out, would have damaging results for all involved. Not only for the conquistadors/colonists but also for the king, who would be seriously harmed by prohibiting the *encomienda* ("such as by a decrease in royal earnings for Your Majesty and the loss of such great dominion as Your Highness already possesses" – "dominion" that implicitly he owes to the bravery of Cortés and his companions). But the best of his subtle and clever logic is the presentation of the institution as beneficial for the natives:

> And the other: that the reason for not apportioning them in *encomienda* seems to be the privation of their liberty which seems to have happened there. . . . Distributing them in the way I distribute them, they are taken out of captivity and set free; because the way they served their previous masters, they were not only captives, but were in an unwarranted form of subjugation.

He proceeds then to develop an argument that would become very popular among the apologists of the Spanish empire and that would be perfected almost half a century later by Hispanic-Peruvian detractors (e.g., Sarmiento de Gamboa [1572]) of the Inka monarchy: the kings and native lords were cruel and bloody tyrants. Thus the recent Spanish regime assumes a redemptive and liberating character.

> Besides taking everything they had, without leaving them with anything for their survival, they also would take their sons and daughters and

relatives and they themselves to be sacrificed to their idols. . . . To frighten some nations into giving good service to the Christians to whom they have been entrusted, they are told that if they do not serve well they will be returned to their old masters, and they fear that more than any other threat. (Cortés 1985, 211)

As was typical, the decision of the Spanish Crown did not come in haste. The emperor ordered that a poll be taken so as to determine the outlook on the matter of the diverse *Spanish* groups in Nueva España (emphasis is added to point out that the discussion was about the natives, but they were not consulted). The result was almost a unanimous choir in favor of *encomiendas*, at least for life, and if possible in perpetuity.

The provisions of Granada in November 1526 marked the triumph of the colonists, colored by the well-known exhortation calling for the natives' good treatment and conversion.

We also command that, as in view of the quality, condition, or ability of those Indians, it has seemed to the aforementioned religious or clergy as a service to God and for the good of the Indians themselves so that they abandon their vices and especially that terrible crime of eating human flesh and so that they be instructed in and taught good behavior and customs and our Christian faith and doctrine and so that they live in a civilized manner, it is appropriate and necessary that they be entrusted to the Christians to make use of them as free persons who can be apportioned by the religious . . . always keeping in mind respect for the service of God. (Konetzke 1953, 1:94–95)

On December 10, 1529, the Council of the Indies faced the dilemma again: the *encomienda* is the cause of the extermination of the natives, but if it is eliminated suddenly the incentive for enrichment that motivates the Spaniards to colonize the New World would disappear. The problem is, therefore, how to obtain the elusive commitment that simultaneously protects the natives and allows for the Spaniards' enrichment, and thus to combine good conscience and increase in assets.

From time to time we have gathered the whole Royal Council and the Council of the Indies as well as the Hacienda Council where all the ordinances, provisions, and instructions that have been made thus far in favor of the freedom of the Indians and their good treatment and conversion to our holy Catholic faith were reviewed, even though the persons entrusted with these tasks have been very remiss. . . . Taking the thinking of all, it has seemed that in service to Your Majesty and in satisfaction of his royal conscience and for the preservation of Nueva España and so that natives there not be decimated by bad treatment, as has happened in other islands, it is appropriate that since God made them free that they should be given full liberty . . . and for that purpose all *enco-miendas* should be taken away from the Spaniards that have conquered them and inhabited them, because in truth this seems to be harmful both to the conscience of Your Majesty and an impediment to the instruction and conversion of the Indians to our holy Catholic faith, which is the principal intention of Your Majesty and also their preservation and increase. (ibid., 131–132)

The instruction concludes with some possible measures to compensate the actual *encomenderos:* increased land holdings and the concession of an Indian tribute during the first year after the dissolution of the *encomiendas.*

Naturally, the problem is that the core element in the colonists' perspective, accumulation of wealth, depends on the forced labor of the natives. Greater land holdings and the provisional tribute would only make sense as an investment through the increased exploitation of the native labor force. Apart from this factor of compulsory labor as a source of enrichment, the incentives are insufficient. The bishop of Nueva España, the Franciscan Juan de Zumárraga, wrote to the emperor on October 4, 1543, expressing subtly the need of some native servile work for the stability of the colony.

It is necessary to provide settlement on the land so that Spaniards may find rest and a perpetual home in it, and that this land may be a mother to them and they be loving children to defend and honor it. This rest and attachment will not come only from the goodness and fertility of the land; do not believe, Your Majesty, that this is enough. (in Gómez Canedo 1977, 97)

In 1545, the Crown had to yield to pressure from the colonists, who in Peru had exploded into armed rebellion (López de Gómara 1946, 155–294), and had to reinstitute the apportioning of Indians, canceled by the New Laws of 1542. Their demands had more power than the ethical denunciations of friars such as Las Casas, who discovered with sorrow that the hierarchy of the religious orders, including the Dominicans, favored the repeal of the prohibition of the *encomiendas.* The thirtieth chapter of the New Laws decreed that "from now on no viceroy, governor, court of law, discoverer, nor any other person could apportion Indians" (Konetzke 1953, 1:219). Three years later this law was abolished:

Because our will is that those who have served us and served in those our Indies will benefit from their being there and have the means to provide for themselves, and also having seen the petitions regarding that law presented by many of the provinces and islands of our Indies . . . we revoke it, and consider said chapter [thirtieth] to have no value or effect. (ibid., 236)

The logic of the centrality of the exploitation of manual labor in colonial development was presented with the clarity of a practical official, the viceroy in Nueva España, Luis de Velasco, to Carlos V in a letter on May 4, 1553.

> There is great displeasure and much poverty among the Spaniards. . . .
> The mines and all the farms that are of value in Nueva España are diminishing as a result of taking away personal servants . . . without these they cannot plough nor obtain supplies. . . . Without Indians, do not let Your Majesty be persuaded that the mines can be utilized; on the contrary, by raising the cost of manual labor for them they are finished, if the Spaniards themselves do not work them, and I doubt they will do so even if they have to die of hunger. . . . Your Majesty should order what is possible to prevent the abandonment of the mines, because after freeing the slaves, which would be shortly, there will be a total collapse in the value of the royal assets and those of individuals because no mine is so rich as to support the payment of wages. (Zavala 1935, 135–136)

He repeated this in a letter to Felipe II, on February 7, 1554: "I consider it impossible for Spaniards to sustain themselves in this land without the service of the Indians . . . because Spaniards do not serve one another except for excessive salaries, and then not to put their hands to field labor, but to manage the farms" (Cuevas [1914] 1975, 189).

In spite of the many efforts provoked by the Spanish Christian conscience to avoid abuses and to regulate the *encomienda* through a labor contract benefiting all the parties involved, maltreatment continued. A memorandum from Mendieta, sent to Spain in 1582, reveals the continuation of grave violations of the human dignity of the natives. The Franciscan recommended five measures, and his insistence showed that the seriousness of the problem and the offenses continued.

1. "That no free Indian be compelled to work in the mines, because . . . to send them to the mines is to send them to die . . ."
2. "That for no service should the Indians be sent away from their homes more than four or five leagues . . ."
3. That the number of Indians for *encomienda* not be larger than what the town can provide easily . . ."
4. "That in no way should they be caused to miss Sunday mass . . ."
5. "That for each day of service they be given a *real* and food, and be treated well. . . ." (Gómez Canedo 1977, 126–127)

The Debate on Perpetuity

On May 4, 1544, twelve friars of the Order of Preachers (known commonly as Dominicans; trans. note) prepared a defense of the *encomiendas* as necessary, first, to the economic well-being of the Spaniards in the New World; second, for the spiritual and religious benefit of the natives. They also insisted that the concession be granted in perpetuity, as an indispensable measure to sustain the prosperity of the Castilian colonies in the Americas. The document deserves to be cited extensively, among other things, for its defense of the social division between rich and poor, favorable for "the authority of the divine cult."

> The perpetuity of the faith and Christian religion of the natives of this land depends on the perpetuity of the Spaniards there [it had previously been stated that "the Indians do not have such constancy nor natural inclination to sustain the faith they have received without the Spaniards"]. And . . . because in this land there cannot be perpetuity without rich men, nor rich men without *encomiendas;* because neither mines, nor silk, nor wool, nor cattle, nor seeds, nor inheritance can be had without the service of the Indians, . . . it follows clearly that it is necessary for the service of God and the perpetuity of the land, and the stability of the faith of the natives, that the Spanish have assigned towns; because in the well-ordered republic it is important to have rich men. . . . It is necessary for the authority of the divine worship that there be rich men and that they have towns, because the Indians being poor cannot offer alms to the churches [they are poor, it is alleged, because, "the Indians of that condition are weak and not greedy, and they content themselves with their daily sustenance"]. (Pacheco et al. 1864–1884, 7:533–540)[15]

It was not an entirely new theme. Years before, Pedro Mártir had defended the idea of the perpetuity of the apportioning system, arguing that if apportionments were only granted temporarily the *encomenderos* would rush to obtain the greatest possible benefit to the consequent spiritual and physical detriment of the natives. Only the permanence of the *encomienda* and the juridical power to will them as inheritance can satisfy the preoccupation with maintaining native manual labor (Anglería 1964–1965, 2.4.7:607). Three Jeronomite fathers (Bernardino de Manzanedo, Luis de Figueroa, and Alonso de Santo Domingo), in a study carried out by order of Cardinal Cisneros in Española (1516–1518), arrived at the same conclusion by reasoning: "One of the things that has destroyed these unfortunate Indians is to go from hand to hand, and have new masters every day" (Pacheco et al. 1864–1884, 1:352). It is an attempt to legitimate, through an appeal to the spiritual well-being of the natives, the permanence of forced manual labor for the economic benefit of the colonists.

Hernán Cortés, in a similar manner, stressed the perpetuity of the *encomienda* as doubly beneficial: economically for the Spaniards; physically and spiritually for the natives. The Indian *encomienda*, bequeathed by inheritance, becomes in his clever letter to Carlos V, the magic wand that would produce all kinds of benefits to the Crown, the colonists, and the natives.

> In this manner two things will be done: one, the good order for the preservation of the natives, and the other, the profit and sustenance of the Spaniards, and from these two the result will be the service of our Lord God and the increase in the assets of Your Majesty. . . . It is very beneficial for Your Majesty to order the natives of these parts to give themselves to the Spaniards in *perpetuity* . . . because in this way each one would look on them as their own and would cultivate them as a legacy to be passed on to . . . descendants. (Cortés 1985, 212; emphasis added; Pacheco et al. 1864–1884, 26:445)

The same argument, on the eve of the approval of the New Laws, was set forth by the representatives of Mexico City on November 28, 1542:

> That Your Majesty have mercy on those who have been entrusted some Indians in your royal name, and make the *encomienda in perpetuity* . . . because if the distribution is in perpetuity they will choose farms for planting wheat and other seeds, and hold and raise cattle, and vineyards and other things. . . . The very natives will benefit because if they are held in perpetuity they will be treated well and will try to increase and remain. (Cuevas [1914] 1975, 109–110; emphasis added)

In 1546, Carlos V gave in on this crucial point: the apportioning could be made in perpetuity.

> Know that the provincials of the Order of Saint Dominic and Saint Augustine and Gonzalo López, procurator of Nueva España, came to us and told us that although they were grateful about the revoking of the order relating to the right of inheritance to the Indians, that was not truly the general remedy for that land, but rather the apportioning in perpetuity so that they will be content and tranquil; and they gave us many just reasons. (Konetzke 1953, 1:240–241)

The opponents of the *encomiendas*, however, led by the tenacious Las Casas, did not give up; they maintained an arduous battle to avoid the fulfillment of that decree. A decade later, Felipe III, at the urging of the *encomenderos*, especially the Peruvians and their creditors, leaned in favor

of the sale in perpetuity and on September 5, 1556, issued a royal decree
with the following decision:

> Having considered and discussed this matter various times and having
> heard the opinion of many persons . . . who agreed that the province
> of Peru could not be sustained, preserved, and increased in the way that
> it has been up to now unless the right of perpetuity is granted, I, having
> found to be true the many causes and reasons advanced . . . have
> resolved to grant the right of perpetuity and order it to be enforced
> without any delay, and I also do so because the needs are great and
> powerful, and my kingdoms and states are in such a worn and dilapidated
> state, and I am under so many obligations to sustain and protect them . . .
> and above all because there is no possible help from other sources with
> enough to pay the large amounts owed. (in Zavala 1935, 205–206)[16]

The philosophical principles prevailing in the first disputes over the
apportioning of Indians are set aside in favor of fiscal considerations, above
all those related to the needs of the creditors of the monarch, whose royal
coffers were consumed by excessive international commitments and the
multiplicity of armed conflicts.

However, the perpetuity of the *encomiendas*, so strongly urged by Felipe
II ("without any delay") in the above communiqué, was not implemented.
On the contrary, it caused an intense battle among the principal actors
of the American drama, from the monarch to the native chiefs, and of
course the untiring Las Casas, who through letter after letter, memorandum after memorandum, concentrated his last energies in fighting against
the sale in perpetuity of the *encomiendas*.[17] Although many reasons were
given for opposing the royal decision, among them that the acknowledged
juridical freedom of the natives was being violated and that the economic
benefits for the Crown would be meager, the principal factor in stopping
it was the reiterated warning that a legislative measure of this kind would
facilitate the creation of powerful *criollo* castes, free from the control of the
Crown. In the long run this would lead to the rupture of loyalty to the
motherland, an evident omen of the sentiments that at the beginning of
the nineteenth century were nurtured by Hispano-American *criollo* leaders.

The Council of the Indies in its response to the young monarch recommended the suspension of the measure:

> In this matter of perpetuity . . . Y. M. would forever lose and alienate
> this great kingdom of yours that no other Christian prince or infidel
> possesses . . . and Y. M. would lose vassals. . . . The *encomenderos* would
> do their own will, and they could if they so wished exempt themselves
> from the dominion of Y. M. (Konetzke 1953, 1:358–359)

The representatives of the Crown in the negotiations with the colonists assumed a similar posture. In 1562, they wrote the monarch:

> It seems to us that one of the greatest inconveniences of perpetuity was and is that if perpetuity is granted in general, in thirty or forty years the descendants and successors would not have much love for the monarchs or realms of Spain or for their way of doing things, for they would not have known them. Rather, being born here, they would detest them as is regularly seen when a kingdom is governed by others, even if they be descendants of Spaniards . . . and they would easily rise up and not obey the monarchs of Castilla. (in Las Casas 1969, lxii–lxiii)

A few years earlier, in response to the monarch's decision, Las Casas had already cleverly raised the specter of republican *criollo* independence. "When the children and heirs see themselves so rich and powerful, and understand that their parents conquered the land and bought it from Your Majesty for so many millions, . . . would they fear to rise up . . . not knowing and hating to hear the name of the king?" (ibid., 88, 104).

The result is that the supposedly final ruling of Felipe II was suspended during all of his long reign, and the fight over perpetuity continued throughout the second half of the sixteenth century. The Crown kept distancing itself from the measure to avoid increasing the autonomous power of the colonists and tried to transform the *encomiendas* into royal favors, keeping their ultimate jurisdiction in the monarch's hands. The colonists reiterated from time to time the overused argument of the multiple benefits of perpetuity. That argument is found, among many other sources, in the *"Anónimo de Yucay"* (in Salvá [1848] 1964, 438).

> It would be fortunate for the Indians to give them Spanish lords in perpetuity . . . because in that way they would treat the Indians very well and as their own, and the Spaniards would become fond of this land and would forget Spain . . . making the kingdom very well ordered.

It was not until the eighteenth century that the system of *encomiendas* was eliminated.[18] Although in some regions the ban took many decades to take root, the order was issued by Felipe V on July 12, 1720 (in Konetzke 1953, 3:175–178). The decisive factor was not theoretical considerations in favor of the well-being of the natives, but the fiscal needs of the Crown, above all related to the military strengthening of Spain. The monarchs decided not to share with the *criollos* the tributes from the work and the assets of the natives. Belatedly and despoiled of every evangelical dressing, the old proposal defended by Bartolomé de las Casas was realized.

Whether or not that was a great triumph for the natives is debatable.

7

Rational Creatures
or Bruta Animalia?

Mine majordomos

[They] are like asses . . . are beastly in their vices . . . are not capable of doctrine . . . are traitors, cruel and vengeful, who never forgive; highly inimical toward religion, lazy, thieves . . . and of low judgment and spirit; do not keep faith or order . . . are as cowardly as hares, dirty as pigs; eat lice, spiders, and raw worms . . . do not have any human artistry or skills . . . they turn into brute animals; in all, I say that God never created people so set in vice and bestialities.

Fray Tomás Ortíz

The enemy of the same human race . . . inspired some of his satellites who, to please him, have not hesitated to publish abroad that the Indians . . . should be treated as dumb brutes created for our service, pretending that they are incapable of receiving the Catholic faith.

We . . . consider, however, that the Indians are truly human beings . . . [and] we decree and declare with our apostolic authority that the said Indians, even though they be outside the faith of Jesus Christ, are not to be deprived of their freedom; nor should they in any way be enslaved.

Pope Paul III

Bestiality of the Indians

The debate over the freedom and servitude of the natives is linked to different appraisals of their nature. The first great philosophical and theological dispute about the New World centered on the *humanity or bestiality of its inhabitants*.[1]

At the same time, some native peoples questioned the humanity or divinity of the Spaniards (Friederici 1986, 1:167–171). The first aborigines found by Columbus believed that he and his companions were celestial beings. According to the Admiral, they exclaimed: "Come and see the men who have come from heaven" (Varela 1986, 65). Moctezuma, perplexed at the possibility of the divine origin of Cortés and his cohorts, was fatally indecisive. An account in Nahuatl (the primary native language of Mexico) says that the Mexican chief "had the belief that they were gods, he took them to be gods." That caused him anguish and terror, which led him to say, according to the same account: "My heart is wounded unto death! Like it [is] being submerged in chile [hot pepper], it suffers great anguish, it is burning . . . !" (Sahagún [1482] 1985, 12.6–8:765–766).[2] Also, according to Acosta (1985, 5.3.220), the Peruvian natives called the Spaniards *viracochas* [divine], "for they believed they were children of heaven."[3]

Alonso de Ercilla (1984 [1945], 1:54 [39]; 2:58 [41]) considered that one of the reasons for the initial triumph of the Spaniards over the Araucans was that the Araucans "feared them as immortal gods . . . ; and our people were mistaken as supernatural." But soon, the Chilean native warriors "seeing they were born from man and woman . . . they perceived their stupid error, rage and shame blazed out from knowledge that their conquerors were mortal." The most interesting anecdote is of an incident that took place in Puerto Rico when a group of natives submerged a Spaniard in water to discover his mortality, and consequently his humanness (López de Gómara 1946, 180).[4] In general, the inhabitants of the continent soon discovered the humanness of the Europeans, not only because of their mortality, but also because of their intense greed.[5]

On occasion the natives were labeled as subhuman, "barbarians," or "beasts from a European perspective." Vitoria (Urdanoz 1960, 650) directly refers to those who claimed that the legitimacy of Spanish hegemony over "the barbarians of the New World" was based on the anthropological inferiority of the latter, "who really do not seem to be far from brute beasts." Las Casas refers to the judgment expressed by Gregorio, a scholar in the Castilian court in the 1520s, at the beginning of the debates over the nature of the natives, according to which "those Indians . . . are like talking animals" (Las Casas 1986, 2.3.12:472). It really was a debate about the rationality of the natives. According to Acosta (1952, 4.3:332), there were many Europeans who thought that the natives "were quadrupeds rather than rational men."

Ginés de Sepúlveda (1951, 35, 63) thought of the natives as *humunculos* ("little men in whom there is hardly any trace of humanness"; "hardly men"). John L. Phelan (1974, 293) summarizes his precise posture: "The Indians lacked *humanitas* . . . that quality of mind and spirit that makes a specific people competent to attain civilization." Based on that evaluation, Sepúlveda justifies their loss of dominion over their lands, their forced servitude, and the imposition of Christianity upon them. Sepúlveda is an Aristotelian humanist scholar. He uses the Aristotelian thesis on the difference between the nature of free humans and servants to justify the suitability of imposing a regime by masters on the natives of the continent. "The differing condition of men produces just forms of government and diverse types of just empires. In fact, men who are moral, human, and intelligent are apt for a civil empire, which is proper for free persons, or royal power."

"Men who are moral, human, and intelligent" and "free persons" are, above all, the Spaniards (and in general Christian Western Europeans). Since they possess genuine *humanitas*, a civil government befits their rationality and liberty. But there is another type of human being: "the barbarians . . . who have little discretion." There are two possible reasons for this inferiority, this lack of *humanitas*. "Either they are servants by nature, as they say exist in several regions of the world,[6] or because of their depraved customs . . . they cannot fulfill their duty in any other way." The natives of the Americas fit both descriptions: the natural-geographic and the socio-moral. "One and the other cause concur in the case of those barbarians." They do not qualify, therefore, for a government similar to the one enjoyed by Iberian subjects, but for a regime that Ginés de Sepúlveda (1951, 119–122) calls *"dominio heril"* [domination by masters], for a species in between free man and slave.

> Therefore, the difference between those who are free by nature and servants by nature, is the same that should exist between government applied to the Spaniards and that which is applied to those barbarians by natural law. The empire, therefore, should be shaped in such a way that the barbarians, in part by fear and force, in part by benevolence and equity, would be maintained within the limits of duty in such a way that they would not or could not plot uprisings against Spanish domination.

The nature of Sepúlveda's opinion about this issue rests, to a certain extent, on acceptance as original and authentic of the variable that appears in parts of his *Demócrates segundo* indicating the drastic difference between the inferiority of the natives and the superiority of the Spaniards ("as children are to adults, women to men") adds "denique quam simiae prope dixerim ab hominibus" ("finally, one could say as monkeys are to men"). Menéndez Pelayo included it in his 1892 Spanish edition. It also appeared in the edition published in Mexico by the Fondo de Cultura Económica (1941, 100). Angel Losada (Ginés de Sepúlveda 1951, 33), in the edition used here, discarded it.

We suspect that the phrase was eliminated by Sepúlveda himself from the original version to soften his thesis and attain the necessary authority to publish his book, especially after Pope Paul III's bull *Sublimis Deus* (1537), which affirmed the full humanity of the natives. Sepúlveda mentions the bull in his short treatise "Proposiciones temerarias, escandalosas y heréticas que notó el doctor Sepúlveda en el libro de la conquista de Indias, que fray Bartolomé de Las Casas, obispo que fué de Chiapa, hizo imprimir 'sin licencia' en Sevilla, año de 1552, cuyo título comienza: 'Aquí se contiene una disputa o controversia' " (Rash, scandalous, and heretical propositions noted by Dr. Sepúlveda in the book about the conquest of the Indies that Fray Bartolomé de las Casas, former bishop of Chiapa, had published 'without license' in Sevilla in 1552, whose title begins: 'Here is contained a dispute or controversy') (in Fabié [1879] 1966, 71:338). This treatise reflects the softening of his negative opinion in respect to the American natives. In a key passage he clarifies:

> The conquest of the Indies to bring those barbarians into subjection, eradicate their idolatry, and force them to keep the laws of nature even against their will, and after subjugating them, to preach the gospel *to them with Christian meekness without any force*, is a just and holy thing. And after they have been subjected, they shall not be killed or enslaved, or deprived of their estates, but made vassals of the king of Castilla . . . and that which is taken by force, outside the rights of war, is theft and shall be returned. (ibid., 351; emphasis added)[7]

The central differences between Sepúlveda and Las Casas, however, perdures since the latter (a) repudiates the concept of conquest, for it necessarily implies the violent usurpation of political sovereignty; (b) rejects the idea that conversion should be preceded or be conditioned by force of war; (c) censures the *encomiendas*, which Sepúlveda, on the contrary, includes as part of his "domination by masters"; (d) insists on the necessity of the Castilian empire being the object of a free autodetermination of the native communities, which for Sepúlveda would be absurd, because of the impossibility of obtaining a free and rational decision from nations not made up of men who are moral, human, intelligent, and "free."[8]

Maybe the first degrading affirmation about the natives was uttered by Dr. Diego Alvarez de Chanca, who accompanied Columbus on his second journey and sent a detailed report to Sevilla. In contempt of their eating habits ("they eat whatever snakes and geckos and spiders and whatever worms they find on the ground"), he asserts: "Their bestiality surpasses that of any other beast in the world" (in Fernández de Navarrete 1945, 1:349). The epithet "beastly" endured. It is found in innumerable descriptions of the social customs of the natives. Even José de Acosta, who considered himself a friend and protector of the natives, upon discovering that the Quechuas did not consider female premarital virginity an indispensable prerequisite to personal honor, is morally outraged and imputes bestiality to them. "The greater and almost divine honor that other peoples attribute to virginity, the greater seems the effrontery and ignominy of the attitude that these beasts have toward it" (Acosta 1952, 6.20:587).

Francisco López de Gómara (1946, 290) tells about the presentation that the Dominican friar Tomás Ortíz, who became the first bishop of Santa Marta, made to the Council of the Indies to defend the enslavement of natives:

The men from the mainland in the Indies eat human flesh and are more given to sodomy than all generations ever.[9] A state of justice does not exist among them . . . they are like asses, dumb, crazy in a mindless way; for them it is nothing to kill themselves and others; they do not tell the truth unless it is to their own benefit; they are irresolute; do not know what advice is; are very ungrateful . . . are beastly in their vices . . . are not capable of doctrine . . . are traitors, cruel and vengeful, who never forgive; highly inimical toward religion, lazy, thieves . . . and of low judgment and spirit; do not keep faith or order . . . are as cowardly as hares, dirty as pigs; eat lice, spiders, and raw worms . . . do not have any human artistry or skills . . . they turn into brute animals; in all, I say that God never created people so set in vice and bestialities.[10]

The Rationality of the Indian and Servile Work

The natives are declared beasts to legitimize converting them into property, into slaves. Beatriz Pastor (1984, 95, 101) is right: "It would become the metamorphosis of *man* into a *thing*, passing through a first metamorphosis of man into a beast . . . which would climax in the transformation of man into a commodity." A similar perception is reflected by Sebastián Ramírez de Fuenleal, bishop of Santo Domingo, when writing to Carlos V, on May 15, 1533, criticizing the opinion of Fray Domingo de Betanzos, who labeled the natives as beasts before the Council of the Indies. "Fr. Domingo de Betanzos . . . agreed to affirm what those people who want to consider them as beasts say so that they can seize their property" (in Cuevas 1946, 1:256).[11]

The same thesis is underscored by Julián Garcés, Dominican friar and first bishop of Tlaxcala, in an extensive letter sent to Pope Paul III shortly before he issued his famous bull *Sublimis Deus*. Garcés censures:

The false doctrine of those who instigated by the devil's suggestions affirm that the Indians are incapable of our religion (*incapaces religionis nostrae*). This voice, which is really from Satan . . . is a voice coming from the avarice of Christians, who are so greedy that to quench their thirst they want to establish that rational creatures (*rationabiles creaturas*) made in the likeness of God are beasts and stupid . . . with the only aim of using them in their service at will. . . . And hence some Spaniards . . . have come to think that it is not sinful to devalue, destroy, or kill them. (Xirau 1973, 90–92)

For Garcés, on the contrary, the American natives "are entitled to be called rational, and have full sense and mind" (in ibid.).[12]

The same approach was taken six decades later by Mendieta (1980, 1.5:28):

> [Due] to the craving for gold and silver . . . worldly men, without feel-ings for God nor charity toward their neighbors, have always reported that these peoples are beastly, without judgment or understanding, full of vices and abominations, implying that they are incapable of doc-trine . . . believing these things and other similar ones, to which the devil our enemy and greed for the things of this world easily persuade some . . . so that no attention be given to the souls God has created in these lands, but only to money and other temporal goods that would be gotten from them.

Fray Antonio de Remesal ([1619] 1932, 1.16.1:206), in his critical evalua-tion of the initial intent to dehumanize the natives by pretending that they were *bruta animalia* (irrational animals), integrated the adventurers' avarice and greed with the popular theological vision of a historically active Lucifer. According to this Dominican historian, this unhealthy opinion started in Española, which had become "a school of Satan."

> Thus these [Spaniards], who used so much cruelty and inhumanity against the Indians, though scolded and reprehended by the preachers of the gospel and by the pious . . . came to deny such a clear and evi-dent principle that Indians are men, and thus rob them of their very personhood, deprive them of their children and their estates as if they did not have any more control over their things than the wild animals of the field. That diabolical opinion started in the island of Española, and it was in great measure so as to finish off the former inhabitants of the island, and since all the people who came to that new world of the Indies passed first through that island, it was like entering into a school of Satan to learn this hellish outlook and belief.

Fray Domingo de Betanzos, who, as we said before, had been criti-cized by Bishop Ramírez de Fuenleal for calling the natives beasts before the Council of the Indies, in order to free his conscience before his death, made a retraction and admitted the link between the brutalization of the natives and the greedy exploitation of their work.

> I, Fray Domingo de Betanzos, friar of Saint Dominic, who because I spoke many times on matters relating to the Indians concerning their defects, and placed a memorandum before the Council of the Indies . . .

treating of these defects, saying that they were beasts and were sinful and that God had sentenced them and they would all perish . . . and as a result some people out of greed have caused great destruction and death to the Indians; and have wanted to excuse their conduct, seeking authorization for it in many statements they attributed to me. . . . I say to you and beg you . . . not to give any credence to anything I wrote, preached, or spoke against the Indians . . . for my words are harmful and worthy of retraction . . . being prejudicial and an obstacle to the preaching of the faith, and not helpful to the health of those souls and bodies. (in Las Casas 1962, 184–186)

The priest and official representative Tomás López (in Hanke 1985, 1964) inverted the description of bestiality and applied it to those who exploit the work and life of the natives: "Even though we had falsely said that the Indians are beasts, it is the Spaniards who have become savage animals." The bestiality of the Spaniards is shown in "that they give such great care to their own beasts that as a result the Indians suffer for lack of food."

Acosta (1985, 6.1:280) also pointed to the close link between disregard for the rational nature of the natives and their use as beasts of burden. He criticized "the false opinion that is commonly had of them as unintelligent people, bestial and without understanding." More important still, he perceived the self-interest that underlies that depreciation: "They employ so much deceit in committing many great injuries against them, using them as if they were animals."

It is Las Casas who above all fully realized the material interest behind the description of the natives as *bruta animalia:* then they can be utilized as beasts of burden for the enrichment of the colonists. What seems to be a theoretic posture in respect to the nature of reality is in fact, according to his demythologizing criticism, a badly concealed justification for the use of the natives as means of production: "Those that are esteemed and appreciated less than beasts . . . are taken as means and instruments to acquire riches" (Las Casas 1965, 1:719). The cause of the bestialization of the natives has been "the vehement, blind, and disorderly greed from which all harm and evil come." In order to utilize the work of the natives without any consideration for them they "defamed them, and caused those who had not seen them to be in doubt as to their human or animal nature." Together with this "infamy," there is another assertion that Las Casas stigmatized as "bestial heresy": namely, "that they are incapable of Catholic faith" (Las Casas 1986, 2.1.1:206–207; 3.3.99:167).

The position taken in regard to the subhumanness of the American natives did not come, according to Las Casas, from a genuine philosophical analysis of their reasoning faculties. It arose, rather, from the heart of conquerors and *encomenderos*, among them Francisco de Garay, Juan Ponce de León, Pedro García de Carrión, and "other neighbors of the island [Española] . . . who had many Indians in servitude."

> All or some of them were the first . . . to defame the Indians at court by saying they could not govern themselves and needed tutors; and that wickedness continued to grow until they debased them to the point of saying they were incapable of faith, which is not a small heresy, and made them equal to beasts . . . and that they could not govern themselves in order to . . . make use of them in that hellish servitude in which they placed them . . . and so as to make them work. (Las Casas 1986, 2.3.8:455–456)

It is not sufficient to affirm, as Maravall (1974, 322) does in a valuable work, that the positive and negative images of the natives "should not be taken to be a testimony of reality, but as imagined representations of the exotic worlds, ideologically constituted and dependent, above all, on the vision that one or other persons have of ancient societies." One has to take a forward step and point out the central element in the "dispute of the New World": that is, the legality or not of exploiting the manual labor of the natives and the expropriation of their possessions and goods. It is true that such images are "ideologically constituted," but one has to show their decisive convergence with the antagonistic socioeconomic projects.

A few years ago, there was a cordial but intense divergence on the central point of that dispute between Lewis Hanke and Lino Gómez Canedo. According to Hanke (1985, 22–81), the question centered on the nature or essence of the natives: are they human beings or irrational beasts? According to Gómez Canedo (1967, 1:29–51), the axis of the debate, on the contrary, was not the humanity of the aborigines, something which in his opinion had not really been denied, but whether they had a right to their unconditional freedom, to control of their possessions and lands, and could they be compelled to work for the primary well-being of the Castilians. It seems that the analysis of the texts reveals how intertwined both issues were. However, the weight of the debate favored Gómez Canedo's position. In spite of the sometimes extremely denigrating words of such persons as Tomás de Ortíz, very few people were ready to deny that the Indians were closer to the Europeans than to irrational beasts. The problem was whether they were endowed with an *inferior rationality* that would make it impossible for them to be fully instructed in the Christian faith and to govern themselves adequately as persons or as nations, a situation that would bring with it the necessity for some sort of compulsory tutelage. When the dean of Santo Domingo in Española, Rodrigo de Bastidas, suggests before the Council of the Indies that American natives are "all beastly and incapable, and live and die bestially," he does not think he is stating a fact of anthropological philosophy, but that he is describing the savagery or cultural barbarism of the native peoples (in Hanke 1985, 77).[13] Such a state of nature can have diverse implications, but those who defend it concur at least that it implies incapacity for self-government and the need for an enforced work regime.

Las Casas, upon recognizing the full humanity of the natives, insisted that their full individual and collective liberty be respected. He faced not only a "dehumanizing concept" of the natives, but also its corollary: their utilization as mere instruments of enrichment. In his letter to Bartolomé Carranza de Miranda, August 1555, he reiterated his criticism "of the blindness and diabolical evil . . . which the Spaniards themselves perpetrated: namely, to have defamed those Indians as beasts," an evaluation that is used to establish a supposedly despotic government whose true finality is "to rob them and oppress them and hold them in servitude" — then, with greater prophetic indignation, he adds: "to become rich through blood" (in Fabié [1879] 1966, 71:414, 416).

"All the Nations of the World Are Human"

The Las Casas position is built on the thesis that the natives are creatures "endowed with reason," (Las Casas 1965, 1239) with "lively understanding," (1989, 17), created like the Europeans in the image and likeness of God. He stresses the equal nature of Europeans and natives, since "there is only one . . . species of rational creatures . . . dispersed throughout the world" (Las Casas 1942, 13). It is fitting, therefore, to recognize their full humanity as beings endowed with intellect, who also constitute *imago et similitudo Dei.*[14] Phelan (1974, 302) has indicated with good reason that the identification of human nature in Las Casas has two roots: the ontological definition of the rational unity of the human species from classic Greco-Roman philosophy, and the medieval ideal of the universality of divine grace.

Compared to other Europeans, Las Casas sometimes gets carried away by his great love of the natives and magnifies their virtues, both intellectual and ethical, thus becoming one of the main sources of the modern myth of the "noble savage" (Abellán 1976).

> Our native nations . . . are endowed with true genius; and more so that
> in them there are individuals in greater numbers than in other nations
> of the earth with a very perceptive understanding of the principles gov-
> erning human life [*ingeniosiores ad regimen humanae vitae*]. (Las Casas
> 1942, 3)

> They live in very large cities in which they wisely administer every-
> thing . . . with justice and equity, governed really by laws that in many
> aspects are superior to ours and could have gained the admiration of
> the wise men from Athens. (Las Casas 1974, 43)

But this point should not be overly exaggerated. The central and
decisive emphasis of Las Casas is not on the superiority of the natives,
untouched by avarice and European corruption (his enthusiasm for the
natives does not lessen his heartfelt preference for the literary and theological culture of the West), but in the profound ontological and religious
unity between human beings on both sides of the ocean.

To a dehumanizing and mercantilist vision he juxtaposes the full
humanity of the natives. When debating with his ideological rivals, he
focuses the polemic on the destiny of the souls of the natives: they are
perfectly capable of understanding and accepting the Christian faith. In
his dispute of 1519 with the bishop of Darién, Juan de Quevedo, he asserts:
"Those people . . . with which the New World is teeming and filled, are
very capable of the Christian faith and of every virtue and good habit
through reason and Christian doctrine, and of their very *natura* [nature]
are free" (Las Casas 1986, 3.3.149:343). The accomplishment of a rational
and pacific conversion of "those peoples" should be the regulatory norm
of the Spanish Crown in the lands that Providence has granted it.

The idea that the natives have defects in their humanity—to consider
them "beasts incapable of doctrine and virtue" who allegedly lack the
"quality of human nature" —Las Casas considers "scandalous and false
science and perverse conscience." Such ideas imply an affront to the "dignity of the rational creature," and still worse, to God, who is responsible
for "consenting to create . . . [this] monstrous species . . . lacking in
understanding and without talent for governing human life" (ibid.,
1:13–20). For the Dominican friar, "all nations of the world are human and
there is only one definition for each and all of them: they are all rational;
all possess understanding and will and freedom, formed to the image and
likeness of God" (ibid., 2.2.58:396).

To demonstrate this thesis he writes a monumental work: *Apologética
historia sumaria*, the most impressive effort on the part of a white and Christian European to demonstrate the rational integrity and full humanity of
non-European, non-white and non-Christian nations.[15] The whole purpose

of this extraordinary work is to demonstrate in a multiplicity of ways the same thesis we have seen, namely: "All nations of the world are human" (Las Casas 1967, 1.3.48:257–258). This universal rationality and capacity for intelligent self-determination is denied in the case of the natives so as to exploit their work without scruples. The Spaniards, who wanted to obtain the most wealth possible by means of "harsh slavery" and "heavy oppression" of "innumerable peoples," without any religious or ethical impediment, invented the false idea that the native Americans were

> so far from the reason common to all men, that they were not capable of governing themselves . . . they had no qualms in affirming that those men were beasts or almost beasts . . . and that, therefore, they could use them at will. (Las Casas 1942, 363)

Las Casas reaffirms that "these gentle people from our Indies are human nations" are "reasonable," endowed with reason, because "no nation in the world was excluded from this human and universal property by Divine Providence." If some of its nations seem "primitive and barbaric" (Las Casas 1967, 1.3.48:257–258; see Las Casas 1986, 2.1.175:171), so had in the past many communities considered cultured and civilized today, such as Spain. It is a matter of educating them with persuasive arguments suited to their intelligence and pleasing to their will.

The idea that the American natives "are human nations" implies something more than the affirmation that they should not be enslaved, that they are individually free. It implies also collective and political freedom. As a result, in his reply to Bishop Quevedo, Las Casas not only insisted that the natives are individually free and fit to receive the Christian faith, but he also defends "their right to lordship." "By nature they are free and have their natural lords and kings who govern their realms" (ibid., 3.3.149:343). It was in defense of this thesis that he dedicated the extensive juridical-political treatise *Los tesoros del Perú* (1563). From this anthropological conception Las Casas developed his frustrated utopia, in which the Spanish Christian empire would sustain, not abolish, the original political structures of the native nations and respect their autonomy and self-determination.

As José Maravall (1974, 315–327) points out, Las Casas, while defending the full humanity of the natives, lays down the bases for a new *cosmopolitanism*, which he bases partly on the revival of classic stoicism, and partly on the empirical proof of the similarity between the inhabitants of the old and new continents. Note, however, that Las Casas maintains the medieval ideal of the *orbis christianus*, the preeminently theological and religious character of the unity of the human species. In the acute debate with Quevedo, he affirms the correlation between the unity of the human race and the universality of the Christian faith: "Our Christian religion is the same and can be adapted to all the nations of the world and from all it equally receives, and it does not take from any of them their lordships nor does it subjugate them" (Las Casas 1986, 3.3.149:343).

I do not share the hypothesis of Maravall on the "obvious level of secularization" of the thought of Las Casas. In his long treatise on the injustice of all forms of slavery to which the natives have been subjected, Las Casas stresses, without neglecting the demand of the natural law and universal morality, the biblical and evangelical demands. The principal problem for the European is that in violating divine law one incurs *mortal sin*, putting the *salvation of one's soul* in grave danger.

> Since the Spaniards have the Indians unjustly as slaves and against their conscience, they are always in mortal sin, and therefore do not live the Christian life and are impeded from their salvation. . . . Your Majesty is obliged by divine precept to order the Spaniards that the Indians they have in the Indies as slaves and whom they deprived of their liberty should be returned to their original state. (Las Casas 1965, 1:601)

The accent is not on the obvious fact that the "bodily differences between them [Spaniards and Indians] are few and do not alter the human figure, and that reproduction between individuals from the different sexes was possible" (Maravall 1974, 324), but on the ontological similarity of a common rationality, and on the same capacity to respond effectively to saving divine grace. Las Casas creates a peculiar and fertile convergence between stoic rational cosmopolitanism, the Christian conception of the unity of the human race, and the verification of the substantial similarity between Europeans and natives. All of that results in the categoric statement we have cited: "All the nations of the world are human."

Aristotle and the "Barbarians"

Las Casas is ready to use in a positive way the philosophical premise of his antagonists: the argument made by Aristotle, in the first book of *Politics*, about natural slavery. Although on some occasions he said that the peripatetic philosopher "was a gentile and was burning in hell" (Las Casas 1986, 3.3.149:343), he knows perfectly well the precarious nature of that position, especially among his brother friars, followers of Saint Thomas Aquinas, the great theologizer of Aristotle. So he tries, with greater reflective serenity, to refute the idea that American natives belong to the Aristotelian category of servants by nature. Three characteristics are indications of their full humanness: the harmony of their physical presence ("they are of a very good disposition"); prudence and wisdom in their political life ("they have an orderly republic, they have gubernatorial and elective prudence"); and their individual intelligence ("they have sufficient science and ability to govern themselves") (ibid., 3.3.151:348–351). In the course of his exegesis he develops a line of interpretation that is, however, foreign to *Politics* and that is more in keeping with his universal cosmopolitanism than with the Aristotelian intention. Thus, Aristotle's category of servant becomes a strange monster, difficult to find, contrary to the intention of the Greek thinker of stressing the superiority of the Hellenists over the barbarians to justify the servitude of the latter.

A similar exposition is found in Diego de Covarrubias, in his treatise of 1547, "De iustitia belli adversus indos," (Of the justice of the war against the Indians) (in Pereña 1956, 205), in which this disciple of Vitoria concludes that the American natives do not fall within the category of the natural slave in Aristotle.

> I understand that his words refer to men created by nature in such a way that they roam in the fields, like vagabonds without law, without any political organization; in short, I would say men born to obey and to serve others just like beasts and wild animals which they resemble, and in reference to whom Aristotle says that one can exercise over them the art of the hunt as against beasts. But I doubt that Indians can be counted as being like them. . . . They live in cities, towns, and villages, they appoint kings whom they obey, and they practice many other things that demonstrate that they have knowledge of mechanical arts and of morality, and *are endowed with reason.* (emphasis added)

Las Casas and Covarrubias reflect the theoretical problem that the Aristotelian conception of the slave by nature posed for the Spanish theologians who attempted to explain the cultural inferiority of the natives. The main difficulty comes from the incompatibility between the Aristotelian idea of some beings who by reason of their being congenitally inferior exist by nature to serve and who can then be justly subjugated by force, and the Christian vision of the essential unity of the entire human race, strengthened in the course of time by the stoic conception of the universality of reason. This causes difficulties at both ends: on the one hand, those like Sepúlveda try to utilize the Aristotelian notion to legitimate the conquest and the domination of the natives by masters, since they easily come into conflict with Christian doctrine as to the essential unity of all human beings; and on the other hand, those like Las Casas and

Covarrubias attempt to show that the servants by nature to whom Aristotle refers are beings that, in historical reality, are almost nonexistent, without noting that the Hellenic philosopher seems to refer to great multitudes of barbarians. Vitoria (Urdanoz 1960, 664–665, 723–724) tries to resolve the problem through educational tutelage. But he hesitates when faced with the possibility that such an explanation will serve to legitimate the armed conquest of the natives. Those who participated in the debate, however, did not perceive that the problem was created, mostly, by their use of an ahistorical hermeneutics incapable of placing Aristotle's texts in their specific temporal and cultural context, one that was very different from that created in the sixteenth century in the confrontation between Europeans and American natives.[16]

Las Casas does not admit that the lack of a civilizing development in various indigenous nations justifies individual slavery or the loss of their collective lordship. Rather, that lack should stimulate an arduous process of education, to be carried out through peaceful, gentle, and persuasive means, and not violently or by war. It cannot be forgotten that centuries earlier Spain was a nation of few cultural achievements. In some texts he is willing to recognize serious moral defects and political imprudence in the peoples and nations of the Americas.[17] But he considers that they can be overcome through a persuasive and pacific process of integration into Christian culture and ethics.

Las Casas creates a taxonomy of the different meanings of the word "barbarian" in a section later added to his *Apologética* (1967, vol. 2, ch. 264–267:637–654). It is a type of postlude in cultural philosophy, written at the end of his combative existence. He distinguishes four variations in the concept. The first refers to the actions and attitudes of a human being generally reasonable but sometimes allowing himself to be possessed by great flares of passion and wildness, to the point of committing a "barbaric act." The second denotes those cultures that do not yet have a literature, or do not speak our language correctly, or have different political characteristics. The third implies rude and wild beings, beastly in conduct and customs, the only ones to whom the term can be applied without correctives. Finally, the term "barbarians" is applied to the infidels, and these can either be guilty and consider themselves enemies of Christianity, such as the Turks, or not guilty by reason of not having heard preaching about Christ. The natives of the New World fall in the second category and in the second subdivision of the fourth. As a result of both of these reasons they cannot be declared irrational, inept for self-government, or incapable of accepting and fully understanding the Christian faith.

A Diminished Victory

The Las Casas position won out on the theological and juridical levels. In the theological realm, this was thanks to the *Sublimis Deus* bull of Pope Paul III, according to which:

> The sublime God so loved the human race that He created man in such wise . . . and endowed him with capacity to attain to the inaccessible and invisible Supreme Good and behold it face to face. . . . [A]ll are capable of receiving the doctrines of the faith.
>
> The enemy of the human race, who opposes all good deeds in order to bring men to destruction . . . he inspired his satellites who, to please him, have not hesitated to publish abroad that the Indians . . . should be treated as dumb brutes created for our service, pretending that they are incapable of receiving the Catholic faith.
>
> We . . . consider, however, that the Indians are truly human beings and that they are . . . capable of understanding the Catholic faith. . . .
>
> By virtue of our apostolic authority We define and declare . . . that said Indians, and all other people who may later be discovered by Christians, are by no means to be deprived of their liberty or the possession of their property, even though they be outside the faith of Jesus Christ; and that they may and should, freely and legitimately, enjoy their liberty and the possession of their property; nor should they be in any way enslaved; should the contrary happen it shall be null and of no effect.
>
> . . . [A]nd said Indians and other peoples should be converted to the faith of Jesus Christ by preaching the word of God and by the example of good and holy living.[18]

Las Casas also triumphed in the juridical field with the New Laws, which stressed the will of Spanish authorities as follows:

> Because our principal will and intent has always been and is to preserve and increase the Indians and that they be . . . treated as free persons . . . we charge and command the Council [of the Indies] to always give much attention and special care above all to the preservation and good government and treatment of the Indians . . . and we order that from now on in no way whatsoever may the Indians be enslaved. (Konetzke 1953, 1:217)

Sublimis Deus links rationality with the ability to fully assimilate the Christian religion. The *indófobos* (Indian foes) deny the rationality of the natives or drastically restrict it. Their denial is not motivated by philosophical reasoning, but is advanced as a pretext so as to justify the imposition of servile labor on the natives. Their central objective is social subjugation: "And they effectively reduce them to servitude, burdening them with as much work as they load on the irrational animals in their service." If they cannot be fully Christian, if they have deficient intelligence, then they could be enslaved and have their goods confiscated. If, on the contrary, they are identical in nature to the Europeans, "they cannot be deprived of their liberty, nor of dominion over their own things." The dispute centers on two concurrent axes: the divergent evaluations of Indian rationality and the legitimacy of imposing on them forced labor to benefit the European economy.

The thesis of the rational inferiority of Indians, of their subhuman-ness or semi-bestiality, defeated at the theoretical level of theology and jurisprudence, was kept alive and in bloom. It was reiterated by Bernardo de Vargas Machuca (in Fabié [1879] 1966, 225–227; emphasis added), gover-nor of the island of Margarita, in his fierce criticism of the Las Casas work *Brevísima destrucción de las Indias*. According to this calloused veteran of multiple battles against the Indians, the American natives, thanks to Satan's pernicious influence, are *bruta animalia*.

> The devil's malice ordinarily attempts to take away reason from humans so as to convert them into *brute animals*, the way that he has possessed these Indians for such a long time. . . . They are by all means the cruelest people on earth, they are as beastly as they are cruel, and it is my opinion and that of many who have dealt with them, that if you wish a picture of cruelty all you need to do is picture an Indian . . . people without . . . reason, vicious and without honor . . . they are more beastly than irra-tional animals. . . . Most of them are idolaters and talk to the Devil.

In the introduction and exhortation to the reading of this work, Zoyl Diez Flores, friend and colleague of Vargas Machuca, adds his negative appraisal of the natives:

> These peoples are by nature barbarians and without any prudence, con-taminated by barbaric vices. . . . And that is how they could be forced into subjection by arms; and the war of natural law against them is just because those who do not have by nature the openness to be induced into better living by the doctrine of words, it is necessary to place them under the yoke as beasts. (ibid., 212; emphasis added)

During the middle of the seventeenth century, Juan de Solórzano y Pereyra, in his *Política indiana* (1930, 1.9:92–94), articulates after the will of divine providence and the discovery/occupation a third valid title to legiti-mate the Castilian domination of the New World, the so often repeated thesis about the intellectual inferiority of the natives:

The just and legitimate establishment of the supreme domination of our Monarchs was possible: because they were such barbarians, uncultured, and primitive that *they hardly deserved to be called men.* . . . From which we can take the third title, and we cannot underrate those who are in such a primitive condition that it is not good to leave them free for *they lack reason* . . . as they say it was really the case in many parts. And Fr. Tomás Ortíz, bishop of Darién, in the presence of the Emperor Carlos V dared to state it about all of them in general. Because those who are so brutish, and barbaric, are considered as beasts more than as men. . . . To make them Christian, it was necessary to make them men first . . . and force them, and teach them so they could be considered and treated as such.

Oviedo goes a step further in the dehumanization of the natives in the famous passage where he demonizes them. While Las Casas lamented the depopulation of the island of Española, Oviedo (1851, 1.1.5.3:141) affirmed: "Satan has now been uprooted from this island: he has ceased to be here with the extermination of most of the Indians, and because those who are left are very few and at the service of the Christians."[19]

Ironically, the depreciation of the natives is also found in many of their protectors' texts. There are many who, when valiantly facing the exploitation suffered by the natives, assumed a clearly paternal posture that considered their defendants as "children," "invalids" in need of someone to act on their behalf or speak for them. In a report to Felipe II, the Council of the Indies defends Castilian perpetual sovereignty over the Indian nations, for they "have not arrived at adulthood, but are as minor children with bad habits who have a perennial need of tutors" (Pereña in Las Casas 1969, lxxviii). More intense is the loving but subjugating paternalism reflected by the Augustinian Pedro Xuárez de Escobar.

All these Indians are like little birds in their nests, who have not yet grown wings nor will grow them to learn to fly alone, but who always have need of their caring parents to bring fat and nourishment to their nests so they will not die of hunger and perish. . . . I wish Y. M. to know that the religious alone are their fathers and mothers, their scholars and procurators, their defenders and protectors . . . with them they rest while crying and complaining as children with their mothers. . . . [Place] your eyes of mercy on these miserable Indians to do them so much good so that they not be abandoned by their religious ministers nor deprived of them, because the day the religious are missing that will be their end. (in Cuevas [1914] 1975, 311–312)[20]

Mendieta also asserts that in order for the American natives to be saved there is a need to link persuasive preaching and exemplary life to the authority of the "spiritual fathers" whom the natives are "to fear and respect, as children do their parents, and as children taught in school by their teachers." Mendieta, whose sympathy for the natives is undeniable, defends the ecclesiastical norm barring natives from priestly ordination or religious vows because they have a peculiar characteristic: "they are not good for giving orders or governing, but for being ordered and governed . . . are not good for being teachers only disciples, nor to be prelates, but only . . . to be subjects." These "childish people" do not have the quality of character, nor the authority or firmness needed to be priests (Mendieta 1980, 1.4:26; 4.23:448–449; 4.46:563).[21]

Also Acosta (1952, 1.17:126), in a similar trend of thought, states this about the American natives: "There is no more docile nation . . . they have a desire to imitate what they see; with those who have power and authority they are extremely submissive, and immediately do what they are ordered." That was a virtue frequently praised by friars and monks—it constituted the subjective source for their unquestioned authority. Underneath, a subtle contempt persists.

Education of the Natives

In spite of *Sublimis Deus*, some clerics refused for years to give the eucharist to many natives, as they considered them incapable of being true Christians. During the first century of colonial domination they were not accepted into the priesthood either. In 1544, several important Dominicans in New Spain were opposed to allowing the Indians to study for the priesthood:

> No fruit can be expected from their study . . . because they have not the ability to understand surely and correctly certain things of the faith nor their reasons, nor is their language abundant enough to serve to explain the faith without great improprieties that can easily lead to errors. And it follows that they should not be ordained, for it would be better for their reputation if they are not. Because even the sacrament of the eucharist is not given to them, for numerous reasons given by many learned and religious persons. . . . It is therefore very necessary that they should be removed from study. (Pacheco et al. 1864–1884, 7:541–542)

Their thesis did not go without controversy. Years before, a group of Franciscans in Mexico, led by the Provincial Fray Jacobo de Testera, in a letter to the emperor, May 6, 1533, had articulated the opposite position:

Whatever they say about their incapability, how can one be so incapable who has created such sumptuous buildings, shown such care in the creation of handiwork of such subtlety . . . and finally, [been] so capable in exhibiting such discipline in ethical, political, and economic life? . . . What shall we say of the children of the natives from this land?

They write, read, sing plain chant and counterpoint with the organ, they compose, teach others; the music and rejoicing of ecclesiastical song is within them; and they preach to the people the sermons we teach them, and deliver them with great spirit. . . . And that sovereign God who works hidden miracles in their hearts knows it, and even through their actions it would be seen by those who are not blinded by malice or ignorance. (in Cuevas 1946, 1:262).

The Franciscan Bernardino de Sahagún (1985, 20) reaffirms what was explicitly stated before by his brother friars.

It is very certain that all these people are our brothers proceeding from the same trunk of Adam like us, are our neighbors. . . . They have ability for all the mechanical arts . . . are also capable of learning all the liberal arts, and holy theology, as experience shows in all those who have been taught these sciences.

Here we can see the humanizing effect of Christian doctrine on the monogenetic origin of all humanity. All human beings, independently of their actual cultural developments, are descendants of Adam, the first man created by God. All, therefore, have an identical transcendent spiritual finality.[22] All can be educated to serve in the holy priesthood.

Sahagún (1985, 583) relates his efforts to facilitate the liberal education of the natives. When his efforts begin to show fruit, there arises firm opposition from many Spaniards: "Laymen as well as ecclesiastics began to oppose this business and to have many objections against it." The root of that opposition seems to be philosophical, that is, doubts about the rational capacity of the natives, but in reality it arises from an astute fear that the Spaniards' educational monopoly, the basis for their social and economic hegemony, would be eroded. What need do field workers and laborers have of higher education? Robert Ricard (1986, 347), who cannot be accused of being antagonistic toward the Catholic missionary work in Mexico, astutely asserted: "The principal cause of the vehement opposition to the college at Tlatelolco on the part of the clergy and general opinion arose precisely because the majority of Spaniards in Mexico did not wish to see Indians being formed for the priesthood."[23]

The possibility of entering the priesthood was closed to the natives during the sixteenth century in all of the Americas. In Nueva España, in 1555, the ecclesiastical council decided against the creation of a native clergy.

In Peru, the First Limeño Council in 1552 and the second in 1567 decided the same thing. The second council affirmed: "The Council feels, and orders it to be observed thus, that these Indians . . . should not be initiated in any sacred order." Acosta defends this statute with words that, in spite of his reiterated sympathy toward the natives, do not cease to be offensive. "The severity with which the sacred writings reprove priests that come from the dregs of the people is to be admired. . . . They consider it great wickedness to be given ministers who are commoners and evil" (Acosta 1952, 1.6.19, 581; 582).[24]

In 1568, a royal decree was issued reprimanding the bishop of Quito for having

> conferred orders on [ordained] mestizos . . . which, as you may consider, is a grave inconvenience for many reasons and mainly because . . . they are not the persons who should be given those orders for they are not devout, virtuous, and fit. . . . For now you should not in any way, confer sacred orders on those mestizos. (Konetzke 1953, 1:436)

Aware of the intention of the ecclesiastical Peruvian authorities to ordain mestizo priests, Felipe II, on December 2, 1578, forbade it by means of a royal decree "until after having considered it, you are advised as to what should be done" (Konetzke 1953, 514). This "consideration" took a decade. On August 31, 1588, the same monarch after an intense debate in the Council of the Indies determined that mestizo priests could be ordained and mestizos could take religious vows if they were of proven virtue and knowledge. The decree does not grant this same right to pure-blooded Indians, who remained excluded from the religious state during all of the sixteenth century (Konetzke 1953, 595–596).

According to Ricard (1986, 23, 349, 355), the exclusion of natives from the priesthood was a grave error.

> The Mexican church, like that of Peru . . . was as a result an incomplete foundation. Or better, a Mexican church was not founded, and barely the bases were established for a *criolla* church; what was founded, was first and above all a Spanish church, organized according to the Spanish model, directed by Spaniards and where the native faithful played the role of second-rate Christians. . . . It was not a national church; it was a colonial church. . . . Even religious life in its most humble forms was forbidden to the Indians. . . . This error kept the Mexican church from becoming deeply rooted in the nation and gave it the aspect of a foreign institution that remained intimately dependent on the metropolis.[25]

The discussion was in the first instance theological, but if we remember the indissoluble link between theological discourse and politics that we posited earlier as a fundamental hermeneutical key to decipher the debates surrounding the conquest, we shall see its extra-ecclesial implications. If the natives have a capacity for the priesthood and the spiritual guidance of souls, will they not also have it for conducting their own affairs in self-government and the temporal management of their affairs? The question of education is indissolubly linked to the problem of personal liberty and the self-determination of nations. The intellectual formation indispensable for priestly ordination would have been the first step to the full assumption of their own governance, first in ecclesiastical matters and later in social and political ones.[26] To avoid this possible consequence the testimonies about the inveterate "vices" of the natives were multiplied: "lack of authority, inebriation, ineptitude for intellectual work, for the guidance of souls, and for celibacy" (Ricard 1986, 349).

The situation in Hispanic America was not exceptional. Both Iberian nations (Spain and Portugal) failed to promote the formation of native clergy in their vast ultramarine empires. Only at the end of the eighteenth century when it was already too late to save the vast Spanish-American empire did the Crown hurry to promote the formation of an indigenous clergy.[27] The royal decrees could not prevent the imminent political debacle (Boxer 1978, 1–30).

8

The Battle of the Gods

*City of Hell: Heavy punishments; Prince of Darkness;
the rich, avaricious, ungrateful, lascivious, arrogant;
punishment of the haughty wealthy and sinners
who do not fear God.*

They are in error and deceived by the devils, enemies of the human race, concurring in abominable vices and sins, which will bring them to damnation and to suffer the sorrows and eternal fire of hell.

Gerónimo de Mendieta

I think that it is by divine consent that so many of them die because of the evil they commit against the divine majesty. . . . One should believe that it was the divine will not to allow such an idolatrous and perverse people to escape, and that this divine will also wished to sow the holy faith in that land, inhabiting it with Christian people who were Spaniards.

Bernardo de Vargas Machuca

Satanic Idolatry

In the sixteenth century, colonists, conquerors, friars, defenders, or detractors of the human dignity of the natives lacked respect for *cultural diversity* in the crucial matter of religion. From the prism of Spanish Catholicism, the native religions were considered false and idolatrous, the adoration of false gods caused by satanic forces. There were intense debates over whether Christianization should be by peaceful or persuasive means, or if military force was legitimate. But in general, the different parties were in agreement on the false and demonic nature of native worship and the urgency to abolish it.

That disregard for native worship is found in the Spanish texts of the first century of the conquest, from Ramón Pané, the first to try to understand the mythology and religion of the American natives, to Gerónimo de Mendieta. When speaking of the beliefs of the native Taínos in Española, Pané (1987, 35) says: "The things that those simple ignorant people believe that their idols [cemíes] do, or better, those devils . . ."[1] Anglería (1964–1965, 1.9.1:198) summarizes the lost treatise by Pané and reflects a similar opinion when referring to Taíno religious images. "All have been already subjugated by the Christians and without exception the obstinate ones are dead, without any trace of the *zemes* [cemíes], which have been taken to Spain so that we could understand the effrontery and deceit of their devils."

The opinion from Anglería is not surprising, but that Las Casas, who also read the lost manuscript, shared the same vision of Taíno religion as diabolical deceit definitely is.

[The Arawaks] did not have idols, only rarely, and then not for worship, but only to be used imaginatively by certain priests used by the devil. . . .

They did not have external or visible ceremonies, but only a few, and these were conducted by those priests whom the devil appointed as his ministers. (Las Casas 1967, 1.3.120:632)

In another passage of his *Apologética historia sumaria* (1.3.71–74:369–387), Las Casas develops a more complex vision of Indian idolatry with three components: (a) it comes from the inherent human impulse to know and venerate God (natural inclination to latria); (b) that impulse toward the divine is distorted by the perverse action of the devils (becoming idolatry); and (c) this parody of authentic worship becomes embedded by custom. In another section, Las Casas makes a theologically interesting remark that he, however, does not develop: the American natives initially "had a special knowledge of the true God" —he does not say how they had arrived at it— "and they went to him with his sacrifices, worship, and veneration," but "the main enemy of humanity," Satan, linked fatally to the abundant sins and the lack of doctrinal continuity, deceived them and led them "by mistaken paths" (1.3.121:47). Las Casas cannot free himself from his orthodox Catholic vision and, in the first instance, considers idolatry "a universal plague of the human race," labeling their rites and ceremonies as "execrable" and their myths as "fictions . . . and trickery" (1.3.127:663; 2.166–167:176–179). He agreed with his missionary colleagues that idolatry should be completely eliminated, but exclusively through persuasive and reasonable preaching and the patient example of a genuine Christian life, excluding violence.

Hernán Cortés (1985, 64) relates, as worthy of praise, his actions in the Aztec pantheon:

The greatest of these idols and those in which they placed most faith and trust I ordered to be dragged from their places and flung down the stairs and I had the chapels where they had them cleansed . . . and I placed in them the image of our Lady and other saints, all of which was deeply felt by Mutezuma [sic] and the inhabitants; who first told me not to do it.

The conqueror did not heed the protests of the Aztec lords, or even less, their helpless sorrow upon seeing their gods and religious customs defiled and being unable to come to their defense. That was followed by an old missionary tradition of converting the major temple into a place for Christian worship. Political violence is also accompanied by violence against sacred traditions.

Cortés and his companion and chronicler Bernal Díaz del Castillo differ on the consequences of this desacralization in the major temple. Cortés understands it to mean the strengthening of Spanish power. Díaz del

Castillo (1986, 209), probably with greater insight, sees it as an act that provokes anger in the Aztec hierarchy and accelerates the war of insurrection.

> Because in the great temple we had placed the image of our Lady and the cross upon an altar we had built, and we read the holy gospel and said mass, it seems that the Uichilobos and the Texcatepucas talked to their popes, and told them . . . that they did not want to be where those figures were, or that they would not be there if they killed us . . . and to tell Montezuma and all his captains to begin the war and kill us.

Fray Toribio de Motolinía, on his part, reflects the majority opinion among Catholic Spaniards when he warmly praises the Cortés action and rates it as one of the greatest heroic acts in the history of Christianity. According to this Franciscan defender of Cortés, "it is worthy of note the strength and daring God gave him in order to destroy and topple the main idols of Mexico." It is an act filled with symbolic meaning: the triumph of Christianity over idolatrous worship, which is nothing more than devil service.

> When Marqués del Valle [Cortés] entered this land, God our Lord was gravely offended and men suffered very cruel deaths [referring to human sacrifices], and the devil our adversary was well served by all the idolatry. (Benavente 1984, 205)

One of the orders in "Ordenanzas de buen gobierno," issued by Cortés in 1524 stating his colonizing purposes, is the instruction to destroy the idols and forbid all native religious practices.

> I order that all persons in Nueva España who have Indians in *repartimientos*, be obliged to take away their idols and admonish them from now on they cannot have them . . . and forbid their rituals and ancient ceremonies. (Pacheco et al. 1864–1884, 26:140, 142)

According to Mendieta (1980, 3.13:214), the Franciscan missionaries – known as the "twelve apostles" – who came to Nueva España in 1524 explained the theory of idolatry as devil worship in their first talk with Aztec priests and officials: "They are in error and deceived by the devils, enemies of the human race, concurring in abominable vices and sins, which will bring them to damnation and to suffer the sorrows and eternal fire of hell."

Pedro de Cieza de León ([1553] 1962, 27–28; emphasis added) reflects the same opinion with respect to Peru. He explains the intention of his chronicles:

> We and all these Indians, have our origins in our ancient parents Adam and Eve, and the Son of God came down to earth from heaven on behalf

of all men, and clothed in our humanity he met a cruel death on the
cross to redeem us and to free us from the power of the devil, *the devil
who possessed these peoples*, with permission from God, [and] kept them
oppressed and captive for such a long time; it is just for the whole world
to know now the way in which such great multitudes of peoples like
these Indians have become members of the holy mother church, by the
work of the Spaniards.

There is an effort on the part of Spanish missionaries to show how
every meaningful moment of mythology and native religion is "full of lies
and devoid of reason." Because the oral mythical traditions point to the
autochthonous origin of the peoples of the Americas, Acosta (1985, 1.25:64)
considered them false and combats them through references to Genesis,
"which teaches us that all men come from the first man," and that,
therefore, the natives come from "the old world." Acosta, like Las Casas,
is concerned about the origin of idolatry, which in the sixteenth century
is found to have greater universality than the authentic faith. This fact,
which in some insightful observers could lead to relativism and meta-
physical skepticism is, according to the Jesuit theologian and missionary,
an expression of the transcendental and cosmic battle between God and
Satan. The latter, due to his pride and homicidal hate, continually invents
idolatrous cults, fallacious satires of authentic latria that result in the
perdition of the deceived followers. Idolatry is, in its depths, a "dirty trick"
of Lucifer. The myths of the natives are no more than "lies from the one
who loves nothing more than the harm and perdition of men" (ibid.,
5.1:217–218; 10:34; 17:245).

In many Spanish texts the criticism of idolatry as satanic is accompanied
by a denunciation of human sacrifice, anthropophagy, and sodomy, which
constitute something of a "black legend" against the natives. In the
"*Memorial*" (Memorandum) by Fernández Enciso (1516), the *Historia General*
(1552) of López de Gómara, and the "Tratado del derecho y la justicia de
la guerra que tienen los reyes de España contra las naciones de la India
Occidental" (1559) (Treatise on the lawful and just war by the monarchs
of Spain against the nations of the Western Indies) by the Dominican friar
Vicente Palatino de Curzola, among many other "testimonies" and
"opinions," these fateful abominations are reiterated not only as mortal
sins of the natives but as the legitimate causes of the just war, loss of
sovereignty, and even captivity.

Due to sins against nature and enormous vices some nations can be justly
punished. . . . Thus, the Indians who sacrifice human victims to the
demons. . . . Besides, everywhere they are sodomites, eat human

flesh. . . . These Indians are also drunkards, liars, traitors, enemies of
all virtue and kindness. (Hanke and Millares 1977, 36)

Acosta (1985, 5.19–21:248–254; 28:271) details as revealing the diabolical
essence of indigenous idolatry, the human sacrifices carried out by the
natives of Mexico and Peru. His fundamental objective is never ethnological
nor anthropological, but theological and above all apologetic: to show the
"rabid hate" that Satan, "its cruel adversary," has against humanity. Therefore, Satan seeks "the perdition of men's souls and bodies . . . and the
human blood shed in various ways in honor of Satan was infinite." The
homicidal practices of indigenous worship are proof of the corrupting and
debasing nature of idolatry, which is "an abyss of every evil." Therefore
he takes seriously the task of relating the "falsehood and superstitions"
of the Indians "while they were gentiles," so that those charged with their
religious and cultural instruction can recognize them and "not tolerate
them." Again the face of inquisitorial censure appears.

Las Casas, on the contrary, on some occasions daringly, presents a controversial defense of human sacrifice, arguing that it reflects the natives'
high esteem of the divine, to whom instead of animals they offer what
is most valuable: persons. "I held and justified many conclusions that no
one before me dared touch on or write about, and one of them was that
to offer humans to a false or true God (taking the false one to be true) . . . is
not against natural law or reason" (Las Casas 1969, App. 10:238). In his
controversy with Sepúlveda, he digs out the strange passage on Jephthah's
holocaust of his daughter to God (Judg. 11:1–12:7; Heb. 11:32) to try to show
that the human sacrifices carried out by the native nations were not as
detestable, from the perspective of natural reason, as some had alleged
(Las Casas 1965, 413–415). As was to be expected, this defense of human
sacrifice as a religious manifestation of devotion that does not necessarily
violate the natural or divine law placed him in a vulnerable position, which
did not escape Sepúlveda: in his violent reply he accused the bishop of
Chiapas of having a position "impia et plusquam heretica" (impious and
worse than heretical) (in Fabié [1879] 1966, 71:340–345). It is not clear how
this risky rationalization of human sacrifice is in harmony with his vision
of the satanic character of native religiosity.

Cannibalism is another ritual characteristic despised by the Spaniards.
The scruples of Cortés, however, are not too great when his native allies
eat the Aztecs defeated in battle.

With the cry of "Santiago" on our lips we suddenly burst upon them . . .
in such a way that in this ambush more than five hundred fell, including

all their principal men and these the most hardy and valiant. That night our native allies dined well enough, for all those that we killed they cut to pieces and took off with them to eat. (Cortés 1985, 154–157)

On another occasion, when Cortés learns that the Aztecs, besieged and hungry ("we found roots and bark from trees that had been chewed . . ."), would come out at night to fish and search for roots and weeds to eat he prepared an ambush. Upon attacking them he learned that they were from among "the most wretched of the citizens . . . nearly all unarmed and mainly women and children." His bellicose reaction is of intense cruelty: "We inflicted such slaughter on them . . ." Finally he points out that, thanks to that massacre, "we returned to our camp with a large booty and *victuals for our allies*" (ibid., 154–157).[2] In view of the Spaniards' sanctimonious denunciation of Indian anthropophagy it is ironic to note that Alvar Núñez Cabeza de Vaca (Morales Padrón 1988, 14:27) later related that a group of North American Indians was scandalized by the unusual act of endo-cannibalism committed by some Spaniards ("five Christians . . . went to such an extreme that they ate each other") when their life was threatened by excessive hunger.

As an example of the "Christian" reaction of some Spaniards to indigenous sodomy, Fernández Enciso relates the example, in the conquering expedition to Darién, made of the young men that the chiefs dressed as women and used for their pleasure: "We took them and burnt them" (Pacheco et al. 1864–1884, 449).[3]

Destruction of Idols

The disregard for Indian religion resulted in a great historical loss, caused by Christian zeal for the destruction of Indian places of worship and their objects of adoration. Perhaps the first to show disregard was Dr. Chanca, Columbus's companion on his second journey. About the natives of Española he says: "Truly they are idolaters, because in their houses there are figures of many types; I have asked them and they reply that it is something from Turey, which means from heaven." He proceeds to throw the *cemíes* into the fire; the natives' sorrow is immediate, "and it was so painful for them that they wanted to cry" (in Fernandez de Navarrete 1945, 1:348).

The first bishop of Mexico, Juan de Zumárraga, joyously counted that by 1531 they had destroyed in Nueva España more than five hundred temples and twenty thousand idols (Höffner 1957, 500). The destruction of the ancient places of worship was defended by considering them to be "temples of devils," as the Augustinian friar Nicolás de Witte in 1554 called them (in Cuevas 1975, 222). The obsession to abolish any ritual considered idolatrous caused the conscious and systematic obliteration of irreplaceable, often irrecoverable, cultural creations.[4]

The concept of evangelization that prevailed in the Americas was different from that practiced later by the Jesuits in Asia. While the latter developed an integrated evangelization theory and practice,[5] discovering in Oriental religions providential seeds of divine grace, in the Americas there prevailed the idea of a radical antithesis between Christianity and native idolatry "at the service of the devil." The first bishops of Mexico, Oaxaca, and Guatemala affirmed, on November 30, 1537: "The first commandment obliges us all to destroy idolatry" (Ricard 1986, 165). This perception led to an unrelenting war against native religions, a holy war, a true battle of gods and myths that climaxed in the uprooting and destruction of a valuable part of the cultural heritage of humanity.

Ricard (1986, 409–417) makes a distinction between two concepts of Christian mission. One he calls "tabula rasa," which globally rejects the religious traditions of the people to be evangelized and posits a total rupture with them; the other he calls "providential preparation," which discovers in the native cults, "segments of truth" that should be utilized and assumed by theology. He points out that in Spanish missionary work in the Americas the first conception prevailed. This led the missionaries to attempt

> to destroy not only idolatry in itself but also a large portion of anything that could be a reminder of it. Destroying the temples to end all the celebrations of paganism, uprooting the idols, teaching children to search diligently for the idols, and keeping a watchful eye on everything that in secret could lead the Indians to revive their ancient paganism—thus, in the religious domain, at least, the total rupture is proclaimed (ibid., 411).

Mendieta (1980, 3.20:227–228) relates with great pleasure the destruction and burning of temples on January 1, 1525:

> Idolatry remained . . . while the temples of the idols remained standing. It was clear that the ministers of the devils would go there to exercise their roles and convoke the people and preach to them, and do their customary ceremonies. And as a result the [friars] agreed to start destroying and burning the temples without stopping until all were razed to the ground, and the idols also destroyed. . . . They did it so, starting in

Texcoco, where the temples were very beautiful and towered, and this was in the year 1525, on the first day of the year. After that followed those of Mexico, Tlaxcala, and Guexozingo. . . . Thus fell the walls of Jericho.

The confrontation between Europeans and the natives of the Americas was perceived by the Europeans as a divine, transcendental, and cosmic battle in which the victor was God and the loser, Satan. "No matter how hard the devil tried, Jesus Christ vanquished him from the kingdom that he had here" (ibid., 18:224). The devastation of the pagan temples is the visible and tangible expression of the Christian deity's victory over the eternal adversary.

In Peru, the other region in the continent with temples and sacred places that revealed in their architecture and art an advanced degree of civilization, Pedro Cieza de León (1962, 57:179) rejoices in the speedy progress of the policies imposed by Pizarro of demolishing the gentile temples and substituting Christian religious symbols for them.

> The ancient temples, which they generally called *guacas*, have all been destroyed and profaned and the idols broken and the devil, for his wickedness, thrown out of those places where out of human sinfulness he was so esteemed and revered; and the cross has been placed there.[6]

Fray Bernardino de Sahagún (1985, 10:579) justifies this war without quarter against native religion:

> It was necessary to destroy all the idolatrous things and buildings and even the customs of the republic, which had been mixed with idolatrous rituals and accompanied by idolatrous ceremonies, which were present in almost all the customs that the republic had, and for this reason it was necessary to destroy them all . . . so that nothing would have a trace of idolatry.

His extraordinary work, a rich source of ethnographic knowledge about Nahuatl culture, is framed within a medical perspective. He studies the rituals, ceremonies, symbols, and indigenous customs as symptoms of a grave illness, labeled diabolical idolatry.

> The doctor cannot correctly prescribe medication for the sick patient without first knowing the humor or the cause of the illness . . . the preachers and confessors are doctors of souls; to cure spiritual illnesses they should know the medicines and the spiritual illnesses. . . . The sins of idolatry and idolatrous rituals, superstitions, omens, ablutions, and ceremonies have not all disappeared. (ibid., 17)

Sahagún gathers the religious and cultural traditions of the Mexican pre-Colombian peoples so "that they can be cured from their blindness."

He warns the Mexicans to accept the fact that "Huitzilopochtli is not a god . . . nor any of the others you used to adore, none are gods, all are devils." The widespread idolatry that Mexico suffered before the arrival of European Christians "was the cause of your ancestors' great travails . . . and death." It also caused the one and true God to send the Christians to punish the natives, "to destroy them and their gods . . . because God abhors idolaters above all other sinners." Sahagún knew that idolatry persisted and that the Indians managed to keep alive clandestinely their religious traditions. That is why he exhorts his readers to denounce any signs of such ceremonies at once "to those who are charged with spiritual or temporal government in order to correct it immediately." He describes, in the greatest possible detail, the ancient rituals and ceremonies so that the "diligent preachers and confessors" can detect any vestige of their presence, "for they are like a rash that sickens the faith." One has to be alert and in battle gear against satanic idolatry because "I know for a fact that the devil never sleeps nor can forget the honor that these natives paid him, and is waiting for the moment to . . . return to his old lordship, . . . and it is good for us to have weapons ready to meet him." In that constant battle against Satan and idolatry, the otherwise gentle Franciscan takes on the role of an inquisitor: "One cannot consider that person to be a good Christian who does not persecute this sin and its authors" (ibid., 429, 58–59, 285, 189, 64).[7]

In general, one can say about Sahagún's work, like that of almost all the "ethnographic" production of the friars who preserved in writing the forbidden customs and religious beliefs of the natives, that they were works resulting from ideological battles and were a substantial portion of the theological weapons drawn against the native convictions. Their objective was to provide information on "the cruelties used by the devil in that land and on the hardships he imposed on the poor Indians only to lead them to eternal damnation" (Motolinía 1984, 1.11:49). Nonetheless, these works contain valuable information for the historical reconstruction of the social life of many Indian nations. Their ideological goals notwithstanding, the writers show intellectual curiosity and the desire to inform "so that it be known how strange and diverse is the ingenuity and skill of humans" (in Morales Padrón 1988, 30:62). These works are key materials in the development of modern anthropology and ethnography. In general, however, the prevailing idea in them is that the native religious, philosophical, and moral convictions are inferior and should be abolished.

Sahagún is sufficiently sensitive to realize that a fatal effect of this eradication of indigenous values and convictions is the collapse of the native social ethic, with the consequent idleness, cynicism, and alcoholism. When "they were reduced to Spain's way of life in divine matters as well as human . . . they lost all discipline," and "vices and sensuality prevail." His *Historia* (1985, 578–585) has an underlying pessimism about the fruits of the missionary work in Mexico ("this becomes worse every day") and a growing negative vision of the natives. He attributes his pessimism to the climate in a fatalistic classic fashion ("I think this is caused by the climate, or the constellations of this land").[8]

He does not notice, however, the damaging effect of a typical practice of the first missionaries: the use of children to spy on the idolatrous practices of their parents and other adults. This widespread prying by children accelerated the bankruptcy of social discipline. Sahagún criticizes the fact that some parents punished their children, even killing them, without realizing the social rupture that the friars had caused through the manipulation of children as denouncers. His colleague Motolinía (1984, 3.14:174–181) also praises the children, especially those chieftains' children who dedicated themselves to denouncing the religious practices of their parents. He gathers stories about the martyrdom of some of those children. Mendieta (1980, 3.17:221) also highlights the decisive role of the converted children as "ministers of idolatry's destruction." None of the missionaries showed any sensitivity toward the anguish of the parents nor a full understanding of the family or of the social disruption this family-destroying policy produced. It was considered a holy war, with cosmic dimensions, of the true faith against false idolatry; of God against Satan.

Sahagún dedicated himself for several difficult decades to the study of the customs and traditions of the Mexican aborigines. His work was unpublished for centuries, victim of an order issued by Felipe II, backed by the Holy Office, in 1577 forbidding any writings on native culture. The disregard for native religions caused his laborious work to be forgotten for centuries, as well as the loss of many works in the native languages written by the missionaries.[9]

Acosta (1952, 3.20–21:297–306), like Sahagún, points to the paradox that the social mores of the natives had markedly waned after the arrival of the Spaniards in spite of the fact that uplifting the natives' ethics is one of the justifications cited for the Iberian domination. He is principally concerned about the vice of alcoholism, affecting the body, customs, and the faith of the natives: "Wretched servitude of these poor creatures who, as they are little different from the beast by birth, . . . try diligently and with every effort to become worse than beasts." But he does not perceive that the uncontrolled spread of that vice is an effect of the debasing assaults on their natural convictions; on the contrary, he sees it as caused by the strong resistance of Satan to his dethronement ("the cause of such frequent drunkenness is the devil"). He notices that the natives do not really look for intoxication, but for the suspension of judgment and conscience. He is, however, so submerged in his missionary ideology that their desire to escape and run away from reality does not show him anything; it merely confirms what his old theology books tell him: the devil is tenacious in his malice.

Similarly, Mendieta justifies the inclusion of accounts about the ancient traditions of the original Mexicans in his *Historia eclesiástica indiana*. We can find in them, he asserts, "every vile action that can come to the human mind, and how their natural understanding is perverted by lack of faith and grace, for it comes to believe and take for certain the follies and nonsense that these infidel Indians believed." As in the case of Motolinía and Sahagún, Mendieta attempts to present Mexican mythology on the origin of the universe and of society. His judgment on that mythology leaves no doubt as to his perspective. It is "nonsense and lies that end nowhere." He joins those who repeatedly warned about being vigilant over popular native songs and dances because, even though some of them could be considered simply as popular music, "all are filled with idolatrous memories." The famous Indian calendar, which some intended to value as an autochthonous cultural relic, he considered not only a "silly fiction," but above all, "a dangerous thing" because it brings to the memory of the natives "their infidelity and ancient idolatry." It is therefore very important that all calendar reproductions be destroyed so that it be erased from memory and "the Indians would follow only the calendar . . . which the Roman Catholic Church has and uses" (Mendieta 1980, 2, 75; 32:143; 2.3:80; 2.14:97–99).

There is an interesting paradox in Sahagún (1985, 11:706–708), Mendieta (1980, 5.9–10:588–592), and Acosta (1952, 43–49). The three religious were eager to defend the natives from the tendentious lies told about their alleged intellectual inferiority and little capacity for the Christian faith. They cannot, however, hide their growing pessimism over the natives' rationality and prudence, and therefore their capacity for a peaceful Christianization compared with the natives of the Orient, and with the great Asiatic cultures and traditions.

The devastation aimed at the religious cultures of the natives also reached the hospitable community of the Yucatán Mayas. Diego de Lando (1959, 41:105), a Franciscan missionary, relates: "We found a great many of their books in their writing, and because they did not have anything that was not full of superstitions and lies from the devil, we burned them all, which they felt very deeply and with great sorrow."[10]

Although there is no doubt that a religious objective was the primary thrust of the iconoclastic anti-idolatry movements in the New World, another factor should not be forgotten, one that was present above all among the secular actors: the desire to take over the wealth surrounding the idols. That motive does not escape the acumen of Motolinía (1984, 3.20:201): "Mixed with the great zeal for finding idols was no small greed" (also Mendieta 1980, 3.21:228). The good Franciscan was not wrong. Passion for riches led, in Peru, to the profanation and ransacking of the tombs of the Inka hierarchy and, in Nueva España, to the search for pre-Hispanic sacred images.

In this context, it is appropriate to note the criticism made by Las Casas (1974, 7:63–70) of the iconoclastic destruction of idols carried out by Hernán Cortés in Mexico. He agrees that the native religions are a demonic captivity and that the native cults should be eradicated. But, and the difference is crucial, he believes in the natives' right to self-determination and that they should be the ones to eliminate idolatry and their altars after their authentic and sincere conversion. What is important is to uproot, through persuasion, the idols from the hearts of the natives, and they themselves would then eliminate the manifestations of pagan idolatry. Cortés, obviously, did not share this method and style of evangelization.

> First, the idols should be uprooted from their hearts, that is, the concept and esteem they have of them as gods, through constant, diligent, and continuous doctrine and painting for them the concept and truth of the true God and then, they themselves, seeing their error and deceit, will dethrone and destroy with their own hands and all their will the idols they venerated as their God or gods. (Las Casas 1986, 3.3.97:232)

Today, as one might expect in view of the great strides made in anthropological and ethnological research, even Catholic writers express great reserve at the pejorative descriptions directed against the "evil abominations" of the natives, and in the case of ritual anthropophagy and human sacrifice they discover "a profoundly religious disposition" (Höffner 1957, 135).

An issue that has not been adequately analyzed remains as a challenge to researchers: the relationship between the devaluing of native religion, the eradication of the complex vision of values and ideals (which, like any spiritual worldview, always gives human meaning to both being and doing), and the demographic catastrophe suffered by the natives of the Americas in the sixteenth century. "Not from bread alone" do humans live; that is a universally valid truth. If our gods have been dethroned and uprooted, if our myths have become the object of scorn and unrelenting criticism, has life any meaning and value? The sadness of the natives, so often stressed by their friar friends—does it not mask the incurable melancholy of those who have experienced the irreversible profanation of their sacred space and time? Acosta (1952, 6.8:290) points out that, "regarding the tradition, . . . [the Indians] were very diligent, and the young received as being sacred what the elders told them."[11] What effect can the scorn with which the Europeans handled that "tradition" have had on the desire to live in dignity? The profanation of the sacred has always had fatal consequences on the social conscience of nations whose existence is rooted in the preservation of the collective religious memory.

Death comes not only from physical mistreatment. Downgrading of native culture and religion, present in both Indian haters and promoters, could have also brought it about. Edmundo O'Gorman is correct: the process that he has called "the invention of America" was characterized by cultural assimilation that "implied the cancellation, because it lacked true historical significance, of the particular and unique meaning of the autochthonous cultural life of the Americas. . . . In fact, there is no other meaning to the providentialist Christian interpretation of the history of the American natives" (in Acosta 1985, li).

Oviedo (1851, 1.3.6:69–74) notes the relation between the religion of the natives and their death, but through an inverse rationalization. The aboriginal cults are diabolical idolatries that, as such, were accompanied by "big, ugly, and great sins and abominations on the part of these savage and bestial peoples." Their tragic misfortune is divine retribution: "God had to punish and destroy them in these islands for their vices and sacrifices to the devil." The death of the Indians is divine punishment.

This ethnocentric vision reached deeply in providentialist circles. It was picked up at the beginning of the seventeenth century by Vargas Machuca and Solórzano. According to the first, the displacement of the population of the Antilles and their substitution by the Spaniards is an expression of a dual providential judgment. God has punished the natives for their abominations and rewarded the Spaniards for their virtues.

> I think that it is by divine consent that so many of them die because of the evil they commit against the divine majesty. . . . One should believe that it was the divine will not to allow such an idolatrous and perverse people to escape, and that this divine will also wished to sow the holy faith in that land, inhabiting it with Christian people who were Spaniards. . . . [God] favors the Spaniards in those regions, whereas the idolatrous Indians incur disfavor. (in Fabié 1966, 71:241, 253–254)

According to Solórzano (1930, 1.1.12:126–127), the "demographic catastrophe" of the natives is due to the "secret judgments" that God "has used to diminish them. . . . All of which seems [to be] and must be, because of heavenly wrath and punishment. . . . God disposed it thus perhaps because of their grave sins and their ancient, abominable, and enduring idolatries."[12]

In the middle of the twentieth century, prominent Spanish theologians still firmly defended the "civilizing and Christianizing" activity carried out against the autochthonous cultures and religions of the Americas in the sixteenth century. For example:

> Our country was not content with having an empire nor with domina-
> tion . . . it went, above all, to civilize, to Christianize the New World,
> to erase the cultural differences that naturally existed between the old
> and the new world. Official Spain, its Court and its Monarchs . . . along
> with spiritual and religious Spain saw in the Indians true brothers,
> inferior yes, due to culture and customs, but always as men, rational
> beings, needing to be educated, uplifted, rescued for faith and civiliza-
> tion. (Carro 1944, 1:115)

The author of these lines, Venancio Diego Carro, who wrote the prin-cipal work of his time on the ideas of the Spanish Catholic theologians about the conquest of the Americas, does not seem to realize the hidden, enslaving violence in that benevolent mission to "erase the cultural dif-ferences" between Europeans and the indigenous peoples.

9

A Holocaust of Natives

*Mine overseer: He punishes cruelly
the Indian chiefs, with no consideration
of justice, and he abuses the poor
in the mines without mercy.*

The slaves who died in the mines produced such a stench that it caused the plague, especially in the mines of Guaxaca, where for about half a square league you could hardly walk without stepping on dead bodies or on bones; and so many birds and ravens came to eat that they greatly shadowed the sun, and many towns were depopulated.

Fray Toribio de Motolinía

Their bodies are maltreated with harshness like dung on the ground that is stepped upon.

Dominicans and Franciscans in Española

A Demographic Catastrophe

The theoretical affirmation—theological and juridical—of the humanity of the American natives could not prevent their social degradation and despoiling. Neither did it prevent a great many of them, including whole ethnic groups, from *simply ceasing to exist*. Without hyperbole it can be affirmed that "from the perspective of the conquered, the conquest was a true cataclysm. . . . The encounter with Europeans was synonymous with death" (Flores Galindo 1987, 39). The Franciscan Sahagún (1985, 11.12–13:706–710) wrote something similar in 1576 when he observed that after the Spaniards arrived in the "West Indies," they found "a diversity of people . . . innumerable peoples," but of these, "many have already perished and of those remaining many are close to perishing."

The problem with many excellent studies on the ethics of the debate about the New World is that they remain at the abstract theoretical level, without asking the concrete effects the events had on the life and existence of the original inhabitants. Authors of great critical insight who dissect the tendentiously apologetic and panegyric treatises about the Spanish empire conclude, in the last analysis, by eulogizing the triumph of the spirit of liberty and justice in the Spanish governmental theory for the Indies without subjecting that vision to the test of the consequences of that theory on the existence of those who were to be Christianized and civilized. The natives remain always as objects of the debates and disputes and never emerge as historical subjects and protagonists.

While the theoretical debates among theologians, jurists, court officials, and the church were in progress, the tragic breakdown of ancient indigenous cultures and the annihilation of the New World's original inhabitants was inexorably advancing. In this respect, Höffner's severe judgment, in a work filled with sympathy for the Spain of the sixteenth century, seems on target when he asserts:

> Aztec and Inka civilizations were only at the beginning of their development when they were destroyed by the conquerors. We cannot guess what values could have been created by an uninterrupted cultural evolution. But we should confess that the destruction of Indian culture . . . represents a grave and irreplaceable loss for humanity. (Höffner 1957, 172–173)

He says of their decimation: "The New World witnessed such a horrible enslavement and extermination of its inhabitants that the blood freezes in our veins" (ibid., xxxiii). He concludes, in spite of his Catholicism and Hispanophilia:

> No matter how much respect the daring deeds and the almost superhuman hardships the conquerors endured evoke in us, we have to recognize, however, that the pagan Indians deserve, before the tribunal of humanity and of Christianity, a more favorable verdict than the one passed by Christian conquerors and their brood of soldiers. (ibid., 208)

A key point in any evaluation of the intense debates that accompanied the conquest of America has to be the historical experience of the conquered. It is difficult to sustain the strange thesis that the accounts of the natives' sufferings are nothing more than a "black legend" created by the fantasy and imagination of Las Casas. The contemporary witnesses who closely link the death of the natives with the violent greed of the newly arrived Spaniards are countless and their case overwhelming. They lugubriously reiterate the many ways in which the blood of the first became the source of riches for the second. Let us review, by way of example, fragments from those testimonies (see Comas 1951).

The Jeronomite fathers who visited Española between 1516 and 1519 cannot be accused of being anti-Spanish. Their attitude was different from that of Pedro de Córdoba, Antonio de Montesinos, and Las Casas. For this reason their testimony about the death of the natives and Spanish blame for it assumes greater significance.

> Your Holiness . . . you ought to know that at the time that the Spaniards came to this island there were many thousands or even hundreds of thousands of Indians in it, and because of our sins they went so fast that by the time we arrived here, a little more than a year ago, we found so few that it is like the leftover remains on the tree branches after the harvest. (in Pacheco et al. 1864–1884, 1:300)

In the 1530s the royal official Pascual de Andagoya tells how the native towns in the region then called Darién, the southeastern isthmus of Central America, had been desolated.

> The captains and men who left for those regions . . . would take on their return many chained Indians. . . . The captains divided the imprisoned Indians among their soldiers. . . . No one was punished even if he had committed great cruelty. In that way they desolated the land a hundred leagues from Darién. All the captives who arrived in that village were assigned to work in the gold mines . . . and since they arrived exhausted by the long journey and the heavy burdens, and since the land was very different from theirs and not healthy, all would die. (in Sauer 1984, 422)

Around the same time, August 12, 1533, the Dominican friar Francisco de Mayorga complained in a letter about the abuse suffered by the natives of Nueva España and predicted their extinction if it did not cease (in Cuevas 1975, 46–47).

> My heart cries upon seeing the loss and destruction of these poor ones and how little fruit we get from it, with all their hard work and too many jobs. . . . They have so much work and they are so weak that they have no time to clean or fix their houses, or their orchards. And the loss and destruction is so obvious . . . that they have already lost hope.

Motolinía (1984, 1.1, 17) described the homicidal effects of "mining work" to which the Indians were subjected in the passage at the head of this chapter.[1]

Luis Sánchez writes to the Council of the Indies on August 26, 1566:

> The reason that so many lands have been depopulated . . . : The first thing is the cruel and unjust wars that the Spaniards have waged and wage against the Indians, killing them, taking their lands, and frightening them away. . . . Secondly, the thing that has destroyed the Indians is slavery, . . . the apportioning of the Indians, because the Spaniards do not use them as vassals but as slaves and enemies. . . .
>
> From whence it follows that I count about one thousand five hundred leagues have been depopulated by the Spaniards, which were once teeming with Indians, and in most of them they have left no one, and in the others so few people remain that you can call them depopulated.
>
> The cause of this evil is that all of us who go to the Indies have the intention of returning to Spain very rich, which is impossible . . . except at the expense of the sweat and blood of the Indians. (Pacheco et al. 1864–1884, 11:163–164)

We have similar testimonies about Nueva España from the Franciscan friar Luis de Villalpando in a letter to Carlos V, October 15, 1550 (in Gómez Canedo 1977, 233):

I write this with great bitterness in my heart, seeing that there is no remedy for the way this poor people are perishing . . . that all want to devour the Indians . . . and they have no other alternative nor protection but death . . . and this is why in many provinces of this Nueva España there were Indians like grass and all have died and been exterminated and the provinces are barren . . . some of them as barren as the islands of Española and Cuba.

Also in reference to the mortality of the natives, something similar is reported by the royal official Alonso de Zorita (in Pacheco et al. 1864–1884, 2:104, 107, 113).

Because of the labors and cruelty that have been used against them and due to plagues among them, there is not a third left of the people who once lived here. . . . And this has destroyed and diminished them everywhere, and will exterminate them if it is not remedied in time, because some have ceased to exist in some places. . . . And I heard many Spaniards say in the new Kingdom of Nueva Granada [Colombia] that from there to the government building in Popayan one could not get lost because the bones of the dead showed the way.

Zorita rises to a tone of indignation upon contemplating the death of the wretched natives.

Who will be able to recount the misery and labors endured by these most pitiful and unfortunate peoples, without any assistance nor human help, persecuted, afflicted, and forsaken? Who is not against them? Who does not persecute and afflict them? It has even been heard publicly in some circles that when there is no water for Spanish farms, they will be watered with the blood of the Indians. (ibid., 117–118)

In the Americas of the sixteenth century the demographic statistics on the natives lose their abstractness and become frightening. According to Sherburne Cook and Woodrow Borah (1971, 1:viii), the Mexican native population was reduced from about 25.2 million in 1518 to 1.37 million in 1595.[2] Noble David Cook (1981, 114) calculates that the number of natives in Peru diminished from 9 million in 1520 to 1.3 million in 1570. The Antillean depopulation was also enormous. According to Rolando Mellafe (1964, 21), at the time of the Spaniards' arrival there were in Española around one hundred thousand natives; in 1570, "there were hardly 500."[3] In an attempt to save the Antillean natives, a truly endangered species, the Crown issued in 1542 an order as part of the New Laws ensuring their good treatment and an exemption from paying tribute:

It is our will and we order that the Indians who are presently alive in the islands of San Juan, Cuba, and Española, for now and until it is our will, shall not be burdened with the payment of tribute nor other royal, personal, nor mixed services any more than the Spaniards do in those islands. Let them relax so that they can multiply and be instructed in the things of our holy Catholic faith. (Konetzke 1953, 1:220)

It was a useless and belated effort. With greater objectivity, Oviedo (1851, 1.3.6:73) points out the near extinction of the Caribbean aborigines: "There is little that can be done in this island [Española] and in San Juan and Cuba and Jamaica for the same has happened in all of them: namely, the death and extermination of the Indians." It is not something that disturbs his sleep nor perturbs his conscience. The natives of Puerto Rico, Santo Domingo, and Cuba came to be ethnological curiosities of the past, museum pieces. Zavala (1935, 39) correctly expresses the unfortunate outcome: "The protective theory and laws arrived too late to help the Antillean Indians. The clash between the Spanish race and the indigenous race annihilated the latter." It is sadly ironic that such "protective theories and laws" came about precisely as a way of protesting the inhumane treatment of the natives in the Caribbean islands.

The prominent historian of Latin American cultures Pedro Henríquez Ureña (1964, 35) has described this drastic population reduction as an "ethnic tragedy." The Cuban historian Fernando Ortíz (1978, 95) calls it a *"democidio"* (democide). Córdova (1968, 27) speaks of a "genocidal process not willfully sought, but incredibly effective."[4] The Peruvian Gustavo Gutiérrez (1989, 10) calls it a "demographic collapse." Nicholás Sánchez Albornoz (1986, 7) refers to it as a "demographic disaster." The British professor R. A. Zambardino (1978, 708) calls it "one of the greatest demographic catastrophes ever known." Even more categorically stated, the North American scientist William Denevan (1976, 7) affirms: "The discovery of America was followed by possibly the greatest demographic disaster in history." The noted historian and Spanish economist Jaime Vicens Vives (1972, 353) uses similar expressions: "demographic catastrophe . . . one of the worst ones in human history."

Vicens Vives cannot keep his Spanish sentiments from interfering in his historical evaluations; he attributes the catastrophe principally to an indigenous version of the theories of Malthus—the population was more than the land could feed in the long term—and to the primitive agricultural techniques. In his opinion, that implies "that before the arrival of the Spaniards the aboriginal population was condemned to a disaster." Even if we accept the hypothesis that Mexican agriculture could not sustain the native population of 1518, the question is obvious: Without the incursion of the invaders would such a cataclysmic mortality have occurred, or would there not have been rather a leveling off of demographic growth?[5]

The dispute about the cause of the extinction of the Antillean natives and the serious decrease in population in other parts of the Americas during the sixteenth century is unending, partly due to the presence of ideological motives, on the one hand, and to the methodological difficulty of approaching the question, on the other. What is impossible to deny is the proportionally inverse growth in the Spanish population and the reduction of the aboriginal inhabitants. This was already pointed out in 1554 by Fray Bernardo de Alburquerque, then Dominican Provincial and later bishop of Antequere (Oaxaca):

> Since the Spaniards in this land are many and growing and increasing every day, and the Indians that live near them are caused great harm because the Spaniards are so many, . . . and the Indians are decreasing each day, we now have not even a tenth of those that were here twenty years ago. (in Cuevas 1975, 180–181)

It was repeated again three decades later by Fray Gaspar de Recarte, in his assertion that "by their [Spaniards'] increase in numbers the work of the Indians increases and they are diminishing" (ibid., 385). A decade later Mendieta (1980, 1.15:62–63) repeated it: "The Indians increase and multiply . . . where they are free from the moths that are the Spaniards." We are faced, then, with a true holocaust of natives.[6]

The Right to Human Existence

The primordial human right is the *right to exist*. Any other right presupposes existence as a reality not placed in jeopardy arbitrarily. This principle gives priority to the problem of the poor and wretched. The existence of the needy is threatened by hunger, violence, illnesses uncared for, maltreatment, and excessive work. The oppressed poor are unprotected in the face of the violence of the powerful. Their vulnerability and precariousness are a threat to their very lives, not just to their liberty and happiness. Their fragility and abandonment become a threat to ethical and religious conscience (see Sobrino 1986, 1–7).

The many projects that Bartolomé de las Casas planned for the communities to be established and legalized in the New World, beyond their many variables, have something in common—respect for the right of the native, an incarnation of the right of the poor of the Gospels to exist, to be. The vital essential necessities—food, health, housing, work—acquire theological transcendence. For Las Casas the Old Testament text is key: "Bread is life to the destitute, and to deprive them of it is murder. To rob your neighbor of his livelihood is to kill him, and he who defrauds a worker of his wages sheds blood" (Ecclus. 34:21-22, REB). The hunger that the conquered Indians suffered was a crime, and even more, a sin against the divine law of the solidarity of all humanity. Therefore he insisted:

> Because their lives depend on having food, and in its absence has come their death; therefore, so that the Indians may have something to eat in the haciendas and the mines and in all other works in which they are engaged, give them bread, meat and fish, poultry, and pepper . . . two pieces of *casabi* [bread made from yucca or mandioca; trans. note]. (Las Casas 1972, 83)

He also stressed the problem of health in the context of the *right to be*. Faced with the continued reiteration of many scholars that the principal cause of the "extinction of so many indigenous populations during the first years of the European invasion into America" was the "biological law of lack of immunity to infections" (Konetzke 1972, 96), it is important to note the effort made by Las Casas to demystify the "natural" theory of the mortality rates. It was not mainly the supposed biological weakness of the natives and their lack of immunological strength. Many elements were central to the magnitude of the deaths caused by illness. The breakdown of agricultural production due to war and mining exploitation was decisive. That created an arbitrary scarcity, accompanied by the physical weakening of the natives. Other factors were the lack of care of the sick, the conditions not conducive to their recovery, and the overcrowding in homes and work situations that facilitated contagion.[7] What Las Casas (1986, 2.2.14:255-256) witnessed in the Antilles was terrifying; thus his testimony is significant:

> If they [the Indians] became ill, which happened frequently, due to the many grueling and unusual types of work and because they were by nature delicate, they [the Spaniards] did not believe them, and without mercy called them dogs, and told them that they complained because they were lazy and did not want to work; and besides those abuses, they were kicked and hit; and as soon as their illness increased they would be freed to go to their lands, 20, 30, and 50 leagues away, with only some garlic roots and casaba for the road. The poor ones would leave and fall by the first brook, where they would die in despair; others would go farther, but very few would make it to their lands, and I came across some dead bodies on the roads and some under trees in their last agony, and others with the moans of death and crying as best they could: Hunger! Hunger!

Ortwin Sauer (1984, 307), a North American scholar who cannot be called pro-Las Casas, analyzes what he calls "the destruction of the social aboriginal structure." About the illnesses from the mines he writes:

> Mining camps ignored every sanitation measure. The Indians lived on top of each other and worked the same way . . . so that the conditions were ideal for infectious contagion of the Indian population living on an inadequate diet [Spaniards had restricted hunting and fishing], depressed by excessive work, and dispirited by the loss of their natural form of life.

This explanation is not different from that of many chroniclers of the sixteenth century. The Franciscan Fray Jerónimo de San Miguel wrote to the Council of the Indies, September 11, 1551, pained by the death of the natives of Nueva Granada, especially those charged with the transportation of Spanish goods via the Magdalena River. The immediate cause of death for many was sickness that in such primitive sanitary conditions easily became epidemics. Fray Jerónimo, however, lifts the veil and denounces as the ultimate and real cause of the tragedy the avarice that values enrichment more than the life of the natives.

> It is certainly a pity to see these poor ones all day standing while rowing and dying during such long journeys, . . . for even though the work is heavy, food is scarce and miserable, because often to fit more merchandise aboard they do not put the necessary food for the Indians, and, as a result, upon their return home they become gravely ill and many of them die. (in Gómez Canedo 1977, 135)

At the end of the second decade of the sixteenth century, the Antillean Indians were struck by a terrible epidemic of smallpox, which resulted in some belated efforts aimed at stopping their extinction. Las Casas (1986, 3.3.128:270) insists on placing the medical problem in the context of social oppression.

> Around the years 18 and 19 [1500s] . . . a terrible plague caused the death of almost everyone, leaving only very few alive. That was smallpox that hit the poor Indians and was brought by someone from Castilla . . . and because it was a destructive plague, all would shortly die. This was combined with their thinness and lack of substance because of the scarcity of food, and their nakedness, sleeping on the floor, excessive work, and little or no health care and protection from those who used them.[8]

The fatal effect of depression and anguish on those who have been weakened and humiliated has been recognized by doctors and psychiatrists, and this condition can on occasion cause death (see Frankl 1986,

11–94). Las Casas is an eloquent witness to the profound sadness and melancholy of the dispossessed Indians. "Some, from pure sadness, seeing that their life, so bitter and full of calamities, will never find consolation nor any remedy whatever, withered and emaciated, fall dead"; "very profound sadness fell upon them . . . [without] any hope of freedom" (Las Casas 1965, 2:755; 1986, 1.1.106:419).[9] Fray Miguel de Salamanca, in 1520, speaking before the Council of the Indies, asserted that one of the causes for the rapid death rate of the natives was their "discontent . . . and despair" (Las Casas 1986, 3.3.136:300). This depression led many to collective suicide in order to escape a life irreversibly marred by despair.[10]

The Dominican Pedro de Córdova (J. M. Pérez 1988, 133), in a letter to the king, probably in 1517, described the tragic consequences of the natives' despair:

> Due to the illnesses and hard work, the Indians chose and are choosing to kill themselves, preferring death rather than such strange work, and in some cases hundreds have killed themselves together so as not to subject themselves to such hard servitude. . . . The women, exhausted from work, avoid conceiving and giving birth; so that they would not have work upon work with pregnancy and delivery, and many becoming pregnant have ingested things to abort and have aborted the creatures, and others, after delivery, have killed their own children with their own hands, so as not to place them under such hard servitude.[11]

The situation of the natives is so lamentable that the Dominicans and Franciscans in Española, in a collective letter to the Jeronomite fathers in 1517, dramatically express the tragedy: "Their bodies are maltreated with harshness like dung on the ground that is stepped upon" (J. M. Pérez 1988, 126).[12]

This position was not universally shared. Motolinía (1984, 216) in his 1555 criticism of the treatises published three years earlier by Las Casas suggests that the depopulation of Mexico was a divine punishment for idolatry and the sins of the natives. Thus, the substitution (Spaniards for aborigines) of the population that took place was similar in its manifestation and its origins to what the Old Testament relates (Israelites and Canaanites).[13] A similar vision is shared by Oviedo (1851, 1.3.6:74): "God had to punish and desolate them in these islands because of their viciousness and the sacrifices to the devil."

Francisco Guerra (1986, 41, 42, 58) has recently criticized Las Casas because in his *Brevísima relación* he stresses war and servitude as "the two principal and general ways" of indigenous depopulation. In all Las Casas's clamor to defend the Indians, he failed to report that epidemics were the main cause of their depopulation. According to Guerra, the truth is that in the New World "the important demographic changes are always the result of epidemics." It is not, therefore, a "genocide" but a "sanitary disaster."

> There were new lands with new men, and the effect of sickness was devastating. . . . And this panorama of pain of which we, to our sorrow, were protagonists with the discovery of America, proves only one thing, that Las Casas was unjust with the discoverers. The natives of the Americas were victimized by sickness, not by the Spaniards.

In this view, it was a matter of mosquitoes, lice, fleas, bacteria, viruses, and germs![14] Missing is a critical and concrete analysis of the social context of the epidemics, their relation to the breakdown of the social order, the disaster in agricultural production, the degradation of autochthonous values, and the use of natives as instruments for the avaricious search for precious metals. The strange thing is that such factors are overwhelmingly present in innumerable testimonies from contemporaries.

Some analysts place excessive emphasis on serious epidemics, above all smallpox, in what Todorov (1987, 69) calls an unintended "bacteriological war" against the natives. They fail to give attention, however, to common and ordinary illnesses—colds, flues—which in conditions of excessive work, inadequate nutrition, constant exposure to rain, change of environment, and maltreatment can be and generally are fatal. Las Casas (1967, 1.2.34:176) suggests this phenomenon by pointing out that "any accidental illness immediately makes them lose weight, emaciates them, and dispatches them . . . because they have been placed under such burdensome work since we got here."[15]

This integral perspective concerning the sickness of the natives is not exclusive to Las Casas. Mendieta (1980, 4.37:523), at the end of the sixteenth century, wrote in a similar vein:

> For myself I think that in respect to all the plagues that have come upon these poor Indians, some are from the onerous apportioning where they are ill-treated . . . and given excessive work that grinds and breaks their bodies.

10

Black Slavery

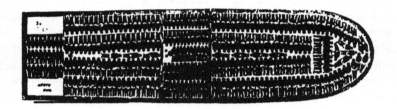

The remedy for the Christians is this, surely, that Your Highness agree to lend to each of these islands five or six hundred blacks, or whatever number seems necessary to be distributed among the residents who have no one else except Indians; and for the settlers who would come later, from three, or four, or six, depending on what the person feels is best, that they be sold on credit, and the blacks be mortgaged for the same amount.

Bartolomé de las Casas (1531)

This advice with regard to providing licenses to bring black slaves to these lands was first given by the cleric Casas, not aware of the injustice of the Portuguese then taking and enslaving them; that advice, after he realized the situation, he would not give again for anything in the world, for he always considered that they [the blacks] were unjustly and tyrannically made slaves, the same as the Indians.

Bartolomé de las Casas (1560?)

A *"New Slavery"*

The demographic collapse suffered by the natives of the Americas necessitated the substitution of servile manual laborers. One cannot speak of the conquest of the Americas nor of the servitude of its aborigines without making a necessary digression, given the Antillean origin of these reflections. The conquest of the Americas is the starting point for the modern system of slavery.

The introduction of African serfs was concurrent with European expansion in the Americas. Mellafe (1964, 23, 26) correctly notes: "Black slaves were objects of commerce who arrived everywhere with the conquest itself, not after it. . . . There were two elements that were never absent from the baggage of an important conqueror, whether his retinue was large or small: horses and black slaves."

African slavery arising at the end of the fifteenth century differed significantly from traditional European serfdom (see Finley 1980 and Klein 1986, 1–20), where the slaves played a relatively limited role in the production of goods, prevalent from the decline of the Roman Empire to the end of the fifteenth century:

1. Slavery and blackness became almost synonymous terms (cf. Tannenbaum 1946, 110–112, n. 236). After the initial serfdom imposed on the American natives was revoked, they were acknowledged, at least in theory, as free vassals. But then the grand-scale black slave market began, which could be called a new slavery. From that moment on, slavery was linked intimately with the black race in a long history of oppression and resistance.

The enslavement of Africans was not initiated by Christians. When the Portuguese arrived in the middle of the fifteenth century at the Western coast of Africa they found a substantial slave trade. But it was the Europeans who multiplied it and catapulted it into a new means of production. And this was possible because of the domination and colonization of the New World.

2. In the Americas, slavery took on a new ideological and paradoxical justification: the civilizing and evangelizing of the African. This position is put forward, naturally, in treatises by white European Christian intellectuals. The Spanish Jesuit theologian Luis de Molina, at the end of the sixteenth century, includes this apology as coming from the Europeans involved in the slave trade:

> They are surprised if someone expresses doubt, and they maintain that blacks who are sold and led to other places are treated gently. They are

of the opinion that by being among us in this way, they [the slaves] are converted to Christianity and also enjoy a better material life than what they had before, where they were naked and had to be content with miserable nutrition.[1]

In this way the medieval slave system was drastically distorted from its original design by Christendom. The containment wall of slavery disappeared and the bases for its extraordinary increase were established. The paradox of simultaneous evangelization and exploitation of Africans was well expressed by Deive (1980, 377):

> The attitude of the church toward slavery centered officially on its interest in having black pagan idolaters received, through previous indoctrination and baptism, into the benefits and consolation of Catholicism. The Crown shared that view and also tried to see to it that black slaves received religious instruction. Nevertheless, the interest . . . in having the slaves embrace Christian doctrine was not due only to apostolic zeal. . . . The Christianization of Africans also sought their easy subjection and was . . . a technique used to justify the market in black slaves. . . . The body of the slave was chained so as to reward him with a soul that could be saved.[2]

It is important to remember that the church and the ecclesiastical organizations were also slaveholders, and not infrequently engaged in the buying and selling of black human merchandise. In fact, at the time the Society of Jesus was banned from many parts of America in 1767, it was the institution with the greatest number of African American slaves in the Western hemisphere.

3. The number of slaves increased dramatically. The statistics of this "black market" [literally] are impressive. Klein (1986, 21) calculates that between 10 and 15 million African slaves were imported into the New World during the time of the slave market.[3] In 1589, a report of the *Casa de Contratación* in Sevilla indicated that black slaves were the most important merchandise for export to the Indies, and in 1594, 47.9 percent of ships arriving in the Americas were taken up with the black trade (Mellafe 1964, 59–60; Konetzke 1972, 69). Deive (1980, 678–679) is correct in saying that during the fifteenth century, "The demand for African slaves . . . on a scale so great that it would bleed Africa for several centuries . . . started as a consequence of the discovery of America." This had a decisive role in shaping the history of some parts of the continent such as the Caribbean, Brazil, and the southern region of the United States.

4. The exploitation of slave labor was intensified. While conventional slavery maintained a traditional mode of production, black slavery in the Americas set in place the necessary elements for a new mode of production resting on a different relation to labor: *capitalism*. Modern systems of

colonialism and slavery and their relations to the rise of the *capitalist system* are intimately linked to the domination of Europe over the Americas initiated on October 12, 1492.[4]

African Slavery and Christian Conscience

During the sixteenth century the theological, juridical, and philosophical defense of the natives abounded; not so, however, in the case of the black slaves. The disparity is striking.

The attitude of Bartolomé de las Casas regarding black slavery constitutes one of the most controversial elements for his biographers, whether these be impartial, apologists, or detractors of his work (see Zavala 1944; Brady 1966; Ortiz 1978; the Pérez Fernández study in Las Casas 1989). In his memoranda from between 1516 and 1518, in a famous letter to the Council of the Indies written in 1532, and in a memo in 1542, Las Casas suggests the importation of slaves to accomplish certain labors that at the time were being done by the natives (Las Casas 1972, 65, 79, 120–122, 130, 138, 140; Fabié [1879] 1966, 70:484–485). Those texts show without shadow of doubt that for several decades Las Casas promoted African slavery as one of the necessary measures to simultaneously solve the demographic crisis of the native population and the colonists' serious economic problems. From this a peculiar "black legend" has emerged against Las Casas, according to which he is responsible for the introduction of African slavery into the Americas. In that interpretation, his aim would have been to transfer the labor productive of riches from one oppressed group, the natives, to another equally exploited group, the Africans.

Several points should be made in response to that anti-Las Casas "black legend."

1. Contrary to what is still being affirmed, the introduction of African slaves preceded the first suggestions by Las Casas by more than a decade. In no way were his suggestions either the efficient or circumstantial cause.[5] He was partially responsible for that error by having apparently affirmed on occasions something he wrote in his *Historia de las Indias:* "This advice by which permission was given to bring black slaves to these lands was first offered by the cleric Casas" (1986, 3.3.102:177). His self-consciousness of being a privileged actor in the historical drama of the Indies made Las Casas assign to himself the paternity, which really did not belong to him, of having suggested the introduction of black slaves into the Antillean islands.

The truth is that Las Casas shared an opinion commonly held by those who wished to avoid the total extinction of the Antillean natives. Fray Pedro de Córdoba, together with his Dominican brothers, urged the introduction of black slaves in an opinion presented to the Jeronomite fathers who visited Española between 1516 and 1518 at the request of Cardinal Cisneros (Deive 1980, 31–36). In a memorandum filled with passion in defense of the natives of the Americas, he advises: "For the temporal remedy of the Christians and their haciendas, Your Highness should grant license to bring slaves, and even if they did not have money to pay for them now, Your Highness would send them and sell them on credit for some time" (in Pacheco et al. 1864–1884, 2:214; J. M. Pérez 1988, App. 1, 121).

In 1517, the Franciscan Fray Pedro Mexía reiterated the proposal to substitute black labor for Indian labor: "That each person with Indians in *encomienda* . . . be deprived of them . . . and be given in remuneration for each five Indians taken away, a male or female slave." Mexía believed that if two thousand slaves, "half male, half female" were introduced in Española the double problem of rapid extinction of the aborigines and the economic crisis of the colony would be solved (in Gómez Canedo 1977, App. 220).

The Jeronomite fathers made a similar recommendation to Cardinal Cisneros, regent of the Castilian Crown: "Grant a general license to these islands, especially San Juan, so that they can bring black bozales [newly enslaved blacks; trans. note] there because experience shows their great usefulness, and also to help these Indians . . . as well as for the great benefit that would come to Your Highnesses through them" (Deive 1980, 84–85). They repeat the same suggestion on January 18, 1518, regarding all the other Antillean Islands in process of colonization in a letter to the new monarch, Carlos: "Especially that black bozals may be brought to them and that they be of the quality that is suited for this area" (in Pacheco et al. 1864–1884, 1:298–299).

Alonso de Zuazo, a judge residing in Española, named by Cardinal Cisneros, recommended on January 22, 1518: "To give general license to bring blacks, strong people for work, the opposite of the natives who are so weak they can only serve in labor requiring little endurance." Two years later, his successor would insist: "Blacks are highly desirable" (ibid., 293, 418). Also, a poll taken in 1520 in Española about the economic crisis the island was experiencing reveals a widely held opinion by the Castilian inhabitants:

> It would be fitting that Your Highnesses would send seven or eight thousand blacks, bought with the income from these islands, and send

them to be distributed among the residents of this island . . . and with that I [Francisco de Vallejo] think that this island would be populated and the income from it for Your Highnesses would increase. (ibid., 406)

The request for slaves was constant from colonists and *encomenderos*, from whom it was to be expected; it was also constant from religious leaders, including those who distinguish themselves for their generosity and solidarity with the natives. Bishop Sebastián Ramírez de Fuenleal, on August 11, 1531, asserted: "The entire population and the preservation of this island [Española] and that of San Juan and even Cuba depend on bringing blacks to mine gold and benefit the other endeavors" (Deive 1980, 84–85).

Deive (27–49) fully shows the financial pertinence of those recommendations, which, independently of the sympathy the writers seem to have with the sad condition of the Indians, were mainly intended to solve the growing scarcity of slave labor at a time when there were plans to increase the economic exploitation of the Antillean possessions. Importing Africans seemed to be the effective remedy for the ethical problems with Indians and for the mercantile difficulty. Bataillon (1976, 134) asserts that, regarding the introduction of black slaves in the Americas, "Las Casas played an unimportant role."

2. Las Casas never denied the legality of certain types of slavery. He accepted the traditional concept of *ius gentium*, which stated the legality of enslaving those captured during a just war. That idea, as we have seen, has biblical (Deut. 20:14) and classical (Aristotle, *Politics*, 1.3–8) origins, modified by the exception of not subjecting Christians to forced serfdom. Initially, he did not question the argument devised by the Portuguese Crown that the Africans were Moors and Saracens, and therefore could be legally subjected to forced labor.

Las Casas maintained, beginning in the early 1520s, that the natives of the New World were unjustly enslaved. Their subjection to serfdom was against ethics and law. That was the thesis he defended in his "Tratado sobre la materia de los indios que se han hecho esclavos" (Treaty on the subject of the Indians who have been enslaved) (1965, 1:500–641). That extensive dissertation about the injustice and illegality of the serfdom of the New World's natives has as a premise, however, the legitimacy and legality of the enslavement of other peoples in other circumstances based on the tenets of human law accepted by Christianity. Without this premise his argument would be absurd. At the end of the fifteenth century, three groups could be enslaved in Europe and Spain: Saracens, Slavs (so frequently subjected to forced serfdom that their ethnic name would become the term used for institutional slavery), and African blacks. In general, Las Casas did not question the legality of their subjugation.

It does not seem correct, however, to affirm, as Deive (1980, 57, 59) does, that "for Las Casas, the slavery of blacks was a natural state . . . something logical and proper to their nature."[6] In the view of Las Casas, their "natural state," like that of the rest of humanity, is freedom. The serfdom of Africans arises from historical, religious, and wartime reasons that Las Casas first admitted and finally questioned.

It is possible to detect, however, in contrast to his idyllic perspective of the "noble savage" native to the Americas, that his view of Africans is never liberated from certain racist hues that are typical of European white culture, for example, "others as black as Ethiopians, as deformed in their faces and bodies" (Las Casas 1986, 1.1.24:131). Here Las Casas shows he shared in the general devaluing of black physiognomy characteristic of his time.[7] The problem is that in Western metaphysics from Plato to Kant there are such intimate links between truth, virtue, and beauty that if one of these elements is questioned in reference to blacks—for example, beauty—it is almost impossible to avoid devaluing them also in the other two. As a result the theoretical bases for legitimizing racism and slavery are established.

3. At first Las Casas did not limit slavery exclusively to blacks. In some of his recommendations about the possible importation of manual labor, he spoke of "black or white" slaves. In 1531, he repeated the need to import slaves to the Antillean islands, who could be "black or Moors" (Fabié [1879] 1966, 70:485). With the rapid expansion of the African "black market," however, white slavery became an exotic species in process of extinction. The Crown also never regarded the importation of Islamic slaves favorably for it considered them to be a contaminating religious influence, and it avoided their importation by means of edicts and decrees (Mellafe 1964, 54). In 1542, Las Casas would conceive of slavery in the Americas as exclusively black by recommending that as a remedy for the difficulties of the Iberians settled permanently in the New World, "you would order some black slaves be lent or sold on credit" (in Fabié [1879] 1966, 71:461).

4. Las Casas could not imagine the extraordinary exploitation of black labor that would be the cause of the sale of millions of human beings. He seemed to envision importing *ladino* slaves, not the systematic raids designed to capture massive numbers of Africans. His suggestions about the importation of Africans reveal that the numbers he had in mind were relatively small. According to Deive (1980, 66): "Las Casas, who was in Spain [1517–1520], could have read every memorandum and petition regarding blacks arriving at the court, and he vehemently opposed the

importation of bozals, insisting that the slaves should be *ladinos* and that the island should be settled with Castilian farmers."

However, Deive does not draw out the obvious conclusion, namely, that Las Casas did not suggest that the Africans would become the new exploited ones in the Antillean Spanish possessions, but that they would be minority servants on whose shoulders would rest the principal load of productive work for the joined societies of Castilian farmers and Indian towns. In his recommendations dating to 1516–1518, the importation of relatively small numbers of black slaves predominates: "two black male and two black female slaves" for the Castilian families settled in the Antillean islands, evidently for domestic service, and "twenty black males and females" for whoever established a sugar mill (Las Casas 1972, 138, 140; in Fabié [1879] 1966, 70:458–459). In his detailed plan for the peaceful colonization of the northern coast of what is today South America, the total number of black slaves who should be imported in ten years is only 500 (Las Casas 1986, 3.3.132:283). In 1542, he speaks of "some black slaves" (in Fabié [1879] 1966, 71:461). When compared to the history of the massive importation of black manual labor into the Antilles, those numbers are infinitesimal.

5. Las Casas never proposed that the slaves should become the main social base for productive labor. On the contrary, his memoranda contain proposals for communal labor that would fall primarily on the shoulders of Spanish and Indian farmers. They propose a utopia where labor is shared, in gospel-like fraternity between Spaniards and natives, sharing work and profit. In his memorandum of 1518 he insists that the Crown "should order that farmers be provided . . . and that a proclamation be made that all working men who wish to go could go" (Las Casas 1972, 140). Two years earlier he had suggested to Cardinal Cisneros:

> May your very reverend lord order that forty [Spanish] farmers, more or less according to the situation in each place, go to every village or city now existing or to be established later in these islands, along with their [Spanish] wives and children; [that these farmers be taken] from among those who are in excess or in need [in Spain] to settle [in the islands] permanently. And that each may have five Indians with their wives and children as companions to be their colleagues and work together; and after taking His Highness's portion, the rest should be shared *fraternally* by the farmer and his five Indians . . . and they [the Indians], seeing the Christians work, will be in a better disposition to imitate what they see, and at the same time they will mix through the marriages of the sons of the ones with the daughters of the others, etc. And peoples and fruits will be multiplied . . . and the islands will be

ennobled and become, therefore, the best and richest ones in the world. (ibid., 61–62)

It is a utopian vision, if you will, of a mixed [*mestiza*] farming society, whose goods come from the labor of its members, not from the exploitation of enslaved captives. This mixing is based on the work in collaboration and the fraternity of indigenous and Castilian residents. He repeated the same idea decades later, when reflecting on those first memoranda; in his *Historia de las Indias* (1986, 3.3.102:179), he writes on what should have been done in time to avoid the extinction of the Antillean natives:

> Send true settlers, namely, farmers, who would live from the cultivation of such rich lands as these, those freely granted by their owners and native inhabitants, the Indians, from their own free will, and who would intermarry, and from them one of the best republics would be created, perhaps the most Christian and peaceful in the world, and do not send the kind of villainous people who robbed, scandalized, destroyed, devastated, and threw them into hell, resulting in an unbelievable disgrace to the faith.

Las Casas insisted for decades that farmers should be sent to the Antilles, as he repeated many times, people who "will not live from the sweat of others." In a letter in 1559 he asserts that the remedy for Española is "to settle it with simple farmers who are in abundance in those kingdoms [Spain]" (in Pérez de Tudela 1958, 5:463).

It is still true, however, that in 1531 and in 1542, Las Casas felt himself pulled by the mirage of African slavery as a key factor in the solution of the economic problems of Castilian colonists in the Antillean islands, an indispensable element for freeing the natives from cruel exploitation. In the extensive and emotional letter of January 20, 1531, to the Council of the Indies, fifteen years after his first memorandum, he takes up once again with even greater stress his suggestion in respect to slavery.

> The remedy for the Christians is this, surely, that Your Highness agree to lend to each of these islands five or six hundred blacks, or whatever number seems necessary to be distributed among the residents who have no one else except Indians; and for the settlers who would come later, from three, or four, or six, depending on what the person feels is best, that they be sold on credit, and the blacks be mortgaged for the same amount.

Las Casas is concerned in that letter with lowering the cost of the acquisition of blacks by the colonists, criticizing the exclusive sale of importers' licenses by the Crown, because in the end the cost was passed on to the colonists. "My Lords, one of the big reasons that have caused this land to be lost and not to have been settled more than it has been . . . is not having freely granted a license to import blacks to whoever wants to bring them." He alludes to his recommendations from 1516 to 1518, whose aim was to "remedy and free and give new life to the Indians who were oppressed, to take them out of their captivity," recommendations that included, as a significant factor, the importation of slaves. By lamenting the fact that those plans failed, due to his absence from the scene while he was in the Dominican novitiate, he reflects again his intense messianic self-consciousness. "But it was for little benefit . . . because I did not take part any more in the decisions since God took me out for my own greater safety" (in Fabié [1879] 1966, 70:484–486).

In 1552, he returned to his old idea that the only type of colonization that would be at the same time just and profitable would be that of farmers. "The soil of that entire region is very fertile and useful for enriching all those who wish to go there without despoiling the Indians. And productive working farmers, not lazy as the warriors are, are fit to go there" (Las Casas 1965, 1:449).

6. As a final point, and one that his critics neglect, Las Casas became convinced that the raids on the Africans did not fit within the just war criteria; therefore, their enslavement was also illegal. In *Historia de las Indias* (3.3.102:177) he recognized the cruel violence committed in the course of the capturing and trading of the Africans, and he severely condemned those events as "unjust and tyrannical":

> This advice with regard to providing licenses to bring black slaves to these lands was first given by the cleric Casas, not aware of the injustice of the Portuguese then taking and enslaving them; that advice, after he realized the situation, he would not give again for anything in the world, for he always considered that they [the blacks] were unjustly and tyrannically made slaves, the same as the Indians.

Las Casas indicated that, contrary to his initial expectations of some four thousand blacks, more than one hundred thousand (ibid., 3.3.129:275) were taken to the Indies, without reducing the maltreatment of the Indians nor preventing the extinction of the Antillean natives. "There was no benefit for the Indians, for whose welfare and freedom it was ordained, because in the end, they remained captives until there were no more to kill" (ibid., 3.3.102:178). It was also his opinion that the slave trade did not benefit Spain economically and that those who truly gained were the foreigners who dominated the market of blacks. The figure of one hundred thousand that he provides, as all the other figures he gave, should be taken cautiously.

He points out with sadness and indignation that the increase in demand for slaves provoked the increase in the hunts and raids for Africans:

> The consequence is also that since the Portuguese have been stealing from Guinea, and enslaving the blacks in a most unjust way, seeing that we . . . bought them for a good price, daily they have been and continue to be in a rush to steal and capture the Africans by every evil and iniquitous means possible. (ibid., 3.3.129:275)

Conscious that the enslavement of Africans had been based on the premise that they were Saracens and Moors, and therefore, "enemies of Christianity," Las Casas begins to distinguish Moslems, a risky matter in the highly anti-Islamic climate of his day, in an attempt to overcome the often cited threefold classification made by Cardinal Cayetano of infidels (namely, those who are by law but not in fact subjects of Christian princes [i.e., the Turks] and are therefore enemies of Christianity; those who by law and fact are under Christian princes [e.g., the Jews]; and those who, neither by law nor fact, have any relationship to Christians [e.g., the American natives]). Even though the Africans were "Moors," they did not belong to the groups who robbed Christian Europeans, had not injured the Iberian countries in any way, and therefore, the acts of war and enslavement against them were unjust. By law and by fact they did not fall under the jurisdiction of Christian European authorities.

> And this is the blindness . . . that has fallen on worldly Christians who believe that they can mug, rob, capture, and kill infidels since they are not baptized. Certainly, even though [the Africans] were Moors, they should not be captured, nor robbed, nor mugged, since they were not the ones who infest Berbería and the Levante and do harm to Christianity, and these people were quite different from those, in very different provinces and conditions. (ibid., 1.1.22:120)

Worse yet, Portuguese avarice through the slave market stirred, in turn, the enslaving actions of Moors [Arabs] and other blacks.

> The Portuguese did not see either that the Moors, knowing [the Portuguese's] avarice in making black slaves, provoked [the blacks] to make war and ransacked them . . . without just cause, to sell them as slaves . . . since the blacks see the Portuguese are so eager for slaves, out of avarice . . . they steal and capture as many as they can. (ibid., 120–121, 144)[8]

The Portuguese have the right to establish beneficial bilateral commercial relations with the infidel Africans; they also have the duty of missionary activity: "to deal with them peacefully, giving them an example of Christianity, so that . . . they [the Africans] would love the Christian religion and Jesus Christ" (ibid., 1.1.22:120). The Lusitanian Crown definitely does not have a right to continue the sequence of "violence and robberies, deceit and fraud in which the Portuguese have always engaged against those lands and peoples" (ibid., 27:141–142).

He admits ruefully his earlier naïveté about the physical endurance of blacks compared to the natives.

> Earlier, before there were mills, we held the opinion on this island [Española] that if blacks were not hanged they would never die, because we had never seen a black man die from illness. . . . But after they were put in the sugar mills, due to the heavy work they endured and from drinking the sugar molasses that they made, . . . they experienced death and epidemics; in this way many of them die every day. (ibid., 3.3.129:275–276)[9]

This tragic situation makes him conscious of grave sin, and on this occasion he has to declare himself an accomplice. "The cleric, shortly after giving that advice, became repentant, judging himself to be guilty . . . because he later saw and learned . . . that the captivity of the blacks was as unjust as that of the Indians" (Las Casas 1986, 3.3.129:275).[10] The denouncing prophet sorrowfully turns the weapons of his criticism against himself. It must not have been at all easy for a human being so deeply endowed with a messianic conscience and sense of his providential self-worth to intone this mea culpa.

Those are pages of vibrant force, unique for their time. Fernando Ortíz (1978, 107) says about them: "Against the infamy of enslavement and slave markets, Las Casas spoke with more promptitude, vigor, and depth than any other humanist, Spaniard, foreigner, cleric, or lay person until the days of the Enlightenment." And Pérez Fernández (in Las Casas 1989, "Estudio Preliminar," 123) concludes: "Father Las Casas is a defender of blacks against their enslavement in Africa. . . . He was the first one *to defend* them, and even more . . . he was the only one who defended them until the end of the sixteenth century." It may, perhaps, not be incorrect to affirm that the assertions I have alluded to by Las Casas in *Historia de las Indias* constituted the most severe criticism of African slavery until the work in the seventeenth century (1627) of the Jesuit Alonso de Sandoval.[11]

Why is it that his self-criticism and amendment of his earlier suggestions about slavery did not impede the rise of the "black legend" against Las Casas, the accusation that he was an enthusiastic proponent of exchanging the forced manual labor of the natives for that of blacks? In my opinion, it is because the *Historia de las Indias* remained unpublished for more than three centuries. Not until its publication at the end of the nineteenth century (1875) were his strong expressions against African slavery read.[12]

Admittedly, these pages critical of African slavery constituted a minuscule fraction of his writings in defense of the Indians. A few years before adding these clarifications to *Historia de las Indias,* he printed an extensive and passionate treatise declaring that "all the Indians who have been enslaved in the Indies of the Ocean sea . . . have been unjustly enslaved" and should be freed (Las Casas 1965, 1:505). About the black slaves, neither he nor any of the friars who were defenders of the American natives wrote anything similar. Correctly, Deive (1980, 714–715) points out that the strong polemic of Las Casas against Sepúlveda in their famous Valladolid debate (1550–1551) concerning the freedom of the American natives took place at a time when "the enslavement of black men [and black women!] was firmly rooted in the New World. However, the blacks remained totally at the margin of the dispute." He adds critically:

> Certainly Las Casas, after advocating the enslavement of blacks, confessed his guilt by considering it as unjust as that of the Indians, but there is no indication whatever that allows one to suppose that the most fervent defender of the Indian publicly condemned the subjection of the African.[13]

It seems, therefore, that Robert Brady (1966, 47) goes too far in his apologia of Las Casas. It is too much to claim that "the humane [!] treatment that the blacks received was the result of the Defender of the Indians being also the Defender of Blacks." Brady shares the notion, disseminated by many scholars, that enslavement in the Iberian colonies was less cruel than enslavement in the colonies of other European powers.[14] Hence his reference to the "humane treatment" supposedly received by the slaves in Spanish territories. He considers Las Casas responsible for this difference, but the evidence he presents is scanty and weak. Besides, the alleged divergence in the treatment of the slaves cannot be argued exclusively on the basis of the comparative analysis of the legal codes. In the case of Spain's possessions, the famous dictum "I obey but do not comply" must be understood as applying.

It also seems to me that Hanke (in Las Casas 1965, 1:xviii) goes further than the facts and texts allow one to affirm when he asserts: "It is true that Las Casas began as a defender of Indians only, but he later also opposed the enslavement of blacks for the same reasons; thus he worked for the freedom of all peoples of the world." It is certain that in the end he theoretically opposed the enslavement of Africans, and basically for the same reasons that he claimed full liberty for the natives of the Americas. But there is no doubt that he "did not work for the freedom of all peoples of the world," if by that is meant that he made an effort for the abolition of African serfdom. The strange thing is that Hanke writes this sentence as part of a prologue to the modern Mexican edition of the Las Casas *Tratados* of 1552, all dedicated to the freedom of the American natives, with scarce if any references to the tragic situation of the Africans. From the time he returned to Spain for the last time in 1547 until his death in 1566, he dedicated his passionate efforts to the well-being of the first, not of the latter.

Equally outlandish seems the assessment by Ortíz (1978, 116) with which he concludes his excellent essay: "Si a las Casas se le puede llamar 'apóstol de los indios,' también fué 'apóstol de los negros'" (If Las Casas can be called "apostle to the Indians," he was also "apostle to the blacks"). For his part, Manuel Giménez Fernández in the second prologue to the Mexican edition of *Tratados* (1965, 1:lxxxvii) refers to the "tolerance of institutionalized slavery of blacks" on the part of Las Casas at the beginning of his public career as a "forgivable mistake." Las Casas judged it more severely: ". . . became repentant, judging himself to be guilty . . ."

Here arises a problem that only a careful paleographic study of *Historia de las Indias* could resolve: When did Las Casas make the denunciations of African slavery of which he writes? Alain Milhou (1975–1976, 63), in a provocative work, asserts that they came late. "Perhaps not before 1560, in which he wrote chapters 102 and 129 of the third book of *Historia*." In Milhou's opinion, the first conscious awareness for Las Casas, not yet made definite, proceeds from his reading a book by Joâo de Barros about Portuguese journeys and conquests, *Dos feitos que os portugueses fizeram no descobrimento e conquista dos mares e terras do Oriente* (Portuguese exploits in the discovery and conquest of seas and lands in the Orient), known best as *Décadas de Asia*, which was published in 1552. Similarly, Pérez Fernández (in Las Casas 1989, 35) understands that chapters 22 to 27 of the first book of *Historia de las Indias*, where Las Casas criticizes the Portuguese violent conquest of Africans, must have been written late, "toward 1558 or 1559 itself." In that case, Hanke's affirmation and that of the legions who followed Hanke would be incorrect that in the Valladolid debate the theoretical and dogmatic fundamental axis of Las Casas was "[all] humanity is one."

Why the relative silence of Las Casas about African slavery ("relative" when compared to the voluminous flow of his passionate writings on behalf of Indian freedom)? Las Casas was *Spanish and Catholic*. The raids against Africans were primarily a sin of the Portuguese; the exploitation of the Indians was, on the contrary, a violation of divine and natural law on the part of Spain. Las Casas has for his country the same attachment that the prophets of the Old Testament had toward the biblical Israel. If this is true, instead of being stubbornly anti-Spanish, as it has been suggested so often by his detractors, his denunciations came from his passionate and fiery nationalism. In his "Brevísima relación," after a lugubrious account of the interminable and morbid sequence of "cruelties and tyrannies" committed by the Spaniards in the New World, he affirms his providential role in appealing to the Christian and ethical conscience of his country.

> I, Fray Bartolomé de las Casas o Casaus, friar of Saint Dominic, was called . . . by the mercy of God . . . and by the compassion that I have for my country, which is Castilla, so that God will not destroy it because of the great sins against its faith and honor it has committed, and against its neighbors . . . (Las Casas 1989, 193–195)

He is concerned with denouncing the "destruction of the Indies" as a sin of Spain. He considers himself God's prophet, chosen as a beacon of the Spanish nation's conscience, which in his opinion, is the missionary vanguard of the Catholic faith. The sin against the Africans, on the contrary, is Portuguese transgression, and therefore a priority for Lusitanian prophets. He has no problem in characterizing it as "very execrable tyranny" (Las Casas 1986, 2.1.150:73). But he does not think that his providential role is to insist on its denunciation.

Besides, Las Casas attempted always to walk on solid paths of ecclesiastical orthodoxy. In the Spain of the sixteenth century, in which so many notable figures were given such a hard time by the Inquisition, that meant confronting authorized papal declarations. There is a marked difference between the papal declarations dealing with Indian and African slavery. In the fifteenth century various bulls and papal decrees—*Dudum cum ad nos* (1436) and *Rex regum* (1443) of Eugene IV; *Divino amore communiti* (1452) and *Romanus pontifex* (1455) of Nicholas V; *Inter caetera* (1456) of Callistus III; and *Aeterni regis* (1481) of Sixtus IV—endorsed the forced serfdom of black Africans carried out by the Portuguese Crown. On the contrary, the bull *Inter caetera* (1493) of Alexander VI insists on the conversion of the American natives, implying their freedom, and *Sublimis Deus* (1537) of Paul III proclaims their freedom and threatens enslavers with excommunication.

As a Spaniard and man of the church, therefore, Las Casas felt firmly compelled to protest viva voce against indigenous slavery. He questioned African slavery in his *Historia de las Indias* but without the same dedication or devotion. And he avoided making direct negative judgments about the papal bulls that directly authorized the enslavement of Africans.[15]

There were many clerics whose obvious sensitivity toward the suffering of the natives was not accompanied by a similar sentiment toward blacks. I differ therefore with Zavala (1984, 102–103) when he alleges, in spite of the scant evidence he provides, that "the just analysis that dared draw out of Christian principles liberal conclusions favorable to blacks . . . was not absent . . . as it had not been absent before with respect to the Indians . . . [due to the] word of theologians and jurists who came to see the problem clearly."[16] On the contrary, Fernando Mires (1987, 219; cf. 1986, 131–138) is correct in his critical assertion that "if on some occasions the church was committed to defend some Indian interests, that did not occur in the case of the blacks. In other words, it was not the official politics of the church to defend the blacks."[17]

Part III

A Theological Critique of the Conquest

11

The Theological-Juridical Debate

The priest punishes and gives orders—
but he should not do so, being a priest.

We came to conquer this land so that all may come to know God and
his holy Catholic faith . . . and so that you will understand and abandon the diabolical and beastly life you lead.

Francisco Pizarro

They have the very highest cause of all, and many other causes in all
justice which they, the Indians, have by natural, divine, and human law,
and that is to quarter them [their enemies] if they have the strength and
arms needed, and to throw them out of their lands.

Bartolomé de las Casas

Theory and Reality

Spanish domination over the "islands and mainland of the Ocean sea"
caused fiery questioning and ardent debates in respect to the justice of
the armed conquest and Christianization of its inhabitants. Lively and
intense discussions continued throughout the sixteenth century among
Spanish theologians and jurists, who debated the issues passionately and
creatively.

The questions were many, as we have seen in the course of this work.
Do the Europeans have the right to take possession of and conquer the
lands and inhabitants of the New World? Are the wars against the indigenous nations that do not accept Spain's temporal and spiritual sovereignty
just? Can the colonists force the indigenous peoples to work in the extraction of mineral resources? Are the differences in the cultural life of
Spaniards and American natives relative and historically conditioned, or
do they express an essential inequality "almost as those between humans
and beasts"? (Ginés de Sepúlveda 1951, 38).

Are the natives free or servants by nature? Are they noble savages or
vicious idolaters? Do they have culture or are they uncivilized? Do they
or do they not have a right to their lands and possessions? Should the
Christian faith be preached to them peacefully, respecting their right to
reject it, or should it be imposed on them, forcing them to be baptized?
Does conversion precede colonization, or vice versa?

The theological-juridical debate was exemplary and took on an exceptional intellectual and emotional intensity. If the denunciatory writings of
Bartolomé de las Casas have provided abundant ammunition to the
infamous "black legend," it is also true that the cordial and attentive reception that they received from the royal court and the Council of the Indies

reflects their interest in combining political and material expansion with the spiritual well-being of both Europeans and American natives. The North American Sauer (1984, 10) rightly asserts that "the Spaniards were the most severe and insistent critics of the sad state of their own colonies." While the critical scourges that were the treatises of Las Casas were printed and widely distributed, the main anti-Indian writing of his rival Sepúlveda was only published four centuries after it was penned.[1] It is difficult to deny the conclusive affirmation of the North American historian Hanke (1967, 15):

> The Spanish conquest of the Americas was more than an extraordinary military and political feat . . . ; it was also one of the greatest attempts the world has seen to make Christian principles prevail in the relations between peoples. This attempt became basically a fiery defense of the rights of the Indians which rested on two of the basic presuppositions that a Christian can make, namely: that all men are equal before God, and that a Christian is responsible for the well-being of his brothers, no matter how alien or humble they may be.

The markedly confessional character of the Spanish state, which converted the conquest into missionary activity, and the subordination of the church to the Crown, which in turn made a state venture of the propagation of the faith, conferred on the intense debates a unique character, unequaled in history. *Every theological dispute about the New World and its inhabitants took on a political character and vice versa; every political disagreement over the relationship of Spain to the natives became a theological debate.* This phenomenon explains the public preeminence of all the writings and expositions of such theologians as Las Casas, Sepúlveda, and Vitoria, and the religious tones given to many political decrees from the Council of the Indies.

The theoretical debates, from a particular time and space, touched perennial problems deeply: Is humanity one or diverse? Are some human beings superior in intelligence and prudence, and do they therefore have a right to special privileges and unique responsibilities? Is the domination of some nations by others justified because of natural or historical inequalities? Do valuable mineral resources belong to the inhabitants of the territory where they are, or to whoever can invest in their development?

From those questions, with Francisco de Vitoria's help, modern international law was born. It is important to clarify, however, that it is an international law conceived from the perspective of the conquerors, which ultimately served to legitimize armed conquest. Many times we forget the markedly bellicose character of the law of nations in Vitoria. It is no accident that his two lectures on the Indians gravitate toward the legitimacy of the objective and methods of the wars against the "barbarians of the New World." There is a serious historical contradiction between the theoretical promulgation of the human dignity of the American natives and their displacement, oppression, and decimation. This perspective of imperial power is what gives an abstract character to the theoretical equality of sovereign nations propounded by Vitoria.[2] It does not reveal the profound inequality in economic, social, and military power between the empire and the occupied territory, which shatters the theoretical schema of equality and reciprocity. In general, it would not be untrue to assert that the promoters of the human rights of the American natives win at the level of theory but are defeated in the historical practice of conquest.

Pope Paul III's bull *Sublimis Deus*, June 2, 1537, asserts the humanity, rationality, and freedom of the natives. The papal decree, in contrast to the opinion promoted by "the enemy of the human race itself," asserts that "the Indians are true men . . . and can in no way be deprived of their freedom." The New Laws of 1542 recognized the individual autonomy of the natives and officially and formally declared the benevolent will of the empire: "Because our main intention and will has always been and is the preservation and increase of the Indians and that they be treated as free persons . . ."

Well and good, but their concrete predominant experience is defeat, suffering, decimation, and subjugation. Juan Friede (1976, 59) has made the same judgment more emphatically:

> At a distance of several thousand miles from central power . . . no royal decision was capable of abolishing as if by magic the self-interest that was leading to the "destruction" of the native population. America lived its own life, almost, it could be said, on the fringes of legal dispositions. . . . It structured its society by the facts, not the laws.

This does not deprive of merit the titanic efforts of Las Casas and other jurists and religious to promote just and humane legislation for the natives of the New World. These efforts reflect an important idea that Bataillon (1976, 41) captures well: "Throughout the constant lack of compliance for the Laws of the Indies the *need for legal justice* persisted." The aspiration for the creation of a just and reasonable system of law comes through in such works as *De indis*, by Vitoria, and *Los Tesoros del Perú*, by Las Casas. The latter surprisingly suggests that there is only one remedy for the cruel exploitation to which the natives are subjected: to promote the juridical nullity of all the events. "There is no other solution nor can we think of another one outside this one; namely, that all the actions that have taken place, in reference to and against the natives, be taken as null by law [*nulla de iure*]" (Las Casas 1958, 337–341). Many pages of Las Casas reflect that juridical conscience, deeply humanistic and at the same time idealist and utopian.

Zavala (1984, 96–97) is right in affirming that those intense theoretical debates were not "academic boasting nor juridical frills; rather, they provided the spiritual base for an administrative regime which, faced with the facts, would have its virtues and limitations tested daily." But it is a non sequitur to deduce from that correct assessment the strange thesis that "the historical reality, though dominated by avarice, remained subject to the attraction of superior principles of human dignity."[3] There is no doubt that the battle between avarice and dignity constitutes an extraordinary struggle. In the case of the American natives and the African blacks, it also carried with it an exceptionally high human cost.

Juan Manzano (1948, 62), too, errs in his excessive theoretical and legalistic enthusiasm by saying that the collective effort of a great number of friars on behalf of the natives "was to see itself crowned with the most complete success," above all thanks to the legislative actions of 1542.[4] If that had been true, the American natives would not have seen themselves marginalized from the structures of power in their own lands, nor would the writings of Las Casas in his final two decades have had the bitter and denunciatory tone that characterizes them.

> Since the laws were published . . . those in charge . . . have not wished to comply with the laws . . . because they do not like to abandon the usurped haciendas they have, or grant freedom to the Indians they hold in perpetual captivity. Where they have ceased to kill them quickly with swords, they kill them little by little with personal services and other unjust and intolerable demands. And up to now the king is not powerful enough to stop it. (Las Casas 1989, 197–199)

Later, Manzano (1948, 191) admits that "this success attributed to the theologians of the Order of Saint Dominic, although considerable, was not absolute or complete."[5] The problem is that both affirmations, besides being mutually incompatible, gravitate to the level of theological and juridical abstraction. For Las Casas the primary and crucial matter was not theoretical diatribe but historical action: the concrete life of the inhabitants of the New World.

Venancio Carro (1944, 2:309, 317, 321), in his important work on Spanish juridical theology of the sixteenth century, confuses the prevalent theories in theological schools, especially Salamanca, with the historical reality of the conquest and colonization. He affirms that his extensive work of more than nine hundred pages is dedicated to "examining the conquest and colonization of the New World as it was in reality." It is a promise to which, to be truthful, he does not dedicate a single page. He analyzes an impressive number of peninsular writers, above all the Dominicans, based on the theoretical premise that the "true defense of human freedoms and rights is possible only within the principles of Christian theological-juridical science." He arrives at the impressive and triumphalistic conclusion that "the conquest and colonization of the Hispano-American world was the most humane and Christian that has occurred in the history of all the nations." In all that voluminous account of "the conquest and colonization of the New World as it was in reality," there is not one single dead, hungry, or maltreated Indian. A word of thanks here to Francisco de Vitoria, Domingo de Soto, and Domingo Bañez!

In a similar triumphalistic line, Antonio Ybot León (1948), in a study of the theological counseling committees of the Spanish Crown, concludes that starting from "the purest principles of the law of nations according to the divine origin of man," they produced "an entire body of normative and operative doctrine" and "binding norms of government" that imprinted the Spanish regime in the Indies with "its singular and exclusive distinguishing style in the history of all empires." Ybot León calls this style "a deliberate attempt to govern according to the precepts of justice and Christian law, of which the theologians were the natural definers." The relationship seems simple and direct: theological principles on the human dignity of the Indians—humanist legislation—benevolent government. Ybot León is not inclined, however, to study the possible empirical relationship between "the theory that maintained the great Spanish task in a missionary stance" and the reality of the way of the cross of the natives.

The contradiction between the legal decrees and the experience of illegal applications and the sense of powerlessness on the part of the Iberian authorities is clearly evident in a communique that on July 3, 1549, was sent to the emperor by the Council of the Indies affirming its frustration:

> . . . because those who go on these conquests do not carry with them people who would refrain from doing as they please nor anyone who will accuse them of the evil they have done. For such is the greed of those who go on these conquests and so humble and fearful are the people they go to that we have no assurance that any instruction given to them [the conquerors and colonists] will be observed." (in Jaime González Rodriguez in Ramos et al. 1984, 216)

Something not much different had been stated by a Dr. Montano in 1547, who said that in spite of the benevolent legislation for the Indies approved by the Castilian court, "everything is done under cover in such a way that the Indians continue in the same condition of servitude as before" (in Milhou 1975–1976, 30). Anglería (1964–1965, 2.7.4:607) presents a similar testimony when, after stressing the conscientious job accomplished by the Council of the Indies in the enactment of beneficial legislation of the Indies, he bitterly concludes:

> But, what is happening? Our people, transported across an ocean to such strange, changing, and distant worlds, . . . and far from the authorities, allowed themselves to be carried away by the blind greed of gold, and those who leave here meeker than lambs, change as soon as they arrive there into wild wolves, forgetting all the royal commands.[6]

From their profound solidarity with the oppressed Antillean natives, the Dominican friars in Española accuse the Spanish colonists of making "fun of the provisions that in this matter [the good treatment of the natives] are provided by the Council." They recognize that they cannot "tame the rabid and disorderly greed of five hundred or a thousand men who come not knowing once there any subjection to God, even less to Your Majesty, . . . in order to come back loaded with gold" (in Pacheco et al. 1864–1884, 2:245). In the same way Las Casas, in his letter to the Council of the Indies of 1531, denounces the corruption that quickly afflicts the royal officials who go to the New World with the specific task of enforcing the laws.

> Those who come here to give orders become daring and lose their fear of God and faith in their king and fidelity to him and respect for the people, and then they make a pact with the devil, to whom they give their souls so they can rob . . . for they see that the king and his Council are far away. (in Fabié [1879] 1966, 70:482)[7]

The strange contradiction between the abundant decrees and laws that the Crown and the Council of the Indies approved for the benefit and protection of the Indians and the blatant and intense injustice that they suffered was eloquently noted by Alonso de Zorita (in Pacheco et al. 1864–1884, 2:117–118; emphasis added), who in passing pointed out the saying that in the course of time became famous: "acato pero no cumplo" (I obey but do not comply).

> The will of Y. M. and of your Royal Council is clearly known, and it is known and understood by means of the daily instructions sent on behalf of those poor natural inhabitants, and for their increase and preservation. But they are *obeyed without being complied with*, and therefore they continue to be lost sight of, nor is there anyone who exactly knows what

Y. M. has ordered. What instructions, decrees, letters are sent by the Emperor our Lord [Carlos V], already in heaven! And how many and how necessary the ones sent daily by Y. M. [Felipe II] and how little they prevail. . . . I am certain that what a philosopher used to say is very fitting: just as where there are many doctors and medicines, health is absent, where there are many laws, justice is lacking.

Mendieta ([1596] 1980, 1.16:66), at the end of the same century, would issue the same complaint, censuring the colossal discrepancy between legislative justice and socioeconomic abuse, while at the same time pointing out the "temporary advantages" that serve as hermeneutical key for understanding the divorce between them.

Seeing that our Catholic Monarchs in Spain provided innumerable decrees, orders, and commands for and on behalf of the Indians, . . . it is a marvel that not even one of those who have governed in your royal name in the Indies was in any way inclined or interested principally in that duty . . . but only in that with which he could burden the hands of the poor ones who can do little or do not know how to or dare speak or act for themselves, and they (the royal representatives) behave in this way out of respect for their own interests and temporal benefit.

According to this Franciscan friar, in America "there is no other law nor right nor statute, except what will benefit the Spaniard justly or unjustly, and make the Indian suffer and grieve" (ibid., 4.46:561).

The historian José María Ots Capdequí (1986, 14) points out that, on the part of a government official in the Indies, the act of "obeying but not complying" reached the point of being formalized as a brief ceremony. "Upon receipt of a Royal Decree, whose fulfillment was not considered pertinent, the viceroy, president, or governor would place it solemnly on his head as sign of compliance and reverence, at the same time declaring that its fulfillment was placed in abeyance."

The theological-juridical debates were exceptionally intense in the Spain of the Golden Age. They were initiated by missionaries and theologians and eventually ended by them. If Montesinos, Las Casas, and Vitoria reflect the freshness and vigor of a debate in its fiery beginnings, Acosta by the end of the century already reflects the fatigue and exhaustion in the polemical impulse. The opportunistic pragmatism prevails, shielded by a pious evangelistic intention.

Granted that dominion of the Indies has been usurped unjustly, it is still better to believe and proclaim . . . that by law and right it is inappropriate to doubt the right of Christian princes to govern the Indies, which besides is very useful for the eternal salvation of the natives.

Acosta (1952, 2.11:186–187) promotes a policy of a strong hand against those who question the justice of the conquest. "If . . . they are not repressed with a strong hand, one cannot tell the evils and universal ruin that will follow, and the very serious disturbance and disorder in all things." The time for debate and lively polemics, stimulating to the juridical and theological mentality, has been left behind. Under the severe scrutiny of the Inquisition and of bureaucracy, the clash of ideas is avoided and the publication of divergent opinions is made difficult.[8]

The Cross and the Sword

In the entire process of conquest and evangelization of the Americas the relationship between the cross and the sword was problematic and complex. The sword, superior military technology, determined the outcome. The cross represented the final objective that the Spanish protagonists accepted, at least in juridical and theological theory. Paradoxically, the sword had religious and spiritual objectives, while the cross was invested with political and temporal characteristics.

It is significant that before Sepúlveda wrote his apologia for the Spanish wars against the Indians in *Demócrates segundo*, against the initial pacifism of some Protestant reformers he wrote a treatise—*Demócrates primo* (1525)— theologically defending war as a possible just action for Christians (i.e., against the Turks). In the same way, Vitoria immediately after his theological lectures on the justice of the Spanish domination of the New World—*De indis* (1538)—delivers others on just war—*De iure belli* (1539). The link between the cross and the sword is expressed again in the Augustinian clothing of the holy war, cultivated during centuries of crusades against the infidels.

The connection between the two is quite evident in the account that the Chontal Maya made about the execution of Cuauhtémoc (Léon Portilla 1987, 93–95). The Spaniards are convinced that his subjection is a fake and that he is planning an armed revolt. They decide, therefore, to kill him. But first they take precautionary religious steps and baptize the Aztec monarch. In this way, the Christian sacrament is linked to the conquering violence. The body of the chief is killed while at the same time an attempt is made to redeem his soul.

The Inka king Atahualpa also is baptized before his execution. In his case, the sacrament serves as amelioration of his execution, which was by hanging and burning. After his execution he is buried as a Christian, with the appropriate liturgical ceremonies ("the Governor, with the other Spaniards, took him very solemnly, with all possible honors, to be buried in the church") (Jerez 1947, 344–345). Baptism serves as an ironic exchange: eternal salvation of the soul in exchange for the temporal death of the body. In the case of Atahualpa, it is linked to the adoration of mammon: as a useless ransom for his life the indigenous monarch gives Francisco Pizarro an enormous amount of gold, a tragic forecast of the riches that the Spaniards could acquire if they overcame and subjected the natives.[9]

Atahualpa and his attendants were surprised and trapped. Pizarro had invited Atahualpa to Caxamarca to explain to him the purpose of the Spaniards' arrival. After the king refused to accept the exhortation to accept the Christian faith made by Fray Vicente de Valverde, according to a Quechua account:

> Fray Vicente entered . . . carrying a cross in his right hand and a breviary in the left. And he said to the Inka Atahualpa that he [Vicente] also is an ambassador and messenger from another lord, very great indeed, and a friend of God, and he [Atahualpa] should become his [God's] friend and adore the cross and believe the gospel of God and that everything else was not worthy of adoration, that it was false.
> The Inka Atahualpa responded that he did not have to adore anyone except the sun, which never dies . . . and gods who also have their law: those he obeyed. . . . Fray Vicente called out and said: Here, gentlemen, these gentile Indians are against our faith! And Don Francisco Pizarro and Don Diego de Almagro, on their part, raised their voices and said: Go forth, warriors, against those infidels who oppose our Christian faith! (in Léon Portilla 1987, 144)

The Spanish chronicler of the conquest of Peru and personal secretary of Pizarro, Francisco de Jerez (1947, 332–333), relates this scene with different details. He admits, however, that the order to attack Atahualpa and his warriors was given after Valverde informed Pizarro that the Inka chief "had thrown the sacred scriptures to the ground." Following the messianic cry of "Santiago" [James], the Castilian artillery and cavalry attacked by surprise, causing the Inka warriors to flee, and allowing for the imprisonment of the Inka monarch. Pizarro then explains the providential and religious cause of his victory:

> We came to conquer this land so that all may come to know God and his holy Catholic faith . . . and so that you will understand and abandon the diabolical and beastly life you lead. . . . And if you have been taken prisoner and your people scattered and killed, it is because . . . you threw on the ground the book where God's words are, therefore our

Lord allowed your pride to be wounded and did not permit an Indian
to hurt any Christian.[10]

He who carried the cross becomes the legitimizing agent of the one
who uses the sword; the requirement of conversion becomes the death
sentence.

Symptomatic of the close link between religious and military power
in the conquest of the Americas is the description given by Robert Ricard
(1986, 265–266) of the convents and monasteries that the friars built in
Nueva España during the first years of evangelization.

> The convent of the sixteenth century, besides its primary aim, had two
> purposes: to serve as a fortress if needed and as a refuge for Spaniards
> in the not remote case of an Indian uprising. In that way the two con-
> quests were mutually allied and strengthened: the spiritual and the
> military. And this explains, also, the military value of many convents . . .
> true fortified castles.

Therefore, when Doctor Luis de Anguis, professor of the Decretal Chair
of the University of Mexico, protested in a letter to Felipe II (February 20,
1561) because of what was in his opinion the excessive size of the monasteries and convents, he received a reply that was more military than
religious: "They answered that they built them that way so that when
necessary they could serve Y. M. as a fortress" (in Cuevas [1914] 1975, 262).

Alonso de Ercilla relates in his epic *La Araucana* (1569–1589) (1984 [1945],
34:582–583 [302–303]) the conversion and final torment of Caupolicán, the
last of the great Araucan chiefs who rebelled against Spain. His sudden
acceptance of the Christian faith, after his defeat and arrest, caused great
joy among the Spaniards, who after instructing him in his new religion,
baptizing him, and celebrating his conversion, proceeded nevertheless to
execute him in a horrendous way: by impalement and transfixment with
arrows.

> Yet, God changed him in a moment,
> Working with His Hand Almighty.
> Bright with faith and understanding,
> He desired he a Christian's christening.
> Piteous joy did he elicit
> From surrounding folk Castilian,
> Causing all admiring wonder,
> Awing red barbarians present.
> On that mournful day, yet happy
> Solemnly they then baptized him,
> And whilst scanty time permitted,

In the true faith gave instructions.
Dense platoons of armored gentry
Hemmed him in and soon escorted
Him out to suffer death accepted
In the hope of God's hereafter.

In other respects, the battle between the cross (friars and ecclesiastics as defenders of the Indians) and the sword (conquerors and colonists) is one of the most interesting chapters in the long and labyrinthian relationship between church and state, between spiritual and worldly powers. Occasionally the evangelizers tried to redeem the soul of the American native without chaining the body, but this was not the general practice. The most famous example of peaceful evangelization was the religious activity of Las Casas in Vera Paz, Guatemala.

As was mentioned in chapter 3, with a decree in 1526 the Spanish Crown tried to control and moderate the violence of the sword by requiring the inclusion of religious men or clerics in every expedition. Thus, the armed actions against the natives required the previous authorization of the religious "signed with their names" (in Konetzke 1953, 1:92, 94). Demetrio Ramos (Ramos et al. 1984, 716) has assessed the outcome in the following way: "The system of 1526 failed. . . . The moral power of the two 'religious men or clerics' on which rested the responsibility of conscience, had no efficacy at all."

The theological-juridical idea of the *just war*, promoted by Saint Augustine, had the double and difficult task of moderating the cruelty of war and at the same time admitting that on some occasions a nation could and even should use arms in response to a grave injury (see Russell 1975). Spanish theologians and jurists tried to demonstrate that the armed conflict against the indigenous peoples fulfilled the criteria for a just war. Sepúlveda was an extreme case, but Vitoria did the same, while defining and restricting the reasons and causes. In general, Spanish scholars made the just war concept the conceptual fundamental axis for their analysis of the double confrontation for Catholic armies at that time: against Turks and Muslims, on the one hand, and against the indigenous peoples, on the other. From Vitoria to Spanish Jesuit theologian Francisco Suárez, the problem of the legitimacy of the war against the "infidels" was central to Castilian academic circles.

Although for those thinkers, the main criterion for determining the legality of a military conflict derived from the injury received and not vindicated (Vitoria: "La única y sola causa justa de hacer la guerra es la injuria recibida" [The one and only just cause to make war is the injury received] [in Urdanoz 1960, 825]), it was easy to devalue infidels and gentiles based on the religious motives of virulent holy wars. In that case, the Spanish theologians sometimes approved of extremes of horrendous cruelty. The Jesuit Luis de Molina in *De iustitia et iure*, (2.122, n. 4. in Höffner 1957, 455) recommends the killing of infidel enemies,

> if from it [the killing] there is some usefulness for the church, and even for the guilty ones. For example, when dealing with gentiles, those who can hardly be expected to convert or abandon their sinful life. In that case, it would be without doubt holy and legitimate to kill them all, or at least, as many as would be considered necessary to achieve that aim. On the one hand, such an execution would be just in itself, and, on the other, a manifestation, also, of love of God and neighbor. It would serve the good of the church and of the executors of the order and even of the executed ones themselves, for death would impede them from continuing accumulating sin on top of sin. They would suffer less punishment in the eternal flames than if they had continued to live in this world.

This reference shows the subtle line separating the just war from the holy war, and the ferocity and violence that always accompanies the holy war.

Las Casas adopted the opposite position: the wars the Indians wage against the Spaniards are just. Two indispensable factors are missing from the Spanish wars to rate them as legitimate: a just cause ("No war is just if there is no cause for declaring war. . . . But the infidel people [the Indians] . . . have not done any damage to the Christian people for which they deserve to be attacked by war" [Las Casas 1942, 515]) and true authority (the attacks by the conquerors, according to Las Casas, have been carried out without true royal consent).

For Las Casas the Indian wars on the Spanish, on the contrary, fulfill the formal criteria that grants them legitimacy: they are declared by the true authority of the territories in question, are for defense, and respond to incalculable damages that have not been vindicated. The Spaniards are blind and cannot see that:

> [The wars] were, are, and always will be unjust, evil, tyrannical, and detestable wherever for such a cause and under that title [i.e., refusal to accept the *Requerimiento*], they are or will be waged against the inhabitants and dwellers of the Indies; they are condemned by all natural, human, and divine law; therefore, wars of these infidels against every Spaniard and against every Christian who starts such a war are very just. (Las Casas 1986, 3.3.58:30)
>
> They have the very highest cause of all, and many other causes in all justice which they, the Indians, have by natural, divine, and human law, and that is to quarter them if they have the strength and arms

needed, and to throw them out of their lands, because of their very unjust behavior, filled with every iniquity, and condemned by all the laws
that are in force among them . . . reason, therefore to make war against
them (the Spaniards). (Las Casas 1989, 101)

The wars of the Spaniards violate all the natural rights of the indigenous
nations and constitute, also, a repugnant procedure contrary to the one
that ought to be followed in the conversion of the natives. This, according
to Las Casas, should be characterized by persuasion of their understanding
and attraction of their will, both absent from armed conflicts. Faced with
the opinion of those who alleged that war would achieve more positive
results, such as the eradication of cannibalism and idolatrous human
sacrifice, he replied that generally there are more victims as a result of
armed conflict than those who could be saved from cannibalism or ritual
sacrifices, and that the desire to impose the faith by force was more in keeping with the followers of Mohammed than with the Christians.

It is an error, however, to label the posture of Las Casas as "extreme
pacifism," as Urdanoz has done (see 1960, 629, n. 269). Although he considers armed conflict "the worst evil" and "a plague of the body and the
soul" (Las Casas 1974, 298, 360), it is a distortion of his position to classify
it as pacifism, if that term is understood as the unconditional rejection of
any military action. Two observations need to be made here.

First, Las Casas distinguishes between the use of arms for defending
the state and the nation from external aggressors, which he considers valid,
and armed action for the spread of the gospel, which is illegal.

But do not think that as a result armed conflicts are forbidden to Christian princes when needed for the defense of their republics. For it is one
thing to speak about the way the law of Jesus Christ should be preached,
and therefore of assembling, propagating, and preserving Christianity
where it reigns spiritually, and it is something else to speak of ways of
preserving a human republic in accordance with right reason, which tells
us that sometimes it is necessary to undertake war to defend it and free
it from tyranny. (Las Casas 1942, 491)

Secondly, Las Casas holds that there are times when a prince may
defend or preach the Christian faith by means of war. Three traditional
examples that he supports are: (a) the recovery of the Holy Land — reason
for the Crusades; (b) the reconquest of the Iberian peninsula from the
Moors; and (c) in general, the battle against the Muslims, "enemies of the
faith, usurpers of Christian kingdoms" (Las Casas 1965, 1037).[11] Those are,
in his opinion, defensive actions against the offenses committed by
Muslims against Christianity. Even at times when there can be a truce,

for example, against the Ottoman Turks, that does not alter the fact that "we have a just war against them, not only when they are actually waging it against us but even when they stop, because we have a very long experience of their intention to harm us; so our war against them cannot be called war but legitimate defense" (Las Casas 1986, 1.1.25:134).

Las Casas is willing to go further and justify armed action to defend the preaching of the gospel and the missionaries from the aggressive actions of hostile infidels. "Our war would be just against them if they maliciously pursue or disturb or impede our faith and Christian religion, or without legitimate cause kill its priests and preachers" (ibid.). But it has to be proven that there is no genuine "legitimate cause" for the violent action of the infidels and the resistance to preaching is done "maliciously" and not in response to injustice previously committed by Spanish Christians (1974, ch. 25, 168–175).

In his extensive apologia against Sepúlveda, Las Casas accepts in principle the tenet of Vitoria on the legality of utilizing arms to defend the innocent victims who are sacrificed by infidels on the altars of their gods and those executed for cannibalistic purposes. However, in his opinion, reality contradicts the appropriateness of such armed intervention since it would be accompanied by greater damage to more innocent people than the few instances, according to his unique accounting system, of those who are sacrificed or eaten by the peoples of the Americas (ibid., 185–194).[12] Faithful to his usual style, he gathers extensive quotes from theological and juridical authorities to demonstrate the injustice of such military ventures.

He is also ready to validate wars against the heretics (such as the famous wars against the Albigensians and Hussites). "The Apostolic See may grant and cede the kingdoms of heretics to the Catholic Monarchs . . . and give them [Catholics] orders to war against them and eradicate them." Of course, this is granted on one condition: "that it can be accomplished without great loss, killings, and damages," which is in keeping with the war criterion of proportionality (Las Casas 1965, 1037).[13]

Las Casas establishes a distinction in the treatment of the heretics and the infidel natives. The first can be compelled by ecclesiastical and state force as a result of disobeying their baptismal vow; not the second. Thus, he tries to evade the relevance of the quotes that Sepúlveda uses from the epistles of Saint Augustine in which he defends the state repression of heretics.

> It is of little use for the doctor [Sepúlveda] to use against the Indians what Saint Augustine said of the heretics, since the heretics can be subjected by force to the faith which they promised by baptism, for they are already subjects of the church. This is not true of the Indians because

they are not subjects as they have not received baptism. (Las Casas 1965, 381)

In respect to the basis of this key distinction between "infidel" and "heretic," it is my opinion that we need to modify John Phelan's (1974, 298) judgment that Las Casas tried to "replace an Augustinian idea with a Thomistic one" by insisting that being an orthodox Christian is not a prerequisite for the validity of one's political and personal rights, "an idea for a long time identified with Saint Augustine." More precisely, what Las Casas is proposing is that the Augustinian thesis is valid with respect to the heretics, not to the infidels whose separation from the Christian faith comes from "invincible ignorance."

Las Casas is walking on very orthodox paths. Aquinas expounded the distinction between heretic and infidel. Cardinal Cayetano (Tomás de Vio Caietano) made a further distinction: namely, the category of infidel with invincible (i.e., inculpable) ignorance, and therefore, guiltless for being pagan. The distinctions of the latter became the restraining wall against the universalist theocratic concepts that advocated the holy war against infidelity, for infidelity was an alleged intolerable offense against God.[14] In a key passage, Cayetano distinguished between the infidels who by law and by fact (*de iure et de facto*) are under the jurisdiction of Christianity, those who by law but not by fact are, and those who neither by law nor fact are legitimate subjects. The natives of the New World belonged to the third category:

> The owners of these lands, although infidels [those who have not committed any injury against Christianity], are their legitimate owners . . . [and] their infidelity does not deprive them of their dominion, for dominion ensues from natural law and infidelity from divine law, which does not destroy natural law. . . . No king nor emperor, not even the Roman church itself, can wage war against them to occupy their lands and dominate them in temporal matters, for there is no cause for a just war. . . . Whereas we would seriously sin if we wished to spread the faith in Jesus Christ in this manner, and would not obtain legitimate jurisdiction, but rather would be committing grave robbery and would be obliged to make restitution for these unjust opponents and owners. To those infidels there should be sent good men who by their preaching and example would convert them to God and not such as those who oppress them, despoil them, scandalize and subject them, and make them twice the children of hell, in the style of the Pharisees.[15]

At the same time, however, the cruel persecution of the heretics is justified. Aquinas (*Summa* 2-2.10.8), after insisting that the infidels should not be obliged to convert "because the act of faith belongs to the will" (*quia credere voluntatis est*), says of the heretics and apostates that they "should be subjected even to bodily compulsion so that they may fulfill what they have promised and profess what they at one time received."

Las Casas does not separate himself from that intolerance of theological heterodoxy. After repeating the dogmatic motto *extra ecclesiam nulla salus* (outside the church there is no salvation), he warns that, unlike the American natives, "the heretics should be expelled from the church by means of spiritual punishment, excommunication. If they stubbornly persist in their error, they should be consumed by the flames," since there "cannot be salvation in the absence of the holy Catholic faith" (Las Casas 1967, 1.3.45:238; 1974, 163–164, 304–312).[16] That was the common doctrine of the theologians of the Roman church in general. Domingo de Soto, critic of the attempts to enforce the conversion of the natives by war, also established the distinction between the infidels who never had the Christian faith preached to them and the heretics. Against the latter, punishment is legitimate—even capital punishment: "Certainly it is licit to compel the second ones [the heretics] with threats and terrors; and even to inflict capital punishment. . . . But not so against the first [the infidels]."[17]

However, the wars against the natives do not fall within any of the categories outlined above. The American natives "are not Turks nor Moors who pester and maltreat us" (Las Casas 1986, 3.3.120:241). They are not heretics either. The norms of the just war do not apply against the infidels who do no harm to Christianity. After a long time of confrontations between Christian Europe and the Islamic "infidels," many have made the mistake of identifying infidelity as a legitimate cause for war.

> It is from there the confusion comes that we now have. Some advocate the extension of what the doctors [scholars] affirm of the Moors and Turks, persecutors of the Christian name and violent occupiers of the kingdoms of Christianity, to the infidels who never knew nor were obliged to know that there were Christian people in the world, and therefore had never offended them. (Las Casas 1965, 1039)

Juan de Zumárraga, bishop of Mexico, also expressed his criticism of armed invasions against the Indian nations, insisting in a letter of April 4, 1537, after hearing the account of the situation in Peru from one of the friars, "that the conquest be taken away . . . ; they are an opprobrious injury to Christianity and our Catholic faith. In all this land what has happened has been only butchery" (in Cuevas 1975, 83; also cited by Pérez Fernández in Ramos et al. 1984, 132–133).

A Franciscan follower of Las Casas, Fray Gaspar de Recarte, in a brief of September 24, 1584, stressed the injustice of the Castilian wars of conquest, and, in contrast, the justice of the wars of resistance and defense on the part of the natives.

Because the infidel natives, by natural law and the law of nations, are legitimate and true lords of these lands and kingdoms, they can justly *manu armata* [by armed force] impede entry into their lands to all and every [person] who wishes to come into them against the expressed or implied will of those Indians, and proceed against them as enemies and violators of the natural law and law of nations, even to the point of killing them if necessary. . . . And the Spaniards cannot resist them *manu armata*, even under the title of defense. (in Gómez Canedo 1977, 282)

This, however, was a minority view. Another Spanish bishop, Vasco de Quiroga, expressed the predominant opinion on the favorable interrelation between the sword and the cross to constitute an *imperium fidei* [the rule of the Christian faith] in the "testimonial of erection of the Cathedral of Michoacán," his diocese:

It pleased the Divine Will to place at the head of the kingdoms of Spain such famous heroes, who did not only defeat the swords and war machinery of the barbarians, but who, generous with their lives and their patrimony, penetrated . . . unknown and very remote regions and having defeated the monster of idolatry, they planted everywhere, amid the clapping and happy anticipation of the Christian religion, the gospel of life, for the universal triumph of the banner of the cross. (in Zavala 1971, 263–264, 448)[18]

It is the sword of the conquerors that allows the "universal triumph of the banner of the cross" that is carried by the religious. The *imperium fidei* is extended through force and the violence of war. Pope Clement VIII, on the first centenary of the first Colombian journey, in the bull *Excelsia divinae potentiae,* celebrates

the conversion of such an extraordinary number of New World countries . . . Nueva España, America, Brasil, Peru, and all the vast adjacent lands.

Let us bless God for all this, then, for in his great mercy he has willed, in new ways, to call men also during this time to cease being children of wrath so that they can be led to living hope and to the knowledge of his Son Jesus Christ, Our Lord.

The unity of the faith and the nation could not be absent. The pope, on March 21, 1592, exhorts the inhabitants of the conquered lands to be fully loyal to the Spanish Crown:

In conclusion, we warmly commend you in the Lord to show fidelity and obedience to our very dear son in Christ, Felipe the Catholic King of Spain and the Indies, your prince, to whom the Apostolic See granted power and the mission to procure the salvation of those nations. (in Terradas Soler 1962, 118–120)

12

Evangelization and Violence

Sacrament of baptism

We trust that during the entire time you are on earth, you will compel and use your zeal in making the barbarian nations come to know God, maker and founder of all things, not only through edicts and admonitions, but also through force and arms if necessary so that their souls may share in the kingdom of heaven.

                                                                    Pope Clement VII

Without doubt, and experience confirms it, the barbarians are of a servile nature, and if you do not make use of fear and compel them by force . . . they refuse to obey. What should be done then? . . . It is necessary to use the whip. . . . In this way they are forced to enter salvation even if it is against their will.

                                                                    José de Acosta

Missionary Action or Evangelizing Conquest?

If the purpose of the Spanish empire was the eternal spiritual salvation of the American natives, did it have the legitimate authority to impose its religion on them? This question painfully touches on the task that all European protagonists considered essential: to spread the Christian faith. Giménez Fernández (in the prologue to Las Casas 1965, 65, 1:lviii) correctly asserts that there has not always been "sufficient appreciation of the transcendence of the new problems that the evangelization of the Amerindian masses posed to the churchmen of the first half of the sixteenth century." It is a crucial moment for the expansion of Christianity. In consequence of its evangelization of the New World, Christianity ceased being a provincial European confession and became a global religion.

The first impression that Columbus noted after the warm reception from the natives is that they could be converted without violence. "I recognized that they were people who would be freed and converted to our holy faith better by love than by force. . . . I believe that they would quickly become Christian" (Varela 1986, 62–63). He perceived only a linguistic problem and he thought it could easily be overcome. It was only a matter of some friars learning the native language before the aborigines would be converted. "I have said that . . . if devout religious (friars) who would learn their language are sent to them, they will all soon become Christians" (ibid., 92).

The validity of this judgment, however, is highly questionable as it was made only hours after establishing contact with strangers with whom there was no possibility of adequate communication. That rash judgment does not exclude the other alternative; namely, that if the natives did not accept the invitation to become Catholics, besides the expropriation of their lands and the obligation to perform hard and rigorous work, force would predominate over love (the Admiral carefully noted the primitive character of their military technology). What was never doubted by the Europeans was the need to make the autochthonous cults illegitimate, to destroy them, and to substitute Christianity for them, either by "love" or "force."

The intimate link between the evangelization of the natives and the enrichment of the Spaniards is also evident in Columbus's texts.

> They do not have any sect and are not idolaters . . . and they all believe that God is in heaven and that we surely came from heaven. . . . So Your Majesties should decide to make them Christian, for I believe that if you begin now, there will be multitudes of peoples converted in a short time; and our holy faith and you will gain many kingdoms and riches. . . . Without doubt, there are great quantities of gold in these lands. (ibid., 94)

A great many Europeans, among them friars and priests, adopted the norm expressed by Motolinía (1984, 211): "It is fitting that the holy gospel be preached throughout these lands and those who do not willingly wish to listen to the holy gospel of Jesus Christ, *be forced* to do so; for here that old proverb is applicable 'better good by force than bad by one's will.' "[1]

That was also the vision held by the first friar who tried to understand the mythical and religious world of the natives. Fray Ramón Pané, "a poor hermit of the Order of Saint Jerome" (1987, 21), accompanied Columbus on his second trip to America (ibid., "Estudio preliminar," 4). The Admiral commissioned him to study the language and the customs of Taínos in Española. That gave rise to the brief account that has been called "the first book written in the New World in a European language" (ibid., 1). In the end, his advice for the evangelization of the natives was:

> [Some] were inclined to believe easily. But with others *force* is needed, for all do not have the same nature. As there were some [the first converts] who started well and ended better, there will be some who will start well and later laugh at the things they have been taught; those need *force and punishment.* (ibid., 55; emphasis added)[2]

The problem concerned Ginés de Sepúlveda (1951, 64–65, 71), above all, who proposed a high degree of external force, arguing that:

> Those who go away from the Christian religion wander on the path of error and walk toward a sure precipice, unless even against their will we retrieve them by whatever means possible. . . . Thus I affirm that those barbarians should not only be invited, but also compelled to do good, that is to be just and religious.

Sepúlveda transformed the justification made by Saint Augustine of state force against heretics into a weapon that links preaching with *terror*.

> I say that the barbarians should be controlled not only so that they listen to the preachers but also to add threats to doctrine and advice and thus spread terror. . . . When healthy doctrine is added to useful terror not only to have the light of truth scatter the darkness of error, but also that the force of terror may break bad habits, then as I said, we rejoice in the salvation of many. (ibid., 73)

The salvation of barbarians would be extremely difficult and laborious if only rational and affective persuasions were used. The rootedness of old traditions, repression by the priestly castes, and barbaric habits conspired against the acceptance of the Christian faith. Sepúlveda distrusted the capacity of the natives to understand European theology. Unlike other pagans, the natives of the New World were not able to develop a monotheistic and spiritual idea of God nor overcome the savage custom of human sacrifice. They did not possess the required rationality to be entrusted with such crucial matters as religion for their exclusive decisions and deliberations. To accomplish their conversion the compelling force of the state was required. He injected, as usual, an Aristotelian argument into the debate: "A great portion of humanity obeys more through force than by words and reasoning, and are more compelled by punishment than guided by honesty" (ibid., 74).[3]

The use of military force for missionary purposes did not originate with Sepúlveda, as is illustrated by the passage that heads this chapter, taken from a letter dated May 8, 1529, from Pope Clement VII to Carlos V (in Zavala 1971, 349; Hanke 1937, 77).[4] The pope advocates use of "force and arms if necessary" to bring souls to God.

Acosta gathered the experience of the evangelizing conquest in his work *De procuranda indorum salute* (1588). After praising "the ancient and apostolic way of preaching the gospel among barbarians . . . without any military machinery," he insisted that, regarding the majority of the American natives, such a procedure would be "extreme foolishness."

> The manner and command of the apostles, where it could be followed comfortably, was the best and preferred; but where it could not be followed, as was the usual case among barbarians, it was not prudent to place oneself at risk, under the guise of greater holiness, to lose one's life without in any way saving the soul of the neighbor.

In the case of the savages who inhabit many regions of the Americas, a certain degree of state force was required so that they could come to accept a civilized and cultured life, an indispensable factor for genuine Christian existence. "These people made to live like beasts have little room for human customs." It is true that during apostolic times many preachers of the gospel were martyred. But those who executed them "were men of reason." To try the way of peace in bringing the faith to the barbarians of the Indies, without any military assistance, "would be like pretending to establish friendship with wild boars and crocodiles." Such a martyrdom had nothing to do with religious differences; it would only "provide one's flesh for a more savory feast to their palate." In the case of the evangelization of the Indies, it was necessary that soldiers accompany the priest (Acosta 1952, 2.8:169–172).

Acosta's treatise tries to be a kind of manual for missionaries. Its notion of the missionary task is framed within the sophisticated taxonomy of the "barbarian" nations. There are in his opinion three types of barbarians. First, there are those "who are not too far from right reason." They have laws, judges, and stable and reasonable civil institutions. Above all, they have a literary culture. They should have the faith preached in the apostolic manner. However, Acosta cannot find one example of a nation in the New World that falls under this category. All the peoples he finds of this type are in the Orient: Chinese, Japanese, and Hindus.[5]

The second type are those with reasonable social institutions who have not attained a literary culture nor deep philosophical or civil concepts. They suffer also from having "such monstrous rites, customs, and laws . . . that if they are not constrained by a superior power, they would hardly receive the light of the gospel and accept customs worthy of humans." The more advanced nations of the New World are in this category: the Aztecs and the Inkas. Their evangelization and civilizing efforts first require conquest and political domination, although "their laws and customs not contrary to the gospel" should be preserved, if possible.

"There are in the New World a great many" of those who fall under the third category of barbarians, described as "savage-like wild animals who hardly have any human sentiments; without laws, nor pacts, nor judges, nor republics" (Acosta 1952, "Proemio," 46–48). The Jesuit missionary is not sparing in the negativity of his judgment. "It would take a long time to enumerate all their abominations . . . in everything they are equal to wild beasts" (ibid., 2.3:145). Their conversion requires that they be first dominated and subjugated. "Aristotle referred to this type of barbarian, saying that they have to be hunted as beasts and tamed by force." Christian sensibility leads Acosta to change the analogy from bestiality to childishness: "For all those who are hardly men, or are half men, it is fitting that they be taught how to be men and to instruct them like children." But traditional pedagogy has never given up physical discipline to achieve its ends: "They have to be contained by suitable force and power and be obliged to leave the jungle and gather in towns, and, even against their will in a way, to force them to enter the kingdom of heaven" (ibid., 46–48).[6]

Acosta was a missionary who was interested not in great feats of martyrdom but in achieving the greatest possible effectiveness in the transcendent process of evangelizing the natives. And he did not believe that it could be done without military force. He found through experience that where natives have been left to their own devices "there has been little stability and security in the Christian faith and religion . . . it has decayed and is threatened with ruin." While among "Indians who are subjugated, Christianity is growing and improving" (Acosta 1985, 7.28:377). No matter how much he insisted on his love for the American natives, he could not avoid the serious undervaluing of their culture and customs, always comparing them to beings of inferior rationality, as are, in the traditional perspective, children, women, and beasts: "Because the Indians have an intelligence that is little and childish like that of children and women, or better still beasts" (Acosta 1952, 2.15:199).

The case of the American natives was unique, for it demanded the conjunction of "two disparate things such as are the gospel and war." If there should be insistence on preaching strictly along apostolic and peaceful lines it would impede the Christianization of the aborigines. In his opinion, the condition of the "barbarians of this New World" is such that "like wild animals," if "the necessary force" or "voluntary violence" is not used, "they will never come to know the freedom and nature of the children of God." In the Americas it is possible to "reconcile such disparate things as violence and freedom" (ibid., 2.1:137).

Although Acosta insists that the barbarism of the American natives does not mean they are subhuman, but only that their savage customs have suffocated their inherent rationality ("the barbarians are not such by nature, but by preference and custom; they are children and insane by choice, not in their own natural self" [ibid., 5:161]), he does not have any illusions about following a peaceful and free missionary method. His pragmatism demands severity and coercion.

> Without doubt, and experience confirms it, the barbarians are of a servile nature, and if you do not make use of fear and compel them by force . . . they refuse to obey. What should be done then? . . . It is necessary to use the whip. . . . In this way they are forced to enter salvation even if it is against their will. (ibid., 1.7:85–89)

Acosta is ready to consider the possibility of converting indigenous communities without necessarily deposing their pagan princes. But this is an abstract alternative with low probability. He does not have illusions about the natives' need to be in a context of governmental compulsion to preserve their Christianity. For "in the middle of a bad and perverse nation, what hope is there for weak men, poor in intelligence, of useless customs, and fickle by nature, to preserve their faith, if they are not received with open arms by our kings?" It is unlikely that pagan and infidel princes, "with an enraged devil," will allow the free exercise of the Christian faith, the only true and authentic religion. Therefore, it is in keeping with Acosta's pragmatism, "as a general rule and inviolable canon," to dethrone, even *manu militari*, the aboriginal authorities who persist in their paganism and idolatrous convictions (ibid., 3.2:217–221).

Acosta cannot escape a certain disillusionment, similar to that found in missionaries such as Sahagún and Mendieta, regarding the forced evangelization that has been imposed on the natives. "Here is the Samaria of our times" is his stern judgment about the superficial Christianity of the Indians. "They adore Christ and worship their gods. . . . They fear [Christ] in words while the judge or the priest insists; they fear him show-ing a fake appearance of Christianity; but they do not fear him in their hearts, nor do they truly worship him, nor believe with their understanding as it is necessary in justice" (ibid., 1.14–15:113–115). After these critical com-mentaries, so full of bitterness from a missionary who would have very much preferred to preach to less barbaric ethnic communities, he is never-theless left with the hope that after inculcating values and Christian con-cepts by means of severe discipline and rigorous coercion, "the children will be better than their fathers . . . better prepared for the faith."[7]

This is what Gómez Canedo (1977, xvii) has called "protected evan-gelization," and which Vargas Machuca (in Fabié [1879] 1966, 224) reiterates with greater irony and less charity:

> If the [Indians] obey and go to the doctrine of the holy gospel, it is because they have in sight the force of soldiers, for it has not been understood to this day that in the Western Indies, religious coming alone are not effective . . . without soldiers showing their arms. . . . To convert them it is better for religious and the military to come together so that their conversion would be faster.

Las Casas writes his voluminous tome *Del único modo de atraer a todos los pueblos a la verdadera religión* (1942) to refute the arguments for the armed thrust given to evangelization. Behind an extensive and exhaustive theo-retical treatise about the intrinsic relation between Christian faith, freedom, and peaceful preaching, full of biblical, patristic, canonical, philosophical, and theological citations (his passion has little respect for brevity and moderation,[8] and he also pays little attention to the inauthenticity of some documents he naively cites, such as the *Testamentos de los doce patriarcas*), he repeatedly expresses his thesis that conversion is genuine and true only if it is quite free of coercion, and if it is attained through "persuasion of the intellect through reasoning and by invitation and the gentle motion of the will" (Las Casas 1942, 7). Violence corrupts freedom and therefore deforms the faith. "To receive our holy faith . . . freedom of the will . . . is required" (Las Casas 1965, 745).[9] In his dispute with Sepúlveda, he summarizes his thesis: "If faith has to be preached with the same meekness [as Jesus Christ orders], it is an iniquity to first send warriors to subject the people" (Las Casas 1965, 263, 267).

How does Jesus Christ order that the gospel be preached?

> Christ only granted his apostles the license and authority to preach the gospel to those who willingly wanted to listen to it, but he does not force nor inflict any discomfort or unpleasantness on those who do not wish to listen. He did not authorize the apostles or preachers of the faith to force those who would not listen, nor give them authority to punish those who threw them out of their cities. . . . Whoever acts in a contrary manner becomes . . . transgressor of the divine precept. (Las Casas 1942, 177, 183)

Evangelization is corrupted and spoiled if it is used as a pretext in the search for power and domination or greed. It is necessary to guarantee, by word and deed, "that the hearers, and very specifically the infidels, understand that the preachers of the faith do not have any intention of gaining dominion over them through their preaching" and that "the ambition for riches does not move them to preach" (ibid., 249).

A persuasive and pacific style of missionary methodology is very effective with the inhabitants of the New World, whose nature, Las Casas insists many times, is "meek, simple, kind, and docile," which could even be said to be "made by God to be transplanted and transformed from the wild, uncultivated, and bitter grapes of the jungle of their heathenism into the olives or very sweet grapes of his dearest and most precious vineyard." This conversion from docile gentiles into devout Christians would have been very easy if "these peoples . . . had been treated with love and kindness from the beginning" (Las Casas 1986, 1.1.45:226).

If religion is used to legitimize a holy war, one follows "the road of Mohammed" or "Mohammed's law," "which the devil invented and his mimic and apostle Mohammed followed through so many thefts and much bloodshed." Compelling the infidels to listen to preaching after conquering them by force of arms is to become "true imitators of that notorious and very repulsive pseudoprophet and seducer of men, who stained the whole world, Mohammed" (see Las Casas 1965, 357, 445, 455; Las Casas 1942, 459; Las Casas 1986, 1.1.25:134–136).[10]

A similar idea, more concise but similar in its theoretical solidity, is argued by the Franciscan Fray Gaspar de Recarte in an opinion written on November 24, 1584. He considers that using military escorts for the protection of missionary preaching is contrary to natural and evangelical law. To affirm its necessity, therefore, is to concur in a proposition that is heretical, imprudent, and scandalous. The custom of sending armed battalions to assist the evangelizing forays

> has been the most efficacious and total cause of the desolation and loss of the Indies, and of the great many evils and sins that our people have committed there against the Indians who came like sheep and would have accepted the faith if the ferocity of the Spaniards in subjecting them to very heavy works had not been such a hindrance. In view of that, then, . . . the said proposal is heretical, imprudent, and scandalous. (in Gómez Canedo 1977, 274)

Recarte contrasts the peaceful gospel of Christ and the apostles with the gospel proclaimed "with arms, ferocity, and artillery . . . the gospel of mines and of great temporal interests," which is the one preached to the American natives (ibid., 280).

A severe critique of that kind of evangelization was made with mordant force, and under the obvious influence of Las Casas, by the Franciscan Juan de Silva (in Zavala 1971, 405–406) at the beginning of the seventeenth century. He differentiates two types of evangelizing conquests, depending on the first or second phase of the process to acquire dominion over the nations and peoples of the New World. He censures both for not adapting to apostolic preaching norms. Immediately one senses an implicit criticism of Acosta.

> Two ways have been found for the preaching of the gospel in the Indies, one being the one practiced by the first conquerors who carried out everything through weapons, harshness, and cruelty, thinking that it was quite just that the sword should first open the way for the gospel. Such a contrary way to the gentleness and meekness that Christ our Redeemer maintained, taught, and ordered. . . . Another and different way has been found by the Spaniards who are here now and want new entries and discoveries in the lands yet to be conquered and converted . . . namely, that the sword should not go before the gospel, but follow it; that the preachers go to preach first and they should have with them soldiers and warriors for their safety. And there are many learned men from different professions who affirm this to be a safe, just, and

efficient way, saying that we are now in different times and that with such barbaric peoples one cannot follow the way and discipline that Christ our Redeemer taught.

Because of their opposition to the teachings of Christ and his apostles, "without alleging a sacred text, nor having sufficient authority from the Old or New Testaments, nor from the church," these two ways of joining the power of the sword to evangelical preaching "I consider without doubt to be a very imprudent way and a scandalous proposition."[11] The natives should be converted to the Christian faith "non coactione sed persuasione" (not by force but by persuasion; trans. note).

Silva considers the following measures to be indispensable so that the conversion of the natives might proceed efficaciously and in accordance with the gospel: (1) abolish the system of personal serfs "through which our Lord receives many and grave offenses"; (2) stop "all new entries and conquests, which cause so many offenses against God"; (3) that the preachers show "by word and deed, the gentleness and meekness of the law of Christ"; (4) that a promise be given the natives "that by becoming Christians and accepting our faith, they will not lose their freedom, nor be dispossessed from their kingdoms, vassals, their women, nor daughters; nor shall they be urged, nor forced to become personal servants; and that finally no Spaniard would be allowed to offend them in any way" (in Castañeda 1974, 165).

There are, therefore, two different perspectives on the legitimate ways to gain the natives' conversion. The first could be called *evangelizing conquest*, and it proposes to achieve, by force if necessary, dominion over the aborigines as a necessary condition to facilitate their evangelization. The second can be called *missionary action*, and it consists of reasonable persuasion through convincing arguments and adherence of the will through attraction.

Missionary action, lacking armed aggressivity, had vigorous promoters. The first suggestions in this regard seem to have come from Fray Pedro de Córdoba, the head of the Dominicans in Española, who recommended to Carlos V, at the beginning of his reign, that the first approach to the natives should be made by the religious without armed companions.

> Because they are such meek people, so obedient and so good, that if preachers alone would come, without the force and violence of these unfortunate Christians, I think that we could establish among them as excellent a church as was the primitive one.

This suggestion comes from the tragic experience of the Antilleans, "because these islands and mainlands newly discovered and found to have so many people . . . have been and are being destroyed and depopulated through the great cruelty of the Christians." In a way typical of a mentality filled with biblical images, he uses the pharaohs to express the oppression that has victimized the natives. "Pharaoh and the Egyptians were not so cruel against the people of Israel" (in Pacheco et al. 1864–1884, 11: 217–218).[12]

The Dominicans in Española insisted on missionary action without any violent coercion or forced captivity.

> There never was, nor is, nor ever will be such an unfortunate and tyrannized land as these discovered Indies . . . and destruction and desolation continues. . . . Because of the Spaniards' greed to take out gold . . . the island of Española has been depopulated . . . and the island of Cuba, and San Juan and Jamaica. . . . Y. M. already knows that these people cannot be forcibly despoiled, nor be killed for gold. . . . The peoples of the New World given by God to Y. M. can be brought to the gentle yoke of Christ and his faith . . . and all to obey Y. M. without taking their possessions by force, and allowing them to retain their kingdoms, except for the supreme jurisdiction which belongs to Y. M., nor destroying them . . . as is now done until they [the Spaniards] see them die.

In case the Crown and his counselors do not consider the evangelization to be possible without armed action, the Dominicans make a radical suggestion, one that would not be heeded, which was to leave the natives alone in their infidelity and isolation.

> If . . . you deem this to be impossible . . . from now on we beg Y. M., out of the good we wish for your royal conscience and soul, that Y. M. will order them to be left alone, for it is better that they go to hell alone, as before, than for both our people and them to do so, and for the name of Christ to be blasphemed among those people by the bad example of our people; and that Y. M.'s soul, worth more than the whole world, would suffer damage. (in Pacheco et al. 1864–1884, 11:243–249)

In another memo, written at the request of the Jeronomite fathers, they repeated the suggestion. "It is better to allow them to return to their *yucayeques* [Indian regional divisions] than to place them in *encomiendas* with the Christians; for even if their souls do not gain anything, at least they would gain life and multiply, which is better than for them to lose everything" (ibid., 212).

Gaspar de Recarte would take up again the idea of the exclusion of lay Castilians in the missionary penetration of the indigenous territories.

> We could say that just as there cannot be a good form of commonwealth and friendship between wolves and lambs, in the same way there cannot

be a good republic, confederation, or league between Indians and Spaniards, for they are of such different dispositions and conditions: the Spaniards, insolent and extremely haughty . . . the Indians, on the contrary, timid and miserable. . . . These Indies get such little benefit from the Spaniards compared to the very grave harm they cause to the Indians with their way of living and abominable example, so that little would be lost if they had not come to these lands, and even less would be lost if they left them. (in Cuevas 1975, 358, 367)

Bishop Zumárraga, of Mexico, made the suggestion that any future step forward in the penetration of the New World should be done

in an apostolic and Christian way . . . ordering the Spaniards [soldiers], under penalty of death, not to enter any town or Indian home but that the religious enter the towns, and that without weapons the Spaniards begin to understand about bartering and little things like that . . . without harming any Indian nor showing weapons, for the Indians receive them in peace. (ibid., 84)

Another religious, Fray Rodrigo de la Cruz, insisted in a letter to Carlos V that in the zones to be entered next it would be desirable to have only friars, forbidding for a good number of years the entry of the laity. Only in that way would an authentic evangelization be carried out without being corrupted by greed and abuse.

If there was a decree from Y. M. so that if the friars bring from their provinces peaceful people, no Spaniard should be allowed in that land for twenty or thirty years, and that they shall not undergo any of the suffering that these are now enduring, I know that many will come to the yoke of the church who do not come now. (ibid., 160)

Paulino Castañeda (1974, 177–189) has shown that in the conversion and subjection of diverse Indian nations of the New World, the Spanish Crown tried different procedures but never took seriously the few proposals to suspend imperial expansion in the lands of the New World. The so called "doubt of Carlos V" about Peru has been, as discussed in an earlier chapter, unduly inflated.

There does not seem to have been any effect or significant ripples from the suggestion of the Dominican theologian Bartolomé de Carranza, included in an academic lecture given in 1540 at the Colegio de San Gregorio in Valladolid, that Spain become a provisional tutor to the Indian nations, who would come to accept the Christian faith and culture so that "after doing that for sixteen or eighteen years and the soil being well-prepared, when there is no danger of their return to their old way of life (*ad suam sectam*), they should be left in their first and proper freedom since they no longer need a tutor."[13]

Antonio Rumeu de Armas (1975, 61) rightly says that "in America the evangelizing conquest prevailed over the missionary action." The principle of attaining civil and political domination through military action as the first alternative, and then proceeding with Christianization, more or less voluntary, was the more popular strategy. The evangelizing conquest seems to have been the most convenient way, certainly the most common, for carrying out the "subjugation" of the New World for the benefit of the spiritual salvation of the natives, the political interests of the empire, and the economic ones of the colonizers.

The Politicizing of Baptism

Peaceful conversion and violent conversion end up with the same sacrament: *baptism*. In chapter 4 we reproduced a quote from Francisco de Vitoria on the implications of this sacrament in the evangelization of the indigenous peoples and the possibility that "so long as they become true Christians," regardless of how their Christianization was achieved, would imply that the pope could remove the other infidel lords and give them a Christian prince (in Urdanoz 1960, 719).

The phrase "so long as they become true Christians" does not allude to the quality of the belief of the natives but to their *baptism*, which is conceived to have objective sacramental validity, independently of the subject's disposition. In general, the interpreters of Vitoria, be they Spanish theologians such as Urdanoz, or Anglo-Saxon jurists like Brown Scott, do not spend much time on this controversial "legitimate title." Ramón Hernández (1984, 372–373), for example, discusses what Vitoria means by "a good portion" of the Indians but evades the principal problem: What is the meaning of the concept of "true Christian" in reference to a conversion achieved through ignorance and fear? These factors (i.e., ignorance and fear) might be seen to vitiate a political determination but were not seen as invalidating baptisms, even when these took place through compulsion or in ignorance.

The detachment of the sacramental character of baptism from the possible coercion that preceded it was a canonical norm shaped during centuries of the compulsory Christianization of Moors and Jews, especially their children. Even when Vitoria in another context recalls the importance of the correct catechesis of the natives of the New World, in this crucial text he accepts the sacramental validity of forced baptisms or baptisms induced through distinct strategies of pressure and compulsion. The implicit license is given, therefore, in the logic of Vitoria's text for forced baptisms en masse, by intimidation or psychological manipulation.[14]

Baptisms en masse became the common missionary practice. Motolinía (1984, 207) claimed that he and his Franciscan colleagues "had each baptized more than three hundred thousand souls" in Mexico. Mendieta (1980, 3.38:275), after affirming that by 1540 more than six million natives had been baptized, alleged that there was no precedent like it in the history of the church:

> In conversion and baptism in this Nueva España, I think that if you make comparisons over time from the primitive church to our own day no other church has come close. For that let us praise and bless the name of our Lord.

The news about massive indigenous baptisms was repeated, apparently without giving much consideration to education in the Christian faith. In general, the Indians were baptized if they could recite in Latin the Our Father, Hail Mary, Creed, or Hail Holy Queen.[15] The Chilean Mires (1987, 144–145) does not seem to notice that a good portion of the dispute over baptisms en masse has to do with the way in which the sacramental act was carried out, and not with the understanding that the neophytes had of its meaning.[16] The dispute arose because the sacrament was not always administered following all the canonical liturgical norms. "Some stated that the sacrament of baptism should be given to the Indians only following the full solemnity and ceremonials that are ordered by the Church" (Mendieta 1980, 3.36:267; Motolinía 1984, 2.4:86–90).

To answer the criticism, Pope Paul III issued the bull *Altitudo divini consilii* [the highness of divine providence] on June 1, 1537, in which, after insisting that the Western rite prescribed by canon law should be followed as much as possible, he reaffirmed the validity of those baptisms which had been administered, viewing them in the context of sacramental objectivity, characteristic of Catholicism since the time of Saint Augustine.

> With the apostolic authority conferred on us by our Lord Jesus Christ, through blessed Peter and his successors . . . we declare: Whosoever baptized those Indians who came to faith in Christ in the name of the Blessed Trinity without following the ceremonies and solemnity observed by the church, did not sin for they thought rightly it was proper to do so. (in Hernáez 1879, 1:66)

The baptism of the natives was valid and they had been transformed into genuine Christians, and therefore spiritual subjects of the Supreme Pontiff, so long as the officiating priest had carried out the sacramental action with liturgical reference to the Trinity. The subjectivity, intention, or understanding of the baptized was of little importance for sacramental legitimacy.

Baptism as an ecclesiastical fact, as sacrament of entry into the church, became a political act, an affirmation of Spanish imperial sovereignty. Let us return to Vitoria: "If a good portion of the barbarians have been converted to faith in Christ . . . the pope, with reasonable cause, could give them a Christian prince and remove the other infidel lords" (Urdanoz 1960, 719).

From ecclesiastical baptism one moves to political subjugation. Pedro Borges has pointed out that, in general, the Indian peoples were baptized after their chiefs and officials, another indication of the link between political serfdom and religious conversion (Borges 1975). Once more we see the indissoluble link between theological and political factors, as an unavoidable result of an imperial expansion carried out in the name of Christianity.[17]

With respect to forced baptism, Las Casas sternly affirms that those who practiced it committed a "great offense against God"; ". . . doing something against the gospel and against the sacred canons and doctrines of all the saints" (Las Casas 1986, 2.1.165:127; and Pérez de Tudela 1957, "Memorial . . . al rey," 202). He also stresses its damaging effects on the natives.

> The Indians are dominated by perpetual hate and rancor against their oppressors. . . . And therefore, even when they sometimes may say they wish to convert to the Christian faith and one can see that it is so by the external signs they use to show their will; you can always, however, be suspicious that their conversion does not come from a sincere intention nor their free will, but it is a faked conversion, or one accepted to avoid some future evil that they fear would overcome them again, or to obtain some respite from the miseries they suffer in serfdom. (Las Casas 1942, 465)

For the "protector of the Indians," the free consent of the natives is a key factor at every stage of the process of conversion and cannot be sidestepped by objectivistic conceptions of the sacrament of baptism. To baptize natives who have not been properly catechized and who, in some form or another, are forced to the sacrament of baptism constitutes a sacrilege. "It was a great sacrilege to baptize whoever did not know what he was receiving" (Las Casas 1986, 2.1.279:186). With respect to the baptism of a Central American chief carried out by Pedrarias' (Pedro Arias Dávila) troops, Las Casas asserts that it was done

> following the error that the Spaniards and even the clerics and some friars committed in baptizing those infidels without giving them any doctrinal instruction whatever or without their having much or any knowledge of God . . . and for this harm and irreverence done to the sacrament, God will question and inflict punishment not on the Indians but on those who baptized them. (ibid., 3.3.65:51)

The bitter and well-known dispute between Motolinía and Las Casas began, according to Motolinía, when Las Casas refused to baptize a Mexican native who sought the sacrament. The reason seemed to be the doubt that Las Casas felt concerning the catechetical instruction of the native. The incident provoked bitter and permanent resentment in Motolinía (1984, 208). The differences between the two extended to other crucial points. Las Casas was quite right in energetically rejecting the following type of defense, which Motolinía (1984, 3.1:116; 3.4:135) put forward in favor of the Indians: "The Spaniards do not see that if it was not for the friars they would not be able to find anyone to serve them, neither in their homes nor in their farms and that all the Indians would now have perished. . . ." "If we (the Franciscan friars) do not defend the Indians, you would not have anyone to serve you. . . . If we favor them . . . it is so that you may have someone to serve you." The protection of the Indians becomes a matter of preserving servants, courtesy of the gracious friars.[18]

Responding to a consultation on the part of Carlos V, inspired by Las Casas, the school of theology at Salamanca, on July 1, 1541, insisted (as one would expect from theologians) that the baptism of the natives should be preceded by an adequate formation in Christian faith and morality. "It is dangerous and rash to baptize barbarians without due care and without suitable diligence and examination. . . . It is for these reasons that we have hastily baptized many, but few, indeed, [are] true Christians" (in Pacheco et al. 1864–1884, 3:552).[19]

The Episcopal Synod of Lima, in 1550, in making this criticism its own, set out to put a stop to the practice of massive baptisms without authentic conversion or willingness to be baptized. It decreed "that no one may be baptized unwillingly. . . . For in conformity with the doctrine of our Teacher and Redeemer Jesus Christ, no one may be compelled to receive our holy Catholic faith, unless fully persuaded and attracted by its truth and freedom, and by the reward of blessedness." That, admits the prelates, has not always been the missionary custom, to the detriment of genuine Christianity.

> Some, in an inconsiderate manner, baptize Indians who have already the use of reason, without examining first if they come of their own will, or for fear, or to make the *encomenderos* or chiefs happy, and it was also given to those who have not yet the use of reason and are children, without knowing if the parents agree. For which reasons it comes about that, later, to the devaluing of the most holy sacrament of baptism, they return to their gods and ceremonies. (Castañeda 1974, 156–157)

The Jesuit Acosta (1952, 6.2:524) joins in this harsh criticism of the Franciscan baptismal practice and insists that it be regulated by at least one year of catechumenate before giving the sacrament to the neophyte. He is aware that reality contradicts his demanding norms. "Who will not be pained by the fact that baptism was given to many at the beginning and even now to not a few before they know a modicum of Christian doctrine . . . and without even knowing if they wish to be baptized?" That, in his opinion, is one of the causes of the fragility of Indian Christianity.

Speaking for the other side, the Franciscans in Nueva España, the main promoters of baptisms en masse, accused their critics of being like the priest and the Levite in the gospel parable of the Good Samaritan, continuing on their journey and refusing "to have compassion, with the wine of charity and the oil of mercy, on the one who had fallen into the hands of thieves and is gravely wounded" (Mendieta 1980, 3.36:267–268). Becoming attached to ecclesiastical formalities, be it those concerning the depth of catechetical instruction or ceremonial norms, the critics neglect, according to the sons of Saint Francis, the spiritual well-being of the redemption of souls, the primary goal of every authentic missionary effort.

Las Casas tried (1552), in his "*Treinta proposiciones muy jurídicas*" and later in *Los tesoros del Perú* (1563), to go a step further in his criticisms, and to separate baptism from its implicit dimension of political subjugation. From that perspective, the sacrament of initiation into the church would be an absolute expression of divine grace. But it does not necessarily mean, as an indissoluble dimension of its nature, the acceptance of political Castilian hegemony. That second step of a political nature, which according to Las Casas ought to be taken by the Indian nations for the well-being and permanence of the Catholic faith in the New World, would be the direct object of a subsequent act of self-determination on the part of the indigenous nations, free from all military coercion.

The second work by Las Casas (1958, 227–269) mentioned above stressed the restrictively spiritual character of the baptism of the natives, which does not in any way reduce their autonomy and political independence. Baptism does not automatically lead to civil subjection. The converted nations retain their full faculty for freely accepting or denying the supreme authority of the Castilian Crown. "Those peoples and nations, even after receiving the faith . . . may still not hold as valid or accept that institution [referring to the Alexandrian bulls of 1493]" (ibid., 243).

It was an audacious proposition, which was creatively in advance of the customs and habits of his time. But like other ideas of Las Casas, it was framed in the context of a utopian vision of the possibility of building a Christian empire, a vision that was atrociously squelched by far grosser ambitious political and economic interests.

13

Prophecy and Oppression

"Good government":
They cut off the head
of Tupac Amaru in Cuzco.

You are all in mortal sin and you live and die in it because of your cruelty
and tyranny against these innocent peoples. Tell me, who gave you the
right to declare such a hateful war against these people? . . . Why do
you oppress them to the point . . . that from the excessive work you force
upon them . . . you kill them in order to mine and acquire gold each
day? . . . Are these people not men? Don't they have rational souls? Are
you not obliged to love them as you love yourselves? . . . You can be certain that in this state, you will have no more salvation than Moors or
Turks who lack faith in Jesus Christ and do not want it.

Fray Antonio de Montesinos

I also saw the sermon that was delivered by a Dominican friar called
Antonio Montesino [sic], and even though he always preached in scandalous ways, what he said has left me in astonishment because what
he said does not have any good theological foundation nor canons nor
laws according to what the scholars, theologians, and canon lawyers say
who have seen the grant that our very Holy Father Alexander VI made
to us . . . so it is reasonable that you will impose on the one who
preached it . . . some punishment because his error was very great.

Fernando V, the Catholic

Biblical Hermeneutics and Prophetic Word

As is to be expected in a dispute dominated by theologians, the
Hebrew-Christian scriptures were the object of heated and contradictory
interpretations.

According to Columbus and Las Casas, the discovery of America by
Spain had been foretold by Isaiah (60:9) (Varela 1986, 226; Las Casas 1986,
1.1.127:486). The insatiable search for gold becomes, in Columbus's biblicist
mentality, an effort to locate King Solomon's gold mines of the legendary
Ophir mentioned in the Old Testament (1 Kings 9:28; 1 Chron. 29:4;
2 Chron. 8:18). Upon hearing aboriginal accounts of some mines, the
Admiral is convinced that they are the ones from which "Solomon was
brought all at once six hundred and sixty-six *quintals* [100 lbs. weight; trans.
note] of gold. . . . Solomon bought all that gold, precious stones, and
silver" (Varela 1986, 292–293).[1]

There were many references to the Deuteronomic code in respect to
the holy wars between Israel and the Canaanites. The dispute between
Sepúlveda and Las Casas is centered in part on an exegesis of those wars
and their relevance (Gines de Sepúlveda 1951, 117; Las Casas 1965,

1:337–349). According to Sepúlveda, the Deuteronomic war code clarifies the transcendent meaning of the armed conquest of the Americas by Spain and justifies it. According to Las Casas, Sepúlveda "has not researched the scriptures with sufficient determination," since "in this era of grace and piety" he remains obstinate "in his unbending application of the rigid precepts of the Old Testament." This hermeneutical error has a tragic consequence: "It facilitates the way for the cruel invasion by tyrants and looters, and for the oppression, exploitation, and slavery of innocent nations" (Las Casas 1974, 110).

Martín Fernández de Enciso defended the extermination of the Indians, citing the conduct of Joshua against Jericho (Joshua 6).[2] The prophetic texts against idolatry, including the execution of the priests of Baal by Elijah, were used in the eradication of indigenous religions. Matthew 10 was used to attempt to prove the thesis of peaceful evangelization willingly accepted. The promoters of the conversion *manu militari* repeatedly used Luke 14:23 ("Go out on the highways and along the hedgerows and compel them to come in [Vulgate: *compelle eos intrare*], so that my house will be full") (REB) (Gines de Sepúlveda 1951, 22, 75–76).[3]

The friars and churchmen who defended the Indians also used the scriptures. Fray Gaspar de Recarte uses the biblical analogy of pharaonic slavery to describe the forced slavery of the Indians, and also as an apocalyptic threat against the Castilian nation if it does not repent from its unjust actions. "Certainly seeing the life they inflict on the Indians it is nothing more than a perfect picture and transferral of the life that the children of Israel endured in Egypt" (in Cuevas 1975, 378).

Las Casas (1989, 101) likens the attitude of the conquistadors to that of the shepherds chastised by Zechariah (11:4–5): "The Lord my God said to me, 'Act the part of the shepherd of a flock of sheep that are going to be butchered. Their owners kill them and go unpunished. They sell the meat and say, "Praise the Lord! We are rich!"'"

The biblical base (Sir. 34:18–22) for the "conversion" of Las Casas to activism on behalf of the Indians is very well known:

> If you offer as a sacrifice an animal that you have obtained dishonestly, it is defective and unacceptable. The Most High gets no pleasure from sacrifices made by ungodly people; no amount of sacrifices can make up for their sins. A man who steals an animal from the poor to offer as a sacrifice is like a man who kills a boy before his father's eyes. Food means life itself to poor people, and taking it away from them is murder. It is murder to deprive someone of his living or to cheat an employee of his wages. (Las Casas 1989, 918)[4]

The Vulgate text used by Las Casas— "Qui offert sacrificium ex substantia pauperum, quasi qui victimat filium in conspectu patris sui" —has a stronger prophetic thrust. The expression *ex substantia pauperum* — "from the poor's substance" —implies that what has been stolen is decisive for the being and existence of the dispossessed poor; their dispossession leads to the death of the oppressed.

The constant analogy used by the friars who criticized the cruelty of the conquerors is the biblical antithesis between sheep and wolves. Jesus, in his missionary command to the disciples, summarizes the dangers they may encounter: "Listen! I am sending you out just like sheep to a pack of wolves" (Matt. 10:16). That passage was recalled by the Christian church with great intensity at various times of persecution and martyrdom suffered under pagan Roman emperors. For Las Casas it represents a central and evangelical characteristic of missionary preaching (Las Casas 1942, 190–200). When describing, however, the relationship between Christians and natives in the New World, the analogy is inverted: the nonbelievers are the docile sheep and the Christians the ferocious wolves. "To these meek sheep . . . came the Spaniards who of course were recognized as wolves" (Las Casas 1989, 19). This inversion of the biblical analogy illustrates the transferal of the relationship between Christians and gentiles, from the meek and loving to the violent and cruel.

The biblical analogy "sheep-wolves" was popular among critics of forced conversion by war. A notable example is the treatise of the Franciscan Recarte against missionaries being accompanied by soldiers, for in his opinion that is a violation of the mandate of Jesus, who sent his disciples "as sheep among wolves. Not as wolves among sheep, as the soldiers go" (in Gómez Canedo 1977, App., 270).

This biblical analogy is also related by Las Casas to another of the most interpreted and debated texts within the Catholic hermeneutical tradition: Jesus' triple warning to Peter in the last chapter of the fourth Gospel: "Take care of my sheep" (John 21:15–17). Ecclesiastical and papal responsibility lies in "taking care of the sheep." This exegesis was used to insist on the primary and fundamental responsibility of prelates laboring in the Indies to defend Christ's sheep—the poor and oppressed natives—from the wolves: the conquerors, colonists, and *encomenderos* who exploit and enslave them.

> The prelates . . . are much more obliged than other men to defend the poor and the oppressed. . . . Then the bishops of the world of the Indies beyond the ocean are obliged, of divine right and as a requirement for salvation, to continue insisting before the King and the Royal Council

until the already mentioned oppressed (Indians), who are unjustly retained by the Spaniards, sometimes in horrible servitude, are fully restored to their pristine freedom of which they were iniquitously deprived. (Las Casas 1965, 2:619, 623, 1319, 1320)

He criticized the first three prelates to be named bishops of the Antilles for their capitulation before the Castilian Crown in promoting indigenous labor in the gold mines. Pedro de Deza, Fray García de Padilla, and Alonso Manso acceded to the demands that "the Indians shall not be taken away from the work they now do in mining gold, but rather encourage them and advise them to serve even better than before in the mining of gold" (Las Casas 1986, 2.3.2:436–437). In the opinion of Las Casas their assent is tantamount to agreeing to the process that leads to the death of the Antillean natives. They violated the cardinal precept that should guide the church's action and thought.

He was even more critical of the first bishop of the mainland, Fray Juan de Quevedo, a Franciscan, prelate of Santa María de la Antigua del Darién, who sinned against the episcopal norm that demanded "that he place his life in defense of his sheep," but who instead took active part in the distribution of Indian slaves carried out by Pedrarias and his officials in the Central American isthmus (ibid., 3.3.64:46–47). During a confrontation at court in 1519, Las Casas censured Quevedo with extreme words of prophetic indignation:

> You have sinned a thousand times and a thousand more times for not giving your soul for your sheep to free them from the hands of those tyrants who are destroying them. . . . If you do not return all that you brought from there, till the last *cuadrante* [Roman copper coin; trans. note], you will, no more than Judas, be able to gain salvation. (ibid., 47:338)

There is a dramatic rebirth of prophecy in the debates about evangelization and the conquest of America. Many sources in the sixteenth century—homilies, memoranda, treatises, histories, letters—highlight the heightened prophetic tone with denunciations and ethical evocations. Las Casas, for one, continuously stressed the prophetic tradition linking and interlacing peace and justice expressed inter alia in Isaiah's text 32:17: "The fruit of justice will be peace" (Las Casas 1965, 2:599, 627).

In the midst of a theoretical disquisition on the legitimacy of the political authority of infidel princes in divine, natural, and state law, Las Casas distinguished between king and tyrant. To illustrate the nature of the latter he went to the prophetic Old Testament text in Ezekiel 34:2–4: "Vae pastoribus Israel qui pascebant semetipsos."

You are doomed, you shepherds of Israel! You take care of yourselves,
but never tend the sheep. You drink the milk, wear clothes made from
the wool, and kill and eat the finest sheep. But you never tend the sheep.
You have not taken care of the weak ones, healed the ones that are sick,
bandaged the ones that are hurt, brought back the ones that wandered
off, or looked for the ones that were lost. Instead, you treated them
cruelly.

He was not the first one to cite it. Antonio de Montesinos used it in
the Castilian court as the fundamental biblical text in a memo he presented
to defend the natives of the New World. What is unique, however, is that
Las Casas understood the prophetic character of God's word through his
self-understanding of being divinely chosen to be prophet. On many
occasions he alluded to this providential denouncing role he thought to
be his duty in the conquest of America, "to point out to the world, like
the sun, the dangerous state in which many live . . . for they do not take
to be sins crimes that had never been so gravely and abundantly committed
since men started sinning" (Las Casas 1986, 3.3.160:387).

Frequently Las Casas alluded, directly or indirectly, to the biblical tradition that implies *God listens to the clamor of the poor.* He stressed James 5,
one of the New Testament texts with the greatest prophetic power. This
text is an articulation of the condemnation of the rich, according to which
excessive earnings are responsible for the exploitation of the poor, but the
poor cry to God for help and their cries will not be in vain. The text sheds
light, according to Las Casas, on the outcome of the slavery inflicted on
the Indians by the Spaniards – it will give rise to divine wrath: "The cries
from so much bloodshed already reach heaven." "One of the sins that
clamors night and day and reaches God is the oppression of the under-
privileged and miserable poor" (in Fabié [1879] 1966, 70:473; Las Casas 1965,
1:597). Profoundly influenced by Las Casas, the Franciscan Recarte took
up this biblical theme in 1584: "Understand that God is not blind nor deaf,
and that the cries and oppression of these poor people rise to the divine
ears, and if they do not heed them, they will heap upon themselves God's
wrath and his most severe justice" (in Cuevas 1975, 367). In spite of the
later bitter disputes Motolinía had with Las Casas, the former took up the
biblical theme of the cry of the poor and warned the Spaniards responsible for the Indians' anguish that "the blood and death of these you hold
in so low esteem will rise to God, from the land of Peru as well as from
the islands and mainland" (Motolinía 1984, 3.11.167).

Las Casas was fully imbued with *the prophetic biblical and evangelical
traditions favoring the poor and denouncing oppressive power.* Las Casas, as the

Old Testament prophets, perceives the violence and exploitation suffered by the paupers and the oppressed as the locus of God's presence in the world. Solidarity with the poor and censorship of the powerful, so present in prophetic texts and in the accounts of Jesus, nurtured his passionate spirit. A notable example is provided by the following passage that he cites, attributing it as was then the custom to Saint Augustine:

> Can you consider Christian the one who oppresses the needy, who burdens the poor, who covets the belongings of others, the one who becomes rich by making others poor, the one who rejoices in illicit earnings, who eats at the expense of others, who becomes rich to the ruins of others . . . ?
>
> I know there are people so blinded by the profound darkness of malice and avarice that when . . . their power has chained the poor, or dominated the weak, or crushed the innocent with false witness . . . [they] give thanks to God thinking their wickedness has been made possible through divine favor. . . .
>
> And others think that they are justified in extending a small alms taken from the goods of the poor, giving to the one a small portion of what they took from the many. Only one is fed with what causes many to go hungry; and from the clothing stripped from many only a few are clothed. . . .
>
> Can you consider Christian those whose bread has not fed one single hungry person? whose drink has not satiated anyone's thirst? or whose table is not known by any poor person? . . .
>
> Christian are the ones who are merciful to all; who are moved by those who are injured; who do not allow the poor to be oppressed in their presence; those who help the needy; who frequently aid the indigent; those who suffer with those who suffer; who feel the other's pain as their own. . . . Anyone, therefore, who wants to be a friend of the world, becomes the enemy of God (James 4:4).[5]

There is here a vicarious identification between the poor of the Gospels—the primary recipient of divine mercy—Jesus Christ, and the American natives. The Indians, "unjustly oppressed by a very harsh servitude . . . are the poorest of all men" (Las Casas 1958, 53).

The lack of material goods and acquisitive ambition that Europeans at the dawn of capitalism considered to be a grave defect, Las Casas (1989, 17) interpreted as receptivity for the faith. "They are all very poor people who do not own nor want to own temporal goods; hence they are not proud, nor ambitious, nor greedy . . . and are very apt to receive our holy Catholic faith and to be formed in virtuous habits."

According to François Malley (1986, 263), the vicarious identification between the natives and the poor of the gospel, posited by Las Casas, differentiated his theory from the abstract theories developed by other Spanish jurists and theologians about the rights of the Indians.

> It is not a question, as in Vitoria, of considering the Indian as a depository of rights, formally equal to all other men. For Las Casas the Indians are, above all, "our brothers, and Christ has given his life for them." . . . Here is the central theology of Las Casas, which distinguished him from the great theologians of the sixteenth century. They remained at a philosophical and juridical level. . . . The experiences of Las Casas led him to consider the Indians as the poor of the Bible.

A similar observation has been made by Gustavo Gutiérrez, referring in a general way to many religious as "brothers of the poor":

> In the protest from the friars, there is certainly the affirmation of the fundamental equality of all human beings . . . but beyond that and more deeply is the perception that the Indians, or more exactly those Indian nations, are seen as oppressed, as poor, as neighbors *par excellence* deserving love. In a word, human rights without doubt, but not in a liberal and formal egalitarian sense, but along the line of the rights of the poor. . . . We are facing a new right, of deep roots, not merely theological but also biblical. (Gutiérrez 1981, 146)

Las Casas was not the only one to affirm such a vicarious identification. The Dominican Fray Juan de Ramírez wrote decades later (1595), in an explicit reference to biblical prophetic texts such as Isaiah 10:1-2, Habakkuk 2:12, and Micah 3 (in Hanke and Millares 1977, 278-279, 290-291): "They [the Indians] are the oppressed poor and the abject and abused humble ones."

The political and theological relevance is clear in a prophetic homily given by the Dominican friar Antonio de Montesinos on the Fourth Sunday of Advent in 1511, based on the biblical text *ego vox clamantis in deserto* (I am the voice clamoring in the desert) (Matt. 3:3, in turn a quote from Isa. 40:3), which Hanke has called "the first clamor for justice in the Americas" (1967, 40):[6]

> You are all in mortal sin, and you live and die in it because of your cruelty and tyranny against these innocent people. Tell me, who gave you the right to declare such a hateful war against these people . . . ? Why do you oppress them to the point . . . that from the excessive work you force upon them . . . you kill them in order to mine and acquire gold each day? . . . Are these people not men? Don't they have rational souls? Are you not obliged to love them as you love yourselves? . . . You can be certain that in this state, you will have no more salvation than Moors or

Turks who lack faith in Jesus Christ and do not want it. (in Las Casas 1986, 2.3.4:441–442)[7]

As was to be expected, the homily awakened a furious reaction on the part of colonists and *encomenderos*. It created a true commotion, for on that day the church was attended by the main colonial officials. And the commotion was justified. Those leaders of the Catholic faith in the Indies were likened to Moors or Turks, the worst adversaries of Christian Europe at that time. Therefore they labeled him a "scandalous man, a sower of new doctrine . . . in disservice to the king and harm to all inhabitants" (Las Casas 1986, 2.3.4:442).

King Fernando obtained a copy of the sermon and expressed his displeasure to Diego Colón, including his permission to punish the rebellious Dominican severely:

I also saw the sermon that was delivered by a Dominican friar called Antonio Montesino [sic], and even though he always preached in scandalous ways, what he said has left me in astonishment because what he said does not have any good theological foundation nor canons nor laws according to what the scholars, theologians, and canon lawyers say who have seen the grant that our very Holy Father Alexander VI made to us . . . so it is reasonable that you will impose on the one who preached it . . . some punishment because his error was very great. (in Pacheco et al. 1864–1884, 32:375–376)

The "scholars, theologians, and canon lawyers" alluded to were soon confronted by the rise, initiated by this Montesinos sermon, of a libertarian theology that questioned the very root of the ideological legitimations of the subjugation of the American natives. Meanwhile, the king silenced Montesinos and his Dominican brothers in this matter. "They may not speak from the pulpit nor outside, directly or indirectly of this matter, nor of related ones . . . in public nor in secret" (ibid., 377–378).[8]

The Dominican Provincial in Spain, Fray Alfonso de Loaysa, added his censure to that of the king. After alluding to the Alexandrian bulls and to the Iberian acquisition of the New World by "right of war" (*iure belli*), he affirmed the sovereign rights of the Castilian monarchy over the lands and inhabitants of the Americas. He pointed out the possible subversive outcome of his homilies ("and all the Indies, because of your preaching, are ready to rebel"), and he exhorted his religious brothers in Española to "submittere intellectum vestrum" (submit your intellect). This was an argument used countless times for the benefit of ecclesiastical and political authoritarianism (in Carro 1944, 1:62–63).

Montesinos did not allow himself to be silenced. His cry of protest echoed intensely and was received, enlarged, and deepened by Bartolomé de las Casas.

The Sin of the Conquistadors

Labeling the exploitation of the natives as a *sin* was among the central theological themes taken up during the sixteenth century. "All of you are in mortal sin . . . because of your cruelty and tyranny against these innocent peoples," Montesinos asserted in his sermon. No less powerful is the memorandum (1541) by Juan Fernández Angulo, bishop of Santa Marta, to the Council of the Indies: he labeled the Spaniards' conduct as satanic.

> In this area there are no Christians, only devils, nor are there servants of God or the King, but traitors to their laws. . . . The greatest problem I find in bringing the warring Indians to peace . . . is the harsh and cruel treatment that the peaceful ones receive from the Christians. Therefore, they are so fearful and so suspicious that nothing can be more odious and hated than the Christian name. As a result, all over this land in their own language they call them [Spaniards] *yares* which means: devils. . . . For the things they do are not the actions of Christians, nor of men with use of reason, but of devils. (in Las Casas 1989, 119–121)

Las Casas (1972, 61) also called the conduct of the conquerors "abominable sins . . . diminishing and killing the vassals of Your Highness, without considering or having any goal except their own interest." "Inexpiable sins" is a common phrase he uses in rating the conquests and the *encomiendas*, as in the "Octavo remedio" (1965, 2:843). Those are deeds "worthy of eternal damnation" (ibid.) and deserving of being judged as diabolical. Those who oppress the Indians, in spite of calling themselves Christians, are in reality "supporters of the reign of Satan and opponents of the holy church of Christ . . . precursors not of Christ but of the anti-Christ" (Las Casas 1942, 454, 459).

> Consider now . . . what work is this if it exceeds all the cruelty and injustice that can be conceived; and if it fits well with such Christians called devils, and if it would be better to leave the Indians to the devils in hell than to Christians of the Indies. (Las Casas 1989, 189)

Las Casas, in one of his last treatises, sent in 1565 as a codicil to the Council of the Indies, summarized with prophetic ardor and indignation his caustic denunciation of the "inexpiable mortal sin" committed by Castilians in the Indies. He asserted that the king had no authority to declare an unjust war, and that the wars against the natives of the Americas were unjust. He also asserted that those who participated in any way in the conquest and in the economic exploitation of the inhabitants were ipso facto in mortal sin. His ideas in summary were as follows:

> 1. All conquests were very unjust and the work of tyrants. 2. All the kingdoms and lordships of the Indies have been usurped. 3. The *encomiendas* are very iniquitous and bad per se. 4. Both those who grant them and those who hold them sin mortally. 5. The king does not have any more power to justify wars and *encomiendas* than to justify the wars and thefts of the Turks against the Christians. 6. All the treasures from the Indies have been stolen. 7. If those who are guilty do not make restitution, they cannot be saved. 8. The Indians have the right, which will be theirs until judgment day, to make very just war against us and destroy us from the face of the earth. (cited by Pérez de Tudela 1957, clxxxii)[9]

This judgment on the sinful character of the action of the Europeans in America comes from a theological affirmation that still provokes bitter disputes among church officials of many tendencies: "Tyranny is a mortal sin" (Pérez de Tudela 1957, 501, 508). An oppressive regime, even if it in some ways promotes the well-being of the people, is tyrannical, and according to the reasoning of Las Casas is therefore sinful. Sin is, in consequence, a category that has political and social dimensions.

There is an intimate link between the prophetic denunciation of the conquistadors' violent acts and the providentialism of Las Casas. If the discovery of the New World ensues from the divine dispensation to facilitate among the Indians the knowledge and participation in Christ's redemption of the human race as part of the fulfillment of the evangelical missionary command "Go throughout the whole world and preach the gospel to all creation" (Mark 16:15), the actions on the part of Christians who embarrass the faith and impede the command's fulfillment assume an eternally somber character.

The sin of the conquistadors is very grave, according to Las Casas, for besides enslaving or killing the body of the natives and taking away their goods and women, they erect insurmountable obstacles to the salvation of their own souls. First, they discredit the Christian religion. The Christians' violent conduct results in the natives' mistrust of the preachers of the faith and becomes an obstacle to their evangelization. Second, there are many aborigines who die without being baptized or converted, maltreated in the wars and in the servitude imposed by the Spaniards. In that way "many peoples are thrown . . . into hell" (Las Casas 1989, 49). The

Spaniards "go about . . . *sending to hell* the souls that the Son of God redeemed by his blood" (ibid., 141; emphasis added), "for they die without faith or sacraments" (ibid., 139).

The oppression of the Indians becomes, for the evangelical mentality of Las Casas, violence against Jesus Christ.[10] Some of his pages echo the vicarious identification between Jesus and the poor as expressed in the famous parable of the sheep and goats (Matt. 25:31–46). "Because of their greed for gold to this day they have sold and continue to sell Jesus Christ, and deny and renege him" (Las Casas 1989, 113). The offense against the natives is an offense against Jesus. It assumes the characteristics of a new crucifixion for Jesus of Nazareth.

The blood of Christ and that of the Indians have both been shed because of injustice and oppression, according to a homily by Fray Bernardo de Santo Domingo, preached in Cuba, in the presence of *encomenderos* and colonists. His words exude a strong tone of prophetic condemnation.

> We have already preached to you, after we came, about the bad state you are in because you oppress and exhaust and kill these people; not only have you not wanted to make amends, but, we understand, each day you make it worse, shedding *the blood of so many people* who have not wronged you; I ask God that *the blood he shed for them* be the judge and witness against your cruelty on judgment day, when you will have no excuse. (in Las Casas 1986, 3.3.81:100–101; emphasis added)

Initially the issue is the blood of the natives unjustly shed, but the sermon takes on an unexpected christological twist in the mention of the blood of Jesus as the witness in condemnation on judgment day against the conquistadors and *encomenderos*. The blood of the crucified Redeemer is vicariously identified with that of the Indians. The crucifixion takes place anew in the death of the natives.

Some texts in Las Casas express a somber vision of divine providence in line with his prophetic biblical mentality. There is a thread of continuity between prophets and apocalyptists. We have already seen that some writers of the sixteenth century understand the demographic catastrophe as divine punishment, in which case Spain was the chosen nation as instrument of the ire of God against the idolatry and abominations of the natives. In spite of his opposition to the Manichean (and Machiavellian) dichotomy of Spanish virtues and Indian vices, Las Casas on occasions confronted the enigma of the Indians' death from the providential perspective. Why does God allow the holocaust endured by the natives? Will their death be part of the unknown divine design for history? Perhaps "by divine judgment it was determined that these humble peoples would suffer thus." But are they not innocent? They are, but only with "respect to us," in civil law, but they are not so "nor was any man ever so," "with respect to God" (ibid., 2.3.17:492). Therefore, in an enigmatic and tragic triumph of this unique theodicy, their suffering is a payment to divine justice. That, however, should be no reason for Spaniards to rejoice. Because if the divine punishment for the Indians' sins has been terrible, even more terrifying, Las Casas insists, will be the one awaiting their executioners.

> After God by our cruel hands has finished these peoples, he will shower down his wrath upon us because of our violence and tyranny . . . and it would be possible for us to find those we have held in such low esteem in greater number at the right hand on judgment day; and this consideration should cause us great fear day and night. (ibid., 3.3.145:332)

It is a splendidly tragic vision of history, the product of a providentialist perspective that, while exalting the ethical demands of the Creator, cannot avoid stressing the unfathomable depths of the sin of the creatures. The singularity lies in the final irony: at the time of the eschaton, when humans and nations are weighed in the final balance, it is possible that the Indian infidels and barbarians will be better represented among the sheep blessed by God's right hand than the Spanish Christians who will be cursed by God's left hand.

The Wrath of God
and the Sacrament of Penance

From the prophetic perspective, the violent conquest became the source of eschatological condemnation. Prophetic censure expresses divine wrath. "Those conquests . . . [are] very grave mortal sins deserving of terrible and eternal suffering" (Las Casas 1989, 13). "On the day of judgment it will be clearer when God will avenge such horrible and abominable insults as those perpetrated in the Indies by those who call themselves Christians" (ibid., 133).

In his letter of January 20, 1531, to the Council of the Indies, Las Casas confronted its members with the frightening possibility—not considered a literary metaphor then—that they will suffer eternally in hell because of the devastation of the Indians of the New World. "Watch out, your honors, watch out; because I am afraid and doubtful of your salvation."

It is a call full of religious fervor. He reminds the counselors that according to Saint Augustine an empire that is unjustly administered is nothing more than "systematic robbery"; he recalls the Alexandrian bull in which the pope granted jurisdiction over the newfound lands for the benefit of the natives; he mentions the clause in the codicil of Queen Isabel with the warning to treat the Indians well; he concludes with a harsh questioning of their consciences by having them face the crucial decisive moment for every authentic traditional believer, divine judgment of their actions: "Do you have an answer or some excuse?" He answers himself negatively and warns them of the horrible divine punishment that will come to them, inferior only to the one deserved by those responsible for Jesus' crucifixion.

> I firmly believe, because I believe in my God and the God of all, that after the punishment and suffering deserved because of the ungrateful passion of Jesus Christ . . . nothing among all the things that have happened in the world will be so exasperating . . . nor punished on that dreadful day, as this one will be against those unfortunate ones who are responsible. (in Fabié [1879] 1966, 70:477–478)[11]

In the growing threat from the Ottoman Empire, Las Casas (1965, 2:813) sees God's condemnatory judgment. The fate of the Israelites in the Old Testament, desolated and taken into captivity because of their sins, can also be the destiny of Spain for continuing the annihilation of so many human beings "made in the image and likeness of the most blessed Trinity, a God who does not ignore or forget any one of them, for they all are God's vassals and have been redeemed by [Jesus'] precious blood." He dedicates this prophetic condemnation to the *encomenderos* and conquistadors:

> Oh miserable ones, blind and insensitive! Oh men who have been worse than the Saracens and the infidels! Who will defend you from the wrath that is to come, the day of misery and great calamity? Undoubtedly these words refer to you: "You have justified Sodom"; that is, Sodom has been justified compared to your conduct. . . . Thus you always go filling up the measure of your sins, and God's wrath has fallen upon you until the end. For you are not only enemies of your own salvation, but you also impede so many thousands of people from coming to faith and salvation. . . . Therefore, you will suffer great punishment. (Las Casas 1942, 471)

Various attempts were made to deny absolution, part of the sacrament of penance, to conquistadors and *encomenderos* who exploited and despoiled the Indians. Las Casas, who was bishop of Chiapas, Guatemala, and in residence in his diocese from 1545 to 1547, made liberation of the natives and restitution and satisfaction for damages perpetrated against them a prerequisite before the confessor would say *Ego te absolvo* (I absolve you), even when it was a question of a dying person (in which case a notarized will with the requirements mentioned above was exacted). "All are *in solidum* [fully] obliged to make restitution. And they cannot be saved if they have not made restitution and provided satisfaction to the extent possible for them to do so" (Las Casas 1965, 1:439).[12] This penitential demand is the culmination of his treatise *Del único modo:* "All men who are or will be the cause of the war referred to by means of any one of the listed ways of complicity are obliged, as a necessary means of their salvation, to make restitution to the offended infidels of everything that has been stolen from them . . . and to provide concrete, that is total, satisfaction for the damage they have caused (Las Casas 1942, 541).

The advice to the confessors that he drew up while bishop of Chiapas, probably in 1546 but not published until 1552 (in Las Casas 1965, 2:852–913), reveals his project of utilizing his sacramental religious authority for the liberation of the oppressed.

> About Indians held as slaves . . . the confessor should order the penitent without any conditions to free them in a public act in the presence of a scribe, and should pay them everything that they earned for each year or month of work and service, and this is to be done before they come to confession. And also they must ask forgiveness for the injury done . . . because it is very true and well founded . . . that in all of the Indies, from the time they were discovered until today, there has not been nor is there now any Indian who has been justly enslaved. (ibid., 879)

There had been a recent precedent. Erasmus, in his popular treatise *Querela pacis* ([1517] 1964, 986–987), had suggested that priests should not assist dying warriors, nor allow for their burial in church cemeteries. "Those wounded in warring action should be content with a secular burial. . . . Priests consecrated to God should not attend places where war is made, but places where war is ended."

Las Casas does not mention Erasmus, but this omission could be due to the campaign against him raging in Spain. It is probable that he had read *Querela pacis*, which was reprinted ten times in the first year of publication and was quickly translated into several languages, among them Spanish in 1520; the theoretical kinship is evident, especially in the emphasis on the peaceful nature of the gospel.[13]

The refusal of Las Casas as bishop of Chiapas to grant absolution for their sins to those involved in wars or *encomiendas* was not derived from anything new in his thought. He was not affirming anything he had not already stated officially in public. According to his own autobiographical

250 A Violent Evangelism

reflection after his "conversion," he freed the Indians in his *encomienda* and categorically affirmed in a sermon delivered in Cuba on the feast day of the Assumption of Our Lady, August 15, 1514, "their blindness, injustices, tyrannies, and cruelties that they were committing against those innocent and very meek people; how they would not be saved if they were apportioned among them [Spaniards] and . . . their obligation to make restitution" (Las Casas 1986, 3.3.79:95).[14]

In 1531, after spending several years enclosed in a Dominican convent in Española, he wrote to the Council of the Indies:

> Because I still would like you to know that these nations, all of them, have a just reason for war from the beginning of the discovery, and each day these reasons have continued to grow more and more by law and justice against the Christians. . . . And furthermore there has not been any just war so far on the part of the Christians, in general terms . . . and it follows that neither the king nor anyone who has come or passed through here has taken away anything justly or well earned, and they are obliged to make restitution. . . . And this is for me as true as the Holy Gospel.

Note that the formal and official letter by Las Casas concerning the iniquity of the acquisitions and the obligation to make full restitution applied also to the Royal House. The Spanish authorities, because of their jurisdiction in the administration of the Indies, were responsible for the restitution of ill-gained goods, even if they had not taken part in such illegal profits. "You are obliged to make restitution of all the goods and riches that the others steal from these peoples, even though you do not receive much from them" (in Fabié [1879] 1966, 70:483, 478). He would not abandon that idea. He would repeat it to Bartolomé de Carranza in 1555 – "The monarchs of Castilla are obliged, by reason and necessity, to make restitution and to provide satisfaction" (ibid., 71:418) – and in his last letter to the Council of the Indies in 1565:

> All the sins that are committed in this regard in those Indies, and damages and infinite inconveniences that follow, and the obligation to make restitution, will fall on the conscience of Your Majesty and of this Royal Council, and not even a *maravedí* shall be taken as profit from those kingdoms, without the need to make restitution. (Las Casas 1969, 280–281)

The rules for confession issued by Las Casas were the object of intense controversy and were bitterly censured by such different personages as Motolinía[15] and Juan Ginés de Sepúlveda, who managed to have Las Casas accused of treason before the Royal Council and of heresy before the

Inquisition (see "Proposiciones temerarias . . ." in Fabié [1879] 1966, 71:335–351). The "seventh rule" was particularly attacked because of this affirmation:

> All the things that have been done in the Indies, from the Spaniards' entrance to the subjection and serfdom they imposed on these peoples . . . have been against all natural law and civil law and also against divine law; and therefore everything has been unjust, iniquitous, tyrannical, and deserving of every infernal fire, and therefore null, void, and without any value or legal force. (Las Casas 1965, 2:873)

Although it was an unpleasant moment for Las Casas, neither of the accusations took hold. He could not avoid, however, a royal decree being sent on September 28, 1548, to the Royal Audiencia [Royal Tribunal] of Nueva España ordering the gathering of every copy of his guidelines for the confessional, which was thus interdicted and banned (in Manzano 1948, 166, n. 25).[16] He was in the most difficult situation of his life. However, he reiterated his guidelines in a letter sent to the Dominican friars in Chiapas and Guatemala (Las Casas 1969, 235–250), and until the end of his days he firmly maintained, without yielding an inch, the theological and moral correctness of his doctrine on restitution.

Las Casas made obligatory restitution of everything taken by theft, despoliation, or ransacking the crucial norm for the sacrament of confession in America. In "Tratado de las doce dudas" (Pérez de Tudela 1957, 517–522), he vigorously developed the thesis that the position of the church should be judged primarily in reference to this issue: "Whether in their sermons religious men and preachers admonish those who have stolen things to make restitution and do penance, and also through the confessional and talks to the families . . ." Participation in the eucharist and the right to be given Christian burial are also conditioned by this norm.

Las Casas was not the only Spanish theologian of the sixteenth century to be interested in the doctrine of restitution. Domingo de Soto ([1556] 1967, 2.4.6–7:327–381) also gave extensive treatment to the subject. His principal conclusion was: "Restitution of stolen goods is so necessary that without it no one can persevere in the grace of God nor regain it" (ibid., 331).

We find this issue of restitution provides the thematic axis that unifies the pastoral activity of Las Casas. From his sermon before Diego Velázquez in Cuba in 1514 until his petition to Pope Pius V in 1566, restitution is presented as an indispensable prerequisite for attaining justice on earth and spiritual salvation. In the sermon he insists on the "obligation to restitution" to which his hearers are bound (Las Casas 1986, 3.3.79:95); in the petition (in Yáñez 1941, 161–163; Las Casas 1969, App. 15, 284–286) Las Casas requests the Supreme Pontiff to remind "bishops, friars, and clerics" who have become wealthy in the Americas, "that they are obliged by natural and divine law . . . to make restitution of all the gold, silver, and precious gems they have acquired." Las Casas carried to the extreme a principle postulated by Aquinas (*Summa*, 2–2.66.8), namely, that ransacking in an unjust war, or even malicious stealing in a just battle, is a grave sin that requires restitution of stolen goods.

Las Casas unsuccessfully tried to persuade the pope to utilize the powerful weapon of excommunication against the oppressors of the American natives and their theoretical legitimizers.

> I humbly beg Your Holiness that you issue a decree declaring excommunication and anathema on anyone who says that the war against the infidels is just on account of their idolatry, or with a view to preaching the gospel better, especially to those gentiles who at no time have done us any wrong. Or against those who say that the gentiles are not true lords of what they possess. (Yáñez 161–162; Las Casas 1969, 284–286)[17]

The attempts by Las Casas to condition absolution of sins to restitution for the damage perpetrated against the Indians seem anachronistic or ineffective today. It cannot be forgotten, however, that in the sixteenth century, absolution was considered an indispensable mercy from a cleric at the moment of death. The belief that if one confessed one's sins before dying, including the most horrendous ones, and attained sacramental forgiveness, the soul could evade the perpetual torments of hell, was common among the Catholic masses. For those of that mentality, what was at stake was of transcendental significance: eternal personal destiny.

The withdrawal of absolution from conquistadors and *encomenderos* carries a basic and central idea, both in many biblical texts and in critical reflections of any theology that is within the liberating horizon of those who have been aggrieved: *the incompatibility between oppression of the poor and partaking of the sacraments.* Las Casas and other friars are taking up again the biblical and prophetic motto "I want mercy, not sacrifice" (Hos. 6:6; Matt. 9:13). The practice of oppression contradicts the soteriological aim attested by worship. On this point the friars waged a losing battle, but it was one that presents us with a dramatic and indelible monument to evangelic solidarity.

The ban of the confessional of Las Casas did not dissipate the idea of utilizing sacramental power against conquistadors, *encomenderos*, and colonists. Bataillon (1976, 311–314) found in the National Historical Archives of Spain a letter that a Dominican friar, Bartolomé de la Vega, wrote to the interim bishop of Cuzco, Fray Pedro de Toro, on July 3, 1565. Vega forcefully takes up again the idea of forbidding absolution to those who have participated in the oppression of the natives of Peru if the penitent does not do penance and make full restitution.

> None of those named deserves absolution any more than Judas . . . *Omnes praefati indigni sunt absolutione* . . . (all those mentioned are unworthy of absolution). So that you, Reverend Father, hold in your hands . . . the remedy for Peru by not granting any cleric or friar license to absolve any of these people. . . . The reason is that without cause they have taken from the Indians their haciendas and freedom. (Bataillon 1976, 311–314)

The tremendous influence that the Las Casas position on mandatory restitution as indispensable for sacramental absolution had in many circles of the church in Hispanic America has been well researched (cf. Lohmann Villena 1966). Lohmann exaggerates the "ethical correctness" and the "high virtue" of "Christian gentlemen" who when faced with death paid for their ill-obtained goods through acts of restitution, reparation, and adjustments. He does not take into account, on the one hand, the empty and repetitious character of formulas, of expressions of contrition, all suspiciously similar, nor, on the other hand, though I admit this would be extremely laborious but methodologically essential, does he bother to research whether those promises were fulfilled to the letter by the heirs and executors of the will. I am not certain either that those formulas express "ethical sensitivity," as Lohmann suggests. Another possible perspective is more skeptical or perhaps cynical: Those who did not have any scruples in doing whatever was necessary in gaining name and fortune in the earthly kingdom, at their last moment attempted to buy also the celestial realm.

Of no less dramatic and tragic depth are the eschatological condemnations of the cruelties committed by the Christians, spread throughout the texts of converted Indians who use the biblical prophetic scriptures against Christianity. One example is this Mayan text, apparently written by converted Christians, which forecasts, in words reminiscent of the exodus and the apocalypse, the divine punishment of the conquistadors.

> Alas for the unfortunate ones! The poor ones did not protest against those who enslaved them, the Anti-Christ on earth, tiger of the peoples, mountain cat of the people, leech of the poor Indian. But the tears from their eyes will reach up to God and his justice will come down on the world with one blow. (León Portilla 1987, 86)

Prophecy and Patriotism

For centuries there has been an intense debate about the "patriotism of Las Casas." After his death, his writings were used to keep alive the wounds and scars of the Spanish conquest of the Americas. His works throb with a profound tension between his religious conscience and his national identity. It is a dilemma peculiar to the providentialist mentality.

Las Casas perceived the conquest of the Americas from the viewpoint of a paradoxical theological hermeneutics. The Spaniards' encounter with the Indians was a decisive event, "the world's eleventh hour," in fulfillment of the mission gospel command. It was a unique opportunity given by God to the Iberians to play a crucial role in the expansion of Christianity and in the preparation of the apocalyptic *kairos* of the eschaton. Hence its exceptional providential nature. But the conquest was also a colossal sin by the "chosen people" of Spain. The Christian action became, ironically, the main barrier to the redemption of the natives.

In the dialectic of Las Casas between providentialism and sin we re-encounter the prophetic biblical logic. For the prophets of the Old Testament, too, the chosen people transgress their mission and become a mockery of God. Hence God's terrible condemnation. The unfathomable tragedy of prophets, both as found in the Bible and in Las Casas, is the bitterness of belonging to the chosen people who transform their divine election into a sacrilegious blasphemy. As a result, at the end of his life, in his "Testament," frustrated by his failure to protect the natives, he takes up anew the Old Testament tradition of God's curse on the chosen iniquitous nation.

> God has to shower on Spain his rage and wrath because all of it has taken part in ways little or great in the stolen bloodstained riches and in the extermination of those peoples, if it does not do great penance . . . for during seventy years they have been scandalizing, stealing, and extirpating those nations, and to this day have not acknowledged such scandals and infamies of our holy faith, so many thefts, so many injustices . . . as sins. . . . If God determines to destroy Spain, it will be due to the destruction that we have perpetrated in the Indies. (Yáñez, "Testamento," 167–168)

This type of prophetic curse against the Iberian fatherland has been the cause, for many centuries, of accusations made against Las Casas as Hispanophobic. This is like accusing Jeremiah or Isaiah of hating or devaluing Israel, of being anti-Semites. The biblical prophets criticized Israel because of their lofty conception of the ethical and religious mission that is at the heart of the national identity of the people of the Old Testament — and they were denounced for that. Las Casas criticized Spain for the same lofty reasons — and he was denounced for that. Also, let it be said in passing, the prophets of the Old Testament could be accused of exaggeration and hyperbole in relating Israel's sins.

Many colonizers and *encomenderos* harshly attacked Las Casas and asserted that "this cleric does not carry much weight, has little authority or accreditation" (Las Casas 1972, "Informes de Narvaez y Velázquez," 55). Sepúlveda (Las Casas 1965, 1:327) referred to a Las Casas work as "inflammatory libel of our kings and nation," and about all the activity of Las Casas he stated: "His only intention has been to make the whole world understand that the kings of Castilla rule the empire of the Indies against all justice and with tyranny." In a letter to Prince Felipe, September 23, 1549, Sepúlveda writes about his entrenched adversary in an amusing mixture of Spanish and Latin:

> Referring to the confessional of the bishop of Chiapas [Las Casas] and to my book [*Demócrates segundo*] . . . everything turns into a business of two opposing sides, one being the monarchs of Spain whose very just cause is defended by my book; the other, the passionate men in this business whose *caudillo* [leader] is the bishop of Chiapas as he has been in other similar negotiations, *ut est homo natura factiosus, et turbulentus* [for he is a man of a fractious and turbulent nature]. (in Losada 1949, 202)

Motolinía (1984) wrote to Carlos V in 1555 another strong censure of Las Casas:

> Very great is his lack of order and little his humility. . . . I marvel at how Y. M. and your Counselors have been able to suffer for so long such an obnoxious, restless, and importunate man . . . so aggressive and prejudicial . . . in his noises and disturbances, and always . . . looking for evil and sins that have been committed by the Spaniards in this land. . . .
>
> He has tried to learn about only the bad things and not the good. His job has been to write about the sins and events that the Spaniards have done everywhere . . . and certainly this job alone will not take him to heaven.

Motolinía's nationalistic vein is offended by the Las Casas criticisms. "Then, how so? Are the Spanish nation and its prince to be defamed by a rash man who will tomorrow be read by the Indians and other nations?" (ibid., 207–211).

But Las Casas also had entrenched defenders. Pedro de Córdoba, vice-provincial of the Dominicans in Española, wrote to Carlos V in this fashion:

God our Lord has awakened the spirit of a cleric called Bartolomé de las Casas. . . . I speak of him because he is a person of virtue and truth. . . . Your Royal Highness can justly give credence to everything he says, as true minister of God, who has been chosen by God to stop so much damage. (in Pacheco et al. 1864–1884, 11:221; J. M. Pérez 1988, App. 3, 135).

Years later (April 17, 1540), the first bishop and archbishop of Mexico, Zumárraga, called him in another letter to the emperor "a well-liked religious man, of great zeal for souls. . . . He has served God and Y. M. well" (in Cuevas 1975, 1908).

Mendieta ([1596] 1980, 4.1:366), Motolinía's disciple, is another who is not stinting in his praise of Las Casas, writing decades after his death, and apparently unaware of Motolinía's vitriolic epistle:

> I believe, without any doubt, that the glory he enjoys in heaven is very great and of great honor [is] the crown with which he has been crowned for his thirst and hunger for justice and the very holy and persevering zeal with which he pursued until his death to suffer by God's love, living for the poor and deprived of all favors and help.

The controversy over Las Casas was reawakened in the second half of this century after he was severely criticized by the leader of Spanish intellectuals, historians, and philologists, Ramón Menéndez Pidal, in his book *El padre Las Casas, su doble personalidad* (1963). In its attempt to discredit the Las Casas criticism of Spain, Menéndez Pidal's central evaluation rests on a pseudo-psychiatric appraisal: "He was not a saint, nor an impostor, nor malevolent, nor crazy; he was simply paranoic. . . . In order to expunge his total lack of charity, his monstrous and malicious lies in a man of an ascetic life, . . . one has to make use of the only possible explanation, mental illness" (ibid., xiv). Such an evaluation is very reminiscent of the abuses of psychiatry that some regimes have made to repress dissidents. This subjective judgment is linked to a deep-seated ethnocentrism, which today, a time of greater cultural ecumenism, seems obsolete. For example: "A beautiful fantasy [of Las Casas], the absolute equality of all nations, but also a deceiving fantasy. . . . All nations are equal in regard to the sacred rights of their personal dignity, but are very unequal in their mental capacity, and the more inventive nations, who give impulse to civilization, are very different from those who receive it, and very different also are the rights of the one and of the other" (ibid., 385).[18]

Contrary to what certain nationalist circles suggest, the objective of Las Casas was to save Spain from divine condemnation. Although his

Historia de las Indias has been labeled "anti-nationalistic" (Salas 1986, 10), in reality, all of it vibrates with a profound affection for his country. It is a love, however, in the manner of the Old Testament prophets, full of demands for justice and solidarity. His choleric and prophetic denunciation hopes for the repentance of his compatriots, "to impede the scourges of God and the cruelest one he will inflict because of them [events in the New World] on all Spain" (Las Casas 1965, 1:457–459).

14

The God of the Conquerors

Conquest: Guana Capac (Inka) and Candía (Spaniard):
"Do you eat the gold?"
"Yes, we eat the gold."

Gold is extraordinary; gold becomes a treasure, and with it, whoever has it can do anything he wishes in the world, and even send souls to Paradise.

Christopher Columbus

He had a basket full of gold in the form of jewelry and said: "See here the god of the Christians . . ."

Bartolomé de las Casas

Christ or Mammon?

The main theological problem in identifying the true god of the conquistadors may be framed within the context of the biblical choice between God and mammon. The issue is acutely posited by Las Casas in the rhetorical question, Who is the true god of the conquerors: God or gold? The conquistadors, Las Casas asserts, make war against the Indians and enslave them "to reach the goal that is their god: gold" (Las Casas 1989, 99; 1974, 291); "to take out of their blood the riches they take as their god" (Las Casas 1965, 2:673). To this god-gold, he continues, "they sacrificed the Indians, killing them in the mines" (Las Casas 1986, 2.3.36:558). Therefore gold is "bloody and iniquitous" (ibid., 3.3.68:61).[1] The idolatry of mammon is hidden behind rhetorical allegiance to the crucified Christ.

The gold the Spaniards obtain from the mines is in fact extracted from the blood of the Indians. It is "the price of blood and worthy of eternal fire, for there is no *arroba* (twenty-five pounds weight; trans. note) of gold or silver that placed in a balance with the blood of the Indians they kill for these (metals), that would weigh more than the blood"; "gold . . . was mined with the death of the Indians"; "it seems that by nature gold kills men because of the work required to mine it" (Las Casas 1965, 2:809; 1986, 2.2.11:244 and 13:253). These words would not be forgotten. In 1704, the archbishop of Lima and acting viceroy of Peru, Melchor de Liñán, referred to the extraction of silver and gold in the Peruvian altiplano in the following way: "He was certain that those minerals were so drenched by the blood of the Indians, that if the money made from them was wrung, there would be more blood than silver."[2]

The phrase was not original. Already in 1517 some Dominican and Franciscan friars, in a letter to a counselor of the young Carlos V, anticipated it when speaking of the Spaniards' aspirations to high living: "So that they may be clothed in silk, even including their shoes, and not just those, but also their mules, the silk if well wrung would exude blood of Indians, for all the excessive and superfluous expenses incurred here, all come out of the guts of the miserable Indians" (J. M. Pérez 1988, App. 4, 153).

One of the most famous stories told by Las Casas (1989, 43; and 1986, 3.3.21:505, 508; 25:522–524) is that of the tragic end of Chief Hatuey from Santo Domingo, who fled to Cuba. He includes this dialogue between Hatuey and his nobles on the motive for the persecution they endured from the Spaniards.

> "Do you know why they do it?" They said: "No; but only because they are by nature cruel and evil." He said: "They do not do it because of that, but because they adore a god whom they love much and so that we may adore him too, they force us to work and kill us." He had a basket full of gold in the form of jewelry and said: "See here the god of the Christians . . ."[3]

Hatuey was captured, and before he was burned, a Franciscan friar tried to convert him, using the promise of heaven and the threat of hell. Las Casas (1989, 45) tells of the proud reaction of the unfortunate chief.

> [Hatuey], thinking a little, asked the religious man if Christians went to heaven. The religious man answered yes. . . . The chief then said without further thought that he did not want to go there but to hell so as not to be where they were and where he would not see such cruel people. This is the name and honor that God and our faith have earned.[4]

The view that mammon was the true god of the Christian conquistadors had been expressed before by Fray Tomás Ortíz. "I saw that the God and the administration that they teach and preach is 'Give me gold, give me gold' . . . " (in Friede 1953, 43–44). Motolinía (1984, 16), in his exposition of the "ten plagues" that desolated and exterminated a good portion of the Indian population, affirmed the same theme:

> The sixth plague was the gold mines . . . for the Indian slaves who have died in them could not be counted; and *it was the gold of this land like another golden calf adored as god, for they come from Castilla to adore him.* (emphasis added)

The conquest revealed gold as the true god, the idol that motivated the treatment given the inhabitants of the New World by the conquistadors. Such was their greed "that out of their avarice for gold, they have sold and still sell Jesus Christ and deny and renege him" (Las Casas 1989, 113). According to a Quechua account: "You see here the entire Christian law . . . you have idols and silver in your hacienda" (Guamán Poma de Ayala 1988, 1:339). Referring to the Peruvian mines at Potosí, the Dominican

Fray Domingo de Santo Tomás asserted: "Four years ago, to bring an end to this land, a gate to hell was discovered through which each year . . . great quantities of people enter, sacrificed by the Spaniards' greed to their god" (in Armas Medina 1953, 467; Castañeda Delgado 1970, 837). The contradiction between theological theory and avaricious practices reveals the idolatrous character of the conquistadors' religion.

Various conquistadors and the theologians and jurists who supported them justified their armed encounters against the Indians by citing the human sacrifice that some of the Indian nations made to their gods. Sepúlveda, probably through the influence of Cortés, estimated that the Aztecs made some twenty thousand human sacrifices a year (see Losada 1948). Motolinía's estimates (1984, 205) were even higher. He alleged that "the predecessor of Moctezuma, lord of Mexico, called Ahutzoci, offered the Indians [sic; he meant to say idols] in one temple alone and one sacrifice . . . eighty thousand four hundred men." The twenty thousand figure stuck and became a stereotype. One of those who used it was the first bishop and archbishop of Mexico, Juan de Zumárraga, in a letter to a chapter of Franciscans gathered in Tolousse, France, in 1532: "[I]n this city of Mexico they had the yearly custom to sacrifice more than twenty thousand hearts to their idols" (Mendieta [1596] 1980, 4.30:637). Diez Flores, in his introduction to the apologia of Vargas Machuca (1612), alleged that "in the island of Española they say that there are twenty thousand sacrifices a year" (in Fabié [1879] 1966, 71:213).[5]

Besides considering these figures grossly exaggerated, as they in fact were, Las Casas (1965, 1:397) gave in comparison the human sacrifices that the Spaniards made to their idol—*greed*.

> We can truly say that the Spaniards have offered to their goddess, well beloved and worshiped by them, greed, in each year they have been in the Indies . . . more than the Indians sacrificed to their gods in one hundred years.

The contradiction between the adoration of Jesus Christ and mammon artificially disappears if one undervalues the theological theory as a "mere ideological montage created later . . . [by] those who came searching for gold and personal enrichment" (Nenadich Deglans 1986–1987, 22, 26). It would then be mere ideological deceit. The intensity of Spanish and missionary Catholicism indicates a very complex situation, a conflict between opposing goals, all valid at the various levels of historical objectives constituted by the variegated process of conquest, colonization, and evangelization. God, gold, and glory were all pursued by the conquerors. Cortés, for instance, truly wanted the Christianization of the natives, but he also truly wanted to become extremely rich and truly desired to inscribe his name in the annals of history.

In July 1503, while shipwrecked in Jamaica, Columbus writes a long account to the Spanish Monarchs in which he stresses, against the skepticism of some critics, the riches of the newfound lands. It is very instructive to see in that account the real—not merely rhetorical—convergence between temporal domination, the thirst for gold, and the spiritual goal of salvation.

> When I discovered the Indies, I said that it was the wealthiest domain in the world. . . . All this is security for the Christians and assurance of domination, a great hope for the honor and increase of the Christian religion. . . . Gold is extraordinary; gold becomes a treasure, and with it, whoever has it can do anything he wishes in the world, and even send souls to Paradise. (in Varela 1986, 292)

Political "assurance of domination," the possibility of quickly acquiring extraordinary riches, and the "increase of the Christian religion" are intimately linked. Columbus's allusion to the strange power of gold is unique: ". . . even send souls to Paradise." Fernández de Navarrete understands that this is an allusion to the possibility of earning redeeming credits through the pious and charitable works that one can do thanks to ones' riches (1945, 1:428, n. 1).[6] Columbus, however, might have been thinking of a practice in common use that, a few years later, would have enormous consequences: the sale of indulgences.

A good example is the expression used by Cortés to exhort his men before starting the war against the Aztec capital, as told by López de Gómara (1946, 375):

> The main reason for which we came to these parts is to extol and preach faith in Christ, although that is accompanied by honor and profit, which seldom fit in the same bag. . . . Let us go forth, serving God, honoring our nation, giving growth to our king, and let us become rich ourselves; for the Mexican enterprise is for all these purposes.

Missionary zeal, patriotism, search for honor and glory, greed and desire for quick riches: it is the eclectic convergence of multiple motives that constitutes conquest, Christianization, political domination, and expropriation of precious minerals.

Less complex, but more poetic, is the Nahuatl version of Spanish greed for gold. The anonymous informers of Sahagún tell of the enthusiastic reaction of Cortés and his men to the golden presents that the Aztec chief sent when he learned of their proximity to the city. Moctezuma committed a serious error—cultivation and stimulation of the conqueror's avarice. "His face had a smile, they were very happy, they were delighted. As if they were monkeys they raised the gold . . . and their heart was lighter. . . . They desired it with great thirst . . . they were ravenously hungry for that. They thirst for gold as hungry pigs" (Sahagún [1582] 1985, 12.12:70).

Julian Garcés, bishop of Tlaxcala, in his previously mentioned letter to Pope Paul III, probably written in 1535, provides another argument for converting gold from an object of vanity and greed into an instrument for religious promotion. The armed campaigns in Europe against Moslems and Turks can be financed with the gold extracted from the mines of the New World (Hernáez 1879, 1:61). The popularity of this idea, which reveals the deeply rooted aspiration to "rescue" the Holy Land from Islamic hands, can be seen in the fact that Las Casas once asserted that the "riches and temporal treasures" of the Indies should be used in strengthening the Christian troops rather than wasted on the individual greed of conquistadors and *encomenderos*, "so that the enemies [Turks and Moors] of our holy Catholic faith will not dare to battle against it as in the past" (Las Casas 1986, 1.1.76:330).

The idea that gold and silver from the Indies could be used for the most dear traditional goal of Christianity, the recovery of the Holy Land and the defeat of the Moslems, gave vigor to Columbus's ambitious desire to be the key, through his individual control of gold from the Americas, of a future victorious crusade. In his diary, the Admiral expressed his egotistic illusion that the men he left at La Navidad in Española would find great veins of gold. "And in such large quantities that before three years the Monarchs may take on the conquest of the Holy Land. . . . I protested to Your Highnesses that all the earnings from this my enterprise be spent in the conquest of Jerusalem" (Varela 1986, 155).

The Capitulation of Burgos, May 8, 1512 — between the Catholic king Fernando V and the first three bishops to the Americas, García Padilla, Pedro Suárez de Deza, and Alonso Manso — is truly a monument to the Spanish Crown's ability to use the Christian religion for political and economic objectives. The prelates formally committed themselves to endorse the intense labor of Antilleans in the gold mines. The direct beneficiary was of course the Castilian court; the indirect one, at least ideologically, was Christendom. The text shows, also, the caution of the astute monarch who wished to prevent those bishops from starting on the path initiated by the Dominicans in Española, who provoked such scandal through the Montesinos sermon. He understood well the possibility of profitably using religious motivations.

And because of this and no other reason, the Indians will not be prevented directly or indirectly from mining gold as they do now, but

rather will be advised to work harder in obtaining gold, telling them that
it is to be used to make war against the infidels, and other things which
would make them work well. (Hernáez 1879, 1:23)[7]

This idea was reiterated by the Peruvian viceroy Luis Velasco at the
end of 1594. Upon consulting the religious orders about the legitimacy of
making additional distributions of Indians to labor in the mines where
precious metals had recently been found, he advanced the apparently
unquestionable premise that the gold and silver of the Indies was indispensable for "the defense of Christendom," and if the extraction ceased,
besides being prejudicial to the well-being of the natives, "irreparable
damage would be done by our enemies to the realms of Your Majesty and
to those beyond the sea" (in Castañeda 1970, 908).

Acosta, evaluating the conquest and evangelization of the New World,
insisted that Spanish greed had, ironically, a positive providential result.
Neither missionary zeal nor love of neighbor would have been sufficient
to move Castilians to overcome the unknown seas and throw themselves
into the dangerous adventure of the conquest in which many lost their
lives. Gold served as the incentive for the expansion of Christianity. He
rejected, as a result, the attempts by many religious and defenders of the
Indians to forbid or mitigate mining labor. It would be like eliminating the
bait that brings Spaniards, among them the missionaries, the preachers
of the gospel of Christ. (From the gold came the money to build churches
and monasteries and to provide for priests and friars.)

> If the benefit of the mines is abandoned . . . [and] the work of the min-
> ing of metals is neglected, the Indies will be finished, the republic and
> the Indians would perish. That is what the Spaniards look for in under-
> taking such a long navigation of the ocean, and the day that gold and
> silver are lacking, the concourse of people and affluence would disappear;
> and soon the multitude of civilized men and priests would also vanish.
> (Acosta 1952, 289)

He recognized that the natives worked in the mines only against their
will and that the work was exhausting and extremely dangerous.

> The order that forces the Indians to work in the mines is harsh. . . . To
> force to this labor free men who have not done any harm seems inhuman
> and iniquitous. Besides, it has been learned that many in this job die
> or are consumed by exhaustion or perish in accidents. It is horrible to
> relate the appearance of the caves inside the mine in the entrails of the
> earth . . . perpetual and horrendous night, thick and subterranean
> air . . . (ibid., 287)

But this was understood as a temporal evil that had been exchanged
for a spiritual and eternal benefit: the soul's salvation. The Spaniards'

greedy search for precious metals brought to the New World and its barbarians the good news of redemption.

> The salvation of so many millions of souls does not awaken in our soul greed and zeal, unless it is accompanied by gold and silver; and if there are no advantages, the spiritual benefit is of small weight.
>
> Who, then, will not consider with surprise and astonishment the secrets of the Lord's wisdom, who made silver and gold, plague of mortals, into salvation for the Indians? (ibid., 289, 291)

He warned, however, that whoever exploited the natives mercilessly, without considering their physical health or their spiritual salvation, "would have to give an account to God, who is father of the poor and judge of the orphans." He apparently believed that those who managed forced labor in the mines would take seriously this warning about their possible divine judgment after death.[8]

Acosta does not avoid the Hispanophilic and nationalistic providentialism typical of sixteenth-century Iberian theological circles. The exploitation of American silver and gold mines is a "special favor from heaven." God had hidden the Potosí mines until "the reign of Emperor Carlos V of glorious name" and the joining, under Felipe II, of the kingdoms of Spain and the Western and Oriental Indies (this refers to the union of Spain and Portugal, which incorporated under one monarch an enormous realm beyond the sea). This providential gift to Spain of so many riches was inevitably seen as having an anti-Protestant dimension: "Also for the defense of the very Catholic faith and Roman Church . . . opposed and persecuted by the heretics"; "the pious zeal of the Catholic King [Felipe II] spends the riches of the Americas in causes worthy of the Catholic faith" (Acosta 1985, 4.1–8:140–154). Certainly, greed and avarice dominate many conquerors, but because of the steadfastness of missionary zeal, it is precisely those mundane impulses—those "human and earthly means of men who seek themselves more than Jesus Christ," the ones who paradoxically, and thanks to the secret divine dialectic—allow the transferal of Christianity to the Indies and, with it, for "the great Lord's providence," the saving preaching of the true faith (ibid., 7.28:373–377).[9]

The theological valuing of gold as bait for the missionary enterprise did not originate with Acosta. It is already found in the viceroy Francisco de Toledo, who suggests, in a report to the court in 1570, a religious justification for the Indians' mining labor: "The trade from those kingdoms brings silver and gold from the mines here, and if they are not taken advantage of and preserved, the Spaniards who are here will not support the land, and if they are missing, the conversion of the natives will not be achieved"

Levillier 1921–1926, 3:327). Besides, the viceroy asserts, idleness would only lead them to vices and idolatry.

The enigmatic "Anónimo de Yucay," who reflects so well the common perspectives of Spanish colonists in Peru, also similarly theologizes about the Peruvian mines. He makes use of a homely analogy: A father wishes to make a good marriage for an ugly and grotesque daughter and gives her a substantial and attractive dowry; so God has given to these native peoples, "so unskilled and bestial . . . ugly, rustic, dumb . . . and vicious," extraordinary riches to attract a noble and Christian consort. The great riches in silver and gold of Peru is the dowry that God offers to the missionary zeal.

> And thus he gave them mountains of gold and silver, fertile and delightful lands, so that lured by that and for God's sake people would want to go to preach the gospel and baptize them, and those souls would become brides of Jesus Christ. . . . So I say of these Indians, that one of the means of their conversion . . . was these mines and treasures and riches, because we clearly see that where they are present the gospel flies there.

The exploitation of the gold mines was, therefore, "morally necessary." If it was not done, the Castilian Crown would lose its interest in Peru, and "without the King, it is clear that the Catholic faith would cease in these kingdoms. . . . Hence, they are holy and good" ("Anónimo de Yucay," 461–464).[10] The "Anónimo" adds another popular argument of the time: the Peruvian mines contributed decisively and providentially to strengthen the military alliance of Christian princes in the war against the Ottoman Empire.

In contrast, Fray Domingo de San Pedro, at the farewell in 1544 for a group of Dominican missionaries departing for the Indies, warned them to persevere in "holy poverty," a clear warning not to allow themselves to be seduced by avarice, since, above all in the New World, "gold and silver seem to confuse the senses and intoxicate the soul" (in Manzano 1948, 225, n. 4). And Mendieta ([1596] 1980, 4.46:555–563), deeply disappointed by the decadence and corruption of Christianity in the Indies, came to the conclusion that the cause was

> this bad beast and worst animal . . . greed, which has devastated and exterminated the vineyard, demanding adoration (like the Apocalyptic beast) as lady of the universe, making blind men place all their happiness and hope in dirty money, as if there was no other God in which to hope and trust.

Unlike Acosta, Mendieta prayed to "divine mercy" to "sink all the mines in the abyss" so that only the friars and religious, free from the greed for gold and silver, would travel to the Indies (ibid., 37:523).

The Birth of a Theology of Liberation

Enrique Dussel (1981, 406), theologian and historian, has affirmed that "the prophetic conversion" of Las Casas "could be considered the birth of Latin American liberation theology." Gustavo Gutiérrez (1981, 159), while analyzing the liberating theological ideas of the defenders of the rights of the Indians in the sixteenth century, finds a crucial analogy between then and now: "the contradiction . . . between the situation of the poor in Latin America and God's will for justice and love" (cf. Rodríguez León 1989). This dialectical and distressing perception is the point of departure for a theological reflection accompanied by denunciation, solidarity, and liberation.

> Here you can find in Latin America a profound line of theological continuity, arising when Christianity, transplanted by conquerors, friars, and colonists, becomes the religion of the victors and the faith of the victims. That double function of legitimation and denunciation becomes the historical matrix for Latin American theological debates, always characterized by a vital urgency absent from the theoretical abstractions of other regions. (cf. Silva Gotay 1989)

Las Casas took on the key defense of the defenseless. His voice became the voice of protest and denunciations for those whose testimony was ignored by the officials. When he recalls, after the first violent conflicts between the Indians and the Spaniards, the way in which the Catholic Monarchs gave full credibility (1496–1497) to the Admiral's version, he feels and expresses the profound powerlessness of the natives.

> As there was no one to speak for and defend the Indians and their rights and justice . . . they remained judged and forgotten by delinquents, from the beginning of their destruction to their extermination, without anyone feeling their death and loss nor considering them an offense. (Las Casas 1986, 1.1.113:439)

In the middle of the difficult and important conversations, negotiations, and disputes held in reference to the destiny of "the Indies," crucial for the destiny of its inhabitants, no one listened with attention and respect to the main protagonists in their own tragedy. No one paid attention to their anguished voice. This contradiction between the abundance of European texts and the scarce consideration of the Indians' word determined the substance and content of the voice of many religious, such as Las Casas, staunch defenders of the poor and oppressed.

How can one distinguish between a theology with a liberation perspective and religious reflections that legitimized human servitude, in this case, that of the Indians? Las Casas, in a letter of 1549, gives a profound hermeneutical key: "To discern, Father, which is the decisive factor between diverse accounts, and all from credible religious, *opus est solertissima spirituum probare* [the task is to discern the hidden depths of the spirits]." Which is the decisive factor in "this discernment of spirits"? "What moves them: the liberation of captives . . . or the skinning of bodies?" (Bataillon 1976, 261–265; Las Casas 1969, App. 1, 119–124).

The Vision of the Victims

If the juridical and theological disputes between victors and conquerors were intense, the reactions of the victims and conquered were painful and tragic.

We have relatively few original testimonies of the anguished questions of the American natives, but those that have come down to us reflect the tribulation of the victims with a poetic eloquence that is nothing short of that in *The Trojan Women* of Euripides, as in these examples:

> On the roads broken arrows
> the hairs scattered.
> The houses roofless,
> their walls bloodstained.
> Worms roam streets and plazas
> and the walls are smeared with brains.
> Red are the waters, as if dyed,
> and our drink tastes like salt.
>
> (Léon Portilla 1987, 53)

> We hit the adobe walls in our anguish
> and only holes are our inheritance.
> The shields were our guard,
> but shields do not prevent desolation.
>
> (ibid., 78)

> They taught us fear,
> they came to wilt the flowers.
> For their flower to grow,
> ours was damaged and absorbed.
>
> (ibid., 80)

> Red bearded foreigners arrived,
> children of the sun,
> light-skinned men.
> Alas! Let us be sad for their arrival!
> They Christianized us,
> but they pass us from one to the other like animals.
>
> (ibid., 84)

> Allow us to die,
> allow us to perish,
> for our gods have already died.
>
> (ibid., 25)

The Inka Atahualpa bemoans, according to a Quechua account, his imprisonment and defeat:

> A wicked warrior
> has imprisoned me, oh Colla, [Indian tribe; trans. note]
> has ransacked us, Queen,
> now we shall die;
> may our misfortune not become a deluge of tears
> falling by itself;
> so it had to happen.
>
> (ibid., 146)

A Challenge to Reflect

Critical reflection on the conquest of the Americas, from a perspective that links academic honesty and moral integrity, inevitably leads to a consideration of the martyrs who offered their lives for the emancipation of the poor and oppressed in our continent. In our geopolitical context, it is relevant to recall a great ecclesial martyr on American soil: Antonio de Valdivieso, bishop of Nicaragua, assassinated in 1550 because of his defense of the Indians.

> It happened that while preaching in favor of the freedom of the Indians, he reprimanded the conquistadors and governors for the bad treatment given the Indians. They became so angered that they expressed it with words and deeds. . . . Among the soldiers who had unhappily come from Peru, there was one called Juan Bermejo, a man of evil intention. He became a follower of the Conteras brothers, one [of whom was] governor of Nicaragua. . . . He went out accompanied by others . . . and went

to the bishop's house and found him in the company of his assistant, Fray Alonso, and another good cleric, and losing respect for the sacred, he knifed him. (in Dussel 1979, 335–336, from Gonzalez Dávila 1649, 1:235–236)

Careful reflection on that story is of greater benefit than a celebration of the armed conquest of the powerful over the weak. For Christians faithful to the crucified Lord, what is proper is to reveal the blood of Christ shed from the bodies of the American natives and the ill-treated and suffering blacks, offered in sacrifice at the golden altar of mammon. This implies listening to the voice of the martyrs, masterfully expressed in the message that 2,500 aborigines gave Pope John Paul II, on April 8, 1987, in Salta, Argentina.

> Welcome, John Paul II, to these lands that originally belonged to our ancestors and that we do not possess today. In their name and ours, survivors of the massacre and genocide . . . we declare you guest and brother. . . .
>
> We were free, and the land that is the mother of the Indians was ours. We lived from what she gave us generously, and we all ate in abundance. No one went without food. . . . We praised our God through the land in our own language, with our rituals and dances, with instruments we made. Until one day European civilization arrived. It planted the sword, the language, and the cross and made us into crucified nations. Indian blood from yesterday, martyred in defense of its possessions, [is the] seed of the silent martyrs of today who, walking slowly, carry the cross of five centuries. In that cross, brought to America, they [the conquerors] changed the Christ of Judea for the Indian Christ. . . .
>
> May all the blood shed by the ethnocide and genocide that we the aboriginal nations have suffered be the conscience of humanity and serve to establish new relationships based on justice and the fraternity of peoples. (INFORMEDH 1987, 8)

Conclusion

The discovery and conquest of the Americas changed dramatically the history and destiny of humankind. Five hundred years ago, thanks to the nautical audacity and cosmographical ignorance of an Italian mariner at the service of the Spanish Catholic Monarchs, the Atlantic Ocean ceased to be a divider and became the waterway connection between Europe, Africa, and the Americas. The continents that were then separated were conjoined in the birth of modernity and universal Christianity. The peoples and nations that inhabited those far away lands and territories were brought together by the force of European weapons and the strength of Christian faith. For the sake of God, gold, and glory the men and women of Europe traveled thousands of miles through uncharted waters, found unsuspected and unimaginable realms, and completing the geography of the globe, gave birth to a New World. Explorers and farmers, missionaries and artisans, builders and opportunists conquered the lands, exploited its resources and riches, exterminated or evangelized its population, and wrote a splendid history of cruelty and piety.

This discovery and conquest also produced a collision of ideas and conceptual perspectives with no parallel in history. The Spanish empire produced eloquent apologists who defended the military conquest of the Americas, the forced servitude imposed upon its nations, and the coerced Christianization of its peoples. The elegant style and clarity of thought of Juan Ginés de Sepúlveda is an obvious example. Spain also produced eminent thinkers who, like Francisco de Vitoria, dealt theoretically with the complex issue of building a "just dominion," an empire built upon law and faith but also upon expropriation of land and slave labor.

Spain also forged forceful critics, who submitted their beloved nation to the most stringent ethical scrutiny and critique since the time of the biblical prophets. Like the voice of a new Jeremiah or Amos, their irate cry for justice pierced the heavens, chastising without mercy the soul of their country. Those are mistaken who think that the sixteenth century was devoid of the ethical sensitivity necessary to judge critically the injustices of the age. What reader of Bartolomé de las Casas could ever forget the prophetic resonance of his indignant prose, his thirst and hunger for justice, his compassion for those who were treated mercilessly, his unquenchable and tireless search for a new and different kind of encounter between diverse human communities, his faith in the healing grace of God, and his hope that all human beings, whatever their racial and cultural differences, would finally be able to accept his basic axiom that "all nations of the world are human"?

Notes

Chapter 1

1. The Mexican debate, probably the most heated one in the entire Latin American continent, is reviewed by Ortega y Medina (1987, 127–171).

2. Sauer (1984, 216–222) shows how Columbus, in his fourth and last voyage, confronted many indications that there were doubts about his cosmographic and geographic conceptions, but he rejected a change. "In the last voyage he preserved the preconceived ideas of the first. . . . The proof of his error did not enter Columbus's mind." He reproduces maps that Columbus's brother Bartolomé brought to Rome after the death of the Admiral. Those maps tried ingeniously to maintain the Asiatic nature of the American lands, through the hypothesis of the geographic unity between what was known, and China.

3. Varela's affirmation is too categorical. Columbus's last correspondence reveals a profound melancholy due to his inability to find the fabulous riches that he yearned for or the great Oriental empires for reestablishing the contacts made by Marco Polo. Together with his enforced and painful ostracism from Española, this makes it difficult to maintain that the Admiral died "believing that he had achieved his dream."

4. References to *Historia de las Indias,* by Las Casas, appear with volume, book, chapter, and page from the 1986 Mexican edition. Columbus, in his first journey, took letters of presentation from the Spanish Monarchs for the Great Khan, monarch of the Tartar Empire (cf. Las Casas 1986, 1.1.33:174). Beatriz Pastor (1984, 17–107) has provokingly analyzed the "fictionalizing" by Christopher Columbus of the reality of the lands he arrived at, and his insistence on identifying them with fabulous, quasi-mythical places in Asia.

5. The obsession with locating the paradise of Eden in America persisted. In the seventeenth century (1650–1656), Antonio León Pinelo, a peculiar character residing in Lima, wrote a piece with abundant biblical references to demonstrate that this paradise was located between the Marañon and the Amazon rivers. This work was reedited as *El paraíso en el Nuevo Mundo. Comentario apologético, historia natural y peregrina de las Indias Occidentales* (Paradise in the New World: Apologetic Commentary, Exotic and Natural History of the Western Indies) in 1943.

6. More sought after than the earthly paradise were the legendary mines of King Solomon, the biblical Ophir or Tarsis. Biblicists and theologians discussed their possible location in the New World. The Franciscan Bernardino de Sahagún ([1582]

1985, 719) endorsed the idea, while the Jesuit José de Acosta ([1590] 1985, 1:13–14, 40–43) denied it. The Franciscan Fray Toribio de Motolinía (Toribio de Benavente) (1984, 3.11:167) affirms that many Spaniards left their native land and sailed to America searching for the mines "from which King Solomon took very fine gold."

7. "Information and testimony of how the Admiral went to reconnoiter the island of Cuba, and being persuaded that it was the mainland (June 12, 1494)," by the scribe Fernando Pérez de Luna in Fernández de Navarrete (1945, 2:171–178). After all the members of the exploratory expedition took an oath saying that Juana (Cuba) was not an island but "the mainland, the beginning of the Indies, and the final destination for those who wished to come from Spain on foot," Columbus imposed a fine of 10,000 *maravedíes*, one hundred scourges, and the cutting off of the tongue of whoever contradicted what he had certified. See Friederici [1925] 1986, 1:269–270.

8. "Columbus's achievement was an 'exploit' that has nothing to do with the 'discovery of America'" (O'Gorman 1951, 42). "The modern historiographic thesis in regard to this 'exploit,' namely, that Columbus discovered America fortuitously and without ever realizing it, carries within it an insoluble internal contradiction" (ibid., 357).

9. Dussel's evaluation (1988, 36) of O'Gorman's vision seems to me correct: "First, the interpretation of the invention of America places Columbus and the European being as center of the world. Secondly, it takes what was found in the Ocean sea as an entity. This is historically correct and in accord with the reality. In fact, the European considered what he found to be an entity, a thing. He did not respect it as 'Other,' as a world, as something beyond what might be possible in the Columbian world." Dussel has proposed that the fifth centenary, instead of being a festive and celebrative occasion, be one of penance and atonement on the part of the descendants of the invaders toward the indigenous peoples. From the perspective of Las Casas, would we not also have to think of some other type of restitution?

10. Included in Vignaud (1917, 305). Spanish and English translations are included in Vespucci 1951.

11. The famous map of Waldseemüller, long lost and found in 1901 in a German castle, is reprinted in Shirley 1983, 30–31. The concept of "new world" took hold in good measure thanks to Pedro Mártir de Anglería's popular work *De orbe novo* (About the New World), first published in Latin in its entirety in 1530.

12. Las Casas (1986, 1.1.5:38) explains why the newly found lands were called "Indies" (a name that persisted for a long time in official Spanish terminology): "Christopher Columbus inferred that since the Oriental end of India was not known it would have to be the side closest to us approaching from the West; and, therefore, you could call the lands he had discovered the Indies . . . since they were the Oriental part of India *ultra Gangem*." The term "Indies" remained in Spanish juridical and political usage in spite of the fact that Juan López de Palacios Rubios, jurist and counsel to King Fernando, indicated the inadequacy of the term. "The general public, in its ignorance, calls those islands the Indies. They are, however, not the Indies" (Palacios Rubios and Paz 1954, 6). An example of the persistence of this

mistaken toponymy, and not only among the "general public," is the consistorial act concerning the transformation of the parish church of Mexico into a cathedral: "The church founded in the city of Mexico in India (*in civitate Mexicana in India*) was made into a cathedral" (Shiels 1961, 341–342).

13. Las Casas (1986, 2.1.139:40). Also cf. ibid., 163:114–119. A good portion of the discussion centers on the truth of Vespucci's accounts. The problem is accurately identified by Vignaud in the first sentence of his text: "*Nous ne connaissons les voyages de Vespuce que par lui-même*" (We only know about Vespucci's journeys from himself) (Vignaud 1917, 3). But even if essential segments of his narrative are fraudulent, as has been asserted by his detractors beginning with Las Casas, the undeniable truth is that he was the first to publicly point out that the "islands and mainland of the Ocean sea" constituted a different reality, a "new world." By doing so, he contributed to the stimulation of the European utopian imagination. His accounts were an important influence on the writing of Thomas More's *Utopia* (1516). Cf. Uncein Tamayo (1981, 94–97) and above all, the provocative work of Baudet (1965, 32–42), who highlights the historical links between the American natives and the concept of "utopia" developed in the late Renaissance. The most important modern defense of the veracity of Vespucci's journeys and the authenticity of the letters and accounts attributed to him has been accomplished by Levillier in "*Américo Vespucci: Concordancia de sus viajes y cartas con los mapas de la época*" (A. Vespucci: Concordance of his journeys and letters with the maps of the period) (in Vespucci 1951, 13–92). Levillier does not treat, however, an important aspect of the question: the truth of Vespucci's account. Some information supplied by the Florentine navigator about indigenous ways seems fantastic: for example, the strange techniques that, according to him, lustful female aborigines used to excite the male sexual organ (ibid., 181). In general, it is difficult to separate Vespucci's ethnographic description from literary fantasy, resulting in an early manifestation of what today is called "magic realism."

14. Washburn (1962, 1–21) notices the continuous correlation between the verbs "to discover" and "to win" in the royal letters, but without perceiving its meaning as a strategy for expropriation. This may be because his lexicographic hermeneutics lacks theoretical depth.

15. The royal letter to Columbus is dated April 23, 1497.

16. Todorov ([1982] 1987, 35) says: "To name is equivalent to take possession of." This suggestive work includes a good number of provocative reflections.

17. Three Latin editions were published in 1493 in Rome, and before 1500 there were seventeen editions of the letter: two in Castilian, nine in Latin, five in Italian, and one in German.

18. Morales Padrón's explanation is as follows: "Columbus led people to believe that what he found was the Indies of the East, and because the Ionians from Asia Minor could not pronounce the aspirated 'h' and called the Hindus *Indoi*—the word we inherited—the men and women of the future America came to be known as *Indians*" (1955, 7).

19. The Treaties' principal articles are reprinted in Morales Padrón 1979, 41–43, and in Davenport 1917, 1:36–41.

20. The first quote comes from the papal bull *Inter caetera*, May 3, 1493; the second from the bull of the same name of May 4. Reprinted in the Las Casas appendix (1965, 2:1279, 1286).

21. The conscientious German historian Friederici ([1925] 1986, 1:171) defends the thesis of indigenous hospitality. "America's discoverers and conquerors were welcomed, almost everywhere, with open arms—in the islands as well as the continent—by natives whose suspicions had not yet awakened."

22. In *Los tesoros del Perú*, Las Casas argues strongly and clearly for the juridical legitimacy of native sovereignty.

23. Morales Padrón (1955, 8, 59) correctly asserts: "The discovery and the conquest are part of the same process. . . . The discovery was always followed by 'taking possession.'" That was certainly true in the case of Cortés. López de Gómara (1946, 316) describes the first act of Cortés of discovery/taking possession: "He took possession of all that land and what was yet to be discovered in the name of the emperor Don Carlos, king of Castilla. He carried out the customary required procedures, and asked for the testimony of Francisco Hernández, the royal scribe, who was present."

24. *Veri domini* means true owners of the land, with authentic sovereignty over their territories and towns. The phrase comes from the scholastic disputes over whether or not it was politically legitimate to have dominion over the towns and nations of infidels and non-Christians.

25. Levillier's criticism focuses on the three main protagonists of the Spanish debate in the sixteenth century over the nature of the indigenous inhabitants of the New World: Bartolomé de las Casas, Francisco de Vitoria, and Juan Ginés de Sepúlveda. Levillier's conclusion is that they reduced the vast cultural differences of the native peoples to a stereotypical model. He is correct with respect to the last two, who never had direct experience with the peoples and nations of the Americas. I think, however, that he is mistaken in regard to Las Casas, who wrote one of his most extensive works—*Apologética historia sumaria*—precisely to describe for his compatriots the immense cultural variety found among the New World's inhabitants. Patiño (1966, 184) has said of Las Casas that he was "one of the keenest and most faithful observers of society in the Americas." Friederici (1986, 1:175) also praises Las Casas for his "excellent gift for ethnological observations" and affirms that "he was ahead of . . . the ethnology of his own day." Las Casas, however, makes all the natives equal in two ways: he considers them equal and fully rational, contrary to the belief of his theoretical adversaries, and he understands that in general, they are naturally meek, simple, and optimally ready for evangelization.

26. According to Bosch (1986, 138), the first black ladino slaves were brought to the New World by Nicolás de Ovando in 1502. Some experts affirm that a black man was along on the first journey of Columbus, although nothing is known of his role in the endeavor (Varela [1930] 1986, 12). Others believe it is possible that some of the noblemen accompanying Columbus in his second journey brought black slaves for their personal service. Deive (1980, 21) notes that freed black slaves came to Española by 1501 on paid contracts. Sued Badillo (1986, 17–62) makes a

valuable contribution by pointing out the early presence, in the process of conquest, of freed and enfranchised blacks.

27. This instruction does not specify that the slaves be black. Its purpose is to insist that they be ladinos born in Castilla: "Black slaves or other slaves born under Christian masters, our subjects and natives." According to Deive (1980, 35), the introduction of bozales, blacks imported directly from West Africa, was authorized in 1517.

28. Sued Badillo (1986, 175–182) disputes this statement and tries to demonstrate that there was a black rebellion in Puerto Rico, apparently between September and November of 1514. It is not clear, however, if it was an uprising having certain political consequences like the one in Española in 1522, or rather a wild act on the part of a group who made an escape pact. Sued Badillo himself, when reproducing Suazo's report in 1518 regarding the outbreaks of rebellion in Española, recognizes that there were frequent acts of that kind.

29. Powell (1985, 76) notes the presence of rebellious black groups in northern Nueva España (Mexico), who made things more difficult for the Spaniards in their conflicts with the Chichimeca nomads. On the other hand, according to Lockhart (1982, 219), in Peru the predominant relation between different groups was one of hostility and antagonism because of the active participation of blacks in the armed subjugation of the natives.

30. "*Carta de Fray Toribio de Motolinía al Emperador Carlos V*," included as an appendix in *Historia*, 213. See Benavente 1984 in the reference list.

31. "*R.C. para que no pasen a las Indias negros ladinos si no fuese con licencia particular de Su Majestad*" (Royal Letter forbidding the passage to the Indies of black ladinos unless specifically licensed by His Majesty), Sevilla, May 11, 1526 (Konetzke 1953, 1:80–81).

32. Also Sued Badillo (1986, 172–173). Antillean geography, still like a jungle, allowed greater facility for escaping.

33. Deive's investigations show the complexity and diversity of black cultures, and the impossibility of subjecting them to a uniform mold.

34. I know of no better comparative analysis of military technology at the disposal of Americans and Iberians than is found in Alberto Mario Salas 1950.

35. *Animus dominandi* is the spirit of dominion that, according to Morales Padrón (1955, 36), is expressed in the continued seizures of land carried out by discoverers and explorers.

36. The terminology "encounter of two worlds" was supported by the Mexican delegation to the Meeting of National Commissions for the Fifth Centenary of the Discovery of America held in Santo Domingo, July 9–12, 1984. The first critique made above does not apply to the Mexican position due to the vast knowledge that Miguel León Portilla, main creator of his country's declaration, has of the indigenous American cultures. The other critiques, however, apply. The logic behind the declaration forgets the essential nature of the event traditionally called a "discovery"–an imposed seizure of property, guaranteed by force of arms. Cf. Ortega y Medina 1987, 129–130.

37. As translated by G. Dundras Craig in *The Modernist Trend in Spanish American Poetry* (Berkeley: University of California Press, 1934), 67–69.

38. Encyclical, *"Quarto abeunte saeculo,"* in Terradas Soler 1962, 128.

39. "Spanish conquests in America resulted in the formation of the first great colonial empire of modern times" (Lafaye 1988, 10).

Chapter 2

1. According to Dussel (1981, 403), ten times more silver and five times more gold than there was in the old continent was transferred from America to Europe. The classical work about the influence of precious metals in the European economy is Hamilton 1934.

2. These bulls are reprinted in many Spanish anthologies, such as Fernández de Navarrete 1945 (2:34–49, 467–468) and Casas 1965 (2:1277–1290). In English they can be found in Fiske. Even though it is true, as Giménez Fernández (1944, xiii) asserts, that some of them are "improperly called bulls," I maintain the same generic sense for the very same reason as his: the traditionally understood use. Manzano (1948, 8–28) establishes the following distinction between these three pontifical decrees: the first bull decrees the "donation" of the newfound lands; the second delimits Spanish and Portuguese jurisdictions to avoid probable conflicts between both Iberian states; the third expands the "donation" to the "Oriental Indies," the true aim of the "discovery." Alexander VI issued another bull, *Eximiae devotionis*, dated May 3, 1493, the day before *Inter caetera*. The abundance of papal authorized declarations was due, it seems, to the imminent jurisdictional conflict with the Portuguese Crown. The later demarcation between the zones of Portuguese and Spanish sovereignty was agreed on by the Treaty of Tordesillas, June 7, 1494, confirmed by Pope Julius II in the bull *Ea quae* of 1506. These last two bulls and the Treaty of Tordesillas are reprinted in Davenport 1917 (1:64–70, 84–100, 107–111).

3. Translation taken from *The Prince* with translation and introduction by George Bull (Baltimore: Penguin Books, 1961), ch. 18, p. 100.

4. "In the game of give and take that fills the history of the Machiavellian corruptor Ferdinand V and of the simoniacal Alexander VI, there appear from the beginning, very closely linked, the concessions found in the Letters about the Oriental Indies and the surrender by the king . . . of his cousin María Enríquez to the bastard Juan de Borgia. . . . Thus the *Inter caetera* of May 3 is, then, but the first stage of the kinship between the monarchs of Aragón and the favorite sacrilegious son of Alejandro Borgia" (Giménez Fernández 1944, 86–87).

5. The Spanish Catholic theologians of the sixteenth century maintain in general a cautious respect toward Alexander VI, stressing the dignity of the pontifical see and avoiding his personal moral levity. The Dominican friar Miguel de Arcos ([1551] 1977, 6) was one of the few who allowed himself certain critical references to Roman

corruption. "One cannot doubt the authority of the pope in making this concession to the Catholic Monarchs and their successors. But generally speaking, there is something to be feared, not in the authority, but in the fact that, in these days, many things are granted in Rome, where almost nothing that is requested is not granted."

6. On the contrary, Staedler (1937, 363–402) understands that in reality, Alexander had little to do with the writing or approval of the so-called "Alexandrian bulls." In his opinion, they were documents written by the Castilian court and approved by the curia, with little, if any personal participation by the pope. Giménez Fernández seems to me more convincing.

7. According to this document, apparently dating to the eighth century, Emperor Constantine acknowledged that Pope Sylvester had a certain primacy of power in spiritual and temporal matters. This was interpreted by the extreme ultramontanes as a way of acknowledging the successor of Peter as *Vicarius Christi* also in relation to the temporal universal lordship of the Risen Son of God. The humanist critic Lorenzo Valla showed the fraudulent character of the so-called "donation" in his 1439 treatise, *De falso credita et ementita Constantini donatione declamatio*. The Donation of Constantine maintained, however, a certain currency in papalist circles during subsequent decades, until its apocryphal character was generally recognized in the sixteenth century. Las Casas (1969, 224–225) refers to it in his memorandum to Felipe II in 1556, giving it apparent credence, and saying that the acquisition of the Indies by the Crown of Castilla implied a territorial incorporation "six times larger than the donation of the Great Constantine to the Roman Church." Literary criticism was not a strength for Las Casas.

8. In this regard, the summary of the theocratic universalist ideas made by Höffner (1957, 3–95) is very valuable.

9. This posture has its climax in Solórzano y Pereyra ([1648] 1930, 1.1.10:97–105), who proclaimed the pope as "Vice-God on earth," with divine authority to dispose of the kingdoms of the infidels and cede them to Christian princes. His papalism is, in reality, patriotic imperialist regalism.

10. Cardinal Ostiensis, *Lectura in quinque Decretalium gregorianarum libros* (3.34), *"De voto"* (c. 8), *"Quod super"* (3), cited by Leturia (1959, 158–159).

11. According to *Las siete partidas*, searching for the common good of the subjects is what distinguishes the authentic monarch from the "tyrant." This distinction would be greatly utilized by the defenders of the American natives.

12. Pérez Fernández (in a preliminary study to *Brevísima relación* [Las Casas 1989, 173–187]) historically places them in an excellent chronology of Portuguese expansion in Africa.

13. Giménez Fernández (1944, 63–118) includes a detailed chronology of the jurisdictional dispute between both Crowns. See also Morales Padrón 1979 (15–31).

14. The theoretical and diplomatic convergence between these papal bulls of the fifteenth century are discussed with insight and erudition by Leturia (1959, 1:153–204). About the use of the Alexandrian bulls as the juridical and canonical basis of the *Patronato Real* in the Indies, see Gutiérrez de Arce 1954.

15. Spanish summary of *Inter caetera* (May 4, 1493), as reprinted in Fernández de Navarrete 1945 (2:41–47) and Zavala 1971 (213–215). See also Tobar 1954 (9–14). [English rendition here is based on the Latin and English versions in Fiske (1892, 2:580–592); trans. note].

16. In spite of this exaggerated *motu propio*, a good many academics consider that both the idea as well as the text itself of the papal edict came out of the Spanish court. According to Giménez Fernández (1944, 143): "The mention of the *motu propio* is false" because previously, "there existed requests or petitions from the monarchs."

17. Along this same line, the French encyclopedist Jean François Marmontel affirmed that the bull of Alexander VI was the "greatest of all the Borgia crimes" (Höffner 1957, 268). The Portuguese monarchs would do the same in regard to their possessions. Zavala (1971, 348) cites King Joao III when he writes to the ambassador to France in 1530: "All these voyages of exploration on seas and lands are based on legitimate titles through bulls issued a long time ago by the Holy Fathers . . . based on lawful claim, and therefore they are my personal possessions and of my kingdom's Crown, in my peaceful possession, and no one can intrude on them in right reason and in justice." Again, the problem was the French aspirations.

18. For Sepúlveda's position see *"Proposiciones temerarias, escandalosas y heréticas que notó el doctor Sepúlveda en el libro de la conquista de Indias, que fray Bartolomé de las Casas, obispo que fue de Chiapa, hizo imprimir 'sin licencia' en Sevilla, año de 1552, cuyo título comienza: 'Aquí se contiene una disputa o controversia'"* in Fabié [1879] 1966 (71:335–361). The position of Las Casas is found in the many treatises that he had printed in 1552. Domingo de Soto (Casas 1965, 1:229) in his summary of the Valladolid debate, points out that the question should be resolved "according to the bull by Alexander."

19. In a royal edict, July 9, 1520, for example, Carlos V declared: "The Indian isles and mainlands of the Ocean sea which are or will be part of our Castilian Crown, no city or province, or isle nor any other annexed land . . . can be taken away or removed from it . . . for ever more . . . for this . . . is found in the granting bull made to us by our very Holy Father." Reprinted in Las Casas 1969 (*"Estudio preliminar,"* by Pereña, xliv).

20. Spanish scholars generally stress the first factor, neglecting the importance of native rebelliousness, especially in Boriquén. This is in line with the continual omission of the principal protagonist of the conquest—the subjugated native.

21. An excellent analysis is provided by Biermann (1950).

22. Manzano (1948, 29–57) has highlighted the intrinsic link between the Alexandrian edicts understood as investiture of sovereignty and the *Requerimiento*. The same emphasis is found in Solórzano y Peyrera (1930, 1.11, 1:109) who sees the *Requerimiento* as explaining to the natives the papal bulls and the call to obey them.

23. Morales Padrón (1979, 333) calls attention to other instances of *requerimiento* prior to the approval of the *Requerimiento* as an official and formal document. The Turks, in 1683, presented to the besieged city of Vienna a similar ultimatum: "If you become Muslims, you shall be protected. . . . But if in your obstinacy you resist . . . no one will be spared . . . all of you shall be subject to armed action . . .

your goods and possessions shall be pillaged and your children will be deported into slavery" (Höffner 1957, 277).

24. Also in Las Casas 1986 (3.3.57:26–27). Morales Padrón (1979, 338–345) includes various versions.

25. This citation is from the English translation of the Latin apologia prepared by Las Casas for his debate in 1550–1551 with Ginés de Sepúlveda. Like many other works of the Dominican friar, it remained unedited for centuries. [Citations used here are from the English translation used by the author; trans. note.]

26. An infidel, according to Aquinas, is one who does not profess the true faith: "Fides est virtus: cui contrariatur infidelitas" (Faith is a virtue to which infidelity is opposed). Summa theologica (2–2.10.1).

27. This account faithfully reflects the attitude of some native peoples when faced with the peculiar document, even if Las Casas is right in suggesting that Enciso is guilty of creating a "fake fable." (Las Casas 1986, 46).

28. In regard to the Requerimiento, as with almost every other important topic, the Historia of Las Casas presents a point of view diametrically opposed to those of Oviedo y Valdés. The animosity between these historians of the conquest was mutual and deeply rooted. Las Casas criticized Oviedo for "his great many lies," because he "presumed to write the history of what he never saw nor knew" (1986, 2.3.23:518, 517). It was not a mere professional rivalry. While Oviedo was disdainful of the natives of the New World, Las Casas made himself into their greatest defender. Las Casas accused Oviedo of distorting the account of the events because he was involved in the abuses of the natives by Christians: "Oviedo's Historia, when and where it refers to the Indians, always condemns them and excuses the Spaniards from all the evils and despoiling they have caused throughout these lands, as in truth he has been one of them"; "its author has been conquistador, robber, and killer of Indians" (1986, 2.2.9:239; 2.3.23:518). He particularly expresses his anger against Oviedo in his Historia (1986, 3.3.42–46:320–336).

Las Casas made similar accusations about another of the principal chroniclers of the Castilian conquest of the Americas: López de Gómara, of whose historiography he asserts, "It does not go about setting straight but rather excuses the tyranny and abominations of Cortés . . . and the slaughter and condemnation of the sad and unprotected Indians." He condemns him for praising Cortés, "who had only one end, which was to become rich through the blood of these poor, humble, and peaceful peoples" (ibid., 3.3.114:222–223). Las Casas declared war without quarter on every important writer of the discovery and conquest of the Americas who did not consider the defense of the natives as a transcendental duty.

29. The Dominican friar Carro (1944, 1:373) considered him "the first qualified theologian to intervene in the controversies over the Indies."

30. It is reprinted in Pereña et al. 1982 (538, 541). López de Gómara (1946, 228) gives a shortened and reformulated version reputed to have been read to the Inka Atahualpa by Fray Vicente de Valverde.

31. This later version contradicts Biermann's hypothesis (1950) regarding the modification of the Requerimiento. In the crucial part about the warning, it reiterates

the traditional threat: "If you do not wish to come, you can be sure that we shall kill you and make you all slaves, sell you, and take you off to foreign lands and remove you from your native habitat" (Pacheco et al. 1864–1884, 35, 375).

Chapter 3

1. Las Casas cites the codicil of the queen on innumerable occasions as a general norm that should regulate Spanish colonizing policies, but the constant violation of this codicil becomes the root of his bitter prophetic denunciation of the "tyranny" of the Christians over the natives. He uses it, inter alia, in the treatise *"Aquí se contiene una disputa o controversia entre el Obispo Don Fray Bartolomé de Las Casas o Casaus, obispo que fue de la ciudad real de Chiapa y el doctor Ginés de Sepúlveda,"* in Las Casas 1965 (1:425). It is also reproduced by Mendieta ([1596] 1980, 1.1,5:31).

2. The editors of this work mistake the date of the ordinance by a decade, placing it in 1563.

3. For the origin and significance of the *Patronato Real,* see Leturia 1959 (1:1–48) and Shiels 1961. This last volume reproduces the main documents from the fifteenth through the eighteenth centuries on which the jurisdictional demands in the ecclesiastical and spiritual realms by the Spanish Crown were founded. Giménez Fernández (1944, 92–95) maintains that the juridical foundations for the royal authority over the *Patronato* were acquired by the Catholic Monarchs through Alexandrian Apostolic Letters of 1493, especially *Piis fidelium,* antedated on May 4, and *Eximie devotionis,* antedated on May 3. See Tobar 1954 (45–56).

4. This bull should not be confused with *Eximie devotionis* of 1493. See Tobar 1954 (22–39).

5. See Gutiérrez de Arce 1954 (passim). Although Gutiérrez Arce does not favor the conversion of the *Patronato Real* into a royal vicariate for the Indies, he admits that, in practice, the royal jurisdiction in ecclesiastical matters was substantially greater in the Americas than in the Iberian peninsula.

6. This excellent anthology shows to the point of tiresomeness the strength of the *Patronato Real.* Petitions and presentations of ecclesiastical and religious matters are brought to the monarch, not to the Supreme Pontiff.

7. Cortés forbade his troops to blaspheme (that is, to use popular sayings with sacrilegious meaning), under penalty of severe punishment and to avoid the wrath of God when his special help was needed. He also forbade card games, which often give rise to such blasphemies (with one exception: only in "the room where I am"). He was a hardhearted player. See Zavala 1937 (45–54) and 1981 (49–69). The evolution of the political thought of Cortés and of his concept of empire are discussed by Frankl (1963) in an insightful essay.

8. *"Ordenanzas de buen gobierno"* (Ordinances of Good Government) (March 20, 1524), in Pacheco et al. 1864–1884 (26:140).

9. Mendieta ([1596] 1980, 3.1:176) includes the Latin motto of Cortés. Ricard (1986, 75) gives a slightly different version. The Spanish translation used by the author is given by López de Gómara (1946, 301). A different translation is provided by Díaz del Castillo (1986, 20:33). (English version is from the Latin; trans. note).

10. "*Algunos principios que deben servir de punto de partida en la controversia destinada a poner de manifiesto y defender la justicia de los indios*" (Some principles that should serve as starting points in the controversy aimed at revealing and defending the cause of justice for the Indians) in Las Casas 1965 (2:1271). I frequently cite Las Casas because I find that the words from a prominent French Hispanist about Cardinal Jean Daniélou are applicable to the work of Las Casas: "If hagiography should be criticized, the critique must recognize that some lives have an almost paradigmatic value" (Bataillon 1976, 11, n. 9). I hope, however, not to fall into "indiscriminate laudatory zeal," a fault that O'Gorman (Las Casas 1967, clxvii) criticizes in many admirers of the fiery Dominican friar.

11. The Catholic Monarchs took Granada in January of 1492, completing the defeat of the Moors on the Iberian peninsula, and on March 31, 1492, they decreed the expulsion of the Jews.

12. According to Pope Leo XIII, "Columbus truly discovered America shortly before the Church was agitated by a violent storm . . . by God's singular design, to repair the evils inflicted by Europe on the Catholic name." Encyclical "*Quarto abeunte saeculo*" (in Terradas Soler 1962, 133). Something similar had been written three centuries earlier by the Franciscan friar Sahagún: "It seems certain that, at this time and on these lands and with these people, our Lord God has willed to return to the church what the devil stole from her in England, Germany, and France" ([1582] 1985, 20).

13. According to Olaechea Labayen (1958, 161), the repudiation of heterodoxy "had been constituted into something akin to a racist habit" among Spaniards.

14. Lockhart (1982, 213) points out how in Peru, during the first three decades after the conquest, the mestizo children were treated with disdain not because of their racial makeup, but because most were illegitimate—a grave stigma within the Catholic context of strict marital morality. If this is accepted, then the point stressed eloquently by Boxer (1978, 1–38), that the Iberian nations soon developed clearly racist attitudes toward their American, African, and Asiatic vassals, cannot be denied.

15. His ideological rival, Las Casas, also reflects a sense of Spanish religious superiority but in his case as an ethical imperative. His indignation comes from his belief that his country does not behave in a manner befitting its high and unique moral duty.

16. The Puerto Rican theologian Angel Mergal Llera (1949) four decades ago wrote a book with great insight and sensitivity, critically analyzing the confessional Catholic character of sixteenth-century Spanish government from his Protestant and Hispanic perspective.

17. The Jews and the Moors could remain in the country if they abjured their religion and were baptized. This measure of "clemency" did not resolve the problem

of hostility against both minority groups. Those who submitted remained subject to the people's suspicion of the genuine sincerity of their "conversions" (converted Jews were contemptuously dubbed "marranos" and the Moors "moriscos"), and to the untiring energy of the Inquisition. It should be noted that the descendants of Abraham did not fare any better in other Western European cities.

18. Santiago, Chile's capital city, was named to commemorate the multiple miraculous military "interventions" that the holy apostle, patron of Spain, had made on behalf of the devout Iberians against the idolatrous and pagan natives.

19. The Catholic Monarchs issued, on June 22, 1497, a general amnesty to those willing to venture into the newfound lands and "who had committed any homicide or wounded anyone, or any other crime of whatever nature or gravity." There were exceptions, the first one being heresy (in Fernandez de Navarrete 1945, 2:249).

20. On one occasion, Las Casas suggested that the problem of the expansion of the Hussite heretics in Bohemia had been due to the slowness of the Emperor, "who should have had them all knifed before they grew and infested the entire region." The best remedy, not followed by the authorities, to stop John Hus's heresy would have been "to put it down through war." "Carta a Bartolomé Carranza de Miranda" (August 1555), in Fabié [1879] 1966 (71:408–409).

21. In his dispute with Sepúlveda, Las Casas articulated a difference between the treatment of infidels who had never heard of Christ and the heretics. In his opinion, one could only apply to the latter the repressive measures proposed by Saint Augustine (Las Casas 1965, 1:379–381). As to the thesis of Vitoria, Ríos (1957, 102) confuses the terms when referring to the "heresy of the Indians." Vitoria, teacher and excellent scholastic that he was of nuances and distinctions, never used that term to refer to indigenous paganism or infidelity. On the other hand, it is interesting to note the reference by Ríos to a decree from Fernando and Isabel that forbids "those whose Catholic faith was suspect or who were children or grand-children of those condemned by the Inquisition" from emigrating to the New World (ibid., 164). Later, the works of Las Casas would come under the censure of the Council of the Indies and the Inquisition, when at the end of the sixteenth and during the seventeenth century his works were widely used as the "black legend," an ideological weapon of inter-European rivalry based on the writings of Las Casas as an anti-Hispanic witness (Hanke, "Las Casas, historiador" [in Las Casas 1986, xl–xli]).

22. On the providentialist messianism of Columbus, see the brief but insightful contribution by Cummins (1976). The complex and paradoxical fusion of greedy ambition and mystical and messianic providentialism in the mind of Columbus is treated by Carpentier (1979) in a masterly and challenging way. In contrast, Lope de Vega's Famosa Comedia del Nuevo Mundo, descubierto por Cristobal Colón (Famous comedy of the New World discovered by C. C.) falsifies many important historical facts and overly simplifies the tension between both elements.

23. Lafaye (1988, 143): "The continuity between the war against the Moors and the war against the Indians was so evident that the conquistadors called the pagan temples of the New World mosques."

24. The old emblem of Mexico City, made official in 1540, had this providentialism as its motto: *non in multitudine exercitus consistit victoria sed in voluntate Dei* (victory does not come from the size of the army but from the will of God).

25. On this point see Elliott 1989 (27–41), Maravall 1949 (199–227), Frankl 1963 (470–482), and Lejarza 1948 (43–136). Although Hernán Cortés, thanks to his *Cartas de relación*, is a better example of providentialism and messianism, a similar interpretation has been attributed to Francisco Pizarro, the other great prototypal hero of the conquest (cf. Armas Medina 1953, 5–7, 15–21). This work can be placed in the old-style and uncritical tradition of nationalistic and Catholic interpretation.

26. From a letter by Las Casas to the Council of the Indies, probably in 1552. It is included in Bataillon 1976 (286).

27. *Christum ferens* was Columbus's peculiar signature. Las Casas also attributes to divine providence the negative response of the Portuguese king to Columbus's project, since God "had chosen for this ministry the monarchs of Castilla and León." He also considers in the divine will the death of Columbus's wife, "for it is best to be freed from the care and obligation of a wife" (Las Casas 1986, 1.1.28:151).

28. Compare Bataillon 1976, "*Novo mundo e fim do mundo*." He also analyzes the exhaustion, at the end of the sixteenth century, of the mind-set concerned with the end of history, which he calls "millenarian obsession," "eschatological perspective," and "apocalyptic impatience." That is the cause of the marked pessimism evident at the end of the century in missionaries such as Sahagún and Mendieta (350–351).

29. This demonic explanation for the resistance to Columbus's project is also found in Columbus (Varela 1982, 253).

30. Columbus went a step further and tried to calculate the time remaining until the end of history. He also saw his achievement as an eschatological sign according to the biblical command: "The preaching of the gospel in so many places in such a short time is for me a sign." He forecasts a new sign: the taking of the Holy Land, then in the hands of the Muslims, by the Spanish Crown. He held the idea, common at that time, that the riches obtained from the Indies could be used for a new Crusade. He also suggested to Queen Isabel that he could be the providential choice for a new task: the recovery of Jerusalem. In a letter to the pope (1502) he alleges that all of that could have been accomplished had it not been that "Satan has disturbed all this" (Varela 1982, 256, 278, 287).

31. In a similar sense, see Varela's "Prologue" (1982, viii). However, it would be preferable to speak about messianic consciousness rather than "megalomania," as Varela does. Pérez de Tudela (1957, cx), in his excellent introduction to the five volumes of Las Casas's work edited by him, warns that there is an important distinction in the messianic providentialism of Las Casas: "The supreme assurance with which he takes on the role of sacred interpreter of the past and seer of the future."

32. México, D.F.: Fondo de Cultura Económica, 1942. Only chapters six, seven, and eight of this work have been found, but the thesis of Las Casas is repeatedly and clearly expressed in them.

33. The endurance of such providentialism, both religious and nationalistic,

among modern Spanish theologians, even those with high critical ability and erudition, is remarkable. This explains an affirmation of this type: "Our Country [with an uppercase *c*] was not content with having an Empire, nor with dominion . . . it went above all to civilize, Christianize the New World. . . . God chose Spain, in his divine providence, to colonize the New World because it was *ready to give what no other nation could give, for they did not have it. Only the Spain of the Catholic Monarchs, of Emperor Carlos V and Felipe I, could accomplish an enterprise of such magnitude*" (Carro 1944, 1:115, 120–121).

34. According to Salas (1950, 115): "The prolific mention of these wonders could fill hagiography volumes."

35. Armas Medina (1953, 5–7) continues the Jesuitical tradition of recounting the "miracles" that James the Apostle and the Virgin Mary allegedly worked in favor of the Spanish Christians against the native infidels.

Chapter 4

1. Salas (1986, 183, n. 16) criticizes Friede for lapsing into "anachronisms," i.e., for using concepts more suited to the political conflicts of the nineteenth and twentieth centuries than to those of the sixteenth.

2. This design by Las Casas is not sufficiently flexible in distinguishing between the true Indian government, "primary and intrinsic," and what is despotic and tyrannical. From a perspective that is not at all disinterested, some ideologues of the Castilian conquest would try to show that the Aztec and Inka empires belonged to the latter category. In this way, the conquest would be transformed into liberation. This is apologetic historiography, without doubt, but it touches a sensitive point on which Las Casas appears vulnerable.

3. The most extensive exposition of the Alexandrian bulls as legitimating foundation for the Castilian empire over the New World is found in "*Tratado comprobatorio*" (Las Casas 1965).

4. Although Todorov ([1982] 1987, 182–194) cites this passage, he misses the meaning of Las Casas's criticism, making him simply into a more sophisticated and subtle exponent of "colonialist ideology." In my opinion, Todorov errs in three ways: (1) he equates as similarly excessive the positions of Las Casas and Motolinía; (2) he neglects the emphasis in Las Casas on the primary economic advantage for the Indians (his theory about a benevolent empire); and above all, (3) he does not in any way account for the many times Las Casas insists on the free exercise of self-determination, the autonomous consent on the part of native peoples and nations.

5. The difference between this argument and Vitoria's "sixth legitimate title" is that Las Casas underscores the conviction of the juridical nullity of all supposed oaths of fidelity taken by the native chiefs and nations up to then (1563).

6. Cuevas ([1914] 1975, 178–179) reprints a "reasonable opinion by an unknown theologian, on the title of domination by the king of Spain over the Indies' peoples and lands," from 1554, which also insists on the Indians' consent as an indispensable condition for the legitimacy of the imperial regime. "For the only title that Your Majesty has is this: that the Indians, or most of them, wish to be your vassals willingly and be thus honored, and in this way, Your Majesty is their natural king as of the Spaniards, and thus in good conscience receive moderate tributes by nurturing them in justice and Christianity." That anonymous "reasonable opinion" coincides in many ideas with Las Casas. It shares, for example, the belief that "the land belongs to the Indians, by dominion *iure gentium* (law of nations)," also giving them full authority over the mineral resources that the Spaniards had been exploiting (176). It is risky, however, to attribute its literary paternity to Las Casas without greater external evidence.

7. The excellent analysis by Pereña (Las Casas 1969, xxl–xlvi) is more on target. He traces with dexterity the evolution of what is called the "democratic thesis" of Las Casas, according to which the apostolic grant has to be submitted to the approval of the native peoples and nations, the same as any other important claim that the Castilian Crown might pretend to make over their collective lives. I do not, however, use the nomenclature he uses because today the term "democratic" has connotations that would be anachronistic to attribute to Las Casas, among them the constitutional precept of universal suffrage and religious pluralism.

8. Las Casas took the distinction between jurisdiction *in actu* and *in potentia* from Thomas Aquinas, *Summa theologica* 3.8.3. This passage is cited directly in *Apologia* (Las Casas 1974, 164–165).

9. Las Casas never considers the possibility of the native communities becoming subjects of Castilla while retaining their natural religion. He shares the common Spanish concept of an indissoluble link between church and state, Hispanicity and Catholicism.

10. In *Los tesoros del Perú* ([1563] 1958, 451–455) Las Casas proposes something new: that the Spaniards who have sinned by their abuses of the Indians remain in the native communities, as a way of penitential atonement, to serve them and thus compensate for the past wickedness.

11. He was not alone on this position. From the university chair, the canon lawyer and theologian Diego de Covarrubias asserted that: "The Indians, in all justice, can forbid the Spaniards to take gold from their provinces or fish for pearls even in public rivers; because if the prince and the republic of the Indians have dominion over their provinces . . . they could, in all justice, forbid the entrance in their territories to foreigners who go in search of gold and metals and fishing for pearls (Pereña 1956, 220). With that posture Covarrubias presents an implicit criticism to the first "legitimate title" that Francisco de Vitoria advances to justify the Spanish empire over the "barbarians of the New World."

12. In another text Las Casas affirms: "Enrique de Segusia . . . erred . . . against all logic and even against natural and divine law, when he said that with the

coming of Christ all dominion and jurisdiction from infidels was taken away and transferred to believers. Such error is very harmful and opposed to Sacred Scripture" (Las Casas 1969, 30).

13. Among them Manzano (1948, 126–134), Armas Medina (1953, 521–540), Ramos Pérez (1976, 109–110), and Queraltó Moreno (1976, 186–187).

14. The possible author of this interesting anti–Las Casas document is still discussed. See the summary of the various hypotheses in Gutiérrez 1989 (56, n. 2).

15. Supposedly, Carlos V, because of the pressures from the Las Casas denunciations and Vitoria's prudence, decided to retain dominion over the indigenous nations, but not in perpetuity. "He promised to leave them when they were capable of preserving the Catholic faith" (Salvá [1848] 1964, 13:433). Bataillon (1976, 17–21, 317–351) is a severe critic of the anonymous writer. See also Lucena 1984 (163–198). The observation about Las Casas's objective made by Pérez de Tudela (1958, 496) is on target: "Las Casas's ardent objective is to legitimate what had been acquired, give a foundation in divine and human law to the imperial edifice; never to bring it down."

16. One should note, however, that Las Casas did not in any way vacillate in equally cataloging as a wicked, diabolical strategy the various defenses of the system of conquests and *encomiendas* offered by some friars, as he does in a letter of 1549 sent to Domingo de Soto: "It is an old artifice of Satan to use as his instruments and ministers the most religious persons of the highest reputation and esteem to complete his edifice" (in Las Casas 1969, App. 1, 121). This line of reasoning is foreign to our modern and secular mentality but not to the mentality of a time in which the existence of Satan as an evil being was taken seriously, as shown in the work of the Renaissance painters Hieronymus Bosch and Pieter Brueghel.

17. According to Abril-Castelló, it was already too late for Spain to abandon its territorial acquisitions. It is a way of saying that by 1551–1552 Spain's overseas empire was considered an accomplished and irreversible event. "*La bipolarización Sepúlveda-Las Casas y sus consecuencias: La revolución de la duodécima réplica*" (in Ramos et al. 1984, 229–288).

18. Gómez Canedo (1977, 74), who is not very sympathetic toward the controversial Dominican friar, calls it a "clumsy colonization project." There is some truth in that judgment.

19. This supposed "second conversion" arises not only from the disastrous failure of his intent to inhabit and peacefully evangelize the northern coast of South America but from the increased doubts of conscience about the agreements he had made with the colonizers, from whom he had tried "to buy the gospel." He came to think that the destruction of the Spanish town by the rebellious natives had been a "divine judgment to punish and harm them for joining those whom he thought did not help him in God's name nor to save souls, who were perishing in those provinces due to their greed to become rich. This offended God by staining the purity of his very spiritual enterprise" (Las Casas 1986, 3.3.159:382).

20. In another writing he speaks bitterly of "the corruption and blemish of the treasures stolen from the Indies. They blemish the hands, and even more, the souls

of the many who sent them, from which stemmed their blindness to destroy them [the natives], without any scruples" (Las Casas 1989, 197).

21. "The violent death which they still suffer, and perish . . . many of them in my presence . . ." (Yáñez 1941, 166–167).

22. Vitoria seems to rely on the following accord reached at the Fourth Council of Toledo (A.D. 633), referring then to the Jews who had been coerced into being baptized: "It is desirable that they be obliged to keep the faith which they have received, even if by force or need, so that God's name not be blasphemed nor the faith be devalued." Cited at the end of the sixteenth century with an explanation similar to Vitoria's by the Jesuit José de Acosta ([1588] 1952, 2.11:186).

23. Carro (1944, 2:243) gives only one page of his extensive two-volume work to a quick and superficial analysis of this fourth "legitimate title" and in doing so transforms Vitoria's "good number" ("*bona pars*") into "large number" without mentioning any reason for doing so.

24. Hamilton (1963) criticizes the notion, common among Hispanic Catholic scholars, that Vitoria is the "founding father" of international law.

25. In general, this treaty is disappointing. It attempts to establish particular norms for justice in the wars against the indigenous peoples of the New World, but it forgets them completely in the course of its treatise.

26. Carro (1944, 2:163) is a good example of how Spanish nationalism interferes with a good critical sense. After defending Vitoria's analysis of the "legitimate titles" for the conquest, he interjects this very revealing commentary: "The history of the conquest is filled with treason by the Indians."

27. "Protected by an international law based on reciprocity, [Vitoria] provides in reality a legal base for the wars of colonization" (Todorov 1987, 161).

28. See also Pérez de Tudela's essay (1958, 471): "The lectures of the great Dominican teacher [Vitoria] did not become a damaging doctrine for Castilian domination of the Indies. . . . He offered at least seven doors to undertake a bellicose action . . . against the Indians." For a sharp criticism of Vitoria's *De indis* from the perspective of Las Casas, see Martínez 1974.

29. Also cited in Manzano 1948 (83–84), Pereña 1984 (297), and Gómez Robledo (in Vitoria 1985, xix–xx).

30. The royal reprimand would, however, postpone the publication of the lectures until 1557 in France.

31. I do not see the basis for Deive's (1980, 714) affirmation that "Father Vitoria . . . initiates the Dominican tradition of Indian defense." When the great theologian from Salamanca gave his lecture *De indis*, more than twenty-seven years (December 1511) had elapsed since the famous sermon by Antonio de Montesinos, who in the name of the Dominican community of Española had condemned the maltreatment to which the native population was subject.

32. The influence of Vitoria's criticism of "the illegitimate titles" on Las Casas is especially evident in the two treatises the latter published in 1552 explaining the theoretical bases for his spiritual and religious conception for a Spanish Christian empire, namely, "*Treinta proposiciones muy jurídicas*" and "*Tratado comprobatorio*" (Las

Casas 1965, 2:914–1233; 1:460–499). The last one reflects a marked influence by the scholastic theologian. However, the conceptual schematas of the two Dominicans are different. The primary objective for Las Casas is to defend the life and liberty of the New World natives; Vitoria defends justice and the legitimacy of the Castilian empire. With less caution than Pérez Fernández, Gustavo Gutiérrez (1989, 55–105) criticizes Vitoria for his "aseptic theological reasoning" and analyzes in a challenging way the ideological use of "legitimate titles" made by the Spanish opposition to the Inka dynasty in Peru, namely, by Francisco de Toledo, Sarmiento de Gamboa, and the writer of "Anónimo de Yucay."

33. On one occasion, however, Vitoria judged the events of the conquest and found them deplorable. He affirmed that upon hearing what was happening in Peru, "the blood freezes in my body . . . *non video quomodo* [I do not see how] to excuse the conquerors for their ultimate irreverence and tyranny" (Vitoria 1967, 137–139).

Chapter 5

1. On "natural liberty" and "natural servitude" in Spanish scholastics, see Arenal 1975–1976 (19–20:67–124).

2. The following affirmation by Soto is typical: "Christians made prisoners by other Christians are not obliged to serve as slaves" ([1556] 1967, 2.4.2.2:290).

3. Carro's judgment is quite severe: "Slavery is one of the problems on which scholastic theology has been less consistent with itself and with Christian religious principles" (1944, 1:169).

4. On the evolution of Catholic ideas on slavery, Maxwell's synopsis (1975) is useful. In 1866, at a time when humanity was ready to end all moral and legal justification for the centuries-old institution of slavery, the Holy Office responded to questions put by the apostolic vicar in Ethiopia by saying slavery "considered in its essential nature is not contrary to divine or natural law; there can be various just titles to slavery that have been pointed out by theologians and canonists." March 20, 1886, *Collectanea S.C. de Propaganda Fide*, Roma, 1907, 1, n. 230, 76–77, as cited by Maxwell (1975, 78–79).

5. To promote acceptance of his idea about slavery by the court counselors in juridical theology, Columbus adds: "and they [the Caribs] would be idolaters." There is a problem. Shortly before, the Admiral had written that the Indians he had found "knew no sect nor idolatry." Apparently he equated the supposed cannibalism of the Caribs with idolatry.

6. Friederici ([1925] 1986, 1:299–305) calls attention to the fact that Columbus and many of the first European navigators to America had learned to hunt for slaves in the Portuguese raids in Africa. He says of the Admiral that he was a "mixture, truly unbearable by any moral sensibility, of Christianity and criminality, devotion

and wickedness: we seem to be listening to a missionary and to a professional slave trader, all at once" (ibid., 303).

7. This precedent established in the Canaries is analyzed by Rumeu de Armas (1975, 46–49; emphasis added). The policy of the Castilian Crown in the conquest of the two islands La Palma (1492–1493) and Tenerife (1494–1496) is instructive in its coincidence with the first encounters between Spaniards and the natives of the Americas. "The natives of the peaceful groups were declared free but *the warring ones* were captured en masse to be transported and sold in the metropolitan slave markets." This opened another door for the legal enslavement of the American natives. Las Casas (1986, 1.1.17–19:90–111) criticizes the violent conquest of the Canary Islands and the enslavement of its natives. He rates that as actions "against all reasonable and natural law, against justice and against charity, where great and grave mortal sins were committed and there was need of restitution" (108–109). According to Professor Harold B. Johnson (in Hanke 1985, App. 2, 203), the exploration and domination of the Canaries was in the hands of private entrepreneurs who enslaved and persecuted the natives. "When the Crown brought the situation under control it forbade those activities, but its intervention was too late since the majority of the natives had already succumbed." In his opinion, "the experience of the Canaries constituted a kind of aborted model for the situation of the Indies." Pérez Fernández (Las Casas 1989, 146–173) provides a valuable chronology of the Iberian occupation and conquest of the Canary Islands.

8. In light of this severe appraisal, it seems to me as baseless as the evaluation that Menéndez Pidal (1942, 12) makes of Las Casas as "domestic historian" of the Columbus family. It is a reflection of his anti–Las Casas prejudices. Las Casas also expressed a severe critical judgment regarding Diego Columbus in an essential matter: namely, his treatment of the natives and his responsibility for their oppression and death (Las Casas 1986, 1.2.51:371).

9. Unfortunately, there are no extant documents or memoranda that shed light on the debates held by "scholars, theologians, and canon lawyers" in respect to this important consultation.

10. Rumeu de Armas (1975, 41–78) is very helpful on this issue of freedom or slavery for the Indians under Queen Isabel. However, a note of clarification is in order. The purpose of this eminent Spanish historian is to stress that, in spite of the many violations in its implementation, Queen Isabel's policy and legislation were exemplary in fully recognizing the American natives' humanity, freedom, and dignity. Even though Las Casas would be in agreement with that thesis, Rumeu de Armas continually criticizes the Dominican friar for his excessive denunciations. Yet the difference in tone between Rumeu and Las Casas, whom Rumeu finds to be strident, rests on Las Casas's stress, which is not on the justice of Castilian legislation, which Las Casas in general does not doubt, but on the life and death, freedom and slavery, of the natives. From that perspective, the *de facto* violations assume greater weight than the purity of the *de iure* determinations. I do not think it is correct to affirm that Las Casas admitted "grudgingly the validity of the pontifical concession and therefore, the full political authority of the Monarchs of

Castilla over the Indians" (ibid., 60). On the contrary, all the arguments of the pugnacious Dominican are justly based on this concession, which he interprets as a command to promote the well-being of the natives. Rumeu de Armas affirms, also, that Las Casas "came to advocate a massive Spanish retreat from America," without providing any specific quotation in which the Protector of the Indians recommends that action (ibid.).

11. I do not understand where Pagden (1982, 29–31) gets the idea that the Catholic Monarchs considered the bulls of Alexander VI of 1493 as granting them the right to enslave the American natives. His exegesis of *Eximiae devotionis* is difficult to sustain. Regarding the American natives, at no time do the Alexandrian bulls use the aggressive language that previous papal edicts used about the Africans ("sarracenos . . . et Christi inimicos" [Saracens and enemies of Christ], in the bull *Romanus pontifex* of Nicholas V, in 1455). I do not know of any royal document that alleges such an interpretation. The decision by the Crown was in favor of the natural freedom of the natives, with three important exceptions: the cannibals, the rebels, and the slaves by purchase. Pagden's interpretation of the reply by King Fernando to the first protests of the Dominican friars against the maltreatment of the Antillean natives is a doubtful one. The king, when claiming his right to require servitude from the natives, always refers to the *encomienda* system, not to slavery. The Spaniards distinguished clearly between these institutions, at least in juridical theory.

12. However, this decree presupposes another one with an initial decision by the Crown favoring the freedom of the natives. That document has not been found.

13. However, a short time later, on July 12, 1503, Guerra received a royal license to take Indian slaves. "He may take from any place where he may discover Indian men or women as slaves . . . as many as he can." And Queen Isabel added that Guerra was "not to do them any harm." It is assumed that they will not be harmed, only enslaved (Pacheco et al. 1864–1884, 31:189). Deive (1980, 8) thinks that this was intended for the Caribs, whose enforced capture and servitude had been ordered. Cristóbal Guerra was accused by Las Casas of being a thief and a maltreater of natives. Las Casas suspected him of being the first to antagonize the natives of South America (Las Casas 1986, 2.1.171:149–154). He died in a battle against them.

14. "Latin America would remain marked by this perfect legalism *in theory*, and injustice and disregard for law in *the facts*" (Dussel 1972, 56).

15. Columbus also adds a mythical reference. Caribs are the only males who supposedly have intimate relations with the legendary Amazons, women warriors who inhabit a neighboring island (Varela 1982, 145; Fernández de Navarrete 1945, 1:321). Ramos (1975, 1:81) has said about them: "Only the Araucans, and for analogous motives, caused the same preoccupation on the part of the Spaniards, even though the Caribs never managed to attain a similar notoriety. They lacked an Ercilla [author of the famous epic about the Araucans quoted later in this chapter; trans. note] capable of elevating their deeds to epic heights. Ramos's work shows the changes in the Spanish vision of the Caribs during the first decades of the colonization of those Antillean islands, and especially the weakness of the initial

hypothesis characterizing them above all as anthropophagous. Sued Badillo (1978, 33–66) in his iconoclastic work demolishes the precarious evidence regarding the supposed Caribbean anthropophagy, which in his opinion has not "an iota of foundation." He calls attention to the convergence between the fantasizing imagination of adventurers in search of fabulous lands and the desire for riches through the unrestricted sale of slaves. Like Ramos, Sued Badillo highlights the intrepidity and courage of the Caribbean natives, who on several occasions stopped Spanish attacks on their bases in the Lesser Antilles. For a brief and precise account of the wars against the Caribs see Cárdenas Ruiz (1981).

16. The words "cannibal" and "Carib" are Colombian neologisms that the Admiral thought expressed native words that referred to anthropophagous savages. Cf. Alegría in Cárdenas Ruiz (1981, 3–6). The Spanish theologian Juan de la Peña confuses both terms and writes of those who *"possunt debellari que occidunt homines ad manducandum, ut sunt Caribales* [sic] *in indiis"* (the Indians who kill men in order to eat them, such as the Caribales, can be subjugated through war). *An sit iustum bellum adversus insulanos* (Can there be a just war against the islanders?) in Pereña 1956 (285).

17. Alonso de Zuazo and Rodigro de Figueroa, two royal officials commissioned in 1519 to investigate the situation, heard many testimonies about alleged anthropophagous Caribs. See Castañeda 1970 (81–90) for their decisions favoring the enslavement of Caribs. However, Figueroa in a letter to Carlos V, July 6, 1520, seems to admit that not all those called Caribs are truly anthropophagous: "some slaves, from among the true Caribs, have been brought . . ." It is an indirect way of acknowledging that many natives imprisoned for their alleged cannibalism are not "true Caribs" (Pacheco et al. 1864–1884, 1:418).

18. Although Columbus and some Spaniards stress the hostility between Caribs and the natives of Española and San Juan Bautista (Puerto Rico), López de Gómara (1946, 180) in his brief account of the war on the second island affirms that the natives asked the supposedly feared neighbors for help against the Spanish invaders: "The conquest of Boriquén [Puerto Rico] cost the lives of many Spaniards because the islanders put up a strong resistance, and to their defense they called Caribs who aim with poisonous herbs." The native war effort was "without success." Oviedo (1851, 1.16.1.6:474) also points to this alliance by indicating that in the uprising that occurred in Puerto Rico, "many Indians, as well as Caribs from neighboring islands and archers with whom they had allied," died. Sued Badillo does not see anything strange in this alliance, for he insists on the ethnic and cultural unity between the Boriquens and Barloventans. That unity, nurtured by complex commercial exchanges, facilitated the exodus of a great many Tainos from Puerto Rico when it was impossible to resist the Castilian invaders. That migration, as Sued Badillo indicates, would have been incomprehensible if there had been the reputed hostility between Caribs and Tainos. Alegría (in Cárdenas 1981, 67–89) concisely presents the traditional vision of the cultural differences between Arawaks and Caribs.

19. Arens (1981, 82–85, 118, 120), in a mordant criticism spiced with delightful

irony, points out with reference to the attributions of cannibalism that have been heaped upon American natives, Africans, and South Pacific islanders, that the Arabs also gave ideological justification for their enslavement of black Africans by alleging that they were anthropophagous. In his demythologizing study, Arens does not miss the ideological character of the "myth of cannibalism." "When examining the ease with which the notion of the cannibalism of others spreads, one can immediately recognize the denial of the humanity of the accused. When they are thus defined, they are barred from the sphere of culture and they are placed in the category of animals. . . . War and annihilation become excusable, while the more refined forms of domination such as slavery and colonization become the true responsibility of the bearers of culture."

20. The attitude of Las Casas is ambiguous. Although in general he reproduces the dualist sketch of Caribs vs. Arawaks characterized by the fierce cannibalism of the first and the pacific benignity of the second, and shares the common notion of his time that Boriquén was the frontier where both ethnic groups clashed ("San Juan . . . was full of natives . . . [and] was attacked by Caribs or eaters of human flesh and against them they were brave and defended their lands well") (Las Casas 1986, 2.2.46:355). On occasion he doubts their existence: ". . . the Caribs, if they exist . . ." (ibid., 2.3.24:521). On other occasions, he questions whether the alleged cannibalism is a legitimate reason for enslaving them. "[Las Casas was] coming and going to Castilla to ensure that no slaves would be made, to free those already enslaved even if they were Caribs, the ones who ate human flesh" (ibid., 3.3.157:373). In another text he insists that even if the anthropophagy accusation is true, there have been many Europeans, including the Iberians, who concurred in antiquity in that "cruel bestiality." This fault is not incompatible with the Caribs' political prudence or capacity for self-government or the command that the Spaniards peacefully evangelize them (Las Casas 1967, 2.3.205:352–356). He criticizes the failure of the alleged missionary justification: "Because from the time the Indies were discovered, until today, the Caribs never knew any preachers, nor did they resist them, only the Spaniards whom they took to be cruel thieves . . . because if the Spaniards acted as good Christians, there would be little or no difficulty in bringing them to the faith, as with the others" (Las Casas 1986, 3.3.89:131). Regarding the original royal decree by which Queen Isabel legalized the servitude of the Caribs, Las Casas thinks this was the result of her innocent ignorance, manipulated by her royal counselors (ibid., 2.2.19:270–273).

21. Castañeda (1970, 121–122) includes decrees from the beginning of the seventeenth century that still allowed war against Caribs and their enslavement as a result of their bellicosity and cannibalism.

22. There is a notable exception in the sixteenth century. Miguel de Montaigne (1968, 1:153, 156, 157) in his essay about the American cannibals in the second half of the sixteenth century affirms: "We call barbaric that which is not part of our custom. . . . It is more barbaric to eat a live man than to eat him dead. And we know . . . (. . . as pretext, for full measure, of piety and religion), that here [Europe] we have at times been dismembering a body full of life with many tortures,

roasting it on a slow fire, and throwing it to the dogs and pigs to be eaten and torn apart. That is more barbaric than roasting and eating a man already dead. . . . We could, therefore, call those nations barbarians in reference to reason, but not in reference to us who supersede them in all kinds of barbarities." Montaigne's vision is more accurate in his biting criticism of European violence and cruelty for religious motives than in his idyllic and mythical description of the cannibalistic nobility of the natives. Be it as it may, Montaigne seems to be a conveyor belt for the idea of the "noble savage" from Las Casas to Rousseau.

23. A similar line of criticism is made by Bataillon (1976, 23): "Regardless of my admiration for the jurist theologian from Salamanca, I also feel uncomfortable with the maneuver that enables him to turn around his fifth *illegitimate* title as a glove and convert it into a fifth *legitimate* title."

24. Zavala (1949) cites a good number of official authorizations of the enslavement of rebellious Indians in a useful monograph.

25. See the decrees of the Council of the Indies and of the Crown authorizing the slavery of the Araucans in Konetzke 1953 (2:135–142).

26. See the anti-Araucan memos by Archbishop Fray Reginaldo de Lizárraga, O.P.; "Parecer acerca de si contra los indios de Arauca es justa la guerra que se les haze y si se pueden dar por esclavos" (1599) (Opinion on whether the war against the Araucan Indians is just and if they can be enslaved), and by Fray Juan de Vacones, O.S.A.; and "Petición en derecho para el rey . . . para que los rebeldes enemigos del reino de Chile sean declarados por esclavos . . ." (1599) (Legal petition for the King . . . so that the rebellious enemies of the kingdom of Chile can be declared slaves), in Hanke and Millares Carlo (1977, 293–312). These are notable expressions of theological support for the war against the Chilean natives and their enforced servitude. They exemplify several memoranda and opinions written by ecclesiastics and religious in favor of the enslavement of Chilean natives after a revolt in 1599. Cf. Jara 1971 (186–230). According to Jara (ibid., 191), "The amen in favor of slavery was general."

27. Also Solórzano y Pereyra ([1648] 1930, 1.2.1:131–140), after affirming the cardinal norm of natural and legal freedom of the American natives, hesitates as to its application to the Araucans.

28. Maravall (1974, 350) calls Las Casas a "Rousseau avant la lettre" (a Rousseau before his time).

29. It is signed by Friars Jacobo de Tastera, Antonio de Ciudad Rodrigo, García de Cisneros, Arnaldus de Basatzio, Alfonsus de Guadalupe, Cristóbal de Zamora, Alonso de Herrera, Andrés de Olmos, Francisco Ximénez, Gaspar de Burguillos, and Toribio de Motolinía.

30. *Ionnais Maioris Comm. in secundum sententiarum* dist. 44, cuestión 3. Paris, 1510. Cited by Leturia (1959, 1:285–286, 297–298). On the position of the Scottish theologian regarding the infidels, among them those of the New World, see Carro 1944 (1:381–389).

31. Sepúlveda translated Aristotle's *Politics* from Greek to Latin and dedicated it to then Prince Felipe, to whom he wrote in 1549 recommending the reading of

that work and bitterly criticizing Las Casas as "homo factiosus et turbulentus" (a divisive and turbulent man) (Losada 1949, 202).

32. Because of the many references—many explicit, some implicit—to the nature and the freedom or servitude of the American natives present in the debates of the time, I quote extensively from the first book of *Politics* of Aristotle (1947, 1:540–545): "This is the general law that should necessarily govern men. When one is inferior to one's equals, as the body is to the soul and the beast is to man . . . one is a slave by nature. . . . It is evident that these are naturally free and the others are naturally slaves. . . . War . . . includes the hunt . . . of those men born to obey, but refusing to subject themselves; it is a war which nature itself has made legitimate."

33. Logan (1932, 466–480) shows that neo-scholasticism inherited the stoic distinction between human equality according to natural law and its possible servitude according to the common norms of human law. The difficulty in reconciling Christian theology with the Aristotelian conception of "servant by nature" shows itself even in Catholic exegetes who favored the Hellenic philosopher, such as O'Neil (1953).

34. It seems however that his directive, like many others, was not adhered to with strict fidelity. In 1543, Las Casas alleged that there were in Sevilla more than ten thousand illegal Indian slaves (Pérez de Tudela, "Memorial" 1957, 5:195). Although this number should be taken with caution, it seems certain that there was a lucrative market of aborigines in Spain. Moya Pons (1978, 106), with his methodical skepticism, thinks that the main motive in the prohibition of the importation of Antillean natives to the Iberian peninsula was to ease the growing shortage of manual workers in the islands, resulting from the serious decrease in the number of Indians, and not out of any humanitarian consideration.

35. On this exceptional attempt to humanize the relations between Spaniards and natives through a new legal code, see Muro Orejón 1959.

Chapter 6

1. The juridical theory insists on the primacy of the religious factor: "The motive and origin of the *encomiendas* was the spiritual and temporal well-being of the Indians and their indoctrination and teaching of the tenets and precepts of our holy Catholic faith" (*Recopilación* 1841, 2.6.9.1:263). According to Las Casas, the practice of distributing natives was started by Christopher Columbus in Española to lessen the growing displeasure of the Castilian colonists, dissatisfied as they were by the scarcity of natural resources and poverty of the tropical environment to sustain a prosperous and wealthy colony (Las Casas 1986, 2.1.156:86–90).

2. Even at the end of the sixteenth century, the Jesuit Acosta (1985, 6.16: 301–302) expresses himself in idyllic terms about the simplicity of the South American natives

(he refers, however, to dressed natives), comparing them to the anchorites of ancient Christianity: "And in this they are almost imitating the monks of ancient institutes as told by the Fathers. In truth, they are people with little avarice and desire for possessions, and they are content to live moderately to the point that if their style of life were so by choice and not by custom or nature, we would say that it was a life of great perfection, and it does not in any way present an obstacle to the reception of the holy gospel, which is such an enemy of pride and greed."

3. Hodgen (1964, 354–385) has stressed that, because of theological and religious considerations, the anti-primitive perspective dominated the sixteenth century.

4. Moya Pons (1978, 49–50) has called attention to the importance of this "secret instruction" because it shows the desire to obtain the greatest possible economic benefits for the Crown.

5. The royal decree is dated December 20, 1503. It was not the first time that the Crown authorized forcing the natives to work. It had already happened on September 16, 1501, in an instruction to Governor Ovando: "Because to gather gold and do the other tasks that we have ordered, it will be necessary to make use of the service of the Indians, *and compel them to work* in our service" (Konetzke 1953, 1:6). However, there is no reference here to a system of *encomiendas* for colonists, but to compulsory work in the mining enterprises of the Crown.

6. According to the jurist Gregorio, in the context of the approval and writing of the Laws of Burgos (1512), although the Crown declared the Indians free vassals it can, due to their vices and idolatry, impose on them as a corrective as well as a punitive measure a "qualified servitude," which corresponds to the *encomienda* (Las Casas 1986, 2.3.12:472–473).

7. Zavala (1935, 6), in the *opus magnum* of this topic, observes: "Note the insistence on the principle of the legal freedom of the entrusted Indian, to distinguish him juridically from the slave, . . . but to a certain extent the difference did not go beyond being a formality because both Indians were expended in the same kinds of work."

8. Pérez de Tudela (1957, 1:xv) rates the theory that regards the *encomienda* as beneficial as an "absolutely false convention" that marks its proponents as "pharisaical."

9. Las Casas dedicated a good portion of his iconoclastic work, *Los Tesoros del Perú*, to denying the obligation of the Indians to pay for the high cost of their evangelization.

10. Lecture in Santo Domingo, Feb. 11, 1989. Moya Pons (1978) agrees with the pharisaical nature of the evangelizing rhetoric about the *encomienda*. On the initial evangelization of the Antilles see Meier (1986).

11. According to Las Casas (1967, 1.3.120:632), part of the problem was lack of knowledge of the Taino language. But this ignorance reflects, in a deeper way, negligence regarding the evangelization of the natives.

12. Córdova (1968) has proposed a thesis that the *encomiendas*, in the initial form they took in the Antillean islands as an intense and in practice unpaid exploitation of the natives' labor, was a factor that hastened their "accelerated depopulation."

I differ from him in his emphasis on the provisional and temporal character of the institution as the key element in this demographic catastrophe. The Indian slaves seem to have suffered an equal mortality rate. The excessive exploitation of manual labor was motivated by the provisional and transient aspirations of the colonists who desired to get rich quickly and then return to Spain as soon as possible. It is when the development of a *criollo* conscience begins that the legal need is felt to preserve manual laborers indefinitely. It is Córdova's merit, however, to pose without ambiguities the main problem in the relationship between manual labor and the acute mortality rates of the Antillean natives, which is missed in the analysis by Fernández Méndez (1984) in his widely read essay about the Puerto Rican natives. Córdova also subjects to a sharp critical scrutiny the observations hastily made by Fernández Méndez on the endurance of the aboriginal Antillean race through *mestizaje*, that is, through the racial intermingling of native, European, and African American communities.

13. The Cortés ordinances show his intention to go down in history not only because of his military deeds but also because of his founding a prosperous colony appropriately called Nueva España. He is perfectly aware that in order to attain his goal he has to avoid what happened in the Antillean islands, where rapid extinction of the Indians ruined their economic attraction.

14. The interests of Cortés are at stake. According to him, he is the main debtor of the Mexican conquest. "Besides, I spent everything I had, which was more than one hundred thousand pesos in gold, without counting that I have borrowed more than thirty thousand besides" (1985, 215).

15. Similar arguments, but expressed more simply, were presented by eight Franciscan friars. See Pacheco et al. (1864-1884, 7:533-540).

16. Cited also by Pereña in "*Estudio preliminar*" (Las Casas 1969, lii-liii). This is a very informative work about the dispute over the possibility of perpetuity through the sale of the *encomiendas*. Since the point of departure was the offer/pressure of the Peruvian colonists, the book by Zavala, rich with the Mexican context of the theme, is not so informative. Pereña also introduces the issue with a useful summary of the juridical Castilian antecedents and the dispute between centralist monarchic tendencies and that of the lords.

17. In 1559 the chiefs in the Peruvian Viceroyalty gave Las Casas, together with Frays Santo Domingo de Santo Tomás and Alonso Méndez, absolute and total power to represent them in the polemic against the offer made by the *encomenderos* (in Las Casas 1969, cii-cvi).

18. For a juridical and theoretical elucidation of the *encomienda* as it was emended after the disputes that followed the abrogation of the thirtieth chapter of the New Laws, see Solórzano y Pereyra [1648] 1930, book 3.

Chapter 7

1. This started a tradition. In general every encounter between Europeans and whites with persons of other races (and with less developed technology) leads to a questioning of the rationality of the latter. Hanke (1959, 96–104) offers a succinct summary. It is an ideological mechanism of domination.

2. According to Díaz del Castillo (1986, 113), Cortés, during the first confrontations with the natives, would hide the dead, "so that the Indians would not see that we were mortals, but believe that we were *teules* [divine] as they would say."

3. Vargas Machuca (in Fabié [1879] 1966, 71:225–226) generalizes this naive deification. "As far as taking the Spaniards as children of the Sun . . . generally it has happened at first sight in all the Indies, and it is the same today in the new conquests, from which you can easily tell that they are barbarians."

4. Lafaye (1988, 181) attributes this incident to the Aztecs. It is not the only mistake in that popular book. On another occasion he blames the Caribs for the death of the men in the La Navidad on Española (ibid., 37).

5. The Mexican Indians, according to Mendieta ([1596] 1980, 2.10:93), thought the Spaniards were "gods, children, and brothers of Quetzalcoatl," until after they witnessed their insatiable greed and "experienced and saw their deeds, then they did not see them as celestial beings." The same is found in Las Casas 1987 (3.122:54).

6. This geographic determinism became a masterpiece of imperialist ideology in attempting to give a pseudo-scientific explanation to the supposed natural servitude of some nations.

7. Abril-Castelló (1984, 274–275), in a provocative article, also suggests Sepúlveda shaded the original text in order to lessen the criticism raised by theologians to the first version of *Demócrates segundo*. Ramos (1976, 165–167) thinks he sees a less denigrating opinion of the natives in the Indian chronicle by Sepúlveda written a few years after *Demócrates segundo*. In spite of this, the ban against its publication was upheld and *Demócrates segundo* did not appear for several centuries.

8. The importance of these significant differences seems to have escaped Quirk (1954, 357–364) in his clever defense of Sepúlveda. Also Arenal (1975–1976, 115–120), when highlighting the ideological kinship between Sepúlveda and his theological adversaries, tames the humanist and Renaissance chronicler too much. Losada (1949, 315) is another who attempts to minimize the theoretical distance between Sepúlveda and his theological adversaries of the sixteenth century: "The variations are in the details and not in the substance, as some scrupulous authors came to believe." Losada's argument is not convincing to me. Some differences are substantial, as Sepúlveda and Las Casas certainly thought themselves. Maybe it is just a reaction to the usual censure of Sepúlveda, due to ignorance of his works.

9. Accusations of sodomy and cannibalism usually went together. Both were joined to the idea that idolatry leads to extreme moral corruption. Pagden (1982, 176) points out that this negative vision has been common in the European

perspective of "primitive societies." Thus, imperialism assumes a face of moral education.

10. This testimony was widely circulated and served as ammunition in the anti-Indian propaganda. It is reproduced by Anglería (1964–1965, 2.4,7:609–610). It is also behind the very unfavorable opinion of the natives given by Oviedo (1851, 1.3.6:72). In fact the extensive refutation made by Las Casas (see 1986, 3.3.142–146:320–336) of Oviedo's pejorative opinion is really addressed to his religious brother, Fray Ortíz. The latter is mentioned again by Solórzano y Pereyra (1930) in the next century. In another context, Las Casas (1967, 2.3.246:552–557) refers to the testimony by Ortíz without mentioning his name and says he is a "religious . . . with a zeal lacking the science of which Saint Paul speaks," and he relates how he ended his ecclesiastical term in the New World ignominiously. What is strange, and mostly unnoticed by the interpreters, is that according to López de Gómara (1946, 290), Ortíz seeks the support of Fray Pedro de Córdoba, the promoter of the Dominican denunciations against the abuse of the natives at the hands of the Spaniards, "from whose hands I have all this in writing."

11. Betanzos also wrote in 1545 that it was God's will to exterminate the natives. He believed that the deadly smallpox epidemic assailing the natives was a sign of that divine disposition (Zavala 1935, 108). He was very inconsistent in his evaluation of the natives.

12. Original Latin in Hernáez 1879 (1:57). The translation is by Gabriel Méndez Plancarte and is reproduced in "Carta de fray Julián Garcés al Papa Paulo III," in Xirau 1973 (87–101).

13. I differ from Hanke in the specific nuances of his interpretation of affirmations such as those of Rodrigo de Bastidas.

14. While Las Casas (1989, 15–17) stresses the meekness and lack of bellicosity ("peaceful and tranquil . . . meek sheep") of the natives as the principal indication of their humanity, Alonso de Ercilla (1984) sees that humanity, above all, in their valor and warring skills.

15. The carefully written preliminary study by Edmund O'Gorman prefacing the Mexican version of the *Apologética* is marred by lack of attention to what I have emphasized here. Fundamentally, it is not, as the great Mexican researcher thinks, a question of anthropological philosophy—the levels of understanding historically achieved by the natives—but primarily a question of domination in the area of politics and labor; namely, the legitimacy of the abrogation of native sovereignty and their being compelled to work.

16. Perhaps the only explanation that considers the historical context, although lacking in depth, is found in Acosta [1588] 1952 (2.5:158), who attributes the texts to Aristotle's need to adulate the imperialist interests of Alexander of Macedonia.

17. One of those rare instances is found in "Tratado comprobatorio": "They suffer many and great defects in their realms because of lack of Christian faith, no matter how well governed they are, they require many laws that are neither just nor reasonable, or not as just or as reasonable as they should be, and they also have strong and barbaric customs." The Castilian Crown is capable of reforming those

defects, "taking away little by little the horrors and defects of their policies which necessarily result from . . . infidelity; and by founding, establishing, and laying the roots of the clean, just, and legitimate way of life that the Christian faith has and teaches" (1965, 2:1137; 1115).

18. Las Casas cites the text in *Del único modo* (365–367). Also in Cuevas 1946 (1:263–265; 1975, 84–86 in Spanish, 499–500 in Latin). About *Sublimis Deus* see Hanke 1937 (65–102). Four days before the bull, the pope had sent the brief *Pastorale officium* to Cardinal Tabera, archbishop of Toledo, authorizing him to "excommunicate *latae sententiae ipso facto incurrenda* any person of whatever status, state, condition, or rank who enslaves the natives" (in Hernáez 1879, 1:101–102). Hernáez also includes another papal brief, a variant of *Sublimis Deus*, entitled *Veritas ipse* (102–103). See also Tobar 1954 (209, 216–217).

Contrary to what some of his apologists have said, based on those statements, Paul III did not reject the institution of slavery itself, only slavery imposed on the American natives. On November 9, 1548, he issued a *motu propio* to confirm the legitimacy of the slave market in Rome and to ban the long-held tradition of manumission of slaves who took refuge in the Senate of the city. "We strictly forbid our beloved children . . . in that city from using their authority to emancipate escaping slaves who claim their freedom, independently of their being Christianized or born to Christian slaves" (in Maxwell 1975, 75).

19. Mendieta ([1596] 1980, 1.12:55) criticizes Oviedo for those words and affirms that the famous chronicler should rather have "cried tears of blood for having taken part with others in the extermination and eradication from the face of the earth of so many million souls created in the image of God and capable of redemption."

20. It is Robert Ricard's (1986) distinction to have called attention, correctly and tactfully, to this paternalistic attitude, which paradoxically constitutes an underestimation of the intellectual abilities and virtues of the character of the natives whom they claim to love passionately. The same observation could be made without excessive criticism regarding the famous "Reglas y ordenanzas de hospitales" (Rules and ordinances for hospitals), by Vasco de Quiroga in Michoacán. His protection of the natives could never be freed from a certain condescending paternalism. In a report for the court as an official, he praises the natives because they are "very docile and very gentle and made like wax to do with them whatever one wants" (in Herrejón 1985, 198). Also useful on this subject is Sylvest 1975.

21. Mendieta's historiography is typical of the period in the central role he assigns to the mendicant friars in the Christianization and pacification of the natives. "Religious men, zealous in the service of God and good of their neighbor" face an extraordinary and transcendental battle, "having as opponents all the devils of hell and all those men who are products of this century, dealing with and working for people who do not have even a breath of spirit." He is one of the first to rationalize a dichotomous vision of dedicated religious as opposed to greedy lay persons as the main hermeneutical key to understanding the Iberian presence in the Americas in the sixteenth century. It is a vision that cannot free itself from the twin sins of narcissism and ethnocentrism. At the edge of the scene, as spectators and suffering patients, are the Indians (Mendieta 1980, 4.31:492).

22. The theological doctrine of the one origin for all humanity does not necessarily imply one common sociopolitical destiny. I do not find among sixteenth-century Spanish theologians the peculiar theory later popularized by some Protestant biblical scholars, according to which Africans and American Indians came from Ham, Noah's cursed son, which gave them the fatal destiny of their forefather: "To be the slave of the slaves of his brothers" (Gen. 9:25, NIV). Perhaps there is a passing allusion to that theory in López de Gómara 1946 (290), where, to legitimate forced labor of the Indians and explain their demographic demise, he affirms: "God maybe allowed the servitude and travail of these sinful peoples as a punishment, for Ham sinned less against his father than these peoples against God, and his children and descendants were cursed to be slaves." Another reference to this theory is found in Juan Suárez de Peralta's (1949, 7) work written around 1580 but published in 1878. He says, "The Indians really come from the cursed Canaan." In the seventeenth century Alonso de Sandoval ([1627] 1987, 1.2:74–75), in the most important work of Spanish theology about blacks, reveals knowledge of that slave theory when he affirmed that "Ethiopians . . . have their origin in Ham, who was the world's first servant and slave." The idea that the American Indians came from Ham was defended in the Protestant Anglo-Saxon world by William Strachey ([1849] 1953, 54–55; cf. Allen 1949, 113–137). There existed the possibility of postulating a polygenetic theory of the origin of humanity, but traditional theological hegemony and literal biblical exegesis impeded it. Apparently, the French theologian Isaac de la Peyrère in 1655 was the first to dare suggest that the American Indians, as well as many other peoples and nations, had an origin different from Adam's as proposed by Christian dogma. The attacks and rejections were so intense that he was forced into retraction (Huddleston 1967, 139–143).

23. On the history of the Colegio de Santa Cruz de Santiago de Tlatelolco and its failure in promoting a native clergy, see Olaechea Labayen 1958 (113–200).

24. Francisco Mateo reiterates, "In a mixed society of whites and Indians, the Indian was the dregs of society. If he were made priest he would be in such an abject and despicable social condition that it would not be decent nor tolerable for society to admit him as a priest" (Acosta 1952, 6.19:581).

25. This issue is treated subtly by Gómez Canedo (1977, 189, n. 70) in his study of Franciscan missionary activities. However, in a footnote, he makes an unusual assertion: "The so often discussed question of whether or not there was an 'indigenous clergy' in colonial America should be phrased in a different way. *Criollos* were also indigenous and it did not take long before they constituted the majority of the clergy in the Americas." That "*criollos* were also indigenous" is an ethnic confusion that comes from his apologetic intentions. In spite of his being dissatisfied with Ricard's criticism, Armas Medina (1953, 372) is obliged to admit the following with regard to Peru: "An undisputed error was made by the missionaries when little by little they did not begin to form an indigenous clergy." Behind this caution in allowing the ordination of neophytes in Christianity hides ethnic prejudice.

26. However, the Franciscan Alfonso de Castro, in a brief treatise in 1543 approved by Vitoria, assumed the opposite argument, namely, that the study of theology

and scriptures would promote obedience to metropolitan authorities. "Sacred Scriptures and Catholic faith teach that you should obey authorities, not only the good and modest ones, but also the wayward ones. . . . It is prudent, not only for the preservation of Catholic faith, but also for the preservation of royal and noble authority, to instruct the natives in Sacred Scriptures and in true theology." "Utrum indigenae novi orbis instruendi sint in mysteriis theologicis at artibus liberalibus," (in Olaechea Labayen 1958, 184). An allusion to ch. 13 in Paul's epistle to the Romans, magna carta of political docility, could not be left out.

27. *"R.D. para que los indios sean admitidos en las religiones, educados en los colegios y promovidos, según su mérito y capacidad, a dignidades y oficios públicos"* (1766) (Royal Decree so that the Indians be admitted to religious orders, educated in colleges and promoted, according to their merit and ability, to honorary and public offices) (in Konetzke 1953, 3.1:333–334).

Chapter 8

1. I find López Baralt's affirmation on "Pané's respect for cultural diversity" to be excessively generous. Fray Ramón did not try to be an "astute anthropologist." His objective was to understand native mythology and religiosity in order to *combat* them. It is López Baralt (1985) who develops an astute vision and interpretation of Taíno culture in her challenging exegesis of Antillean mythology.

2. It needs to be clarified that Cortés ended his permissiveness with the cannibalism of his allies after his victory against the Aztecs. Later he ordered one of his Indian friends to be burned upon discovering that he practiced cannibalism after it had been forbidden (Cortés 1985, 228).

3. Death by burning was the punishment generally used in Castilla for homosexuality and sodomy. See Friederici 1925 (1:219–220). Las Casas also insisted on capital punishment for sodomy, an "abominable vice," which if not punished could provoke divine wrath through plagues, hunger, and earthquakes. In his opinion, however, such legal sanctions were not applicable to the American natives for they were outside Christian jurisdiction (Las Casas 1974, 161–162).

4. On the destruction of the pagan temples see Ricard's (1986, 96–108) discussion, with its undisguised sympathy toward the missionaries. Gómez Canedo (1977, 163), after describing the destruction of the great temples in Texcoco, Mexico, Tlaxcala, and Huejotzingo, gives a strange argument: "In regard to the accusation that in the destruction of the temples and idols great works of art disappeared, without denying that possibility, it should be kept in mind that the destruction was principally . . . done through fire . . . and therefore, it is doubtful that solid works were lost." The truth of the matter is that things that are destroyed generally perish. Fire was not the only means used. The places of worship and the idols were dethroned and hidden. Sometimes the stones from the native altars were

used to build Christian temples, as Motolinía (1984, 1.3:22) explained. The effectiveness of that destruction was great. A good example is the main temple of Mexico City, which was devastated and hidden for 450 years until in 1978, in an excavation to enlarge underground public transportation facilities, it was rediscovered. It was excavated, and since 1982 the ruins have been open to visitors.

5. Later Jesuit missionary practice has brought about a rethinking of the universality of grace, including the possibility of seeing all religions as diverse "paths to salvation" rather than "falsehoods" to be combated and eradicated. See Amaladoss 1986.

6. For the Spanish struggle against Quechua idolatry, see Armas Medina 1953 (570–576).

7. Sahagún (1985, 261) criticizes harshly, for example, those who praise the Aztec calendar. He does it not because of modern science's disregard for astrology but because he thinks it is different from that which is practiced by Christian Europeans, "which has a base in natural astrology," and because that of the Indians is "a lie and diabolic trickery."

8. Mendieta (1980 4.32:496–501) also understands that the heroic era of the Christianization of the Mexican natives is a thing of the past and that they have become cold in their devotion to the new religion. He blames the bad example given by the Iberians: "because the Spaniards who mingle with the Indians are for the most part of little value." Las Casas (1967, 213:231–234) stresses that the conquest brought about an abrupt dissolution of the moral discipline of the natives. "It was after the conquest by the Spaniards that things became rebellious and disorganized." He follows the same line of thought as Motolinía. Cf. Benavente 1971 (2.4:312). See also Mendieta 1980 (75, 124, 138–140).

9. About Sahagún's work, Ricard (1986, 137) says: "All those books not only represent many thankless days of patient and careful work, but many long hours of doubt, sadness, bitterness, and persecution." True, but Ricard seems to be pained more by the suffering of missionaries like Sahagún than by that of the natives mortally wounded by the undervaluing of their traditions implied in Felipe II's decree. The Indians, not the missionaries, were the wounded victims of the royal decree.

10. The irony of history is that a very valuable part of what we today know about the Mayas from Yucatán we owe to Fray Diego's work who, let it be said, burned not just papers in the autos-da-fé. Sahagún (1985, 583) also mentions the destruction of a great many pictographic Mexican documents: "Of these works and writings, most of them were burned." With the passing of time and an increase in academic curiosity (with its claim to a certain autonomy and validity) scholars of native cultures lament the "foolish zeal" that took every traditional document as "witchcraft and magic, and . . . superstition," worthy only of the flames. (Acosta 1952, 6.7:288).

11. We lack good writings where history and fiction converge, on the "battle of the gods" between the Christian missionaries and the aboriginal religions, as was

done so well by the Nigerian Chinua Achebe (1974 and 1984) on the encounter between English evangelists and African Ibo traditions.

12. This was a widespread notion among Spanish colonists. Mendieta (1980, 4.37:518) opposed it with another hypothesis as improbable and strange as the first: that the rapid death of the natives through terrible epidemics was for them a divine favor, a providential grace that freed them from the cruel greed of the Iberians. "God grants them a special favor in taking them out from such an evil and dangerous world . . . rather than that by our greed, ambitions, bad example, and God's abandonment . . . they might lose their faith."

Chapter 9

1. However, in response to the publication in 1552 of various Las Casas treatises against the conqueror and the *encomenderos*, Motolinía came out in their defense in a letter to Carlos V in 1555 in which he alleged "that the Indians of Nueva España are well treated. . . . And there is no such carelessness or tyranny as Las Casas says." He even alleged that "the Indians are rich and the Spaniards are poor and dying of hunger" (1984, 216–217).

2. The work by Cook and Borah has revolutionized the demographic history of the conquest of America and provoked intense controversy. Cf. Rosenblat 1967, Sanders 1976, Henige (May and November) 1978, Zambardino 1978. An excellent summary of the dispute is presented by Denevan (1976, 1–12). The estimates on the pre-Colombian population vary enormously between 8.4 million (Kroeber, 1939) and more than 100 million (Dobyns, 1966).

3. Mellafe's figures come from Rosenblat 1954. Most chroniclers of the sixteenth century gave estimates of one million inhabitants in Española (Sauer 1984, 105–111). That figure is supported by Zambardino (1978, 704). The 500 figure by the middle of the century is taken from Oviedo (1851, 1.3.6:72). The debate over the native population of Española, which was the center of operations for the colonization efforts during the first quarter of a century, is not new. In 1517, a group of Dominican and Franciscan friars, in a letter to Monsieur de Xèvres, gave three very different estimates: 600,000, 1.1 million, and 2 million. They were certain, however, that the number remaining was 12,000. The island had become, they asserted with great sadness, "a desert" (J. M. Pérez 1988, 142). "According to Archbishop Andrés de Carvajal, by 1570 there were 25 residents, all old, poor, and without children" (in Milhou 1975–1976, 28). The differences continue. The figures for the pre-Colombian population of Española range from 60,000 (Verlinden 1968) to 7 million (Cook and Borah 1971, 1:376–410).

4. Todorov (1987, 14): "The sixteenth century may have seen the perpetration of the greatest genocide in human history."

5. Vicens Vives borrows this argument from Cook and Borah (1967). Friederici (1986, 1:236), on the contrary, underscores that "in almost every place that the Spanish conquerors arrived, . . . they found the granaries overflowing or at least well stocked."

6. Those who find the term "holocaust" inappropriate due to its literary appropriation for the Nazi genocide against the Jews will do well to reflect on the following: The only massacre that the Italian Auschwitz survivor Primo Levi (1988, 10) is willing to consider as being at the level of the one suffered by his people is that suffered by the American natives in the sixteenth century.

7. See his description of the misfortune of the sick natives in his "Octavo remedio" (Las Casas 1965, 2:791). Also Fray Pedro de Córdoba, superior of the Dominicans in Española, stresses this factor in a letter to Carlos V: ". . . killing them from hunger and thirst, and in their illness seeing them as lesser than beasts, for the beasts are cured but they are not" (J. M. Pérez 1988, 133).

8. The epidemic seems to have begun in December of 1518 or January of 1519. On its effects and spread to other native towns, see Crosby 1967. He stresses the epidemic diseases as the principal cause of "the spectacular period of mortality among the American natives" in the sixteenth century. However, he recognizes that at the time of the smallpox epidemic most of the Antillean natives had already perished. As part of the process of evading moral responsibility, besides attributing the death of the natives principally to smallpox, some try to blame the black slaves for initiating the epidemic—after all, an affair between blacks and Indians! See Arana Soto 1968 (34). "Smallpox, the terrible epidemic brought from Africa by the blacks": Phelps de Córdova (1989). Motolinía (1984, 1.1:13) attributed the first great smallpox epidemic to a black man in the 1520 Pánfilo Narváez expedition. Sahagún (1985, 585), who stressed the mortal effect of the smallpox epidemics among the Mexican natives, was insightful and honest enough to notice that in many cases the decisive factor was lack of medical and sanitary care and not the so often mentioned lack of physical immunity. "In the epidemics of thirty years ago, most died because there was no one who knew how to bleed them nor administer the appropriate medicines . . . and in this epidemic the same thing is happening . . . and there is no one who can nor wants to help the poor Indians and they die without help or remedy."

9. Deive (1980, 688) calls attention to a similar phenomenon with the captured Africans. After being trapped they were taken to ships, where they were held for long periods before sailing. The loss of liberty and hope for the future and the "continued enclosure of the slaves caused many of them to go mad or to suffer from an illness that was called at that time 'melancolía fija' (fixed melancholy), surely caused by nostalgia for the land and, more than anything else, the desire for freedom. Hence many of them died for lack of a desire to live."

10. According to Las Casas (1986, 3.3.82:103–104), always ready to uncover creative and deep theological meanings in the Indians' via crucis (way of the cross), the collective suicides showed that the natives "felt and witnessed the immortality of the soul . . . which many blind philosophers denied." Friederici (1986, 251–252)

thinks that, without the Christian prohibition against it, the natives "had an easy propensity toward suicide." He gathers many testimonies about collective suicides on the part of the natives who were overcome by deep moral depression.

11. Anglería (1964–1965, 1.3.8:363) wrote something similar: "These simple naked men . . . are so overcome by despair that not a few opt for suicide without worrying in the least about procreating children. Pregnant mothers take abortive medicines to give birth before time because they know that the fruit of their womb would become a slave for the Christians."

12. "Carta latina de dominicos y franciscanos de las Indias a los regentes de España," App. 2. The dung image is inherited by Las Casas (1989, 23), who says the Spanish gave less care and esteem to the natives than to beasts, "as little and even less than to the dung in the plazas."

13. In his letter to the emperor, Motolinía comes through in an apologetic tone that is questionable according to his own accounts, especially his important account of the "ten plagues" in *Historia* (1984, 1.1:13–18). He allows his hostility toward Las Casas to cloud his perspective and he jumps hastily to defend the Spanish empire. His differences with Las Casas touch on very important issues: (a) evaluation of armed conquest as essential to evangelization; (b) appraisal of the instruction of catechumens necessary for baptizing natives. This is another example of the conflicting passions Las Casas awakened during his untiring activism of almost half a century. And, interestingly, that same passion, for or against his work, endures with similar intensity.

14. Strangely enough, after mentioning different factors whose synergistic interrelation would be important to analyze, Borah (1962) also takes refuge in the microbes and germs theory as the principal cause of "the catastrophic fall in the aboriginal population."

15. An example has been discovered by Sued Badillo (1989, 66) in the Archives of the Indies in Sevilla. During an investigation in 1529 in the area of Toa, Puerto Rico, native survivors gave an account of the system of work to which they had been subjected: "[The natives] told how many died and that their death was caused by too much work, and if one of them was ill they [the Spaniards] would say, 'Go to work, it is nothing,' and they would go and then die." A pertinent critique of the excessive emphasis on epidemics, and especially their isolation from the violent breakdown of the Indian social structures, is found in Keen 1971.

Chapter 10

1. Molina is not antislavery. He only tries to distinguish between "just" and "unjust" serfdom. He is even ready to affirm that "slavery, under the Christians, leads to the spiritual well-being of the slaves. It is an act of charity to buy blacks their liberty so that in that way they may become Christians" (*De Iustitia et iure*, disps. 34–35, ns. 6, 9–10 [in Höffner 1957, 465, 472]). However, some Spanish

theologians, without condemning African slavery in a global sense, expressed some important reservations. Domingo de Soto ([1556] 1967, 2.4.2.2:289) says of the Lusitanian black market: "There are, in effect, many who affirm that the unfortunate people are seduced with lies and deceit . . . and sometimes compelled by force and without them realizing it or knowing what it is being done to them, they are shipped and sold. If this is true, neither those who take them by force, buy them, or possess them can have their consciences at peace, until they free them, even if they cannot recover the money they paid."

2. In Deive's view (1980, 386), this paradox was resolved in favor of the commercial interests of the colonists. He indicates that in the sixteenth century the majority of black slaves in Española died without receiving the sacrament of baptism.

3. To that number one would have to add those who did not survive the initial enslavement process. Borah (1962, 182) calculates that for each slave who arrived alive in the Americas, at least two died during capture or the ocean crossing.

4. The so-called "triangular commerce" (precious metals from the Americas, slave labor from Africa and the goods produced, and financial credit from Europe) has been analyzed many times. Deive (1980, 655–693) summarizes the literature.

5. Ortíz (1978, 90–96) gives a detailed description of the official market of black slaves to the Indies between 1500 and 1516. However, even an intellectual of Sánchez Albornoz's (1986, 19) stature seems to insinuate that Las Casas bears special responsibility for the initiation of the black slave trade for the Americas.

6. In general, Spanish scholastic theologians of the sixteenth century distinguished between human freedom according to natural law, and the possibility of human enslavement according to the law of nations. Cf. Soto's ([1556] 1967, book 4) careful treatment of this subject.

7. This devaluing of blackness is found, inter alia, in the opinion the Council of the Indies gave to Felipe II after the monarch recommended in 1556 that the rights of the *encomenderos* could be willed to the natural children if there were no legitimate ones. "Those natural children who will thus be in succession cannot have black mothers so as to restrain such ugly unions, because no one would want to marry the black woman from whom those children are born, and also because as we know from experience they have a pernicious influence in those provinces, hence Your Majesty has ordered that mulattoes shall not be allowed in the Indies." On the contrary, natural children from a white father and an Indian mother should be allowed the right of inheritance when there were no other legitimate children (Konetzke 1953, 1:347).

8. The intensification of the slave raids into Africa, due to the increased market demand for forced labor in the Americas, has been mentioned by some experts on this question. Cf. Deive 1980 (692–693).

9. Deive (1980, 47, 367–373) and Sued Badillo (1986, 156–160) point out the high mortality rate among black slaves in the Antilles.

10. According to Bataillon (1976, 136), "Las Casas was certainly one of the first to become aware of the legal problem posed by the Portuguese slave trade."

11. However, at the time that the Society of Jesus [the Jesuits] was banned from the Americas in 1767, they were the institution with the greatest number of slaves in the Western hemisphere (Bowser 1986, 371).

12. On the causes for the late publication of this extensive and important chronicler, see Hanke (in Las Casas 1986, "Bartolomé de las Casas, historiador," xxxviii–xlvi).

13. In another one of his treatises published in 1552, generally titled "*Octavo remedio*" (1965, 2:735), Las Casas calls attention to the violence suffered by American natives at the hands of blacks. "And we can in truth add all the servants and blacks owned by the master, for all they (the blacks) know is to skin, oppress, and rob them (the Indians)." He mentioned something similar three years later in a letter to Bartolomé Carranza de Miranda (in Fabié [1879] 1966, 71:394).

14. For example: "The Spaniards and Portuguese treated their slaves . . . much better than the French, the English, and the Anglo-Americans" (Friederici 1986, 1:466). The main exponent of this theory has been Tannenbaum (1946). A rigorous criticism of the idea that Anglo-American slavery was qualitatively more oppressive than the others is developed by Davis (1961, 29–61, 223–261; cf. Sio 1965, 289–308).

15. José Martí, in one of the most beautiful pages of his famous children's book *La edad de oro* (1981, 170), when describing the confrontation between Las Casas and the irate colonists in Chiapas, says: "He was on foot, aided by a cane and two good Spaniards and a black man who loved him as a father: because it is true that out of love for the Indians, Las Casas advised early in the conquest that they continue bringing black slaves who supported the heat better, but after he saw them suffer, he beat his breast saying: 'With my blood I wish I could pay for the sin of that advice which I gave out of love for the Indians!'" Perhaps, but in the two decades he lived following the incident related by Martí, he published much on the natural freedom of the natives and nothing except for his notes in the unpublished *Historia de las Indias* about the Africans. Sued Badillo (1986, 57–62) has found in the *Archivo General de Indias* (Sevilla), a deposition in 1547 to the Council of the Indies about a suit between Pedro de Carmona, "of black skin," claiming that according to the testament of his original master, Juan de Almodóvar, "resident of Puerto Rico," his manumission should be recognized, for it had been granted to him seven years earlier. According to Sued Badillo, Carmona traveled to Spain and gained a hearing before the Council of the Indies, thanks to the intervention of Las Casas, who met him in Honduras, took him along on his last journey to the Iberian peninsula, and helped write the allegation. This unique find significantly alters the account that Pérez Fernández (1984, 711–721) makes of the actions of Las Casas in 1547.

16. In an earlier essay, Zavala (1949, 114) indicated that "the legal defense of blacks did not arise as early as that of the Indians." One would have to say, with greater emphasis, that the abolition of black slavery in the Spanish-American world was proclaimed three centuries after the New Laws.

17. In Mires's opinion, this divergence was due to the political interest the Crown and the church had in avoiding the acquisition of excessive power by the colonists

through the *encomiendas*, a factor not present in the slavery relationship with Africans. That relationship did not carry the challenging problems of political sovereignty nor land domination with rich natural resources. That does not mean that there are no significant critical observations about the violence and injustice perpetrated against the enslaved Africans. Tomás de Mercado, Bartolomé de Albornoz, and Alonso de Sandoval contributed significantly to the development of potentially abolitionist thoughts. But, contrary to what happened with the American natives, neither the state nor the church officially proclaimed in Spanish-America the illegality of black slavery until the nineteenth century. On Mercado, Albornoz, and Sandoval, see Davis 1961 (187–196).

Chapter 11

1. Although Sepúlveda blamed Las Casas, above all, for the ban against his *Demócrates segundo*, the host of opponents was wider. Cano, theologian at Salamanca, wrote in 1548, "Your doctrine cannot be admitted with such certainty as not to be able to judge it as all just and very reasonable. This criterion is followed by the schools of Salamanca and Alcalá, which unanimously have refused to grant license for the publication of your book" (in Höffner 1957, 323).

2. This lack of critical judgment is seen in the attempts to highlight the historical importance of Vitoria. It taints the otherwise very fertile analysis by Fernando de los Ríos (1957). Something similar could be said of Scott's (1934) work.

3. See Lockhart 1972 (36–37) for a critique of the attempts to describe the social reality of Spanish colonization through the false shortcut of reading contemporary legal codes.

4. The thesis regarding the "most complete success" explains Manzano's opposition to the publication of the *Tratados* of Las Casas ("Brevísima relación," "Octavo remedio," etc.) in 1552. In his opinion, this was unnecessary since the Dominicans were winning the fight against the *encomenderos* and colonists; it was imprudent since "the consequences would be fatal to the national cause," for they gave rise to the "black anti-Hispanic legend . . . the most horrendous deceit registered by the annals of humanity." The only thing it accomplished was to "strike a mortal blow at the good name of the Spanish nation as soon as they fell into the hands of foreigners, especially heretics" (ibid., 229, 233, 250). It seems a tactful criticism, but soon Manzano reveals the deeper reason for his repudiation of *Tratados* by labeling them works "plagued by the most dangerous and grave errors" (ibid., 248). In reality, in spite of his frequent praise for Las Casas, he disagrees deeply with the vision the bishop of Chiapas had about the relationship between Spaniards and the natives. In Manzano's opinion that relationship was fundamentally beneficial, in spite of some considerable abuses. That was not the perspective of Las Casas. Manzano's critique is not original. It had already been expressed in 1555,

with no less animosity, by Motolinía, who thought that the Dominican friar "dishonored . . . the Spaniards with his writings" (Benavente 1984, "Carta a Carlos V," 211). It was repeated in Peru by "*Anónimo de Yucay*" (439–443), for whom the books of Las Casas "defamed the Christian nation, and among Christians, the Spaniards," thus helping "the English and French heretical Lutherans . . . who say that the Spanish King is a tyrant, . . . that we are thieves in the Indies." The heretics, who are themselves led in reality by "greed for gold and silver," then proceed in armed confrontation against the Castilian overseas empire. The idea that the "black legend" would not have existed had Las Casas not written his *Tratados* is arguable. Friederici ([1925] 1986, 1:393) states that "his pages do not contain, in substance or nature, anything that we cannot read in other works." Those who affirm that Las Casas, especially in his *Brevísima relación*, is the principal culprit of the "black legend," are also mistaken. There were other factors that provoked anti-Spanish stereotypes in England and the Low Countries. Religious antagonism prevailed, as did the threat that the Dutch Calvinists and English Protestants felt in the face of the fierce Catholic fervor of Felipe II in assuming his role as the scourge of "heresies." More influential among the European Protestant audience than the *Brevísima relación* were the many accounts that painted a gloomy picture of the Spanish Inquisition. See Maltby 1982.

5. See Pérez de Tudela 1958 for a keen criticism of the common affirmation that the New Laws represented a total victory for Las Casas.

6. Salas (1986, 59), in his essay on Anglería, sees in these words of the Italian humanist "all the drama of a wise and Christian legislation [that] fails because of distance and human ambition and greed that flow unrestrained in the newfound lands. . . . rudely creating a way of life . . . a reality that in many respects had nothing to do with the *Leyes de Indias*."

7. Much has been said about the breakdown in morality in the passage from Europe to América at the beginning of the conquest and colonization, even causing the coinage of the pregnant concept of "tropicalization of the white man." Although Bataillon (1976, 364) prefers "criollización," to indicate that we are dealing more with a social process than a climatological one, the first phrase seems to me appropriate. It points to the dissolution of ethical inhibitions, which are always fragile and precarious in the presence of the seductive influence of the vegetation and flora of the American jungle, as is so often dealt with in Latin American literature.

8. I consider Hanke's (1967, 28–32) panegyric to the "freedom of speech in [sixteenth-century] Spain" to be hyperbole. It is no accident that many works written during the second half of that century were unpublished for several centuries.

9. Spanish chroniclers and theologians debated with their customary intensity the justice and legitimacy of Atahualpa's execution. Acosta (1952, 2.18:211) censures it, not out of legal concerns but because of missionary convenience. It would have been preferable, he suggested, to have his collaboration so as to evangelize the natives. "Our people gravely erred in the death of Atabalipa [sic], Inka prince, . . . and if the good will of the prince had been gained, the entire Inka empire would have soon received the faith easily."

10. Oviedo (1851, 4.3.48.6:373) recounts that Vicente de Valverde was killed by the natives of the islands of Puná. The tone of divine revenge in the narrative is interesting: "God allowed time and Indians to avenge the imprisonment and death of prince Atabalipa [sic], in which affair the religious superior Fray Vicente had been the intercessor so-called." Valverde was named bishop of Cuzco in 1536 by Carlos V, who gave Valverde the title of "protector e defensor de los yndios de la provincia [del Peru]" (in Armas Medina 1953, 122, n. 51).

11. But as I pointed out in an earlier chapter, in later reflections about African slavery he arrived at the important conclusion that not all Muslims are necessarily "enemies of the faith, usurpers of Christian kingdoms."

12. Contrary to his exaggerated arithmetic of Spanish cruelty, Las Casas understands that the aborigines did not sacrifice more than "thirty, a hundred, or a thousand" persons in a year, and not all of them necessarily "innocent" (ibid., 205). Note that Motolinía (1984, 3.11:167), not at all sympathetic toward Las Casas, recognizes that "the avarice of our Spaniards was more to blame for the destruction and depopulation of this land than all the [human] sacrifices, wars, and homicides that took place there during its time of infidelity."

13. On another occasion he mentions the possible legitimacy of the war against infidel princes who are tyrants and cruel. In that case, the Supreme Pontiff can admonish them to change their despotic ways. If his request is not heeded, "the Supreme Vicar of Christ can order those tyrants who do not make amends or who resist to be compelled by war." This is reminiscent of one of Vitoria's reasons for legitimizing the Spaniards' wars against the natives: defense of the innocent. This perspective would bring him close to the Spanish scholastic Dominicans of the sixteenth century—to Christian humanitarian imperialism—but he never develops it fully (Las Casas 1965, 1009).

14. See his key work: *Secunda secundae partis summae totius theologiae d. Thomae Aquinatis, Thomae a Vio Cajetani commentariis illustrata*. Printed in 1517 for the first time, it was widely read due to the many manuscripts in circulation and the many references made to it. The distinction between infidels is in the commentary to part 2-2.66.8.

15. Ibid. It is included in Leturia 1959 (1:164) and in Zavala's introduction to the treatise by López de Palacios Rubios and Paz (1954, lxxxv–lxxxvi). Las Casas cites it in Latin in his "Tratado de las doce dudas" (1965, 490) and in *Los tesoros del Perú* ([1563] 1958, 260). Although in this passage Cayetano does not make explicit mention to the controversies over the Indies, Las Casas (1986, 2.3.38:563) alleges that he wrote it after being informed by the Dominican friar Hierónimo de Peñafiel about the abuses committed against the natives of the Americas. This text was very influential with many Dominican theologians, among them Vitoria, who developed the same idea in *De indis* (1538) in a section dedicated to a discussion of illegitimate Spanish domination over "the barbarians of the New World"; Bartolomé Carranza, in his lecture *An infideles possint habere dominium super fideles* (1539); Melchor Cano, in his treatise *De dominio indiorum* (1546) (the last two are in Pereña 1956, 38–57, 90–147, respectively); and Fray Miguel de Benavides, in his

statement, "Ynstrucción para el govierno de las Filipinas," in Hanke and Millares 1977 (241). On Cayetano, see Carro 1944 (1:397–408).

16. In his *Apologia* against Sepúlveda, Las Casas indicates that in the lost first book of his work *Del único modo de atraer a todos los pueblos a la verdadera religión* he delved in detail into the distinction between heretics, who can be compelled to fulfill their baptismal vows, and infidels, who do not know Christianity and cannot be forced to obey ecclesiastical precepts (Las Casas 1974, 312).

17. "Et quídem illos secundos non solum minis et terroribus cogere licet, verum . . . capitis suplicio plectere. Priores autem non item" (And indeed it is licit to compel the latter by threats and terror, even . . . inflict capital punishment on them. This may not be done with the former). *In quartum sententiarum commentari,* Salmanticae, 1570 (1:271). Cited in Latin in Castañeda Delgado (1974, 137). Höffner (1957, 114–118) shows there was unanimity among the great scholastic Spanish theologians of the Golden Age (Vitoria, Soto, Bañez, Suárez) in favor of persecution and execution of heretics.

18. Vasco de Quiroga seems to have been a bishop dedicated to the well-being of the natives. Fray Juan de Zumárraga, bishop of Mexico, wrote about him to the Council of the Indies on February 8, 1537: "The deep love that this good man shows them, which he proves with the works and benefits he continually performs on their behalf with great spirit and perseverance . . ." (in Cuevas 1975, 76).

Chapter 12

1. However, Motolinía (1984, 3.5:137), expressing faithfully the duality that characterized the Franciscan mission to Nueva España, recognizes nostalgically that on certain occasions (1532–1533) they tried without success to discover new lands through the southern sea in order "to preach the gospel and word of God there, without being preceded by armed conquest." For that purpose they requested help from their protector Hernán Cortés, the most famous of the violent conquerors.

2. Although every judgment on Pané remains open to revision if the original version of this treaty is found, it seems that he considered correct Bartolomé Colón's punishment of six Indians, subjects of Guarionex, for burying some Christian statues in a farming field. The Spaniards considered it a "sacrilege" and applied the punishment decreed by Castilian law for such a "blasphemous" offense: public burning. According to José Juan Arrom (in Pané 1987, 52–54), the incident was a lamentable mistake. It was the custom of the Taínos to bury their *cemíes* in the fields to secure a good crop. They apparently tried to do the same with the Catholic "cemíes."

3. Sepúlveda is citing Aristotle's *Nicomachean Ethics* (10.9:1180a). The Athenian philosopher, however, is dealing there with the relationship between legislation

and social virtue, not with forced religious conversion.

4. Höffner (1957, 344) writes about Clement VII: "His pontificate, a fateful one for the church, saw the sacking of Rome, apostasy on the part of one third of Europe, the fight against Carlos V, with its intrigues, and also the continuation of nepotism and abuses in the apportioning of benefits."

5. Acosta wrote at a time when the Catholic church's aspiration was to evangelize the great Oriental cultures. There is in this missionary thrust a certain tiredness and disillusion with the "Western Indies." This attitude can be found in Sahagún (1985, 11.12–13:706–710), who, in one of his peculiar personal notes after mentioning the "roads" in America, suddenly changes the subject to talk about a crucially important theme: the destiny of the church in crisis because of the growth of Protestantism. Pessimistically he notes how Palestine, Asia, and Africa have eliminated Catholicism; and in Europe, excepting Italy and the Iberian peninsula, "the church is not obeyed." What about the Western Indies? There are few inhabitants left there and those may perish. Besides, the conversion of the survivors has been superficial and unreliable, "due to the stubbornness of these peoples," so that if the Spaniards leave, "there will be no trace of the preaching that has been carried out." What is then the hope of Catholicism? The evangelization of Eastern Asia, beginning with China, "where there are very intelligent people with great policies and knowledge." In Nueva España and Peru, on the contrary, the church has done "nothing more than to pass through, and scarcely has made a step forward so as to be able to converse with those peoples in the parts of China."

6. Hanke's (1959, 89–90) interpretation of Acosta makes him come excessively close to Las Casas, and mutilates their distinct ideas. He thus falls prey to the temptation, seductive and difficult to avoid, that awaits those who come close to the Spanish conquest of America: seeing the entire saga from the dominating perspective of Las Casas.

7. This hope is seemingly lost by Acosta's modern editor, who permits himself a judgment that is a clear example of the pedantic ethnocentrism that characterizes much of Catholic Spanish literature on the Christianization of the Americas. According to Francisco Mateo (in Acosta 1952, 114, 294): "This rudimentary Christianity of the Peruvian Indians can still be noted today [1952]: their faith is probably very unlike that of a white person and is filled with superstitions. . . . This is due to their feeble intelligence and to their refractory attitude toward white culture. . . . The Indians continued and are still attached to their beliefs and semibarbaric customs. . . . In the outskirts of Quito, La Paz, or Sucre, close to the homes of the Europeans [Europeans?], it does not occur to them to use electricity . . . or eat or dress or wear shoes or build their houses in the manner of the whites." An excellent specimen of social analysis!

8. In his *Apologética historia sumaria* (1967) he includes 2,673 citations from 453 works of 225 authors, according to Martínez (1974, 31). Hanke (1985, 109) refers to the torrential flow of prose from Las Casas as "that strange mixture of passion and erudition." O'Gorman (1951, 131, 142) ironically pokes fun at the Dominican friar's "undigested erudition" and "astonishing credulity" regarding apocryphal texts. Las

Casas (1986, 3.3.79:93) himself mentions his voracious reading and how he used it to find arguments in favor of his cause on behalf of the indigenous: "He never read [he refers to himself in the third person] anything in Latin or Romance languages in forty-four interminable years, in which he did not find a reason or authority to prove and corroborate the justice due these Indian people, and to condemn the injustices, harm, and evil that have been done to them." Pereña (in Las Casas 1969, cxlvii–cxlix) severely criticizes Las Casas's way of citing and shows that "his habit of arguing with the support of authorities in order to achieve political ends" leads him to the distortion of works and authors.

9. Las Casas follows closely the classic Thomistic formula on the necessary correlation between faith and free will: "nullo modo sunt ad fidem compellendi ut ipsi credant: quia credere voluntatis est" (they in no way should be compelled to believe for faith is an act of the will) (*Summa theologica* 2–2.10.8).

10. Las Casas points to an interesting theme that he does not go into deeply: to what extent have anti-Islamic Christians adopted the bellicose missionary methodology of their strongest adversaries?

11. Silva wrote and presented to the Crown a treatise in which he gathered his experiences and reflections during several decades of missionary work in America, entitled *Advertencias importantes acerca del buen gobierno y administración de las Indias, así en lo espiritual como en lo temporal* (Important advice on good government and administration of the Indies, on spiritual and temporal matters), Madrid, 1621.

12. The letter is dated May 28, 1517, and is included in Córdoba 1988 (157–163) and in J. M. Pérez 1988 (131–137).

13. Published and translated for the first time in Pereña 1956 (43). Carranza was known for his iconoclastic positions. His promotion as archbishop of Toledo did not spare him from the claws of the Spanish Inquisition and he spent several years in jail.

14. Soto would draw another obvious conclusion, implicit in the logic of Vitoria, his teacher and friend: If the baptized Indians, independently of the procedure followed in the sacrament, deviate from orthodox Catholicism, they would be subjected to the rigors of ecclesiastical heresy and apostasy. *In quartum sententiarum comentarii*, 1.5.10 (in Höffner 1957, 429).

15. According to Las Casas (1986, 1.3.14:480) they were made to repeat "the Paternoster or Ave Maria or Creed in Latin . . . as you would teach it to parrots." Mendieta (1980, 3.16:219) writes that the natives "used to say their prayers there in Latin. . . . This bore little fruit, for the Indians did not understand what they were saying, nor would they stop their idolatries."

16. A precise summary of the controversy between Dominicans and Franciscans is given by Ricard (1986, 164–180). Ricard's position is perhaps too much in solidarity with the "spiritual conquest of Mexico." He exonerates sixteenth-century Spanish missionaries, asserting that the catechumenate has been absent for most of the history of Christianity's expansion (ibid., 164). Another synthesis of the dispute, even more defensive of the missionaries, is found in Gómez Canedo 1977 (172–180).

17. This dual dimension of baptism—religious sacrament and symbol of transculturation—is always present when Christianity as the specific faith of the

West claims the conversion of followers from other historical-cultural-political worldviews. In this case, as the Jesuit philosopher of India, Michael Amaladoss (1986, 238), asserts, baptism is not just "a purely spiritual act; it is also a sociopolitical event."

18. It was a line of thought that Mendieta ([1596] 1980, 3.22:230–231), colleague and disciple of Motolinía, reiterated with even greater emphasis. In his opinion, if the conquest of Mexico was the work of Hernán Cortés, its preservation was the achievement of the Franciscan friars who placated the natives and held in check several indigenous conspiracies.

19. Among the signers were Francisco de Vitoria and Domingo de Soto. Las Casas says that the consultation had been Vitoria's, and that Las Casas had been its promoter, surely anticipating the answer from the Salamanca scholars (in Pérez de Tudela 1957, "Memorial . . . al rey," 203; in Pacheco et al. 1864–1884, 14:114). Gómez Canedo (1977, 174) calls the decision "fórmula de gabinete universitario" (the academicians' formula). He is not opposed to it, but he insists that the missionary practice required greater flexibility.

Chapter 13

1. On another occasion, in an account for the Catholic Monarchs, he alleges that certainly "King Solomon's mines" are in Española (Varela 1986, 227). The search for such "mines" was not Columbus's exclusive fantasy. The son of Martín Alfonso Pinzón, Arias Pérez, in a suit against the Admiral in 1508, claimed that his father had a writ "from Solomon's time" obtained from the Vatican that indicated the route to reach islands filled with gold, pearls, and precious stones (Las Casas 1986, 1.1.34:177).

2. "Memorial que dió el bachiller Enciso de lo ejecutado por él en defensa de los Reales derechos, en la materia de los indios" (Memorandum presented by Enciso of the things carried out by him in defense of Royal rights on the subject of the Indians) (Manzano [1948, 37], who considers the memorandum to come from around 1525) (in Pacheco et al. 1864–1884, 1.441–450).

3. Luke's text was one of the most widely discussed biblical passages by proponents and opponents of forced conversions by the state. Perhaps the first to use it against heretics was Augustine in his Epistle 93, *Ad Vencentium* (A.D. 408). He cites it as the scriptural basis for canon law and for the formulation of laws against heresy. See *Obras de San Agustín* (8:596–597). Thomas Aquinas also alludes to the biblical passage and to Augustine's Epistle in a similar sense. See *Summa theologica* (2-2.10.8). Covarrubias (in Pereña 1956, 227) also applied it to compulsory conversion but rejected its relevance to the forced conversion of infidels. Acosta (1952, 2.1:137) used the passage to legitimize "appropriate force" or "voluntary violence" in the conversion of the American natives. The Augustinian Juan de Vascones used

it in 1599 to defend the justice of the war against the Araucans and their enslavement. "Petición en derecho para el rey . . . para que los rebeldes enemigos del
reino de Chile sea declarados por esclavos" (Legal petition for the King . . . so that
the rebellious enemies of the Kingdom of Chile can be declared slaves) (in Hanke
and Millares 1977, 307). Even at the beginning of the seventeenth century the *compelle*
passage was used to justify the armed conquest of the native peoples. See the Diez
Flores introduction to the anti–Las Casas work by Vargas Machuca, "Apología y
discursos de las conquistas occidentales" (in Fabié [1879] 1966, 71:213–214). Some
missionaries used the same passage as the biblical justification for compulsory
attendance at liturgy and post-baptismal catechetical instruction. The violation of
this norm frequently carried severe physical punishment, especially public flogging.
See Gómez Canedo 1977 (177–180). In his typical apologetic style, Gómez Canedo
censures those who criticize compulsion as holding on to dreams of "missiologists
in their ivory towers," unacceptable to "veterans, those with experience in apostolic
work."

4. Las Casas (1986, 3.3.79:92–95) tells of his conversion in a bitter critique that
took place in 1514 in Cuba of the conquests and *encomiendas*. Ramos scrutinizes
this testimony in "La 'conversión' de Las Casas en Cuba: El clérigo y Diego
Velázquez," (in Saint-Lu et al. 1974, 247–257). Las Casas (1986, 1.1.24:130) alludes
to the same Sirach text in his biting criticism of the capture of African slaves by
the Portuguese. He also uses it as the basis for his argument that the church should
not accept tithing, gifts, or offerings earned through stolen goods or the forced
labor of Indians (Pérez de Tudela 1957, 520).

5. In Las Casas 1942 (443–451), citing Augustine's *De vita christiana*, considered
today by most scholars as the work of an author with Pelagian tendencies in the
fifth century. J. P. Migne, *Patrología latina* (Paris: 1887), 40:1039–1041.

6. Such a judgment is ethnocentric, of course. The first cries for justice came
from the voices of the natives trampled on by European greed.

7. On the controversy provoked by that sermon, see J. M. Pérez 1988 (passim).

8. The monarch's letter is also found, with modern spelling, in Carro 1944
(1:58–61).

9. The letter with modern spelling is fully reproduced in *De regia potestate* (Las
Casas 1969, 282–283).

10. Besides the biblical prophetic denunciations against the Hebrew monarchy,
it is probable that behind the concept of "tyranny" so often stressed by Las Casas
when characterizing the regime imposed on the Indies, there is also the tradition,
proper to Spanish realism, according to which "he who has title and power of
king, but does not do justice, is a tyrant" (Ríos 1957, 84–85). This tradition manifests
itself in the "tenth reason" found in "Octavo remedio," according to which the
encomiendas are tyrannical because they violate "the laws of Castilla" which postulate
a beneficial relation between the governed and the governing and based on the
consent of the former. "Octavo remedio" (Las Casas 1965, 2:761–763). Also in *Del
único modo* (1942, 493), Las Casas distinguishes between the king and the tyrant.
The first, in contrast to the second, governs by popular consent and for the welfare
of all.

11. In a letter of August 1555 to Bartolomé Carranza de Miranda, confessor of the Crown, Las Casas (in Fabié [1879] 1966, 71:384) stated that God does not have anything "closer to his eyes" than the events in the Indies. The Monarch's actions in that regard would determine his eternal happiness or damnation.

12. "Disputa o controversia," 439. The phrase *in solidum*, which Las Casas constantly repeats, means that the obligation to make restitution not only refers to the private profit of each conqueror, colonist, or *encomendero* but to the benefits acquired by all. It was an idea with a very sharp edge.

13. Las Casas was almost surely influenced by another work of Erasmus, "*Ecclesiastes sive . . . evangelicus*" (1535), in which he proposes the apostolic and peaceful means for evangelization. See the excellent work by Bataillon (1966).

14. Something similar was posited in 1518 by the Dominican friars in Española to the Jeronomite fathers: "The Christians' offenses have been and are great and the goods they have obtained from the work of the Indians we think are unjust; and we think that they owe restitution" (in Pacheco et al. 1864–1884, 26:213).

15. However, in a work prior to his bitter epistle against Las Casas, Motolinía (1984, 3.11:167) had stressed the obligation of the conquistadors and colonists to make restitution for whatever they had obtained from the sweat and blood of the Indians "because all these things will be presented on the day of judgment if they are not first returned here."

16. Bataillon (1976, 30) succinctly says in this regard: "On this question of the *Confesionario*, the bishop of Chiapas was defeated."

17. Pereña considers that a letter (in Las Casas 1969, App. 16, 287–292) from Pius V at the end of 1566, written in Italian and sent to the papal nuncio in Madrid, Juan Bautista Castagna, archbishop of Rosario, Argentina, in which the Supreme Pontiff insists on the good treatment of the American natives is a possible response to this proposal by Las Casas. Useful information on the Las Casas petition and Pius V's letter is found in Pérez Fernández 1981 (762–776).

18. Noted countercritics are: Hanke (1964), Giménez Fernández (1964), and Bataillon (1976, 5–42). Pérez de Tudela (1957, "Estudio," xlvii) rates Las Casas as the paradigmatic expression of the best virtues of the Spanish soul in his praise of "the integrity with which the Sevillian displayed the diamond facets of the purest archetypal soul of old Spain: rationalist idealism, stoic sobriety, cult of valor, intransigent passion for truth and justice, exaltation of the person in an unmeasured offering to altruism; that type of unrealizable madness, in short, which Don Quixote felt and universalized."

Chapter 14

1. On the dilemma of Las Casas between the adoration of the true God and the idolatry of mammon, see Gutiérrez's beautiful text in *Dios o el oro en las Indias* (1989), especially the last chapter, 135–172.

2. Cited during a "consultation of the Council of the Indies" on "the *mita* [distribution of Indians by lot to do public works; trans. note] of forced Indians" at the Potosí mines (in Konetzke 1953, 3:146). A very prudent social historian, James Lockhart (1982, 256), has no qualms affirming about the Peruvian exploitation of gold: "The gold fever in Carabaya and Quito were simply death episodes particularly horrendous."

3. One cannot forget the ethical and prophetic character of the historiography of Las Casas which does not exclude the classical method of inserting discourses and dialogues to illustrate the idea presented and defended, but whose authenticity is scarcely evident. This anecdote about gold as "the god of the Christians" is not original to Las Casas. In 1517, referring to an unnamed Indian chief, a group of friars mentions it in a letter to a counselor of Carlos V: "Carta . . . a Monsieur de Xevres" (in J. M. Pérez 1988, App., 156–157).

4. Twenty-five years before the writing of this account, Las Casas (1972, 54) tells something similar about Indians in general: "They so much abhor the Christian name that they prefer to go to hell, believing that there they would not have to talk to Christians, rather than to Paradise where they would have to talk to them."

5. Since nobody dared to repeat such an absurd accusation against the Antillean Arawaks, I am inclined to think that it is a printing error and that Diez Flores meant to write "Nueva España" instead of "ysla Española."

6. Cummins (1976, 47) finds the Admiral to have "a mystic cult towards gold."

7. The ideological motivation is principally addressed to mitigate the possible ethical scruples of the prelates. It is doubtful that the Arawaks were interested in contributing to the war of Catholic Europe against Moors and Ottomans.

8. Similar ideas relating the Indians' mining work and their spiritual nurture, but without the Jesuit's sensitivity, are found in Solórzano y Pereyra (1648) 1930 (2.15:261–272).

9. Felipe II was strongly supported by Acosta in his attempts to control the Spanish Society of Jesus, which by its constitution seemed to seek exclusive subordination to Rome and the Supreme Pontiff. Cf. John Lynch 1987 (1:335).

10. Acosta (1985, 4.2:143) alludes to this analogy without naming him. In spite of his praise of the Indians' rationality, Acosta does not avoid the typical European ethnocentrism of the times or a demeaning concept of the American natives. In his exegesis of the famous vision of the apostle Peter and the unclean animals (Acts 11:1–18), he suggests that the reptiles, the most repugnant creatures in the vision, are a prophetic reference to the Indians (1952, 1.1:54; 6:79–80).

Resources

Abellán, José Luis. 1976. "Los orígenes españoles del mito del 'buen salvaje.' Fray Bartolomé de Las Casas y su antropología utópica." *Revista de Indias* 36, nos. 145–146 (julio–diciembre):157–179.

Abril-Castelló, Vidal. "La bipolarización Sepúlveda-Las Casas y sus consecuencias: La revolución de la duodécima réplica." In Ramos et al. 1984, 229–288.

Achebe, Chinua. 1974. *Arrow of God.* New York: Anchor Books.

———. 1984. *Things Fall Apart.* New York: Fawcett Crest.

Acosta, José de, S.J. 1952. *De procuranda indorum salute (Predicación del evangelio en las Indias, 1588),* "Proemio." Ed. Francisco Mateo, S.J. Madrid: Colección España Misionera.

———. 1985. *Historia natural y moral de las Indias* (1590). México, D.F.: Fondo de Cultura Económica. [*The Natural and Moral History of the Indies.* 1970. Reprinted from the English translation by Edward Grimston, 1604, and edited with notes and introduction by Clements R. Markham. New York: B. Franklin.]

Alfonso X (the Wise). 1807. *Las siete partidas del rey D. Alfonso el Sabio.* Madrid: Real Academia de la Historia.

Allen, Don Cameron. 1949. *The Legend of Noah: Renaissance Rationalism in Art, Science, and Letters.* Urbana, Ill.: University of Illinois Press.

Alvarez de Chanca, Diego. 1945. "Carta al ayuntamiento de Sevilla." In *Colección de los viages y fines . . . See* Fernández de Navarrete 1945, 1:327–350.

Amaladoss, Michael, S.J. 1986. "Dialogue and Mission: Conflict or convergence?" *International Review of Mission* 75:222–241.

Anglería, Pedro Mártir de. 1953. "Al conde de Tendilla." Ep. 173, April 6, 1497, in *Epistolario,* vol. 1, study and translation by José López de Toro. *Documentos inéditos para la historia de España,* vol. 9. Madrid: Imprenta Góngora.

———. 1964–1965. *De orbe novo.* Latin edition, 1530. *Décadas del nuevo mundo.* 2 vols. Translated by Agustín Millares Carlo and Foreword by Edmundo O'Gorman. México, D.F.: Porrúa. References are for volume, decade, book, and page. [*The Decades of the New World or West India,* by Pietro Martire d'Anghiera. Translation from G. F. de Ovieda y Valdés (1478–1557), R. J. Eden (1480/1491–c. 1534), and Antonio Pigafetta (1480/1491–c. 1534). Ann Arbor, Mich.: University Microfilms, 1966.]

Arana Soto, Salvador. 1968. *Historia de nuestras calamidades.* San Juan.

Arcos, Miguel de. 1977. "Parecer mio sobre un tratado de la guerra que se puede hacer a los indios" (1551). In *Cuerpo de Documentos . . . See* Hanke and Millares 1977.

Arenal, Celestino del. 1975–1976. "La teoría de la servidumbre natural en el pensamiento español de los siglos XVI y XVII." *Historiografía y bibliografía americanistas* 19–20:67–124.

Arens, W. 1981. *El mito del canibalismo: Antropología y antropofagia.* México, D.F.: Siglo XXI.

Armas Medina, Fernando de. 1953. *Cristianización del Perú (1532–1600).* Sevilla: Escuela de Estudios Hispano-Americanos de la Universidad de Sevilla.

Arrom, José Juan. 1987. "Estudio Preliminar." In Ramón Pané, *Relación acerca de las antigüedades de los indios,* ed. José Juan Arrom, 52–54.

Augustine, Saint. 1958. "Carta 93: A Vicente rogatista." In *Obras de San Agustin.* Vol. 8:593–655. Madrid: Biblioteca de Autores Cristianos.

Bataillon, Marcel. 1954. "Novo mundo e fim do mundo." *Revista de Historia* (Sâo Paulo) 18:343–351.

———. 1966. *Erasmo y España: Estudios sobre la historia espiritual de siglo XVI.* México, D.F.: Fondo de Cultura Económica.

———. 1976. *Estudios sobre Bartolomé de las Casas.* Barcelona: Península.

Baudet, Henri. 1965. *Paradise on Earth: Some Thoughts on European Images of Non-European Man.* New Haven, Conn.: Yale University Press.

Benavente, Toribio de. Known as Motolinía. 1971. *Memoriales o libro de las cosas de la Nueva España y de los naturales de ella.* Ed. Edmundo O'Gorman. México, D.F.: UNAM.

———. 1984. *Historia de los indios de la Nueva España: Relación de los ritos antiguos, idolatría y sacrificios de los indios de la Nueva España, y de la maravillosa conversión que Dios en ella ha obrado.* Ed. Edmundo O'Gorman. México, D.F.: Porrúa. "Carta a Carlos V" found here, 203–221.

Biermann, Benno, O.P. 1950. "Das Requerimiento in der Spanishcen Conquista." *Neue Zeitschrift für Missionswissenschaft* 6:94–114.

Borah, Woodrow. 1962. "¿América como modelo? El impacto demográfico de la expansión europea sobre el mundo no-europeo." *Cuadernos americanos* (noviembre–diciembre):176–185.

Borges, Pedro. 1975. "Observaciones sobre la reacción al cristianismo de los aztecas, mayas e incas." In *Estudios sobre política indigenista española en América: Simposio conmemorativo del V centenario del Padre Las Casas,* 71-83. Terceras jornadas americanistas de la Universidad de Valladolid. Valladolid: Universidad de Valladolid.

Bosch, Juan. 1986. *De Cristobal Colón a Fidel Castro: El Caribe, frontera imperial.* 5th ed. Santo Domingo: Alfa y Omega.

Bowser, Frederick P. 1986. "Africans in Spanish American Colonial Society." In *The Cambridge History of Latin America,* ed. Leslie Bethell, vol. 11: *Colonial Latin America.*

Boxer, Charles R. 1978. *The Church Militant and Iberian Expansion, 1440-1770.* Baltimore: Johns Hopkins University Press.

Brady, Robert L. 1966. "The Role of Las Casas in the Emergence of Negro Slavery in the New World." *Revista de historia de America* 61-62 (enero–diciembre), 43-55.

Cárdenas Ruiz, Manuel. 1981. *Crónicas francesas de los indios caribes.* Introduction by Ricardo E. Alegría: "Las primeras noticias sobre los indios caribes," 1-89. Río Piedras: Editorial Universidad de Puerto Rico.

Carpentier, Alejo. 1979. *El arpa y la sombra.* México, D.F.: Siglo XXI.

Carro, Venancio D., O.P. 1944. *La teología y los teólogos juristas españoles ante la conquista de América.* 2 vols. Madrid: Escuela de Estudios Hispano-Americanos de la Universidad de Sevilla.

Castañeda Delgado, Paulino. 1970a. "Un capítulo de ética indiana española: Los trabajos forzados en las minas." *Anuario de estudios americanos* 27:815-916.

———. 1970b. "La política española con los Caribes durante el siglo XVI." *Revista de Indias* 119-122 (enero–diciembre):81-90.

———. 1971. "Las bulas alejandrinas y la extensión del poder indirecto." *Misionalia Hispánica* 83 (mayo–agosto):215-248.

———. 1974. "Los métodos misionales en América. ¿Evangelización pura coacción?" In *Estudios sobre Fray Bartolomé de Las Casas,* André Saint-Lu et al. Sevilla: Universidad de Sevilla.

Cieza de León, Pedro de. 1962. *La crónica del Perú* (1553). Colección Austral, 507. Madrid: Espasa Calpe.

Colección de documentos inéditos relativos al descubrimiento, conquista y organización de las antiguas posesiones españolas de Ultramar. 1885-1931. 2nd series, 24 vols. Madrid: Real Academia de Historia. "Real provisión de la reina doña Juana para que los vecinos de la Española y islas puedan hacer guerra a los caribes y hacerlos esclavos" (3 June 1511), vol. 5.

Coll y Toste, Cayetano, ed. 1914-1927. *Boletín histórico de Puerto Rico. Fuentes documentales para la historia de Puerto Rico.* 14 vols. San Juan.

Comas, Juan. 1951. "Realidad del trato dado a los indígenas de América entre los siglos xv y xx," *América Indígena* XI, 323-370.

Cook, Noble D. 1981. *Demographic Collapse: Indian Peru, 1520–1620*. Cambridge: Cambridge University Press.

Cook, Sherburne, and Woodrow Borah. 1967. "New Demographic Research on the Sixteenth Century in México." In *Latin America History: Essays on Its Study and Teachings, 1898–1965*, ed. Howard F. Cline, 717–722. Austin: University of Texas Press.

———. 1971. *Essays in Population History: Mexico and the Caribbean*. 3 vols.: *Mexico and the Caribbean* (vol. 1, 1971); *Mexico and the Caribbean* (vol. 2, 1974); *Mexico and California* (vol. 3, 1979). Berkeley and Los Angeles: University of California Press.

Córdoba, Pedro de, O.P. 1988. *Doctrina cristiana y cartas*. Biblioteca de Clásicos Dominicanos, vol. 3. Santo Domingo: Fundàción Corripio.

Córdova, Efrén. 1968. "La encomienda y la desaparición de los indios en las Antillas Mayores." *Caribbean Studies* 8, no. 3 (octubre):23–49.

Cortés, Hernán. 1985. *Cartas de relación*. México, D.F.: Editorial Porrúa. [*Five Letters of Cortés to the Emperor: The Spanish Invasion of Mexico and the Conquest of Montezuma's Empire, as Seen Through the Eyes of the Spanish Conqueror*. Translated and with an introduction by J. Bayard Morris. New York: W. W. Norton & Co., 1969/1991. First published in 1928.]

Crosby, Alfred W. 1967. "Conquistador y Pestilencia: The First New World Pandemic and the Fall of the Great Indian Empires." *Hispanic American Historical Review* 47, no. 3 (August):321–337.

Cuevas, Mariano. 1946. *Historia de la iglesia en México*. 5 vols. México, D.F.: Editorial Patria.

———. 1975. *Documentos inéditos del siglo XVI para la historia de México* [1914]. México, D.F.: Editorial Porrúa (Biblioteca Porrúa, 62).

Cummins, J. S. 1976. "Christopher Columbus: Crusader, Visionary, *Servus Dei*." In *Medieval Hispanic Studies Presented to Rita Hamilton*, ed. A. D. Deyermond, 45–55. London: Tamesis Books.

Davenport, Frances G. 1917. *European Treaties Bearing on the History of the United States and Its Dependencies to 1648*. 4 vols. Washington: Carnegie Institution.

Dávila, Gil Gonzales. 1959. *Teatro Eclesiástico de la primitiva iglesia de las Indias Occidentales, vidas de sus arzobispos, obispos, y cosas memorables de sus sedes*. 2 vols. México.

Davis, David Brion. 1961. *The Problem of Slavery in Western Culture*. Ithaca, N.Y.: Cornell University Press.

Deive, Carlos Esteban. 1980. *La esclavitud del negro en Santo Domingo (1492–1844)*. Santo Domingo: Museo del Hombre Dominicano.

Denevan, William M., ed. 1976. *The Native Population of the Americas in 1492*. Madison: University of Wisconsin Press.

Denzinger, Enrique. 1963. *El magisterio de la iglesia. Manual de los símbolos, definiciones y declaraciones de iglesia en materia de y costumbres.* Barcelona: Herder.

Díaz del Castillo, Bernal. 1986. *Historia verdadera de la conquista de la Nueva España.* México, D.F.: Editorial Porrúa. [*The True History of the Conquest of New Spain.* 5 vols. Translation with introduction and notes by Alfred Percival Maudslay. New York: Kraus Reprint 1908/1967.]

Dobyns, Henry F. 1966. "Estimating Aboriginal Population: An Appraisal of Techniques with a New Hemispheric Estimate." *Current Anthropology* 7:395–416.

Dussel, Enrique D. 1979. *El episcopado latinoamericano y la liberación de los pobres (1504–1620).* México, D.F.: Centro de Reflexión Teológica.

———. 1972. *Historia de la iglesia en América Latina.* Barcelona: Editorial Nova Terra. [*A History of the Church in Latin America: Colonialism to Liberation (1492–1979).* Grand Rapids, Mich.: Eerdmans, 1981.]

———. 1981. "Hipótesis para una historia de la teología en América Latina (1492–1980)." In *Materiales para una historia de la teología en América Latina.* VIII Encuentro latinoamericano de CEHILA, Lima, 1980. San José, Costa Rica: CEHILA DEI.

———. 1988. "Otra visión del descubrimiento: El camino hacia un desagravio histórico." *Cuadernos americanos,* nueva época, año 2, vol. 3 (9) (mayo–junio):34–41.

Elliott, John H. 1984. *El viejo mundo y el nuevo, 1492–1650.* Madrid: Alianza Editorial.

———. 1989. "The Mental World of Hernán Cortés." In *Spain and Its World, 1500–1700. Selected Essays,* ed. John H. Elliot, 27–41. New Haven, Conn.: Yale University Press.

Erasmus. 1964. "Querella de la paz" (*Querela pacis,* or The Complaint of Peace). In *Obras escogidas,* ed. Lorenzo Riber. Madrid: Aguilar.

Ercilla, Alonso de. 1984. *La Araucana.* La Habana: Editorial Arte y Literatura. [English lines are from: *The Araucaniad,* trans. Charles Maxwell Lancaster and Paul Thomas Manchester. Nashville: Vanderbilt University Press, 1945. Numbers in brackets in citations correspond to English ed. page numbers.]

Esteve Barba, Francisco. 1964. *Historiografía indiana.* Madrid: Gredos.

Fabié, Antonio M. 1879. *Vida y escritos de don Fray Bartolomé de Las Casas, Obispo de Chiapa.* 2 vols. Madrid: Imprenta de Miguel Ginesta. [Reprinted in the *Colección de documentos inéditos para la historia de España.* Vols. 70–71. Vaduz: Kraus Reprint, 1966.]

Fernández de Navarrete, Marin. 1945. *Colección de los viages y descubrimientos que hicieron por mar los españoles, desde fines del s. XV.* 2 vols. Buenos Aires: Editorial Guarania.

Fernández Méndez, Eugenio. 1984. *Las encomiendas y esclavitud de los indios de Puerto Rico, 1508–1550*. 5th illustrated ed. Río Piedras: Editorial de la Universidad de Puerto Rico.

Finley, Moses I. 1980. *Ancient Slavery and Modern Ideology*. London: Penguin Books.

Fiske, John. 1892. *The Discovery of America: With Some Account of Ancient America and the Spanish Conquest*. 2 vols. Boston: Houghton Mifflin Co.

Flores Galindo, Alberto. 1987. *Buscando un inca: Identidad y utopia en los Andes*. Lima: Instituto de Apoyo Agrario.

Frankl, Víctor. 1963. "Imperio particular e imperio universal en las cartas de relación de Hernán Cortés." *Cuadernos hispanoamericanos* 55, n. 165:443–482.

———. 1986. "Un psicológo en un campo de concentración." In *El hombre en busca de sentido*, 11–94. Barcelona: Herder.

Friede, Juan. 1953. "Fray Bartolomé de Las Casas, exponente del movimiento indigenista español del siglo XVI." *Revista de Indias* 51:25–53.

———. 1976. *Bartolomé de las Casas: Precursor del anticolonialismo*. México, D.F.: Siglo XXI.

Friederici, Georg. 1986. *El carácter del descubrimiento y de la conquista de América: Introducción a la historia de la colonización de América por los pueblos del Viejo Mundo*. México, D.F.: Fondo de Cultura Económica. [Der Charakter der Entdeckung und Eroberung Amerikas durch die Europäer. Stuttgart-Gotha: Verlag Andres Perthes, A.G., 1925–1936.]

García, Antonio. 1984. "El sentido de las primeras denuncias." In *La ética en la conquista de América*, ed. Demetrio Ramos.

Giménez Fernández, Manuel. 1944. *Nuevas consideraciones sobre la historia, sentido y valor de las bulas alejandrinas de 1493 referentes a las Indias*. Sevilla: Escuela de Estudios Hispano-Americanos de la Universidad de Sevilla.

———. 1964. "Sobre Bartolomé de Las Casas." *Anales de la Universidad Hispalense* 24 (Sevilla):1–65.

Ginés de Sepúlveda, Juan. 1951. *Demócrates segundo o de las justas causas de la guerra contra los indios*. Bilingual ed. Introduction, editing, notes, and Spanish translation by Angel Losada. Madrid: Consejo Superior de Investigaciones Científicas.

Gómez Canedo, Lino. 1967. "¿Hombres o bestias? (Nuevo exámen crítico de un viejo tópico)." *Estudios de historia Novohispana*, (México) 1:29–51.

———. 1977. *Evangelización y conquista: Experiencia franciscana en Hispanoamérica*. Contains "Carta a Carlos V," by Franciscan friar Francisco Vitoria, 223–225. México, D.F.: Porrúa.

Gómez Robledo, Antonio. *See* Vitoria 1985.

Góngora, Mario. 1974. "El Nuevo Mundo en el pensamiento escatológico de Campanella." *Anuario de estudios americanos* 31:385–408.

González Rodríguez, Jaime. 1984. "La Junta de Valladolid convocada por el Emperador." In Demetrio Ramos et al., 199–227.

Gotay, Samuel Silva. 1989. *El pensamiento cristiano revolucionario en América Latina: Implicaciones de la teología de la liberación para la sociología de la religión* (4th ed.). Río Piedras: Editorial Huracán.

Guamán Poma de Ayala, Felipe. 1988. *El primer nueva corónica y buen gobierno.* Annotated ed. by John V. Murra and Rolena Adorno. 3 vols. México, D.F.: Siglo XXI.

Guerra, Francisco. 1986. "El efecto demográfico de las epidemias tras el descubrimiento de América." *Revista de Indias* 46, no. 177 (enero-junio):41–58.

Gutiérrez de Arce, Manuel. 1954. "Regio patronato indiano (Ensayo de valoración históricocanónica)." *Anuario de estudios americanos* 11:107–168.

Gutiérrez, Gustavo. 1981. "En busca de los pobres de Jesucristo: evangelización y teología en el siglo xvi." In *Materiales para una historia de la teología en América Latina,* ed. Pablo Richard, 137–163. VIII Encuentro latinoamericano de CEHILA, Lima, Peru.

———. 1989. *Dios o el oro en las Indias (siglo XVI).* Lima: Centro de Estudios y Publicaciones.

Hamilton, Bernice. 1963. *Political Thought in Sixteenth-Century Spain: A Study of the Political Ideas of Vitoria, De Soto, Suárez, and Molina.* Oxford: Oxford University Press.

Hamilton, Earl J. 1934. *American Treasure and the Price Revolution in Spain, 1501–1650.* Cambridge: Harvard University Press.

Hanke, Lewis U. 1937. "Pope Paul III and the American Indians." *Harvard Theological Review* 30:65–102.

———. 1959. *Aristotle and the American Indians: A Study in Race Prejudice in the Modern World.* Chicago: Henry Regnery Co.

———. 1964. "More Heat and Some Light on the Spanish Struggle for Justice in the Conquest of America." *Hispanic American Historical Review* 44, no. 3 (August):293–340.

———. 1967. *La lucha española por la justicia en la conquista de América.* Madrid: Aguilar. [*The Spanish Struggle for Justice in the Conquest of America.* Philadelphia: University of Pennsylvania Press, 1949.]

———. 1985. *La humanidad es una. Estudio acerca de una querella que sobre la capacidad intelectual y religiosa de los indígenas americanos sostuvieron en 1550 Bartolomé de Las Casas y Juan Ginés de Sepúlveda.* México, D.F.: Fondo de Cultura Económica.

Hanke, Lewis U., and Agustín Millares Carlo, eds. 1977. *Cuerpo de documentos del siglo XVI sobre los derechos de España en las Indias y las Filipinas.* México, D.F.: Fondo de Cultura Económica.

Henige, David. 1978a. "On the Contact Population of Hispaniola: History as Higher Mathematics." *Hispanic American Historical Review* 58, no. 2 (May):217–237.

———. 1978b. "Reply," to Zambardino (1978). *Hispanic American Historical Review* 58, no. 4 (November):709–712.

Henríquez Ureña, Pedro. 1964. *Las corrientes literarias en la América hispánica.* México, D.F.: Fondo de Cultura Económica.

Hernáez, Francisco J., S.J. 1879. *Colección de bulas, breves y otros documentos relativos a la iglesia de América y Filipinas.* Vol. 1. Brussels: Imprenta de Alfredo Vromant.

Hernández, Ramón. 1984. "La hipótesis de Francisco de Vitoria." In Ramos et al., 345–381.

Herrejón, Carlos, ed. 1985. *Información en derecho del licenciado Quiroga sobre algunas provisiones del Real Consejo de Indias.* México, D.F.: Secretaría de Educación Pública.

Hodgen, Margaret. 1964. *Early Anthropology in the Sixteenth and Seventeenth Centuries.* Philadelphia: University of Pennsylvania Press.

Höffner, Joseph. 1957. *La ética colonial española del siglo de oro: Cristianismo y dignidad humana.* Madrid: Ediciones Cultura Hispánica.

Huddleston, Lee Eldridge. 1967. *Origins of the American Indians: European Concepts, 1492–1729.* Austin: University of Texas Press.

Jara, Alvaro. 1971. *Guerra y sociedad en Chile: La transformación de la guerra de Arauco y la esclavitud de los indios.* Santiago, Chile: Editorial Universitaria.

Jerez, Francisco de. 1947. *Verdadera relación de la conquista del Perú y provincia del Cuzco, llamada la Nueva Castilla, conquistada por Francisco Pizarro, capitán de la sacra católica real majestad del Emperador nuestro señor* (1534). Vol. 26, Ediciones Atlas. Madrid: Biblioteca de Autores Españoles.

Kant, Immanuel. 1914. "Zum ewigen Frieden" (1795), in *Schriften von 1790–1796 von Immanuel Kant* (herausgegeben von A. Buchenau, E. Cassirer, B. Kellermann). Berlin: Bruno Cassirer.

Keen, Benjamin. 1971. "The White Legend Revisited: A Reply to Professor Hanke's 'Modest Proposal.'" *Hispanic American Historical Review* 51:336–355.

Kennedy, Paul. 1987. *The Rise and Fall of the Great Powers: Economic Change and Military Conflict from 1500 to 2000.* New York: Random House.

Klein, Herbert S. 1986. "The Establishment of African Slavery in Latin America in the Sixteenth Century." In *African Slavery in Latin America and the Caribbean,* ed. H. Klein. New York: Oxford University Press.

Konetzke, Richard. 1953. *Colección de documentos para la historia de la formación social de Hispanoamerica, 1493–1810.* 3 vols. Madrid: Consejo Superior de Investigaciones Científicas.

——. 1972. *América Latina, II: La época colonial.* México, D.F.: Siglo XXI.

Kroeber, Alfred L. 1939. *Cultural and Natural Areas of Native North America.* Berkeley: University of California Publications in American Archaeology and Ethnology 38.

Lafaye, Jacques. 1988. *Los conquistadores.* México, D.F.: Siglo XXI.

Lando, Diego de. 1959. *Relación de las cosas de Yucatán.* México, D.F.: Porrúa.

Las Casas, Bartolomé de. O.P. 1942. *Del único modo de atraer a todos los pueblos a la verdadera religión.* México, D.F.: Fondo de Cultura Económica.

——. 1958. *Los tesoros del Perú.* Ed. Angel Losada. [First edition: *De Thesauris in Peru,* 1563.] Includes amendment to "Tratado comprobatorio" found in his *Tratados,* 85–349. Madrid: Consejo Superior de Investigaciones Científicas.

——. 1962. *Tratado de Indias y el doctor Sepúlveda.* Caracas: Biblioteca Nacional de la Historia.

——. 1965. Prologue to *Tratados,* by Lewis Hanke and Manuel Giménez Fernández. Transcription by Juan Pérez de Tudela and translations by Agustín Millares Carlo and Rafael Moreno. 2 vols. México, D.F.: Fondo de Cultura Económica. These documents are found here and are used extensively in the text: "*Aquí se contiene una disputa o controversia,*" 1:217–459; "*Octavo remedio,*" 2:643–849; "*Tratado comprobatorio del imperio soberano y principado universal que los reyes de Castilla y León tienen sobre las Indias,*" 2:914–1233; "*Treinta proposiciones muy jurídicas,*" 1:460–499.

——. 1967. *Apologética historia sumaria.* 2 vols. Ed. Edmundo O'Gorman. México, D.F.: Universidad Nacional Autónoma.

——. 1969. *De regia potestate* (Derecho de autodeterminación) (Right to self-determination). Vol. 4 of *Corpus Hispanorum de Pace.* "Memorial-sumario a Felipe II sobre la enajenación de los indios." Apéndice 8. Edited and with a preliminary study by Luciano Pereña Vicente. Madrid: Consejo Superior de Investigaciones Científicas.

——. 1972. *Los primeros memoriales de fray Bartolomé de Las Casas.* La Habana: Universidad de La Habana.

——. 1974. *In Defense of the Indians. The Defense of the Most Reverend Lord, Don Fray Bartolomé de las Casas, of the Order of Preachers, Late Bishop of Chiapa, Against the Persecutors and Slanderers of the Peoples of the New World Discovered Across the Seas.* Trans. and ed. Stafford Poole, C.M. De Kalb: Northern Illinois University Press.

——. 1986. Introduction and editing of *Historia de las Indias,* by Lewis Hanke. México, D.F.: Fondo de Cultura Económica. [*History of the Indies: Selections.* New York: Harper & Row, 1971.]

———. 1987. *Los indios de México y Nueva España.* In Antología de *Apologética historia sumaria,* ed. Edmundo O'Gorman. 2 vols. México, D.F.: Universidad Nacional Autónoma.

———. 1989. Introduction and notes to *Brevísima relación de la destrucción de Africa: Preludio de la destrucción de Indias. Primera defensa de los guanches y negros contra su esclavización,* by Isacio Pérez Fernández, O.P. Salamanca-Lima: Editorial San Esteban-Instituto Bartolomé de las Casas.

Lejarza, Fidel de. 1948. "Franciscanismo de Cortés y cortesianismo de los franciscanos." *Missionalia hispánica* 5:43–136.

León Portilla, Miguel. 1987. *El reverso de la conquista: Relaciones aztecas, mayas e incas.* 16th ed. México, D.F.: Editorial Joaquín Moritz.

Leturia, Pedro de, S.J. 1925. "La célebre encíclica de León XII de 24 de septiembre de 1824 sobre la independencia de América, a la luz del Archivo Vaticano." *Razón y fe* 72:31–47.

———. 1947. "La encíclica de Pío VII (30 de enero de 1816)." *Anuario de estudios americanos* 4:423–517.

———. 1959. *Época del real patronato, 1493–1800.* Vol. 1 of *Relaciones entre la Santa Sede e Hispanoamérica, 1493–1835.* Caracas: Sociedad Bolivariana de Venezuela; Rome: Universidad Gregoriana.

Levi, Primo. 1988. *The Drowned and the Saved.* London: Abacus.

Levillier, Roberto. 1935. *Don Francisco de Toledo, supremo organizador del Perú: su vida, su obra (1515–1582).* Buenos Aires: Biblioteca del Congreso Argentino.

———. 1921–1926. *Gobernantes del Perú, cartas y papeles.* In *Documentos del Archivo de Indias* (14 vols.). Madrid: Sucesores de Rivadeneyra 3:327.

Lockhart, James. 1972. "The Social History of Colonial Spanish America: Evolution and Potential." *Latin-American Research Review* 7, no. 1 (Spring):6–45.

———. 1982. *El mundo hispanoperuano, 1532–1560.* México, D.F.: Fondo de Cultura Económica.

Logan, Rayford W. 1932. "The Attitude of the Church Toward Slavery Prior to 1500." *Journal of Negro History* 17:466–480.

Lohmann Villena, Guillermo. 1966. "La restitución por conquistadores y encomenderos: Un aspecto de la incidencia lascasiana en el Perú." *Anuario de estudios americanos* 23:21–89.

López Baralt, Mercedes. 1985. *El mito taíno: Levi-Strauss en las Antillas.* Río Piedras: Editorial Huracán.

López de Gómara, Francisco. 1946. *Historia General de las Indias* (1552) (155–294) and *Segunda parte de la historia general de las Indias: La conquista de Méjico* (295–455). Vol. 22 of *Biblioteca de Autores Españoles,* ed. Enrique de Vedía. Madrid: Ediciones Atlas.

López de Palacios Rubios, Juan, and Matías de Paz. 1954. *De las islas del mar océano* (1–209); *Del dominio de los reyes de España sobre los indios.* Published in one volume with an introduction by Silvio A. Zavala and trans. Agustín Millares Carlo. Buenos Aires-Mexico D.F.: Fondo de Cultura Económica.

Losada, Angel. 1948. "Hernán Cortés en la obra del cronista Sepúlveda." *Revista de Indias* 31–32:127–162.

———. 1949. *Juan Ginés de Sepúlveda a través de su "Epistolario" y nuevos documentos.* Madrid: Consejo Superior de Investigaciones Científicas.

Lucena, Manuel. 1984. "Crisis de la conciencia nacional: Las dudas de Carlos V," 163–198. In Ramos et al.

Lynch, John S. 1987. *Imperio y absolutismo (1516–1598).* Vol. 1 of *España bajo los Austrias.* Barcelona: Ediciones Península.

Malley, François. 1986. "Las Casas y las teologías de la liberación" In *Selecciones de teología* 25, no. 100 (octubre–diciembre):254–264.

Maltby, William S. 1982. *La leyenda negra en Inglaterra: Desarrollo del sentimiento antihispánico, 1558–1660.* México, D.F.: Fondo de Cultura Económica.

Manzano Manzano, Juan. 1948. *La incorporación de las Indias a la corona de Castilla.* Madrid: Ediciones Cultura Hispánica.

Maravall, José Antonio. 1949. "La utopía político-religiosa de los franciscanos en Nueva España." *Estudios americanos* 1:199–227.

———. 1974. "Utopia y primitivismo en Las Casas." *Revista de Occidente* 141 (diciembre):311–388.

Martel de Witte, Charles. 1953, 1954, 1956, 1958. "Les bulles pontificales et l'expansion portugaise au XVe siecle." *Revue d'histoire ecclésiastique* 48:683–718; 49:438–461; 51:413–453, 809–836; 53:5–46, 443–471.

Martí, José. 1981. *La edad de oro.* La Habana: Gente Nueva.

Martínez, Manuel M. 1974. "Las Casas-Vitoria y la bula *Sublimis Deus.*" In *Estudios sobre Fray Bartolomé de Las Casas.* See Saint-Lu 1974:25–51.

Maxwell, John Francis. 1975. *Slavery and the Catholic Church: The History of Catholic Teaching Concerning the Moral Legitimacy of the Institution of Slavery.* Chichester and London: Barry Publishers.

Meier, Johannes. 1986. "La presencia de las órdenes religiosas en el Caribe durante la dominación española (1500–1630)." *Missionalia Hispanica* 43, no. 124:363–372.

Mellafe, Rolando. 1964. *La esclavitud en Hispanoamérica.* Buenos Aires: EUDEBA.

Mendieta, Gerónimo de. 1980. *Historia eclesiástica indiana* [1596]. 3rd facsimile ed. México, D.F.: Editorial Porrúa.

Menéndez Pidal, Ramón. 1942. "La lengua de Cristóbal Colón." In *El estilo de Santa Teresa y otros estudios sobre el siglo XVI*. Buenos Aires: Espasa Calpe.

———. 1963. *El padre Las Casas, su doble personalidad*. Madrid: Espasa Calpe.

Mergal Llera, Angel M. 1949. *Reformismo cristiano y alma española*. México, D.F.-Buenos Aires: La Aurora-Casa Unida de Publicaciones.

Milhou, Alain. 1975–1976. "Las Casas frente a las reivindicaciones de los colonos de la isla Española." *Historiografía y bibliografía americanistas*. 19–20:11–67.

Mires, Fernando. 1986. *En nombre de la cruz: Discusiones teológicas y políticas frente al holocausto de los indios (período de conquista)*. San José: Departamento Ecuménico de Investigaciones.

———. 1987. *La colonización de las almas: Misión y conquista en Hispanoamérica*. San José: Departamento Ecuménico de Investigaciones.

Miró Quesada C., Francisco. 1987. "V Centenario del descubrimiento: ¿celebración o conmemoración?" *Diálogo* (March):31.

Montaigne, Miguel de. 1968. "De los caníbales." In *Ensayos*, vol. 1. Barcelona: Editorial Iberia.

Morales Padrón, Francisco. 1955. "Descubrimiento y toma de posesión." In *Anuario de estudios americanos*, 12:321–380.

———. 1979. *Teoría y leyes de la conquista*. Madrid: Ediciones Cultura Hispánica.

Morales Padrón, Francisco, ed. 1988. "Comentarios de Alvar Nuñez Cabeza de Vaca, adelantado y gobernador del Río de la Plata." In *Naufragios y comentarios* (1552), by Alvar Nuñez Cabeza de Vaca. México, D.F.: Editorial Porrúa.

Motolinía. *See* Benavente, Toribio de.

Movimiento Ecuménico por los Derechos Humanos (Buenos Aires), INFORMEDH, no. 56 (October 1987):8.

Moya Pons, Frank. 1978. *La Española en el siglo XVI, 1493–1520: Trabajo, sociedad y política en la economía del oro*. 3rd ed. Santiago, Dominican Republic: Universidad Católica Madre y Maestra.

Muro Orejón, Antonio. 1959. "Las leyes nuevas, 1542–1543." *Anuario de Estudios Americanos* 16:561–619.

Nenadich Deglans, Ramón. 1986–1987. "La ideología de la conquista y colonización de América." *Método y sentido*, Universidad de Puerto Rico, Colegio Regional de Aguadilla 6/7 (junio):19–28.

Nuñez Cabeza de Vaca, Alvar. 1988. *Naufragios y comentarios* (1552). Ed. Francisco Morales Padrón. México, D.F.: Editorial Porrúa.

O'Gorman, Edmundo. 1951. *La idea del descubrimiento de América: Historia de esa interpretación y crítica de sus fundamentos*. México, D.F.: Universidad Nacional Autónoma de México.

———. 1984. *La invención de America: Investigación acerca de la estructura histórica del Nuevo Mundo y del sentido de su devenir.* México, D.F.: Fondo de Cultura Económica.

O'Neil, Charles J. 1953. "Aristotle's Natural Slave Reexamined." *The New Scholasticism* 27, 3 (July):247–279.

Olaechea Labayen, Juan B. 1958. "Opinión de los teólogos españoles sobre dar estudios mayores a los indios." *Anuario de estudios americanos* 15:113–200.

Ortega y Medina, Juan A. 1987. *La idea colombina del descubrimiento desde México (1836–1986).* México, D.F.: UNAM.

Ortíz, Fernando. 1978. "La 'leyenda negra' contra fray Bartolomé de las Casas." *Cuadernos americanos* 217, no. 2 (marzo–abril):84–116.

Ots Capdequí, José María. 1986. *El estado español en las Indias.* 7th reprint. México, D.F.: Fondo de Cultura Económica.

Otte, Enrique. 1975. "Los jerónimos y el tráfico humano en el Caribe: Una rectificación." *Anuario de estudios americanos* 32:187–204.

Oviedo y Valdés, Gonzalo F. de. 1851. *Historia general y natural de las Indias, islas y tierra firme del mar Océano.* Madrid: Real Academia de Historia. References are to volume, part, book, chapter, and page.

Pacheco, Joaquín F., Francisco de Cárdenas, and Luis Torres de Mendoza, eds. 1864–1884. *Colección de documentos inéditos relativos al descubrimiento, conquista y organización de las antiguas posesiones españolas de América y Oceanía, sacados de los Archivos del Reino y muy especialmente del de Indias.* Vols. 1–31. Madrid: Real Academia de la Historia.

Pagden, Anthony. 1982. *The Fall of Natural Man: The American Indian and the Origins of Comparative Ethnology.* Cambridge: Cambridge University Press.

Pané, Ramón. 1987. *Relación acerca de las antigüedades de los indios.* Ed. José Juan Arrom. México, D.F.: Siglo XXI.

Pastor, Beatriz. 1984. *Discurso narrativo de la conquista de América.* Award-winning essay for Casa de las Américas historical contest in 1983. La Habana: Casa de las Américas.

Patiño, Victor Manuel. 1966. "La historia natural en la obra de Bartolomé de Las Casas." *Revista de historia de América* (México) 61–62:167–186.

Pereña Vicente, Luciano. 1956. *Misión de España en América (1540–1560).* Includes *De iustitia belli adversus indos (1548)*, by Diego de Covarrubias, and Bartolomé de Carranza's 1540 lecture in Valladolid. Madrid: Consejo Superior de Investigaciones Científicas.

———. 1984. "La Escuela de Salamanca y la duda indiana." In Ramos et al. 1984.

Pereña Vicente, Luciano, et al. 1982. "Parecer cerca de dar los yndios perpetuos del Perú a los encomenderos." In *Juan de la Peña: De bello contra insulanos. Intervención de España en América. Escuela española de la paz. Segunda generación, 1560–1585. Posición de la corona*, vol. 9, *Corpus Hispanorum de Pace*. Madrid: Consejo Superior de Investigaciones Científicas.

Pérez, Juan Manuel, O.P. 1988. *¿Éstos no son hombres?* "Carta al Rey de Fray Pedro de Córdoba," Apéndice 3; "Carta del padre fray Pedro de Córdoba al padre fray Antonio Montesino," Apéndice 5. Santo Domingo: Fundación García-Arévalo.

Pérez de Tudela, Juan. 1957. "Estudio crítico preliminar." In *Obras escogidas de Bartolomé de las Casas*. Ediciones Atlas. "Memorial de Fray Bartolomé de las Casas y Fray Rodrigo de Andrada al Rey," vol. 5:181–203. "Tratado de las doce dudas," vol. 110. [trans. Luis N. Rivera Pagán from Latin original], 1958. Madrid: Biblioteca de Autores Españoles.

———. 1958. "La gran reforma carolina de las Indias en 1542." *Revista de Indias* (Madrid) 18:73–74:463–509.

Pérez Fernández, Isacio. 1981. *Inventario documentado de los escritos de Fray Bartolomé de las Casas*. Bayamón, Puerto Rico: CEDOC.

———. 1984. *Cronología documentada de los viajes, estancias y actuaciones de Fray Bartolomé de las Casas*. Bayamón, Puerto Rico: CEDOC.

———. 1988. "Cronología comparada de las intervenciones de Las Casas y Vitoria en los asuntos de América (pauta básica para la comparación de sus doctrinas)." *Studium* (Madrid) 28, fasc. 2:235–264.

Pérez Villanueva, Joaquín, and Bartolomé Escandell Bonet. 1984. *Historia de la Inquisición en España y América*. Vol. 1: *El conocimiento científico y el proceso histórico de la Institución (1478–1834)*. Madrid: Biblioteca de Autores Cristianos, Centro de Estudios Inquisitoriales.

Phelan, John Leddy. 1956. *The Millennial Kingdom of the Franciscans in the New World: A Study of the Writings of Gerónimo de Mendieta (1526–1604)*. Berkeley and Los Angeles: University of California Press.

———. 1974. "El imperio cristiano de Las Casas, el imperio español de Sepúlveda y el imperio milenario de Mendieta." *Revista de Occidente* 141 (diciembre):292–310.

Phelps de Córdova, Loretta. 1989. "Some Slaves Had Smallpox Which Spread, Killing Many." *San Juan Star*, November 21, 1989, p. 18.

Pinelo, Antonio León. 1943. *El paraíso en el Nuevo Mundo. Comentario apologético, historia natural y peregrina de las Indias Occidentales*. Ed. Raúl Porras Barrenechea. Lima: Comité del IV Centenario del Descubrimiento del Amazonas.

Powell, Philip W. 1985. *La guerra chichimeca, 1550–1600*. México, D.F.: Fondo de Cultura Económica.

Queraltó Moreno, Ramón Jesús. 1976. *El pensamiento filosófico-político de Bartolomé de las Casas*. Sevilla: Escuela de Estudios Hispanoamericanos de la Universidad de Sevilla.

Quirk, Robert E. 1954. "Some Notes on a Controversial Controversy: Juan Ginés de Sepúlveda and Natural Servitude," *Hispanic American Historical Review* 34, no. 3 (August):357–364.

Ramos, Demetrio. 1975. "Actitudes ante los Caribes desde su conocimiento indirecto hasta la capitulación de Valladolid de 152." In *Estudios sobre política indigenista española en América: Simposio conmemorativo del V centenario del Padre Las Casas*. Terceras jornadas americanistas de la Universidad de Valladolid. Valladolid: Universidad de Valladolid.

———. 1976. "Sepúlveda, cronista indiano, y los problemas de su crónica." In *Juan Ginés de Sepúlveda y su crónica indiana. En el cuarto centenario de su muerte, 1573–1973*. Valladolid: Universidad de Valladolid.

———. 1984. "El hecho de la conquista de América." In *La ética. See* Ramos et al., 1984.

Ramos, Demetrio, et al. 1984. *La ética en la conquista de América*. Vol. 25, *Corpus Hispanorum de Pace*. Madrid: Consejo Superior de Investigaciones Científicas.

Recopilación de las Leyes de los Reinos de las Indias. 1841. Mandadas a imprimir y publicar por la Magestad Católica del Rey Don Carlos II, Nuestro Señor. 4 vols. 5th ed. Madrid: Boix, Editor. References are to volume, book, title, law, and page.

Remesal, Antonio de. 1932. *Historia general de las Indias Occidentales y particular de la gobernación de Chiapa y Guatemala (1619)*. Guatemala: Biblioteca "Goathemala."

Ricard, Robert. 1986. *La conquista espiritual de México. Ensayo sobre el apostolado y los métodos misioneros de las ordenes mendicantes en la Nueva España de 1523–24 a 1572*. México, D.F.: Fondo de Cultura Económica.

Ríos, Fernando de los. 1957. *Religión y estado en la España del siglo XVI*. México, D.F.: Fondo de Cultura Económica.

Rodríguez León, O.P., Mario A. 1989. *Fray Bartolomé de las Casas y la teología de la liberación: Entrevista a Gustavo Gutiérrez*. Toa Alta, Puerto Rico: Convento Santo Domingo de Guzmàn.

Rosenblat, Angel. 1954. *La población indígena y el mestizaje en América* 2 vols. Buenos Aires: Editorial Nova.

———. 1967. *La población de América en 1492: Viejos y nuevos cálculos*. México, D.F.: Colegio de México.

Rumeu de Armas, Antonio. 1975. "Esclavitud del infiel y primeros atisbos de libertad." In *Estudios sobre política indigenista española en América: Simposio conmemorativo del V centenario del Padre Las Casas*. Terceras jornadas americanistas de la Universidad de Valladolid. Valladolid: Universidad de Valladolid.

Russell, Frederick H. 1975. *The Just War in the Middle Ages.* Cambridge: Cambridge University Press.

Sahagún, Bernardino de. 1985. *Historia general de las cosas de Nueva España* (1582). Ed. Angel María Garibay. México, D.F.: Editorial Porrúa.

Saint-Lu, André. 1974. *Estudios sobre Fray Bartolomé de Las Casas.* Sevilla: Universidad de Sevilla.

Salas, Alberto Mario. 1950. *Las armas de la conquista.* Buenos Aires: Emecé Editores.

———. 1986. *Tres cronistas de Indias: Pedro Mártir de Anglería, Gonzalo Fernández de Oviedo, Fray Bartolomé de las Casas.* 2nd ed. corrected and enlarged. México, D.F.: Fondo de Cultura Económica.

Salvá, Miguel, and Pedro Sainz de Baranda, eds. 1848. "Anónimo de Yucay." In *Colección de documentos inéditos para la historia de España.* Vol. 13:425–469. Madrid: Imprenta de la Viuda de Calero, 1848. [Reprinted by Vaduz: Kraus Reprint, 1964.]

Sánchez Albornoz, Nicolás. 1986. "Population of Colonial Spanish America." In *The Cambridge History of Latin America.* Vol. 2: *Colonial Latin America,* ed. Leslie Bethell, 3–35. Cambridge: Cambridge University Press.

Sanders, William T. 1976. "The Population of the Central Mexican Symbiotic Region, the Basin of Mexico, and the Teotihuacán Valley in the Sixteenth Century." In *The Native Population of the Americas in 1492,* ed. William M. Denevan, 85–150. Madison: University of Wisconsin Press.

Sandoval, Alonso de. 1987. *Naturaleza, policia sagrada i profana, costumbres i ritos, disciplina i catecismo evangelico de todos etiopes.* Sevilla, 1627; revised, 1647. Reedited as *Un tratado sobre la esclavitud.* Introduction, transcription, and translation by Enriqueta Vila Vilar. Madrid: Alianza Editorial.

Sarmiento de Gamboa, Pedro. 1942. *Historia de los incas* [1572]. Buenos Aires: Emecé Editores.

Sauer, Carl Ortwin. 1984. *Descubrimiento y dominación española del Caribe.* México, D.F.: Fondo de Cultura Económica.

Scammel, G. V. 1969. "The New Worlds and Europe in the Sixteenth Century." *Historical Journal* 12 (3):389–412.

Schlaifer, Robert. 1936. "Greek Theories of Slavery from Homer to Aristotle." *Harvard Studies in Classical Philology* 47:165–204.

Scott, James Brown. 1934. *The Spanish Origin of International Law. Francisco de Vitoria and His Law of Nations.* London: Oxford University Press.

Sepúlveda. See Ginés de Sepúlveda.

Servin, Manuel. 1857. "Religious Aspects of Symbolic Acts of Sovereignty." *The Americas* 13:255–267.

Shiels, William Eugene, S.J. 1961. *King and Church: The Rise and Fall of the Patronato Real.* Chicago: Loyola University Press.

Shirley, Rodney W. 1983. *The Mapping of the World: Early Printed World Maps, 1472–1700.* London: Hollander Press.

Sio, Arnold A. 1965. "Interpretations of Slavery: The Slave Status in the Americas." In *Comparative Studies in Society and History* 7, (April): 289–308.

Sobrino, Jon. 1986. "Lo divino de la lucha por los derechos humanos." In *Páginas* (Lima, Perú) 11, no. 18, Separata no. 78, 1–7.

Solórzano y Pereyra, Juan de. 1930. *Política indiana* (1648). Madrid: Compañia Ibero Americana de Publicaciones.

Soto, Domingo de. 1967. *De la justicia y del derecho* (1556). 4 vols. Introduction by Venancio Diego Carro. Trans. Marcelino González Ordoñez. Madrid: Instituto de Estudios Políticos. References are given by volume, book, question, article, and page.

Staedler, E. 1937. "Die 'donatio Alexandrina' und die 'divisio mundi' von 1493. Eine kirchenrechtliche Studie." *Archiv für katolisches Kirchenrecht* 117:3–4 (Mainz):363–402.

Strachey, William. 1953. *The Historie of Travell into Virginia Britania* (w. 1612; pub. 1849). London: Hakluyt Society.

Suárez de Peralta, Juan. 1949. *Tratado del descubrimiento de las Indias y su conquista* [1878]. Reedited as *Noticias históricas de Nueva España.* México, D.F.: Secretaría de Educación Pública.

Sued Badillo, Jalil. 1978. *Los caribes: Realidad o fábula. Ensayo de rectificación histórica.* Río Piedras: Editorial Antillana.

———. 1989. *La mujer indígena y su sociedad.* 2nd ed. Río Piedras: Editorial Cultural.

Sued Badillo, Jalil, and Angel López Cantos. 1986. *Puerto Rico negro.* Río Piedras: Editorial Cultural.

Sylvest, Edwin E., Jr. 1975. *Motifs in Franciscan Mission Theory in Sixteenth Century New Spain Province of the Holy Gospel.* Washington, D.C.: Academy of American Franciscan History.

Tannenbaum, Frank. 1946. *Slave and the Citizen: The Negro in the Americas.* New York: Vintage Books.

Terradas Soler, Juan. 1962. *Una epopeya misionera: La conquista y colonización de America vistas desde Roma.* Madrid: Ediciones y Publicaciones Españolas.

Testamento y codicilio de Isabel la Católica. 1956. Madrid: Dirección General de Relaciones Culturales del Ministerio de Relaciones Exteriores.

Tobar, Balthasar de. 1954. *Compendio bulario índico (ca. 1694)*. Ed. Manuel Gutiérrez de Arce. Sevilla: Publicaciones de la Escuela de Estudios Hispanoamericanos.

Todorov, Tzvetan. 1987. *La conquista de América: La cuestión del otro*. México, D.F.: Siglo XXI. [French original: *La conquête de l'Amérique, la question de l'autre*. 1982.]

Uncein Tamayo, Luis Alberto. 1981. "El humanismo y las Indias." *Revista de historia de América* 92 (julio–diciembre):71–97.

Urdanoz, Teófilo, O.P., ed. 1960. *Obras de Francisco Vitoria: Relaciones teológicas*. *Edición crítica del texto latino, versión española, introducción general e introducciones con el estudio de su doctrina teológico-jurídica*. Madrid: Biblioteca de Autores Cristianos.

Valle, Rafael H. 1946. *Santiago en América*. México, D.F.: Editorial Santiago.

Varela, Consuelo, ed. 1986. *Los cuatro viajes. Testamento*. Madrid: Alianza Editorial. [*The Four voyages of Columbus: A History in Eight Documents, Including Five by Christopher Columbus, in the Original Spanish, with English Translations*. Translated and edited with an introduction and notes by Cecil Jane. Two volumes in one. New York: Dover Publications, 1988. It is a slightly altered and corrected republication of Nos. LXV and LXX of the second series of works published by the Hakluyt Society, London, in 1930 and 1933 respectively.]

Varela, Consuelo. 1982. "Prólogo," *Textos y documentos completos: Relaciones de viajes, cartas y memoriales*. Madrid: Alianza Editorial.

Vega, Lope de. 1968. *Famosa Comedia del Nuevo Mundo, descubierto por Cristobal Colón*. Vol. 215, Ediciones Atlas. Madrid: Biblioteca de Autores Españoles.

Verlinden, Charles. 1951. "Le problème de la continuité en histoire coloniale: de la colonisation médiévale à la colonisation moderne." *Revista de Indias* 11:219–236.

———. 1968. "Le 'repartimiento' de Rodrigo de Albuquerque a Española en 1514: Aux origines d'une importante institution économico-sociale de l'empire espagnol." In *Mélanges offerts à G. Jacquemyns*, 633–646. Brussels: Éditions de l'Institut de Sociologie, Université Libre de Bruxelles.

Vespucci, Amerigo. 1951. *El Nuevo Mundo, cartas relativas a sus viajes y descubrimientos*. Text in Italian, Spanish, and English. Edited with a preliminary study by Roberto Levillier. Buenos Aires: Editorial Nova.

Vicens Vives, Jaime. 1972. *Manual de historia económica*. Barcelona: Editorial Vicens-Vives.

Vignaud, Henry. 1917. *Americ Vespuce, 1451–1512*. Paris: Ernest Leroux, Éditeur.

Villegas, Juan, S.J. 1976. "Providencialismo y denuncia en la 'Historia de las Indias' de Fray Bartolomé de las Casas." In *Bartolomé de las Casas (1474–1974) e historia de la iglesia en América Latina*, 19–44. Edited by the Comisión de Estudios de Historia de la Iglesia en Latinoamérica. Barcelona: Nova Terra.

Vitoria, Francisco de. 1967. *Relectio de indis o libertad de los indios.* Edited by Luciano Pereña Vicente and J. M. Peres Prendes. "Carta de Francisco de Vitoria al P. Arcos," Appendix I, 137–139. Vol. 10, *Corpus Hispanorum de Pace.* Madrid: Consejo Superior de Investigaciones Científicas.

———. 1967. Introduction to *Relecciones. Del estado, De los indios y Del derecho de la guerra*, by Antonio Gómez Robledo, ix–xc. México, D.F.: Editorial Porrúa.

Washburn, Wilcomb E. 1962. "The Meaning of 'Discovery' in the Fifteenth and Sixteenth Centuries." *American Historical Review* 68 (October):1–21.

Weckmann, Luis. 1949. *Las bulas alejandrinas de 1493 y la teoría política del papado medieval: Estudio de la supremacia papal sobre las islas.* México, D.F.: Universidad Nacional Autónoma de México.

Xirau, Ramón, ed. 1973. *Idea y querella de la Nueva Espana.* Madrid: Alianza Editorial.

Yáñez, Agustin, ed. *Fray Bartolomé de Las Casas: Doctrina.* México, D.F.: Universidad Nacional Autónoma de México.

Ybot León, Antonio. 1948. "Juntas de teólogos asesoras del estado para Indias 1512–1550," *Anuario de estudios americanos* 5:397–438.

Zambardino, R. A. 1978. "Critique of David Henige's 'On the Contact Population of Hispaniola: History as Higher Mathematics.'" *Hispanic American Historical Review* 58, no. 4 (November):700–708.

Zavala, Silvio. 1935. *La encomienda indiana.* Madrid: Centro de Estudios Históricos.

———. 1937. "Hernán Cortés y la teoria escolástica de la justa guerra." In *La 'Utopia' de Tomás Moro en la Nueva España y otros estudios.* México, D.F.: Porrúa.

———. 1944. "¿Las Casas esclavista?" *Cuadernos Americanos*, Año 3, 2, 149–154.

———. 1949. "Los trabajadores antillanos en el siglo XVI." In *Estudios indianos*, 95–203. México, D.F.: Colegio Nacional.

———. 1971. *Las instituciones jurídicas en la conquista de América.* 2nd ed. revised and enlarged. México, D.F.: Porrúa.

———. 1981. "Hernán Cortés ante la justificación de la conquista." *Revista de Historia de América* 92 (julio–diciembre):49–69.

———. 1984. *La filosofía política en la conquista de América.* 3rd ed. revised and enlarged. México, D.F.: Fondo de Cultura Económica.

———. 1988. "Exámen del título de la conmemoración del V centenario del descubrimiento de América." *Cuadernos Americanos*, Nueva época, Año 2, vol. 3 (9) (mayo–junio):14–20.

Zorraquín Becú, Ricardo. 1975. "Esquema del derecho internacional de las Indias." *Anuario de estudios americanos* 32:573–597.

Zweig, Stefan. 1942. *Américo Vespucio: Historia de una inmortalidad a la que América debe su nombre.* Buenos Aires: Editorial Claridad.

Subject Index

Acosta, José de, 218, 225, 300n16; Christianization and, 233, 311n9, 314n5, 316n3; Cortés and, 61–62; *De procuranda indorum salute*, 220–223; gold and, 264–265, 274n6; *Historia natural y moral de las Indias*, 61–62; native religion and, 158, 159, 167; native social ethics and, 164–165; taxonomy of barbarians, 102; theological-juridical debates and, 206–207; view of natives, 133, 134, 136, 139, 150, 152, 296n2, 319n10

Africa, 28–29, 290n6. *See also* black slavery

Alexander VI (pope): corruption of, 25–26, 278n5; *Dudum siquidem*, 25 (*see also* Alexandrian bulls); *Inter caetera*, 25, 29–32, 194 (*see also* Alexandrian bulls); Las Casas on, 59; Machiavelli's *The Prince* and, 25; papal authority and, 26–28, 38–41, 66–67; quoted, 24; writing of papal bulls and, 279n6. *See also* Alexandrian bulls

Alexandrian bulls: authorship of, 279n6, 280n16; distinctions among, 278n2; enslavement of natives and, 97–98, 292n11; Las Casas and, 67, 68; *Patronato Real* and, 279n14; *Requerimiento* and, 35, 280n22; Spanish jurisdiction in New World and, 12, 24–32; Vitoria's reinterpretation of, 79–86

America, as name of New World, 5–7

Animus dominandi, 18, 277n35

"*Anónimo de Yucay,*" 64, 74–75, 131, 266, 290n32, 311n4

anthropophagy, 102–103, 158, 159–160, 293n15. *See also* cannibalism

Antilles (Española): alliances among natives and, 293n18; blacks in, 17, 184–185, 277n28; expropriation of, 8, 13; native depopulation in, 170, 173–174, 175, 176, 177, 178, 188, 226–227, 305n3, 306n8; rebellion in, 13; settlement of, 188

Araucans, 105–108, 295n26, 295n27

Arawaks, 293n18, 294n20, 319n5, 319n7

Aristotelian theory, slavery in, 91, 102, 110–111, 144–146, 185, 221

authority. *See* native self-determination; papal authority; royal authority

Aztec calendar, 165, 304n7

Aztec empire, 124

baptism, sacrament of: baptisms en masse and, 230; Las Casas's view of forced baptism and, 231–234; politicization of, 229–234, 316n17; prevention of blasphemy by force and, 289n22; prior to execution, 207–209

barbarians: Acosta's typology of, 221–223; Aristotelian argument and, 144–146; enslavement of, 110–111; European barbarisms and, 294n2; in taxonomy of human types, 102, 146. *See also* bestiality of natives; humanity of natives; slavery

Benavente, Toribio de (Motolinía), 16, 250, 313n1; evangelization and, 219, 230; gold and, 274n6; Las Casas and, 57–58, 240, 255, 305n1, 307n13, 311n4; native depopulation and, 170, 172, 178, 260, 306n8, 312n12; native religion and, 164, 166; providentialist messianism of, 57–58, 61, 157

education of natives and, 44; *encomienda* system and, 116, 120; enslavement of natives and, 100; Montesinos's sermon on justice and, 243
Franciscan monks of Nueva España ("twelve apostles"), 109–110, 157, 316*n*18
freedom. *See* humanity of natives; native self-determination; natural freedom, principle of

genocide. *See* native depopulation
Ginés de Sepúlveda, Juan, 111; Aristotelian theory and, 110, 111, 134–135, 145, 295*n*31, 313*n*3; censure of Las Casas, 250, 255; *Demócrates primo*, 207; *Demócrates segundo o de las justas causas de la guerra contra los indios*, 51, 207, 299*n*7, 310*n*1; dispute between Las Casas and, 25, 31–32, 68–69, 70–71, 78–79, 136, 159, 192, 193, 213, 236–237; forceful conversion of natives and, 219; humanity of natives and, 134–136, 145; just war concept and, 210–211; national religious superiority and, 51; native religion and, 260; printing of writings of, 201; slavery and, 110, 111, 145
gold, 319*n*2; as bait for missionary enterprise, 264–265; as god of conquistadors, 259–266; transferred to Europe, 24, 278*n*1. *See also encomienda* system; greed; mines of King Solomon; mining
greed: anti-idolatry movements and, 166; conversion by force and, 224–225, 227–228; debate on bestiality of natives and, 137–141, 143; gold as god of conquistadors and, 259–266; native depopulation and, 120, 177, 261, 312*n*12; providentialist result of, 264–266

heresy: baptized natives and, 315*n*14; conversion and, 316*n*3; infidels vs. heretics and, 54, 213–215, 284*n*21,

313*n*16; military escorts for missionaries as, 225; use of force against, 50, 53–55, 213–215, 218, 220
Hispanicity: Catholic orthodoxy and, 49–55; elegy to, 18–20; patriotism of Las Casas and, 254–257
Holocaust, 306*n*6
humanity of natives: criteria for, 300*n*14; debate over humanness and, 133–153; doctrine of single origin and, 302*n*22; juridical acceptance of, 147–148; Las Casas's position on, 141–144; persistence of inferiority thesis and, 148–150; theological acceptance of, 147
human sacrifice, 158–159, 261

idolatry: gold as god of conquistadors and, 259–266; moral corruption linked to, 299*n*9; native religion as, 155–160, 290*n*5; origin of, 156; Spanish destruction of temples and, 160–168
Indies: as term, 274*n*12
infidels: definition of, 281*n*26; enslavement of, 90–93, 190; vs. heretics, 54, 213–215, 284*n*21, 313*n*16; just war concept and, 212–213. *See also* Muslims
Inka monarchy: as bloody tyranny, 124–125, 286*n*2; conquest of, 290*n*32, 290*n*33
Inquisition, 51–53, 194, 250–251, 311*n*4, 315*n*13
international law, 79–86, 289*n*24
Isabel (Catholic Monarch): cannibals and, 33, 99; *encomienda* system and, 116, 122; policy on treatment of natives, 25, 43–44, 122, 282*n*1, 291*n*10; Will and Testament of, 25, 43–44, 248, 282*n*1

Jeronomite fathers: and peaceful evangelization, 227–228
Jews, 283*n*11, 283*n*14, 289*n*22
juridical principle: enslavement of Africans and, 190; foundations for royal authority and, 282*n*3; humanity of natives and, 147–148; principle of natural freedom and, 110–112, 291*n*10.

Name Index

Abril-Castelló, Vidal, 70, 288n17, 299n7

Acosta, José de, 218, 225, 300n16; Christianization and, 233, 311n9, 314n5, 316n3; Cortés and, 61–62; *De procuranda indorum salute*, 220–223; gold and, 264–265, 274n6; *Historia natural y moral de las Indias*, 61–62; native religion and, 158, 159, 167; native social ethics and, 164–165; taxonomy of barbarians, 102; theological-juridical debates and, 206–207; view of natives, 133, 134, 136, 139, 150, 152, 296n2, 319n10

Agueybana (native chief), 11

Ahutzoci (native chief), 261

Alburquerque, Bernardo de, 175

Alexander VI (pope): corruption of, 25–26, 278n5; *Dudum siquidem*, 25 (*see also* Alexandrian bulls); *Inter caetera*, 25, 29–32, 194 (*see also* Alexandrian bulls); Las Casas on, 59; Machiavelli's *The Prince* and, 25; papal authority and, 26–28, 38–41, 66–67; quoted, 24; writing of papal bulls and, 279n6

Alfonso X (Alfonso the Wise; king of Castilla), 28, 50, 90

Altamira, Rafael, 93

Alvarez de Chanca, Diego, 136, 160

Amaru, Tupac, 235

Andagoya, Pascual de, 171–172

Andrada, Rodrigo de, 70

Anglería, Pedro Mártir de, 11, 25–26, 90, 118, 128, 155, 205, 300n10, 307n11, 311n6; *De orbe novo*, 274n11

Anguis, Luis de, 209

Aquinas, Thomas (saint), 34, 53–54, 144, 214–215, 252, 281n26, 316n3

Arcos, Miguel de, 278n5

Arenal, Celestino del, 110, 299n8

Arens, W., 293n19

Aristotle, 91, 102, 110–111, 144–146, 221, 295n31, 300n16, 313n3; *Politics*, 144–145, 295n31, 296n32

Armas Medina, Fernando de, 122, 302n25

Atahualpa (Inka chief), 71, 207–209, 269, 311n9

Augustine (saint), 53, 91–92, 210, 213–214, 241, 316n3

Ayora, Juan de, 36–37

Bañez, Domingo, 50

Barros, João de, 193

Bastidas, Rodrigo de, 141

Bataillon, Marcel, 21, 76, 202, 252–253, 308n10, 311n7

Baudet, Henri, 21, 275n13

Benavente, Toribio de (Motolinía), 16, 250, 313n1; evangelization and, 219, 230; gold and, 274n6; Las Casas and, 57–58, 240, 255, 305n1, 307n13, 311n4; native depopulation and, 170, 172, 178, 260, 306n8, 312n12; native religion and, 164, 166; providentialist messianism of, 57–58, 61, 157

Bernardo of Española (Dominican friar), 115

Betanzos, Domingo de, 137, 138–139, 300n11

Biermann, Benno, 281n31

Borah, Woodrow, 173, 307n14

Borges, Pedro, 231

Borgia, Cesar, 25

Borgia, Juan de, 26

Printed in the United States
3019